Forbes Field

# Forbes Field

## Essays and Memories of the Pirates' Historic Ballpark, 1909–1971

EDITED BY DAVID CICOTELLO AND
ANGELO J. LOUISA

*Foreword by Philip J. Lowry*

McFarland & Company, Inc., Publishers
*Jefferson, North Carolina, and London*

LIBRARY OF CONGRESS CATALOGUING-IN-PUBLICATION DATA

Forbes Field : essays and memories of the Pirates' historic
ballpark, 1909–1971 / edited by David Cicotello and
Angelo J. Louisa ; foreword by Philip J. Lowry.
p.     cm.
Includes bibliographical references and index.

ISBN-13: 978-0-7864-2754-3
softcover : 50# alkaline paper ∞

1. Forbes Field (Pittsburgh, Pa.)— History.   2. Pittsburgh Pirates
(Baseball team)— History.   I. Cicotello, David, 1953–   II. Louisa,
Angelo Joseph.
GV416.P57F67   2007      796.357068748'86 — dc22        2006036274

British Library cataloguing data are available

On the cover: Students celebrate the Pirates' World Series win from atop
the University of Pittsburgh's Cathedral of Learning
(Photograph by George Silk, Time & Life Pictures/Getty Images)

Manufactured in the United States of America

*McFarland & Company, Inc., Publishers
Box 611, Jefferson, North Carolina 28640
www.mcfarlandpub.com*

To my mother, whose passion was baseball,
and my father, whose passion was books.
— David Cicotello

To my trinity: my mother, who introduced me to the sport of baseball;
my father, who took me to my first game at Forbes Field;
and my wife, Pam, who did more than her share of household chores
so that I would have time to work on this book.
— Angelo J. Louisa

## The Old Lady of Schenley Park

Named for a general,
Forbes became a battle site:
Pirates in pursuit of pennants,
House of thrills for generations
Of Pittsburgh faithful.
Built in just four months
(Handy steel and concrete),
She rose like a cathedral
Donning her rookie year
October's red, white & blue.
Her roofs offered much more
Than shade:
Buc(k) fans in the bleachers
Gandered Greenberg Gardens,
While those in the right stands
Were treated grand by Roberto.
Her diary embraced magic moments:
Ruth's last three souvenir swats,
Kiner's clouts (sorry, Aunt Minnie),
Waners' brother act,
Hopes and fears of sixty years.
She was paradise
For pitchers and triplers,
But never on Sunday (or any weekday)
Would she yield a no-hitter.
The Old Lady had attractive measurements: 365-457-300;
Her scoreboard never exploded,
Just told short stories,
Day's dramas unfolding in living black and white
One digit at a time.
Her grass was Emerald City green,
Easy on the eyes as
Pie diving at the hot corner,
Wagner scooping up infield crust,
Or Maz in the middle of the DP cascade.
Maz's moment most magical of all:
Series-climactic wave of wooden wand
Turned her into an asylum,
City into celebration,
Fairy tale ending, in the place
Where Pirate fans felt more at home
Than when they were at home.

— Gene "Two Finger" Carney

# ACKNOWLEDGMENTS

We wish to express our gratitude to the following individuals and groups whose contributions made this book possible. Any shortcomings of this book are in no way a reflection of the help that they have given us.

Jim Amato, for assisting us in our attempts to locate a photograph of the Walcott-Charles fight.

Tracie Anderson, for contacting senior citizen centers and AARP branches in Allegheny County.

Gail Ankeny, Windber Recreation and Parks Department, for distributing memory forms.

Pierre N. "Nic" Antoine, for publicizing our project in his newsletter, *Legends of Sports*.

John T. Bird, for advice and encouragement.

Bob Bluthardt, for publicizing our project in the *SABR Ballparks Committee Newsletter*.

Dan Bonk, for encouragement and assistance, and for responding to our questions regarding the dimensions of Forbes Field.

Nelson "Nellie" Briles, Pirates Alumni Association, for assistance in contacting former players.

Becky Bohan Brown, University of Nebraska at Omaha, for producing the news release about our project.

George Campbell, for providing information on contacting senior citizen centers in Allegheny County.

Andrew "Stush" Carrozza, for supplying us with an audio tape of the last game played at Forbes, as well as sharing his own memories of the park.

Louis Cicotello, for his memory of Forbes Field, for listening to his brother's progress reports on the book and for creating the collage that appears in the introduction. He is grateful to Latavia Adams at the University of Nebraska at Omaha for graphic design assistance. More information on his art can be found at www.louiscicotello.com.

Nicholas P. Ciotola, Historical Society of Western Pennsylvania, for assistance in obtaining photographs of boxing events at Forbes Field, particularly the Walcott and Charles fight.

David Finoli, for encouragement and for providing us with photographs of Forbes Field's remaining outfield wall.

Tim Fitzgerald, campus photographer, University of Nebraska at Omaha, for photographic assistance.

Julia Fox, Creighton University, for taking on the onerous job of transcribing the broadcast of the final game played at Forbes Field.

William Gasper, for distributing memory forms, as well as contributing his remembrances of Forbes Field.

Glenn Gearhard, for granting us permission to include memories posted on his website at www.mindspring.com/~gearhard/pirates.html.

Connie Henley, University of Nebraska at Omaha, for transcribing assistance and for typing the bulk of the first draft of the manuscript.

The Rev. John E. Hissrich, for distributing memory forms at Guardian Angel Parish in Pittsburgh, for publishing a notice about our project in the parish bulletin, and for contributing a memory.

Bill Horn, National Baseball Hall of Fame, for assistance in contacting the Permissions Department at the Associated Press.

Fran Hubbard, Bradenton Boosters, for distributing memory forms.

Information Technology Services, University of Nebraska at Omaha, for providing website support.

Christopher Jennison, for encouragement and for sending us various articles about Forbes Field as well as his own memories of the ballpark.

Nelson "Nellie" King, for sharing parts of his memoirs with us and for allowing us to use sections of them in our book.

Ryan Kunhart, for assisting with writing some of the biographical statements for the Pirate memories, for helping with the compilation of the bibliography for the book, and for checking a number of facts and direct quotations.

Angelo J. Louisa's "beagle," Poochie, for tracking down the box scores cited in "The Pirates at Forbes: 62 Memorable Games for 62 Seasons."

Anna Louisa, for promoting interest in contributing to the book, distributing memory forms, helping us to find an important newspaper account, proofreading parts of the book, and submitting her own memories of Forbes Field.

Pam Louisa, for helping with the research of certain parts of the book, assisting with the formatting of the pages, getting Adam Paige to computerize Ron Selter's diagrams, and proofreading most of the book.

Major League Baseball Properties, for assistance in obtaining permission clearance for the radio broadcast of the final game at Forbes Field.

Marian McDonald, University of Nebraska at Omaha, for designing the silhouette of the collage by Louis Cicotello and assisting the editors with the creation of the index.

Jeanette McGillicuddy, a relative of Gene Mack, for information that assisted us in obtaining permission to reprint Mack's original illustration of Forbes Field.

Mr. Bill's Sports Collectibles, for selling us a number of Forbes Field and Pirate photographs at a reasonable price.

Richard S. Morgan, for suggesting we contact Bob Smith, a former Forbes Field usher, and for distributing memory forms.

Trudy Myers, Cambria County Library, for distributing memory forms.

Professor Robert Nash, University of Nebraska at Omaha, for assistance in obtaining scholarly material for the editors.

Fran Neff, University of Nebraska at Omaha, for providing layout and production assistance for the Forbes Field Forever memory form.

Jim O'Brien, for his advice and encouragement, as well as allowing us to reprint an article that he had written about Forbes Field.

Christina "Tina" Oertli, for assisting with writing some of the biographical statements for the Pirate memories and for helping with the compilation of the bibliography for the book.

Sally O'Leary, Pirates Alumni Association, for her assistance in contacting former players.

Dr. John Oyler, for writing a column in the Bridgeville Area News publicizing the book and its editors, as well as contributing his own memories of Forbes Field.

Adam Paige, for computerizing Ron Selter's diagrams.

Robert H. Parks, Franklin D. Roosevelt Presidential Library and Museum, for research assistance regarding FDR's speeches at Forbes Field.

Kenton Peterson, University of Nebraska at Omaha, for providing website maintenance.

Lauren Petit, Creighton University, for copy editing and reformatting the entire book, and for putting up with Angelo J. Louisa's constant badgering.

Gilbert Pietrzak, Carnegie Library of Pittsburgh, for rescuing us by tracking down Pittsburgh newspaper references and quickly sending us photocopies of them.

*Pittsburgh Senior News*, for furnishing information on senior citizen centers and AARP chapters in Allegheny County.

Denis Repp, Forbes Field SABR Chapter, for distributing memory forms.

Sarah Richart, University of Nebraska at Omaha, for handling requests for scans of visual material used in the book.

Monica Robinson, Pirates Alumni Association, for assistance in contacting former players (twice!).

Dan Ross, for advice and encouragement during the initial phase of the book's development.

Rob Ruck, for assistance with locating photos of boxing matches at Forbes Field.

Phyllis Ruffing, for beginning the arduous task of transcribing the broadcast of the final game played at Forbes Field.

Gabriel Schechter, National Baseball Hall of Fame and Museum, for handling our initial request for photographs.

Lynn Schneiderman, Creighton University, for her alacrity in getting us books and reels of microfilm through the university's interlibrary loan system.

Senior Activities Center, Johnstown, Pennsylvania, for distributing memory forms.

Dr. Stevie Smith, for arranging the interview with her father, W. Robert "Bob" Smith.

Windber Public Library, Windber, Pennsylvania, for distributing memory forms.

All those individuals who assisted us in obtaining permission clearance for photographs, drawings, written material, and audio material held in copyright; those private individuals who contributed photographs; and those libraries from which we obtained miscellaneous visual material: Jorge Jaramillo, Associated Press; Barry Chad and Gilbert Pietrzak, Carnegie Library of Pittsburgh; Caitlain LeDonne and Brooke Sansosti, Carnegie Museum of Art; Will Tharreau, Corbis, Inc.; Nicole DiBlasi, Getty Images; Jennifer Reifsteck and Lauren Zabelsky, Historical Society of Western Pennsylvania; Michael J. Young, KDKA; James G. Nelligan, Attorney at Law, Family of Gene Mack; John F. Richnavsky, Moods Image; W. C. Burdick, National Baseball Hall of Fame Library, who also provided prompt identification of a player in the 1909 team photograph; Betsy Benson and Mary Louise Dattilo, *Pittsburgh Magazine/Home and Garden*; David Arrigo and Jim Trdinich, Pittsburgh Pirates Baseball Club; Angelika Kane and Heather Ryan, *Pittsburgh Post-Gazette*; Steve Gietschier, *The Sporting News*; Karen Carpenter, *Sports Illustrated*; and Miriam Meislik, University of Pittsburgh; Matthew Baum, Barbara Bowman, David Finoli, Louise Gargis, and Dr. Stevie Smith; and the Amateur Athletic Foundation of Los Angeles, and the Library of Congress.

All the individuals who assisted us with identifying the players in the 1942 Homestead Grays' team portrait by Charles "Teenie" Harris: Amy Baskette, Curatorial Assistant, National Portrait Gallery; John Brewer; John Holway; Patricia Kelly, Photo Archivist, the National Baseball Hall of Fame Library; Larry Lester; Kerin Shellenbarger, Photo Archivist, Charles "Teenie" Harris Archive, the Carnegie Museum of Art; and Brad Snyder.

All the authors who wrote chapters for this book.

All the AARP chapters in the greater Pittsburgh area that distributed memory forms.

All senior citizen centers in Allegheny, Cambria, and Somerset counties that distributed memory forms.

All the unnamed individuals who distributed memory forms.

All those people who contributed memories to this book, but especially Bobby Bragan, who went out of his way to contact us several times and who sent us a number of his remembrances of "Lady Forbes."

All the contributors whose memories we were delighted to read, but were not able to include because of space limitations: Ken Bauer, Matthew Baum, Craig Biddle, Edward Bolte, John L. Brant, Jr., Pat Brennan, Pete Bridgeman, Julius Brown, Jeremiah Buckley, Nick Buckovich, Bruce Casale, Richard Cheuvront, Brian Conley, Lloyd Creech, Sharon Lee Cubarney, Kevin Cunningham, Rick D'Alessandris, Bill Defoe, Bob Duerr, William Du Pal, Raymond Farzati, Ed Funston, Bethann Gallagher, Bob Gallup, Louise Gargis, Ralph Gigliotti, Anna Grancey, Jim Haller, Harv Harvison, Joe Hobson, Jay R. Jackson, Eric Johnson, Patrick Judycki, Larry Klein, John J. Kulidas, Rev. Frank M. Kurimsky, Edna LeGrande, Lynn Swartz Lippman, John C. Majetich, Gary March, Daniel Miller, Lee Monit, Owen K. Morgan, M.D., Andrew Muha, Ronnie Nelson, S. Nicewarner, Nick Nichols, Cliff Page, Bill Phillips, Christine A. Plonsky, Nancy Premoshis, John Quayle, Ray Rall, K. R. Ready, Norm Reefer, Jeff Richardson, Timothy Riley, Bill Rothenbach, Dave Schollaert, John Slaney, Richard Slater, Jim Slopey, Herbert Soltman, Malcolm Spence, Charlie Stevenson, William L. Symons, Margaret L. Takacs, Brian Thomas, Eddie Ulbrich, Mark Vukch, Steve Wachnowsky, Sean Wallace, Martin Whitehurst, Daniel Witko, and Mary Lon Zimmerman.

# TABLE OF CONTENTS

# FOREWORD

## *Philip J. Lowry*

I am honored to be asked by David Cicotello and Angelo J. Louisa to write this foreword to their outstanding book about the home of the Pirates and the Grays. As a child, I almost grew up at Forbes Field. My father took me to perhaps 15 or 20 games every year. We always rode the #76 trolley car from Wilkinsburg, paying a dime each, getting off on Forbes Avenue, just a block away from the left field bleachers. It cost my dad a dollar for a bleacher seat; it was only a quarter for me. We always sat halfway up, as close to the plate as we could, and we always seemed to sit near a bunch of elderly fans who kept up a constant chatter about the exploits of former greats like Honus Wagner, Pie Traynor, and Josh Gibson. Later, as a teenager, I sold hot dogs and popcorn there.

Forbes Field is what the perfect ballpark should be. It has crazy angles; it is asymmetrical; it has no ugly advertisements; there is ivy on the brick wall in the outfield; but most importantly it sits in the middle of a neighborhood rather than in the middle of a parking lot. If only it had been treated with the same tender loving care that Fenway and Wrigley received, it might live on today, and Pittsburgh fans would have been spared the ugly nightmare that was Three Rivers Stadium. In fact, I have chosen to write this foreword as if that were the case: we will treat our friend, Forbes Field, in the present tense.

Some of its features must be seen to be believed. During World War II, from June 26, 1943, through the end of that season, a huge wooden United States Marine stands against the left field wall, just to the right of the scoreboard. At parade rest, the Marine sergeant is 32 feet high, 15 feet wide at his feet, and he is "in-play."

After batting practice is over, the batting cage is wheeled out into left center field near the 436-foot marker, where it is placed against the brick wall, the only "in-play" batting cage in major league history!

It is very difficult to hit a homer down the left field line, as it is a distant 365 feet to the 25-foot, 5-inch tall green scoreboard. So to help Pirate sluggers Hank Greenberg, and later Ralph Kiner, hit more homers, Greenberg Gardens was created in 1947 (later called Kiner's Korner from 1948 to 1953), a fenced-in area between the scoreboard and a chicken coop wire fence which reduces the home run distance in left field by 30 feet so as to increase home run production.

While it may be difficult to hit a homer to left, it is most definitely not difficult to foul out to the catcher. The backstop is 110 feet from the plate, versus 60 feet in most other parks, so the catcher gets lots of exercise, and batting averages plummet due to lots of foul ball outs.

Back before the ballpark was built, the site was home to Schenley Farms. There was a hothouse and a livery stable, with cows grazing on the pastures overlooking Junction Hollow and Pierre Ravine. The year before the park was built in 1909, Carnegie Tech leveled the site and

1

played a football game there on a rocky field versus Penn on October 31, 1908. Nearly two decades later, in 1925, Pierre Ravine was filled in when the right field stands were built.

Forbes has not just one, but two adjoining streets that are almost always misspelled! Bordering the park on the southwest, along the first base line, is Boquet Street, named after Henry Boquet, a French and Indian War colonel, but most people assume it is named after a bouquet of flowers and incorrectly add a "u" in the middle. And, bordering the park on the northwest, down the third base line, is Sennott Street which is almost always misspelled as "Sonnett."

Many unique events happen here. Chief Wilson sets the still-standing major league record for triples (36) here in 1912. The last-ever major league tripleheader is played here versus the Reds in 1920. Harold Arlin is behind the mic here for the first-ever major league radio broadcast. In 1935, Babe Ruth hits his last three home runs here, including the first-ever ball hit over the right field roof. But in all of its 62 years, Forbes amazingly never hosts a no-hitter!

All that remains now of the old ballpark is a portion of the brick wall at its deepest point just to the left of dead center, where the flag pole and 457-foot marker are preserved opposite Pitt's Wesley W. Posvar Hall, which now occupies the site. Home plate is memorialized here inside the building about ten feet below its original spot; the ballfield's actual former location hovers ten feet up in the air above Roberto Clemente Drive, which winds through (and under) where the ballpark used to live.

I encourage you to read every last page in this book, and soak in all the smells and sights of my very good friend, Forbes Field. Reports of the demise of Forbes Field are greatly exaggerated.

Forbes Field lives on! You are all invited each October 13 to join Pirate fans from across the globe who gather every year by the flag pole at the 457-foot marker to listen to the radio broadcast of the seventh game of the 1960 World Series and celebrate the ending. Amazingly, each year it ends the same way! Bill Mazeroski hits a walk-off home run over Yogi Berra's head, and Bob Prince hysterically announces that "Forbes Field has just been transformed into the world's loudest outdoor insane asylum."

Philip J. Lowry is a member of the Society of American Baseball Research and the author of *Green Cathedrals: The Ultimate Celebration of All 271 Major League Ballparks Past and Present*.

# INTRODUCTION

## David Cicotello and Angelo J. Louisa

On February 28, 1909, the *Pittsburgh Post* reported, "[N]o other baseball project in the world even approaches the magnitude [of] the one now under way" near the entrance of Schenley Park in the affluent section of Oakland. Constructed from 300 railway cars of gravel and sand, 60 cars of steel, 60 cars of brick and lumber, and 45 cars of cement and terra cotta, Forbes Field was unmatched as a stadium when play began there four months later on June 30, 1909. The ballpark, named for British Brigadier John Forbes of the French and Indian War, was situated at the intersection of Louisa and Boquet streets. The former was renamed Sennott in 1910. The latter paralleled the first base line and honored Colonel Henry Boquet, a Swiss mercenary who was the second in command of Forbes' expedition that captured Fort Duquesne for the British in 1758.

Forbes Field was to be the new home of the Pittsburgh Pirates Baseball Club, owned by Barney Dreyfuss. Entrepreneurial and innovative, Dreyfuss seized the opportunity to move the club from Exposition Park along the Allegheny River near downtown Pittsburgh to the outskirts

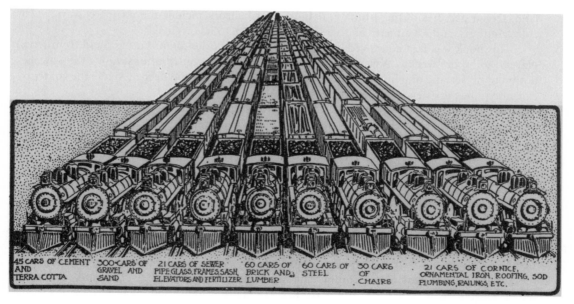

The ingredients for a classic ballpark as illustrated in the *Pittsburgh Post* on February 28, 1909 (*Pittsburgh Post*).

3

of the city. It proved prescient. Transported by the main trolley line via Forbes Avenue to within one block of the park, fans flocked to picturesque Oakland. It was the beginning of a love affair between a team and a neighborhood that lasted nearly 62 years.

According to contemporary accounts, the nouveau concrete and steel design of the park awed spectators. But it was the play on the field that transcended the architecture and captivated the human imagination. An immense source of civic pride, over its lifespan, Forbes Field drew patrons not only for sports but also for nonsporting events such as the circus, the opera, and religious crusades.

History was made at Forbes Field other than between the lines. On October 30, 1911, the first national mine safety demonstration was held there. Planned by the Bureau of Mines, the program was aided by coal operators and miners of the local Pittsburgh district established in 1908. A gathering of 15,000 attended the demonstration, carried out by teams of mining rescue squads from all coal-producing states. Dignitaries who witnessed the event included President William H. Taft.[1]

Soon after its opening, Forbes Field was the inspiration for Rickwood Field, a minor league stadium in Birmingham, Alabama. Built in 1910 by local industrialist Rick Woodward, the park was modeled after Forbes Field while its field dimensions were designed by Connie Mack. Home to the Birmingham Coal Barons, it was later used by the Black Barons of the Negro Leagues. Baseball luminaries Satchel Paige, Josh Gibson, and Willie Mays played there. Abandoned in 1988, the park lay moribund until the local Friends of Rickwood organized and commenced restoration of the facility which continues today. It is the oldest professional ballpark in America still in use.[2]

PNC Park, the current home of the Pirates, was also designed in the spirit of Forbes Field. The club, which had occupied the multi-purpose Three Rivers Stadium for 30 years after leaving Forbes Field, found its new location along the Allegheny River, the same locale that Dreyfuss had abandoned for suburban Oakland. Opened in 2001, PNC Park is one of the neoclassical stadiums in the manner of Oriole Park at Camden Yards in Baltimore and Jacobs Field in Cleveland. Design features of the intimate, natural grass ballpark include masonry archways, terra cotta columns, and asymmetrical dimensions in tribute to its original.[3]

This book was first conceived as a collection of memories about Forbes Field from fans, players, and sportswriters. A website was developed to solicit contributions. Along the way, the notion of preserving oral history evolved into something wider and deeper. While the contents expanded, the persistence of memory never left.

For Angelo J. Louisa, it began on June 16, 1961, Pittsburgh versus St. Louis. It was his first ballgame at Forbes Field and he was nine years old at the time. He rode the charter bus to the ballpark with his father and a number of other people from Bridgeville, Pennsylvania. Walking up the ramp to the second deck on the third base side, he was awestruck by the sight that had opened before his eyes and he thought to himself, "This is the real thing and I'm here."

During the game, he ate peanuts and threw the shells on the concrete floor. This was something that he was taught not to do, but he was surrounded by people who were doing it and enjoying it.

That evening, he saw the entire 1960 starting eight in action: Burgess, Stuart, Mazeroski, Groat, Hoak, Skinner, Virdon, and Clemente. But they were overshadowed by the Cardinals' Bob Gibson, who pitched and hit his way to a victory. The intense right-hander gave up five hits and two earned runs in nine innings and helped his own cause with two hits and a run batted in. The final score was St. Louis 5, Pittsburgh 2 — a losing effort, but the beginning of a winning relationship for a boy and a ballpark.

For David Cicotello, it was a family outing to Forbes Field from Windber, Pennsylvania, to see Pittsburgh versus Los Angeles in a Sunday doubleheader on July 11, 1965. Prior to the first game, he stood at the rail near foul territory along the third base line where the Dodgers were warming up. He had a scorecard in hand. Crowded on either side of him were other kids, pleading for autographs. He got three.

From the second level grandstand along third base, he watched Sandy Koufax pitch the first game. With his back arching during each windup, the Dodger lefty limited the Pirates to two runs on five hits over nine innings and earned the victory, 4–2. Pittsburgh won the second game in 10 innings, 4–3.

The largest crowd in three years was in attendance that day at Forbes Field: 37,631. He still has the 20-cent scorecard with the autographs of Nick Willhite, Willie Crawford, and Maury Wills.

What happened at Forbes Field is also subject to denial and deconstruction, it seems. Late in the 1932 presidential campaign, Governor Franklin D. Roosevelt made a notable speech at the park. In his address, FDR described his point-by-point plan for balancing the federal budget and bringing the nation out of the Depression. This nonsporting event was attended by nearly 50,000 spectators. Four years later, FDR ran for reelection and the country was still mired in the Depression. Republican candidate Alf Landon of Kansas cited Roosevelt's remarks in every address that he gave and attacked the President for failing the nation. Outraged, FDR ordered a return engagement at Forbes Field to explain point-by-point how he had accomplished what he intended to do. According to chief speech writer Samuel Rosenman in his book, *Working with Roosevelt*, the President asked him what explanation he would make. Rosenman responded,

An enthusiastic crowd welcomes Governor Franklin D. Roosevelt to Forbes Field, October 19, 1932 (Bettmann/Corbis).

"Mr. President, the only thing you can say about that 1932 speech is to deny categorically that you ever made it."

When researcher Dan Bonk was consulted regarding discrepancies in Forbes Field's outfield dimensions, he shared this insightful story with us:

About 15 years ago, Len Martin and I interviewed a man named Joe O'Toole. Joe had a long career with the Pirates which culminated as vice president. He was one of those local guys who got a job with the club while in high school in the late '30s or early '40s and stayed a lifetime. He passed away several years ago.

I mentioned to Joe that in my research, it was apparent there were many discrepancies concerning the distances to the outfield walls at Forbes Field. His answer enlightened me and caused me to look at the question ever since from a different perspective.

O'Toole told me that the outfield distances weren't too important to the teams until the 1960s. Painting numbers on the wall was sort of the last thing the club did before the season started and they didn't do it every year. He recalled one year in March, before the season started, the ground

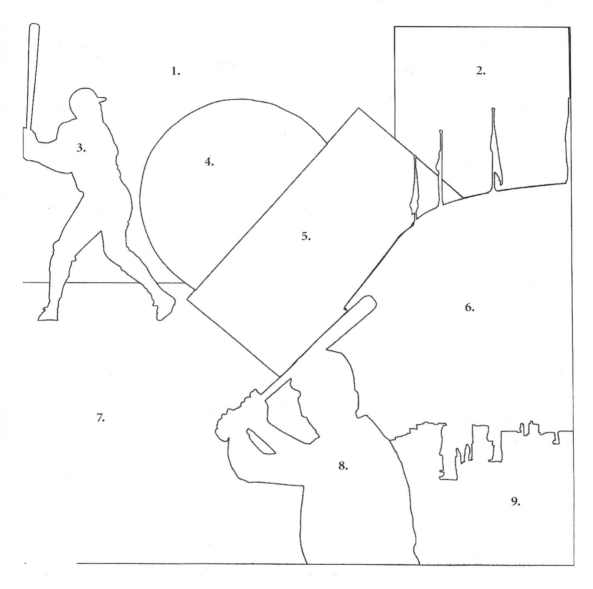

*Opposite and above:* "Forbes Field," paper collage, by Louis Cicotello, copyright 2005. "Forbes Field" depicts the unique architectural character of Forbes Field with several of the important historical events that occurred there and a selection of the renowned athletes from the baseball teams that made it their home field. 1. Detail of Bill Mazeroski hitting his 1960 World Series–winning home run against the New York Yankees. Photograph by Marvin E. Newman, courtesy of *Sports Illustrated.* 2. Detail from team picture of the 1942 Homestead Grays at Forbes Field. Photograph by Charles "Teenie" Harris, courtesy of the Carnegie Museum of Art, Pittsburgh: Heinz Family Fund. 3. Detail of Roberto Clemente's last hit at Forbes Field on June 28, 1970. Photograph by Les Banos, courtesy of the photographer. 4. Detail of an identification badge worn by Forbes Field ushers. Courtesy of SCGaynor Auctions, Inc. 5. Detail of Honus Wagner from the famous T-206 series of cards produced by the American Tobacco Company in 1909. 6. Detail of the main entrance of Forbes Field decorated for the 1909 World Series. Photograph courtesy of the Library of Congress, Prints and Photographs Division, Detroit Publishing Company Collection. 7. Detail of Forbes Field, 1960 World Series. Photograph courtesy of the National Baseball Hall of Fame Library, Cooperstown, N.Y. 8. Detail of Ralph Kiner. Photograph courtesy of the Pittsburgh Pirates Baseball Club. 9. Detail of remaining wall. Photograph courtesy of David Finoli.

crew measured the distances after painting a couple of the numbers on the walls. It was then they realized the measuring rope they were using had been cut and was short by about five feet.

Since paint was expensive and no one wanted to admit a mistake, they let it go. No one noticed and he wasn't sure anyone corrected the mistake the next year. O'Toole said it just didn't matter back then because there was no "tale of the tape" and nobody ever double-checked distances. All they really worried about was selling tickets and making payroll.

Since then, I never lost any sleep over the outfield distances, because I'm not sure you can even believe what you might see in photographs.

The book begins with Sam Bernstein's profile of Barney Dreyfuss, the visionary baseball owner who orchestrated the construction of the modern stadium. Next, Robert Trumpbour contextualizes Dreyfuss's enterprise in the Progressive Era, a critical juncture in American history. As the primary tenant of Forbes Field, the Pittsburgh Pirates played over 4,000 games there. A chronology of milestone games, including 12 selected box scores, are highlighted in "The Pirates at Forbes: 62 Memorable Games for 62 Seasons." David Ogden chronicles the life and times of the Negro Leagues at Forbes Field, for not all the baseball players were white. In his chapter, David Rocchi examines other sporting activities, for not all the athletes who competed there were baseball players. As a tribute to the closing of Forbes Field on June 28, 1970, a play-by-play account of the final game at the park is featured. The first part concludes with Ron Selter's two-part analysis of the historical configurations of Forbes Field.

Fulfilling the original intention of the book, there *are* memories. Growing up in Oakland, Rich Sestili recalls a poignant ballpark experience in his memoir of Forbes Field. Richard Morgan interviews former usher Bob Smith, who also lived in the neighborhood and worked numerous games beginning in 1929. In his contribution, Jim O'Brien covers the annual gathering of fans at the only portion of the outfield wall that stands today, held on the date of Bill Mazeroski's 1960 World Series–clinching home run.

In Lawrence Ritter's *The Glory of Their Times*, the players who were interviewed by the author shared their stories of "what it felt like to be young and a big leaguer." Wilbur Cooper, Pittsburgh's all-time pitching leader in victories, made his debut at Forbes Field in 1912 and expressed a similar sentiment in a letter he wrote to Natt Moll in 1971:

> I just received a paper showing you watching the demolition of our old friend, Forbes Field, and it brought memorys [sic] ... how thrilled I was for so long to hear you through the megaphone announce, "Batterys [sic] for today, Cooper and Schmidt." As Mrs. Schmidt said, "The Sweetest Battery in baseball." Oh yes, they were wonderful days and wonderful memorys [sic] in these late years of life [From the Wilbur Cooper file in the National Baseball Hall of Fame Library].

Included in the book are 58 reminiscences from former players, wives, managers, and club officials that span nearly fifty years of Pittsburgh Pirates baseball history.

The majority of this part is devoted to the fans whose memories recall games and events from the mid-1920s to the final game in 1970. Several members of the media, some who covered the Pirates at Forbes Field, offer their perspectives as well. When reading some memories, it is necessary to suspend our disbelief; with others, it is necessary to remember that recollection is a process by which we "half-perceive, half-create" experience.

A compilation of notable numbers associated with the park's sporting history and a bibliography for readers who wish to pursue the subject further are featured at the end of the book.

Interspersed throughout are various photographs and drawings that capture the neighborhood setting, intimacy, and classic era architecture of Forbes Field, a lost "green cathedral." In his retrospective article published in the *Pittsburgh Press* in 1983, Roy McHugh observed that Forbes Field was a park of "ivy-covered red brick walls that bordered but did not enclose." Neither the view in the park nor the outfield wall was ever spoiled by any commercial advertising. More like Fenway Park and Wrigley Field that were opened in 1912 and 1916, respectively, and remain in use today, Forbes Field evokes a simpler age. Its iconic visual power transcends time and space.

Lady Forbes, during its demolition in 1972, with the left field bleachers and manually operated scoreboard in the shadow of the Cathedral of Learning (courtesy University Archives, University of Pittsburgh).

According to baseball historian Bill James, Forbes Field was "the jewel in the diamond tiara" in its day, ca. 1960s (Pittsburgh Pirates Baseball Club).

The result is a mosaic of interconnecting pieces, forming an enhanced picture of a beloved city neighborhood and its baseball park, built nearly 100 years ago and long gone into oblivion. There is something for the general reader as well as the baseball aficionado. During the final game played at Forbes Field, the broadcast team of Bob Prince, Nellie King, and Gene Osborn paused momentarily during the action to point out to their listening audience that a large home-made banner was visible in the stands with a message written across it: "Forbes Field Forever." Frozen in time and yet timeless, the words resonate in the pages of this book.

## Notes

1. "In the Beginning ... The Early Days of Mine Rescue." Retrieved July 4, 2005, from U.S. Department of Labor, Mine Safety and Health Administration website: http://www.msha.gov/MineRescue/EARLY.htm.

2. Information retrieved July 4, 2005, from Friends of Rickwood website: http://www.rickwood.com.

3. "PNC Park Overview." Retrieved July 4, 2005, from Pittsburgh Pirates website: http://pittsburgh.pirates.mlb.com/NASApp/mlb/pit/ballpark/index.jsp.

# I

# *History and Background*

Fans file through the main entrance of Forbes Field at Sennott and Boquet streets for the 1960 World Series (National Baseball Hall of Fame Library, Cooperstown, N.Y.).

# 1

# BARNEY DREYFUSS AND THE LEGACY OF FORBES FIELD

## Sam Bernstein

In a 1909 issue published a few days after the grand opening of Forbes Field, *Sporting Life* extolled Pittsburgh team owner Barney Dreyfuss: "[He] had the mind to conceive and the courage to execute the plans which have given the world the grandest and most costly ball park in existence, deserves the greatest credit, highest praise, and utmost good fortune for his stupendous enterprise, which has ennobled the National League and enriched the City of Pittsburg [*sic*]."[1] Not bad press for a man who, knowing very little English, had arrived from Freiburg, Germany, 24 years before, with a few dollars in his pocket and an invitation to work in his cousins' bourbon distillery in Paducah, Kentucky.

Barney Dreyfuss was the embodiment of the American dream. Immediately after his arrival, Dreyfuss was motivated and focused. He managed the books for his cousins, Isaac W. and Bernard Bernheim, who sailed to America shortly after the Civil War. Beginning as peddlers, the brothers soon found themselves in Kentucky selling distilled spirits. Eventually, they began processing their own Kentucky bourbon, I. W. Harper, and became a huge success. The Bernheims created opportunities for family members, and they recruited Dreyfuss, who was clerking for a bank in Germany.[2]

The 19-year-old jumped at the invitation to travel to Kentucky, though Dreyfuss needed no incentive to leave his family and board a ship to America in 1885. His parents had a taste of the American dream when they developed a successful mercantile business in Kentucky in 1849, but were forced to return to Germany at the outbreak of the Civil War.[3] In addition, Dreyfuss was encouraged to avoid conscription in the German Army, which could be harsh for a Jewish youth. Barney would also be reuniting with his older sister, Rosa, who had married Bernard Bernheim and was living in Paducah.

Always the workaholic, Dreyfuss toiled six long days at the distillery and studied English at night. When a physician told him that his schedule would affect his health, Dreyfuss took his suggestion to develop a recreational pursuit. His business associates persuaded him that running a baseball club would give him that opportunity.[4] Dreyfuss had developed an appreciation for baseball soon after his arrival in Kentucky.[5] He began by organizing teams using distillery workers as players. As much as he enjoyed the game, Dreyfuss found greater fulfillment in organizing and managing local amateur teams.

The success of the Bernheim Brothers distillery forced the company to expand its operations, and they moved to larger quarters in Louisville in 1888. Dreyfuss was convinced that baseball as a business enterprise had the potential of enormous profit. He convinced his cousins

Five of the 14 players who were transferred from Louisville to Pittsburgh as part of the deal Barney Dreyfuss negotiated in 1900 when he purchased almost a half interest in the Pirates. Top (left to right): Honus Wagner; Tommy Leach. Middle: Fred Clarke. Bottom (left to right): Claude Ritchey; Charles "Deacon" Phillippe.

as well, and with their backing, Dreyfuss joined with some other local distillers and invested in the Louisville Colonels of the American Association. Mordecai Davidson owned the team, but he surrendered the club to the league in 1889, following a disastrous season.[6] In 1892, as Dreyfuss increased his investment, Louisville was admitted into the National League after a merger with the American Association. By 1899, Dreyfuss was the sole owner of the club.

Barney Dreyfuss was aware that major changes were being proposed to restructure the National League. Some owners wanted to restrict cross ownership of teams while others wanted to create a syndication of clubs operated by one individual who would distribute equity shares to club owners in return for absolute control. After much discussion, the magnates of the National League addressed the issue by contracting to an eight-team league and folded the Louisville, Cleveland, Washington, and Baltimore franchises. Anticipating Louisville was headed towards extinction, Dreyfuss brokered a deal that allowed him to purchase almost a half interest in the Pittsburgh Pirates and, by taking a smaller settlement from the National League ($10,000), he negotiated the transfer of the best players from Louisville to Pittsburgh. Among those players were Fred Clarke, Charles "Deacon" Phillippe, Tommy Leach, Claude Ritchey, and the immortal Honus Wagner. Such shrewd transactions quickly earned Dreyfuss recognition as "one of the greatest men connected with the game," whose passion was "dope" (i.e., player information), as he kept his offices "filled with volume after volume of statistics and records."[7]

Within a year, and again borrowing from his cousins, Dreyfuss bought out his partners and operated the Pirates as sole owner for 32 years. On the horizon, however, was the threat of a competing major league led by Western League President Bancroft Johnson who, along with his partners, was beginning to organize and transform the minor Western League to challenge the supremacy of the National League. Skillfully, Dreyfuss kept the American League out of Pittsburgh, lost the fewest players to the raiding new league, and was in the middle of the 1903 agreement that ended the war between the leagues. It was Dreyfuss who cemented the peace between the American and National Leagues when he challenged Boston to a best-of-nine-game competition between the pennant winners in October 1903, the first modern World Series.

When Barney Dreyfuss arrived in Pittsburgh in 1900, the Pirates played their home games at Exposition Park. Built in 1882, Exposition Park, "so-named because circuses and other big tent shows camped there when in town, occupied ground less than 50 yards from the Allegheny River,"[8] near the former site of

Barney Dreyfuss, ca. 1920s (Library and Archives Division, Historical Society of Western Pennsylvania, Pittsburgh, PA).

Three Rivers Stadium. According to Dreyfuss, "[t]he game was growing up, and patrons no longer were willing to put up with nineteenth century conditions."[9]

Dreyfuss contemplated a move away from the river because "[w]hen the Allegheny River overflowed its banks, Exposition Park went under."[10] It was common, especially during Dreyfuss' presidency, to play a game even if the field conditions were unsuitable but advance ticket sales were large. After one such game during which the outfield was flooded and players stood knee deep in water, the press nicknamed center field "Lake Dreyfuss." Other reasons included Dreyfuss' inability to obtain a stadium lease in order to make repairs, his need to prevent other leagues from installing a team in Pittsburgh, and his desire to relocate the club because Exposition Park was in "the wrong neighborhood."[11]

Daniel Bonk observed that "Dreyfuss saw the game as an entertainment vehicle that would need to attract citizens more affluent than the working class."[12] Dreyfuss was ahead of his time when he realized that increasing attendance and increasing the profit per ticket would result in financial success. His search for a site for a new ballpark began in 1903: "When President Dreyfuss came to Pittsburg [*sic*] bringing with him Harry Pulliam as secretary of the Pittsburgh club the fans and the public in general here were content to see the plucky little magnate bring a winning combination to Pittsburgh. Exposition Park looked good enough to them but President Dreyfuss had hardly become a fixture at the head of the Pirate team before he had begun to seek new grounds."[13] As the popularity of the Pirates increased over the years, Dreyfuss began to cultivate friends in high places. One such friend, the industrialist Andrew Carnegie, was instrumental in the development of Forbes Field.

The search for land to build a ballpark that met Dreyfuss' needs coincided with the development of the Oakland section of Pittsburgh by Carnegie. The area was located about three miles from downtown and well connected by trolleys to various neighborhoods. It was dominated by an estate owned by Mary Schenley who had graciously donated 300 acres to Carnegie for a public park.[14] Carnegie later began a movement to develop Oakland as a cultural center of Pittsburgh. Eventually, he endowed the Carnegie Institute there.

Guided by Carnegie, a Schenley estate trustee, Dreyfuss purchased seven acres of land from the estate after Mary Schenley's death. Located adjacent to Schenley Park, the land purchase was "one of the largest real estate deals in Pittsburgh in years."[15] The trustees agreed to allow a ballpark to be built as long as Dreyfuss agreed to a contract under which he "was required to spend a large sum of money to make the ballpark fireproof and of a design that would harmonize with the other structures in the Schenley Park district."[16]

Dreyfuss liked to gamble on horses, and he frequented racetracks in the Northeast, including New York's Belmont Park. Belmont's grandstand was designed by landscape architect Charles W. Leavitt, Jr. Dreyfuss presented his architectural requirements for the construction of a ballpark and invited Leavitt to submit a plan.

A short obituary of Charles Wellford Leavitt, Jr., who died in 1928, described him as a "landscape engineer, designer of many public parks, country clubs, racetracks and large private estates."[17] Leavitt planned such race tracks as Belmont Park and Saratoga, and he was instrumental in the town designs of Camden, New Jersey, and Garden City, New York. He designed cemeteries as well, including the Gate of Heaven Cemetery in Valhalla, New York, where Babe Ruth is buried.[18] Leavitt was born in 1871 in Riverton, New Jersey, and was trained as a civil engineer, holding several positions until he opened his own engineering and landscape architecture firm in 1897. By 1909, he had become an experienced architect of steel and concrete grandstands for sporting venues and a well-known planner of college campuses and estates. However, Leavitt's only baseball park was to be Forbes Field.[19]

Preliminary work on the tract of land began on January 1, 1909, with the Nicola Building Company beginning the actual construction of the stadium two months later. According to William Benswanger, Dreyfuss' son-in-law who served as president of the Pirates after Dreyfuss died in 1932, "The actual work on Forbes Field was a record-breaking achievement. It just required four months to build. Construction started March 1, 1909 and the first game was played June 30, 1909. And this included not only erecting the vast steel stands but also filling in some thirty feet of right field which was [a] partial hollow, before the ground was leveled. Thirty-one years later, when the decision was made to play night ball games, it took four months just to install the light standards!"[20]

Construction site of Forbes Field in December 1908 (Pittsburgh Photographic Library Collection of Carnegie Library of Pittsburgh).

Pirate manager Fred Clarke was deeply involved in the construction and design of the playing field. The *Pittsburgh Post* reported on May 1, 1909, "he [Clarke] paid a visit to Forbes Field, and gave the groundkeeper at the new baseball park some further instructions about the diamond which is now progressing rapidly toward completion."[21] On June 23, the paper reported "[b]efore starting west with the team, Clarke put in a busy day at the new park, testing the apparatus, which he devised and patented, for spreading the great canvas raincover and also for removing it from the diamond. The experiments yesterday were highly satisfactory, and nothing less than hard rains that commence at game time, are likely now to cause postponements on the Pittsburgh baseball program."[22]

At a cost of about one million dollars, Forbes Field was erected and named for British General John Forbes of the French and Indian War, who captured Fort Duquesne in 1758 and renamed it Fort Pitt. Forbes Field opened its gates for the first time on the afternoon of June 30, 1909, for a game with the Chicago Cubs. The Pirates defeated the Cubs 8–1 the day before at the last National League game played at Exposition Park.

Initially, Dreyfuss was criticized for building Forbes Field. Benswanger reported that "[m]any thought Mr. Dreyfuss was making a mistake. He was called 'crazy' for taking such a step and was told 'the park would never be filled.' It was filled the first day."[23] Dan Bonk and Len Martin added that "his critics labeled Forbes Field 'Dreyfuss' Folly' because it was too big, too fancy, and too far from downtown Pittsburgh. Characteristically, Dreyfuss never doubted his decision to build it. On opening day, as he stood inside the main gate, he shook the hands of those who came to congratulate him and told a local reporter, '[t]his is the happiest day of my life.'"[24]

Donald Lancaster wrote that "[o]pening day, June 30, 1909, was a beautiful occasion for a baseball game."[25] The game time was set for 3:30 P.M. against the defending World Series champion Cubs, but fans began arriving at the ballpark as early as 9:00 A.M. to get a 25-cent bleacher seat. A discounted train fare was offered to people going to the game. Streetcar workers had staged a strike at midnight on June 27, but it was quickly settled and service was restored to the stadium by June 29.[26]

The *Pittsburgh Post* ran a special "preview" of Forbes Field on June 27 in which it reported "[t]he humble bleacherite will be as welcome on Forbes Field on opening day as the most austere box-holder."[27] Dreyfuss stated that he would charge the same for opening day as he would for the entire season to encourage the loyalty of the Pittsburgh fans.[28] Seat prices included $10 for a box of eight seats, $8.75 for seven roof boxes, $1 for reserved seats, 75 cents for general admission, 50 cents for bleachers, and 25 cents for the temporary bleachers. Permanent capacity was about 25,000 (the largest in the major leagues), but on Opening Day 30,388 fans crammed into the park.[29]

Dedication ceremonies began at 1:30 P.M., culminating in the first pitch being thrown out by Pittsburgh Mayor William Magee. Many baseball dignitaries attended, including Harry Pulliam, president of the National League and a former Pirate official (and who, tragically, would commit suicide less than one month later); Ban Johnson, president of the American League; and Civil War veteran Al Pratt who had managed the first professional team in Pittsburgh in 1882.[30]

Forbes Field was designed by Leavitt to be "fan friendly." There were ramps instead of steps between decks, and later, elevators were installed to take fans from the entrance to rooftop boxes. The "most innovative feature, however, was the spacious promenade beneath the grandstands at street level. This feature made Forbes Field the only ballpark in the league where everyone in the main grandstand could find cover to wait out rain showers."[31]

The Pirate starting pitcher, Vic Willis, gave up a run in the first when Frank Chance singled home Johnny Evers. There was no scoring until the sixth as Willis and Cub hurler Ed Reulbach were locked in a pitching duel.[32] In the bottom of the sixth, Honus Wagner led off with

Opening Day, June 30, 1909, with a capacity crowd ringing the confines of Forbes Field (*The Index,* July 3, 1909).

a single, Bill Abstein sacrificed "The Flying Dutchman" to second, and Dots Miller knocked Wagner in with a single. The Cubs scored twice in the top of the eighth, and Pittsburgh scored once in the bottom of the inning.

With the Cubs leading 3–2, the Pirates mounted a rally in the ninth, but Fred Clarke hit a ground ball to shortstop Joe Tinker with two on and two out, and Jap Barbeau was forced out at second to end the game.[33] Though the Cubs spoiled Opening Day at Forbes Field, the Pirates went on to win 110 games that season to beat out the Cubs for the 1909 National League pennant by 6½ games.

Pittsburgh's Honus Wagner (center) flanked by Detroit's Davy Jones (left) and Ty Cobb (right) prior to the first game of the 1909 World Series (Pittsburgh Photographic Library Collection of Carnegie Library of Pittsburgh).

Barney Dreyfuss was on a roll, and so was his team. Led by Honus Wagner's seventh batting title and 66 victories from pitchers Howie Camnitz, Vic Willis, and Lefty Leifield, the Pirates marched into the first World Series played in Forbes Field. They were to meet a very successful team, the Detroit Tigers, making its third consecutive trip to the World Series after having won American League pennants but losing in 1907 and 1908 to the Cubs. The 1909 World Series highlighted the only meeting between deadball era superstars Wagner and Ty Cobb, the great outfielder for the Tigers and the American League. By the end of the series, the *Pittsburg Dispatch* would proclaim that Wagner outclassed Cobb on the field, leaving "no doubt as to who is the best baseball player in the world."[34]

The 1909 World Series opened on Friday, October 8, after Barney Dreyfuss had won a coin toss to host the first two games. The record crowd at Forbes was expecting to see their ace, Howie Camnitz (25–6) take the mound, but he had succumbed to a sore throat and fever and was unable to pitch. As Fred Lieb observed, "[i]f all Pittsburgh acclaimed Babe Adams after the Series, many Pirate fans were not so sanguine when they saw their Babe march out to warm up against George Mullin, the big twenty-nine-game winner of the American League champions. 'What's Fred [Clarke] doing sending a boy on a man's errand?' they asked."[35]

The rookie Charles "Babe" Adams outpitched Mullin before a World Series record crowd of 29,264. Although Adams gave up an early run to Detroit, Manager Clarke tied the game with a home run in the fourth inning and Pittsburgh added three more runs on Tiger errors in the fifth and sixth for a 4–1 victory.

"Rosebud" Camnitz may not have fully recovered from his bout of quinsy, and the record crowd of 30,915 watched as Ty Cobb stole home and the Tigers evened-up the series with a 7–2 victory. Camnitz was relieved in the third by Willis, and on the tall right-hander's first pitch, Cobb made his dash to the plate. A controversial call occurred in the first inning of game two in which both umpires on the field lost sight of a ball hit into a crowd of spectators. Starting with the 1910 World Series, four umpires began working each game.[36]

The series shifted to Detroit for the Monday and Tuesday games, October 11 and 12: the Pirates outlasted the Tigers 8–6 on Monday and George Mullin shut out Pittsburgh 5–0 on Tuesday. Thus, the series was tied as the teams headed back to the Smoky City for game five on Wednesday.

The Pirates and Tigers were greeted with raw weather and a crowd of 21,706 at Forbes Field. Babe Adams won his second game, though he gave up two homers early in the contest.

The fans go home disappointed after the Pirates' 7–2 loss to the Tigers in the second game of the 1909 World Series (Library and Archives Division, Historical Society of Western Pennsylvania, Pittsburgh, PA).

Dreyfuss had erected temporary bleachers in center field, and while the Tigers took early advantage of it, a three-run shot by Fred Clarke in the seventh inning to those same bleachers sealed the victory for Pittsburgh, 8–4.

Game six was back in Detroit, where the Tigers were victorious 5–4 despite a furious rally in the ninth inning by the Pirates. The series was now tied three games all. Dreyfuss and Detroit President Frank Navin were again subjected to a coin toss to determine the site of game seven.[37] Navin won, and on October 16 the Tigers drew their biggest series attendance of 17,562. But, the Detroit fans went home disappointed as the Pirates' hero Babe Adams pitched an 8–0 shutout, and Barney Dreyfuss had his first World Series championship. Pittsburgh Mayor William Magee began preparations for a holiday honoring the team: "The national game exemplifies the spirit of the American people as well or better than anything else. Today we are the envy of the entire country. Pittsburg [sic] during the past two weeks has excited the interest of the entire civilized world."[38]

Sixteen years would pass before Dreyfuss would experience another championship. Wagner retired in 1917 and the team was outmatched for the next several seasons. In 1921, Dreyfuss acquired the flaky star shortstop Rabbit Maranville and first baseman Charlie Grimm, who became fan favorites at Forbes Field. Because of his guitar playing and broad grin, Charley Grimm "worked his way into the hearts of Forbes Field patrons."[39]

Still, Dreyfuss could not field a pennant winner because beginning in 1921, the New York Giants proceeded to capture the National League flag four straight years. But then, Dreyfuss engineered a pre-season trade in 1925 sending Grimm, Maranville, and pitcher Wilbur Cooper to the Cubs for pitcher Vic Aldridge, infielder George Grantham, and minor league first baseman Al Niehaus.[40]

The reorganized 1925 Pirates were packed with talented players, including second-year player Kiki Cuyler who put together a career year, batting .357 with 18 homers and 102 RBIs. Pie Traynor, who was later voted the best third baseman of the first 50 years of the 20th century,[41] batted .320 and knocked in 106 runs. Base stealer Max Carey and shortstop Glenn Wright also contributed, as the Pirates finished 8½ games ahead of the Giants and prepared to face the Washington Senators with two of the greatest pitchers of the era, Walter "Big Train" Johnson and Stan Coveleski.

Years later, when he was asked to compare his 1925 Pirate team with the 1960 Pirates, Traynor remarked, "Our team was like the present one in one respect. We always expected to win and never were licked until the last man was out. In the final game of the Series, we handed Walter Johnson a four-run lead in the first inning but we won, 9 to 7."[42]

The old and the new were present for the '25 series: Babe Adams was still in a Pirate uniform,[43] and Dreyfuss had built temporary grandstands in the outfield bringing the capacity of Forbes Field to over 40,000 customers.[44]

Game one featured Walter Johnson who struck out 10 Pirates on his way to a 4–1 victory. Prior to game two, Christy Mathewson, the great pitcher for the New York Giants, died at the age of 45 and the players wore black armbands in his memory. Cuyler and Wright led the Pirates to even up the series by defeating Coveleski, 3–2.

The third game of the series, won by Washington 4–3, was played in Griffith Stadium and highlighted by a notable play. With the Senators leading by one in the eighth, reliever Firpo Marberry had struck out Glenn Wright and George Grantham. Next up was catcher Earl Smith, who lined a drive to right center. Edgar "Sam" Rice leaped up, apparently catching the ball as he fell over the fence and into the stands. The Pirates claimed he dropped the ball and a fan placed it in his glove. Barney Dreyfuss led the charge onto the field to protest the call. The controversy eventually made its way to Commissioner Landis who questioned Rice. He had in his possession several affidavits claiming that Rice never caught the ball and several who said he did. Rice "told [Landis] Judge, the umpire said I did," and Landis decided to not pursue the issue.[45]

The controversy surrounding Rice's catch persisted for many years. Even after he was elected to the Hall of Fame in 1963, Rice continued to be questioned about that now infamous catch whenever he visited Cooperstown. In later years, he wrote a letter to the Hall of Fame, which he requested to be opened only after his death. Rice died in 1974 at the age of 84, and according to his wishes, his letter was opened. In it, he maintained that he had indeed made the catch.[46]

The "Big Train" came on to pitch a 4–0 shutout in game four, and the Pirates had their backs to the wall going into game five, down 3–1. Pittsburgh manager Bill McKechnie handed the ball to Vic Aldridge, the winner of game two. Aldridge beat Coveleski again with the backing of Carey, Traynor, and Cuyler.

The series now returned to Forbes Field for game six on October 13, 1925. Before 43,810 fans, Pirate second baseman Eddie Moore socked a fifth inning home run, breaking a 2–2 tie and forcing a seventh game. For the first time, a World Series champion was to be decided at Forbes Field.

Game seven of the 1925 World Series was played in nasty, wet weather,[47] but before a large crowd of almost 43,000. Walter Johnson took the mound for the third time and faced Vic Aldridge. Johnson had won games one and four, Aldridge two and five. On three day's rest, Aldridge was wild and McKechnie yanked him in favor of Johnny Morrison with one out in the top of the first. Johnson had a 4–0 lead after one, and 6–3 after four. But he, too, may have succumbed to fatigue, giving up 15 hits and 9 runs in eight innings as "[t]he Big Train had jumped the tracks. And the Senators crashed with him, falling 9–7 and losing a World Series they seemingly had locked up a few days earlier. The Pirates' comeback marked the first time a team had rallied from a 3–1 deficit in games to win a best-of-seven Series."[48]

Pittsburgh sportswriter Fred Alger eloquently described the wild celebration in the Pirates' Forbes Field clubhouse. He witnessed "hardened ball players bronzed by the sunshine of seven months of labor on the ball field, supposed to have no feelings, no nerves and no sense of conscience, falling upon each other's neck—some crying from pure joy, others in fond embrace with a brother ball player."[49] National League President John Heydler called the team the "gamest ball club"[50] he had ever seen, and Pirate manager Bill McKechnie understated the outcome when he told reporters that "we had a pretty good ball club after all."[51] As for Barney Dreyfuss, he had his second World Series championship.

In 1926, dissension on the team and petty power struggles[52] caused Pittsburgh to slip to third place behind St. Louis and Cincinnati. For the 1927 season, Dreyfuss cleaned house again and installed Donie Bush as manager. In a very close National League pennant race, three teams—the Pirates, St. Louis Cardinals, and the New York Giants—were within two games of the flag as the season ended, with the Pirates on top.[53] On the strength of the Waner brothers, Paul and Lloyd, and the pitching of Ray Kremer, Lee Meadows, and Carmen Hill, the Pirates prevailed. However, unfortunately, Pittsburgh was to meet the most feared lineup in baseball, the New York Yankees, in the series.

Hall of Fame pitcher Tom Seaver has called the 1927 season "more than just a year in baseball. It was a year in which a legendary ball club was assembled, a club that has become the standard for measuring the best a team can be."[54] The '27 Yankee team had earned the moniker, "Murderers Row," as Babe Ruth hit 60 home runs that season, a record that stood for 34 years. With stars like Lou Gehrig and Earl Combs, New York finished 110-44, 19 games ahead of the Philadelphia Athletics. The Yankees had won their second straight pennant and were looking to avenge a heartbreaking seventh game loss to the Cardinals the previous October.

Sportswriter Fred G. Lieb later noted the 1927 World Series was "a bad memory for Pirate fans."[55] During batting practice before the first game, the Yankee sluggers hit tremendous drives over the walls in Forbes Field. A contemporary account by Richards Vidmer of *The New York Times* described "the Yankees' final practice yesterday [October 4, 1927] was a rather hilarious affair. Babe Ruth left the field in good spirits and five balls somewhere in Schenley Park. The Babe's batting spree left interested onlookers, including the Pirates, open-mouthed in wonder. Most of them had never seen his majesty the ball mauler in action before."[56] The Pirates got swept in four games.

The first two games were held in Pittsburgh. The Forbes Field faithful witnessed poor play by the Pirates including a misplayed fly ball by Paul Waner that led to a run-scoring triple by Lou Gehrig in game one. The costly errors multiplied throughout the series. Following the defeat by the Yankees, a rumor surfaced that Dreyfuss was ready to sell the team. It was conjectured that he "never got over the humiliation."[57]

After game four of the series, Dreyfuss had marched into the gloomy Pirate clubhouse inside Yankee Stadium. While he felt the "crushing setback of his team,"[58] he tried in vain to lift up the spirits of his team after a wild pitch had cost Pittsburgh the game and the series. Donie Bush highly complimented the Yankees, but he also noted his team might have "cracked" under the strain of a tight pennant race.[59] "It is no reflection on the courage of the Pirates," commented sportswriter Frank Graham of the New York *Sun*, "to say that one factor of their World Series defeat was a decided inferiority complex. They weren't afraid of the Yanks; they simply were abashed by them."[60]

*The Sporting News* reported that Dreyfuss "never reconciled himself to the four straight defeats suffered by his team in the 1927 World's Series. His mortification was so great that he had tears in his eyes as he tried to congratulate Col. Jake Ruppert, president of the winning club."[61]

Meanwhile, although Dreyfuss was angry and humiliated by the loss to New York, he began denying rumors that he was about to unload the team. Attending the World Series was Oklahoma oilman Lew Wentz, accompanied by former Pirate manager Fred Clarke.[62] Wentz had an understanding with Dreyfuss that if the Pirates were ever for sale, he was interested. Thinking about selling his team after a downturn in events was characteristic of Dreyfuss who took losing very hard. In 1916, for example, after the National Commission ruled against Dreyfuss in his attempt to obtain the services of George Sisler, Dreyfuss held negotiations with former Boston Braves owner James E. Gaffney and Johnny Evers.[63]

Dreyfuss did not get his price in 1916 and surely wasn't going to sell out in 1927. He wanted to retire and hand over the club to his son, Sam. In fact, Dreyfuss' son had to issue a very strong statement to the press denying that the club was being sold even though "it had been persistently reported in both baseball and business circles that the deal had gone through."[64] Barney Dreyfuss had taught his son well in the business of baseball, so much so that in Sam's obituary, *The New York Times* called the Princeton graduate "one of the best-informed executives in the baseball world."[65]

When Barney Dreyfuss died February 5, 1932, of pneumonia and prostatitis, he was 66 and still in charge of the Pirates. He had retired in 1930 from day-to-day activities and had turned the presidency over to Sam. But before the 1931 season commenced, Sam died of pneumonia. Although Dreyfuss returned for one more season, his heart was not in it as he was emotionally spent by Sam's death.[66] After Dreyfuss died, William Benswanger ran the Pirates until the team was sold to a syndicate headed by John W. Galbreath in 1946.[67]

In his obituary, it was noted that Barney Dreyfuss had gained "the distinction of being the most thoroughly schooled baseball man to be found among major league club owners."[68] He certainly was one of the most innovative owners and had a keen eye for recognizing baseball talent. John Heydler, president of the National League, claimed that Dreyfuss "discovered more great players than any man in the game, and his advice and counsel always were sought by his associates."[69] Branch Rickey echoed that sentiment, telling Lee Allen, historian at the Baseball Hall of Fame, that "Dreyfuss was the best judge of players he had ever seen."[70] Many leading baseball authorities concurred, including Commissioner Landis, Jacob Ruppert, Charles Stoneham, and William Harridge.[71]

The legacy of Barney Dreyfuss is enormous. He was a peacemaker, helping to settle the conflict between the National and American leagues. He was a builder, and the construction of Forbes Field is a testament to his innovation and resourcefulness. He was a facilitator, and when conflicts of interest arose that threatened to tear the structure of the game apart, Barney Dreyfuss was there to mediate the important issues by creating a path towards resolution. Between 1895 and 1932, Dreyfuss was in the middle of every important decision facing professional baseball including syndication, contraction, league conflicts, the Federal League, schedules, and of course, the scandal arising out of the 1919 World Series. Ralph Davis called Dreyfuss "a whole soul,"[72] not only because he was a cool and calculating baseball magnate, the "father" of the modern World Series, and the prime mover behind the construction of Forbes Field, but also because he remained until his death "a 'rooter,' a dyed-in-the-wool baseball enthusiast."[73]

Forbes Field, called "The House of Thrills" by radio announcer Bob Prince,[74] continued as the home of the Pirates until 1970 when it was replaced by Three Rivers Stadium. Dreyfuss' widow, Florence, resisted a movement to rename Forbes as Dreyfuss Field, but in 1934, a monument was erected in the outfield of the park to commemorate Dreyfuss' contributions to Pittsburgh.

One last World Series was played in Forbes Field in 1960. Barney Dreyfuss finally got his long awaited revenge, albeit posthumously, as the Pirates defeated the New York Yankees in seven games.

## Notes

1. *Sporting Life*, July 3, 1909, p. 4.
2. Isaac Wolfe Bernheim, *The Story of the Bernheim Family* (Louisville: John P. Morton & Co., 1910), 64–65.
3. Ibid., 6.
4. John Kieran, "The Passing of Barney Dreyfuss," *New York Times*, February 6, 1932, p. 22.
5. Dennis DeValeria and Jeanne Burke DeValeria, *Honus Wagner: A Biography* (New York: Henry Holt and Company, 1995), 61.
6. Bob Baily, "The Louisville Colonels of 1890," *The National Pastime* 13 (1993): 66.
7. Ralph S. Davis, "Barney Dreyfuss—the Man," *Baseball Magazine* (July 1908): 28.
8. Daniel L Bonk, "Ballpark Figures: The Story of Forbes Field," *Pittsburgh History* (Summer 1993): 55.
9. Ibid.
10. Michael Benson, *Ballparks of North America: A Comprehensive Historical Reference to Baseball Grounds, Yards and Stadiums, 1845 to Present* (Jefferson, NC: McFarland & Company, Publishers, 1989), 310.
11. Bonk, 55.
12. Ibid.
13. Jerpe, James, "Forbes Field, The World's Finest Baseball Grounds," *Pittsburgh Post*, June 27, 1909, p. 6.
14. Bonk, 55.
15. Donald G. Lancaster, "Forbes Field Praised as a Gem When It Opened," *Baseball Research Journal* 15 (1986): 26.
16. Ibid.
17. *New York Times*, April 24, 1928, p. 25.
18. Bonk, 57.
19. Ibid.
20. *Forbes Field 60th Birthday* (Pittsburgh: Century Printing Co., n.d.), 1.
21. *Pittsburgh Post*, May 1, 1909, p. 9.
22. *Pittsburgh Post*, June 23, 1909, p. 12.
23. *Forbes Field 60th Birthday*, 1.
24. Dan Bonk and Len Martin, "Bourbon, Baseball and Barney: The story [*sic*] of Barney Dreyfuss—'Last of the Baseball Squires,'" *A Celebration of Louisville Baseball in the Major and Minor Leagues* (Cleveland: SABR, 1997), 64.
25. Lancaster, 28.
26. *Pittsburgh Post*, June 29, 1909, p. 1.
27. *Pittsburgh Post*, June 27, 1909, p. 6.
28. Ibid.
29. Bonk, 56.
30. Ibid., 57.
31. Ibid., 64.
32. Lancaster, 28.
33. Ibid., 29.
34. *Pittsburg Dispatch*, October 17, 1909, sec. 4, p. 2.
35. Frederick G. Lieb, *The Story of the World Series: An Informal History* (New York: G. P. Putnam's Sons, 1949), 64.
36. Ibid., 65.
37. Lieb, 68.
38. *Pittsburg Dispatch*, October 17, 1909, p. 1.
39. Fred Lieb, "The Pittsburgh Pirates," *The National League*, ed. Ed Fitzgerald (New York: Grosset & Dunlap, 1959), 63.
40. Lieb, "The Pittsburgh Pirates," 65.
41. David Nemec, et al., *20th Century Baseball Chronicle: A Year-By-Year History of Major League Baseball* (Lincolnwood, IL: Publications International, 1992), 113.
42. *The Sporting News*, October 5, 1960, p. 10.
43. Adams pitched one scoreless inning in relief in game four of the 1925 World Series. He was 43 years old.
44. Abby Mendelson, "1925 World Series: 'He looked like he was on springs.'" Downloaded from www.pirateball.com on December 23, 1998.
45. Steve Wulf, "The Secrets of Sam," *Sports Illustrated* (July 19, 1993): 61.
46. Ibid, 64.
47. Mendelson.

48. *The Sporting News*, "History of the World Series: 1925." Downloaded from www.sportingnews.com on December 23, 1998.

49. *Pittsburgh Post*, October 16, 1925, p. 14.

50. Ibid.

51. Ibid., p. 1.

52. Lieb, "The Pittsburgh Pirates," 66–67.

53. Nemec, 122.

54. Tom Seaver with Marty Appel, *Great Moments in Baseball* (New York: Carol Publishing Group, 1992), 88.

55. Lieb, "The Pittsburgh Pirates," 68.

56. G. H. Fleming, *Murderers' Row* (New York: William Morrow and Company, 1985), 370.

57. Lieb, "The Pittsburgh Pirates," 68.

58. *New York Times*, October 9, 1927, p. 5.

59. Ibid.

60. Fleming, 387.

61. *The Sporting News*, October 5, 1960, p. 12.

62. *New York Times*, October 11, 1927, p. 33.

63. *New York Times*, December 15, 1916, p. 14.

64. *New York Times*, October 11, 1927, p. 33.

65. *New York Times*, February 23, 1931, p. 21.

66. *New York Times*, February 6, 1932, p. 21.

67. *New York Times*, January 17, 1972, p. 34.

68. *New York Times*, February 6, 1932, p. 21.

69. Ibid.

70. Lee Allen, *Cooperstown Corner: Columns from The Sporting News* (Cleveland: SABR, 1990), 164.

71. Barney Dreyfuss' acumen for player selection resulted in 26 first division finishes in the 31 years he served as president. The Pirates rewarded Dreyfuss with six pennants and two World Championships.

72. Davis, 28.

73. Ibid., 27.

74. Curt Smith, *Storied Stadiums* (New York: Carroll & Graf Publishers, 2002), 71.

# 2

# Forbes Field and the Progressive Era

## Robert Trumpbour

In a touching essay about a Pittsburgh police officer who attended Opening Day at Forbes Field, Gene Carney, a baseball fan and researcher from Utica, New York, attempts to recapture the feelings that his grandfather must have felt when first exposed to Forbes Field in 1909. To ensure that others would remember Forbes Field and those who were part of the generation that created this legendary ballpark, Carney donated a Forbes Field stickpin, often worn by his grandfather, to the Baseball Hall of Fame in Cooperstown, New York, where it is currently on display.[1] The stickpin was given to attendees of the first ball game at Forbes Field, decades before bat day, batting glove day, bobble-head doll night, and other merchandise-related attendance enticements became a common fixture in major league baseball. It is just one of many ways in which the atmosphere of Forbes Field provided an innovative bridge to baseball as we know it today.

The people of the Progressive Era may have regarded Forbes Field with a sense of awe and reverence, but for very different reasons than today's baseball fans. The fans visiting Pittsburgh's PNC Park for the first time made comparisons to Forbes Field, praising the new ballpark for its intimacy and its quaint representation of a simpler era.[2] The fans attending a professional baseball game in 1909 might have been in awe because of the vast size and scale of Forbes Field. It was an architectural marvel that represented a fundamental shift that was taking place in both society and professional sports.

Trying to capture Progressive Era citizens' perceptions of Forbes Field requires creatively stepping back in time to an era when technology was reshaping more than just baseball. In 1909, as the finishing touches were being put on Forbes Field, modes of transportation and ways of communicating were rapidly changing American society. A fast-paced urban culture, highly dependent on technology, was replacing an agrarian society that reflected the rustic simplicity of Jeffersonian America. In many ways, Pittsburgh was a central part of this transformation of America to a more modern era. The construction of Forbes Field was a reflection of this move towards modernity.

Forbes Field was the first truly modern ballpark of the twentieth century. It included amenities that set the standard for future ballpark construction. Some have cited Harvard Stadium, built in 1903, as the first modern sports facility in America. After all, this facility was the nation's first concrete and steel stadium. But Forbes Field was different in that it was a product of a fast emerging professional sports paradigm, a paradigm that would eventually surpass collegiate athletics, rooted in a commitment to on-field amateurism, as America's spectator sport pref-

Forbes Field as pictured on an Opening Day scorecard, June 30, 1909 (Pittsburgh Pirates Baseball Club).

erence. Beyond that, Harvard's construction was steeped in imitation of classic architecture and features, while Forbes Field combined the modern and ancient in an eclectic manner that more closely resembles today's ballpark-construction strategies. As the 1903 football stadium project unfolded in Cambridge, Massachusetts, some Harvard students emphasized the classical roots of this building, jokingly calling it the "Holliseum," intermingling the names for Rome's ancient edifice and Professor I. N. Hollis, the faculty advisor responsible for construction supervision.

Thoughts of integrating truly modern amenities into the Harvard project did not generally occur, but Pirate owner Barney Dreyfuss and his construction-staff contemporaries made numerous attempts to ensure that Forbes Field was the most modern sports facility possible. In the design of Forbes Field, Dreyfuss introduced many new technologies into the ballpark that had not been considered in previous venues. On-site parking facilities revealed that Dreyfuss may have intuitively known the profound influence that the automobile would exert on American culture. Henry Ford's auto company was a mere six years old, and the famed Model T was introduced in October 1908, so the fate of the automobile was far from certain as Forbes Field planning took place.

Pittsburgh was a hotbed of new technologies at this time, so it should not be shocking that Dreyfuss added automobile parking, telephones, and washing machines (to clean players' uniforms) to the facility. But the use of such technology in a ballpark setting was far ahead of its time. During the early twentieth century, most phone company executives regarded the telephone as a largely utilitarian innovation; it was something used by businessmen to increase manufacturing productivity or to close important deals.[3] But unlike the early Bell Company executives, Dreyfuss saw the social implications of this modern communication device.

Some baseball historians may consider Philadelphia's Shibe Park, opened three months before Forbes Field, as the first modern professional ballpark of the twentieth century. Because it was the first baseball facility to be constructed of concrete and steel rather than the traditional wood, a solid case can be made for such an assertion. Nevertheless, Forbes Field was the first major league ballpark to be built on a truly grand scale. The *Pittsburgh Post* offered readers a comparative illustration of the Forbes Field and Shibe Park projects. It is a comparison that presents compelling evidence that Forbes Field was a truly awesome undertaking.

When Shibe Park opened on April 12, 1909, it was the most elaborate ballpark of its time. Yet according to the *Pittsburgh Post*, Forbes Field was constructed with almost three times more structural steel than its Philadelphia counterpart. Reporters estimated that the raw construction material needed to build Forbes Field would "tax [the] capacity of 537 large freight cars." Beyond that, Shibe Park may have included many ornate architectural features, but it was constructed with a focus on attracting the common man.[4] Forbes Field was intentionally designed to be more upscale, with the hope that such a plan would attract not only the affluent, but the multitude of average citizens clinging to dreams of becoming rich.

Many writers look at Yankee Stadium as the first truly grand baseball edifice, but without Forbes Field as a starting point, current landmarks such as Yankee Stadium, Wrigley Field, and Fenway Park — all considered large and elaborate in their day — may not have been constructed in quite the same manner. Although New York has often led the nation on a number of fronts, including sports, the most hallowed ballpark of that particular city at that time, the Polo Grounds, did not become a fully concrete and steel structure like Forbes Field until after a fire ravaged the elaborate wood-framed landmark on April 13, 1911.

Some individuals may regard Forbes Field as an important part of the sports landscape in a simpler and less confusing time, but such an assessment may be unfair to the people of the Progressive Era. For those who were part of the festivities as Forbes Field opened, the times were anything but simple. Technology was shifting so rapidly that adjusting to the new environment might have been every bit as difficult as our uneasy transition to the computer age.

In 1909, the telephone was rapidly gaining market share over Western Union's popular telegraph, the electric light bulb was gradually replacing the gas lamp, many homes were being wired to receive electricity for the first time, the automobile and streetcar were supplanting the horse as primary forms of transportation, and work methods, even at the most rudimentary level, were moving in a decidedly more scientific direction. The leisure landscape was also changing in dramatic ways. A fledgling film industry and various forms of organized commercial recreation were making inroads on a population willing to try new things. Forbes Field was an important part of that emerging entertainment landscape.

Pittsburgh was a gritty industrial town that regarded business and commerce as its most important attributes. Andrew Carnegie, Charles Schwab, and the Mellons may have chased wealth with a vigor and intensity that defied comparison, but many laborers came to Pittsburgh with similar dreams of accumulating wealth. These workers were often intensely mercenary, too. Immigration historian John Bodnar recounts that "a Polish steelworker in Pittsburgh wrote to his family in Poland not to keep his younger brother in school much longer; an extended education would be unnecessary for the toil required in the Pittsburgh mills."[5] In an attempt to humor its audience, the *Pittsburgh Post* composed the following verse which demonstrated the value that many Pittsburgh residents attached to material success:

> *Pittsburgh is old and smoky,*
> *Is full of fog and wealth;*
> *Not because of foreign aid,*
> *But because it boosts itself.*[6]

Pittsburgh was a city that prided itself as an industrial and technological leader. City newspapers often reflected that pride, despite a quality of life that was very harsh for the typical working-class citizen. Occasional calls for pollution control might be found, but more often than not, the term "Smoky City" was used by reporters as a term of endearment.[7]

Steelmaking, Pittsburgh's leading industry during the Progressive Era, in full production at the Jones & Laughlin Corporation Steel Mill and Coke Ovens, ca. 1912–1920 (Library and Archives Division, Historical Society of Western Pennsylvania, Pittsburgh, PA).

Unlike post–World War II Pittsburgh, the city's problems and uncertainties were exacerbated by a rapidly expanding population base. From 1870 to 1910, the city's population ballooned from 139,256 to 533,905.[8] An influx of immigrants from Eastern Europe created vast tenements of citizens unfamiliar with American culture, while it heavily diluted the old-guard ethnic mix of English, Irish, Scots, and Germans.

This increase in population offered profitable opportunities for city newspapers and recreation-oriented entrepreneurs, but it also presented uncertainties. Sports not only helped to build circulation but also served as a subtle battleground for class distinction.[9] In fact, the entire leisure landscape often served as a hegemonic struggle of various class interests. Affluent citizens pursued two different trajectories in this clash. Some followed the path outlined by Thorstein Veblen in his sociological classic, *Theory of the Leisure Class*, shutting out the unwashed rabble while retreating to hunt clubs and exclusive resorts. More progressive citizens of wealth pushed for improved leisure options for the masses, with the hope that the uplifting inspiration of such endeavors would result in a more productive citizenry. Some of these efforts were inspired by the type of idealism that led to the opening of Jane Addams' Hull House in Chicago, but industrialists such as Andrew Carnegie and Henry Ford were propelled by a desire to control the ideology of recreation in a manner that helped foster a more productive and less cantankerous workforce.[10]

Historian Francis Couvares cogently points out that Carnegie's construction of a museum, music hall, and library for the citizens of Pittsburgh had "an explicit social agenda: to define, create, and disseminate the 'highest culture' and thereby to civilize the inhabitants of the indus-

A Progressive Era ideal — to master nature and order it with aesthetic appeal — is seen in the arrangement of the trees and landscaping at the grand entrance to Schenley Park, with a view of Forbes Field in the background, ca. 1925 (National Baseball Hall of Fame Library, Cooperstown, N.Y.).

trial city."[11] In a similar vein, Roy Lubove argued that "public recreation posed no threat to private economic prerogatives, and had positive advantages as a social control mechanism."[12] Many workers resisted the moralistic intentions of elites, however, including Mary Schenley's donation in 1899 of 300 acres for construction of an idyllic city park. The city's use of some parts of the land for elite leisure activities such as golf and genteel bridle paths further distanced this segment of the populous from partaking in potentially wholesome recreation.

Newspapers often reflected the sensibilities of Progressive Era readership. These publications tended to give more space to park development and high culture activities than to ballpark construction. Because the ballparks of an earlier generation tended to be rickety wooden structures, they were not the source of community pride that they have become today. As a result, the museum or the urban park, not the baseball stadium, was typically regarded as a much more important part of a city's overall development. The popularity of the park movement was spurred in part by a Progressive Era belief that such idyllic cultural assets could tame and civilize unruly children, while providing an uplifting recreational experience to individuals challenged by the rigors of work. Championing this cause was one editorial which argued that open spaces for play provided a child with an outlet to "be trained for future health and usefulness."[13]

Frederick Law Olmstead's park design successes in Boston, Chicago, and most notably, at New York's Central Park, spurred an outpouring of support for pastoral recreation areas throughout the nation.[14] But in Pittsburgh, working-class skepticism about elite intentions encouraged many workers to avoid parks and to seek out various consumer-driven recreational options.

Some of these paid leisure activities were gritty and tawdry, such as the corner bar, the pool hall, the prizefighting ring, and the nickelodeon. Others offered a bit of rural greenery and the veneer of an upscale environment with greater freedom and less threat of well-intentioned upper-class moralizing. Kennywood, an area amusement park featuring assorted mechanical rides and a pastoral backdrop, provided one such outlet to the citizens of Pittsburgh when it opened to the public in 1898.[15]

Major league baseball provided another attractive commercial venue for citizens. Forbes Field's fusion of new technology and architectural innovation with the ballpark's pastoral green appealed to much of the community in differing ways. For elite industrialists, baseball might have been regarded as a back door opportunity to introduce proper values to less privileged spectators. Baseball cultivated acceptance of a meritocracy, where production standards, in the form of player statistics, were accepted. More important, baseball's system of managerial hierarchy and specialized position play, may have taught the notion of bureaucratic efficiency more effectively than a post-game lecture from Max Weber or Frederick Taylor ever could.

The focus on technology in construction and management of the ballpark served to cultivate passive acceptance of elite-inspired innovation. Additionally, the pastoral setting of the baseball field may not have been as uplifting as a high-society country club, but the carefully manicured diamond may have provided an uplifting experience while it inculcated workers with the elite Progressive Era notion of man's ability to master nature. The successful Pittsburgh businessman could enjoy the privacy of box seats while at a ball game, but at the same time, he could watch baseball with the smug belief that some of his subordinates would be unwittingly exposed to various lessons that could contribute to the bottom-line efficiency of the company.

For blue-collar workers, the new ballpark might be regarded as an upscale experience and a chance to visit a well-heeled neighborhood that had amenities unavailable in rickety ethnic tenements. As the twentieth century unfolded, Pittsburgh struggled with typhoid, poor water quality, and substandard housing, but a day at the ballpark, even in the cheapest seats, offered laborers a somewhat pristine diversion from these difficulties. For those within walking distance to the factory, the streetcar ride to Forbes Field may have provided exposure to yet another new urban technology.

The working-class population of 1909 was a diverse mix of ethnicity and experiences. As such, the ballpark visit could be interpreted in a variety of ways. For recent immigrants, a ballpark visit was an opportunity to engage in activity that was thoroughly American. It was also a chance to participate in an uplifting community-binding experience that was a departure from eastern European culture.

For veterans of the mills, watching skillful ballplayers may have evoked memories of an earlier era when craftsmanship was respected in industrial production. By the turn of the century, skilled workers such as iron puddlers and glass shapers were a dying breed, replaced largely by interchangeable semi-skilled labor. These new and more efficient techniques distanced many of the workers from their craft, and shifted power from the individual worker to a Tayloresque supervisor. Veteran workers might regard baseball as a chance to reflect on what the workplace could become if only control could be wrestled from an unsympathetic and disliked supervisor whose perceived aim was to diminish craftsmanship in the workplace.

Pittsburgh's working class often regarded with suspicion business elites and the free leisure opportunities which they offered, making baseball at Forbes Field a more accepted form of leisure among peers than a day at the Carnegie Library. Historian David Koskoff explains that "the heat of the furnaces, the maddening 12-hour day, the marginal wage, [and] the wretched company houses, transformed even the most appreciative south-central European peasant into a labor radical."[16]

Many factory workers correctly determined that the same individuals responsible for oppressive working conditions and repressive labor tactics, including the highly publicized Pinkerton violence at the Homestead mills in 1892, had ulterior motives in their philanthropy. This attitude provided an opportunity for commercial entities, including but not limited to sports venues, to attract the loyal patronage of working-class citizens. Skeptical of the philanthropic intent of the Carnegies, the Mellons, the Schwabs, and a host of upper class moralists, "leisure reform only accelerated the rush of [Pittsburgh's] working people into the arms of merchants of leisure who were fashioning a new mass culture."[17]

In response to this emerging mass culture, newspaper sports sections catered to a broad range of recreational interests. Boxing held appeal for the male bachelor subculture that grew with the influx of mass immigration.[18] College football, particularly the Ivy League variety, appealed to an upper class audience fearful that technology and new riches were softening youthful offspring.[19] Hunt club notices, yacht racing, and a number of other activities appealed to a select elite who wished to partake in an excessive level of conspicuous consumption.[20]

In this vast matrix of recreation choices, professional baseball was a sport that appeared to be a safe haven, or at least an acceptable compromise, for all classes. Not surprisingly, baseball received prominent coverage even when a newspaper's self-interest was not directly tied to the financial success of the home team.[21] Pirate owner Barney Dreyfuss was not directly invested in the local media, yet press coverage of Forbes Field construction was universally favorable. As the project took shape, a number of local editorials and articles praised professional baseball for its positive influence on the populace.[22]

Press coverage of the ballpark project seemed to take three paths: one focused on technology and innovation, the second exhorted community pride, the third praised Dreyfuss and the Pirate staff for civic mindedness or business acumen. Often these three recurrent themes were intertwined.

Dreyfuss, a shrewd entrepreneur, intuitively understood the significance of technology in shaping the urban landscape. He was not afraid to employ new technological solutions to baseball-related problems, turning these innovations into positive press coverage for his team. When Exposition Park's drainage problems threatened his attendance revenues, he was the first owner to use a tarpaulin to cover the infield, a standard practice today. In designing Forbes Field, he placed laundry facilities in the clubhouse. This innovation might seem revolutionary in the context of this era, but it was probably a simple extension of the drive for efficiency that was so central to the commercial environment of Progressive Era Pittsburgh. In the long run, such equipment saved Dreyfuss money and helped to improve his overall profitability.

The Pirates gained press coverage for other technological advances, including use of special box seats, installation of public telephones, design of public lavatories for ladies, importation of special turf from an Ohio sod farm, construction of an underground automobile parking garage, and implementation of innovative crowd control devices such as turnstiles and exit ramps.[23] One story even focused on electric lighting for the new ballpark, with a Cincinnati inventor suggesting that night baseball might be possible.[24] *Pittsburg [sic] Press* reporter G. H. Gillespie called the ballpark project "the acme of modern skill and science."[25]

As Forbes Field neared completion, ballpark construction was frequently trumpeted as a world-class enterprise. One report, replete with pictures, used the exact phrase, "finest athletic field in the world," three times in opening paragraphs, only to rephrase this assertion several times later. If the repetition did not convince the reader, comparative arguments were included specifying why the construction was superior to other cities including Philadelphia's popular venue. Pittsburgh press coverage suggested that Forbes Field brought the city a broad level of community pride. One story boasted that "nothing advertises a city like a good baseball team."[26] Another quoted a St. Louis sportswriter asserting that "there is nothing in the United States that even approaches Forbes Field in size, accessibility, cost, or location."[27] The excitement surrounding Forbes Field's Opening Day was palpable, as ticket requests from distant locations were reported. Published articles often focused on how this ballpark would positively reflect upon the city. Precisely one month before construction finished, President William Howard Taft helped increase interest in the Pirates, sitting with fans in the old ballpark as the Cubs defeated the Pirates.[28]

Newspaper accounts chronicled spectator and celebrity visits to the work site. On June 13, 1909, 10,000 fans were estimated to visit the construction area. Many were so excited that they were seen "climbing into the grandstand and sitting for some time."[29] Explicit instructions regarding ticket purchasing policies were offered frequently. Opening ceremony plans included a concert with two bands, introduction of various dignitaries, including the league president, and a parade of ex-players. The mayor threw the ceremonial first pitch to the city's director of public safety.[30]

Opening Day received lead story status with several photos on page one, a level of coverage not previously granted to ballpark dedications.[31] An editorial triumphantly asserted that "opening day certainly justifies the management's judgement in erecting so worthy a monument to America's most democratic pastime."[32] The opening weekend featured record daytime baseball crowds and a highly publicized evening fireworks show. Tickets for the fireworks offered Pirates management additional Fourth of July revenue since ball games were over before sunset.[33] Dreyfuss astutely looked for new revenue opportunities, attempting to adapt Forbes Field to the changing entertainment landscape of his time. He utilized the ballpark for a variety of non-baseball events when the team was on the road, including "the Hippodrome," billed as "Pittsburgh's combination vaudeville and circus."[34]

There were limits to Dreyfuss' willingness to experiment, however. A key condition of these non-baseball events was that "scenery must be moveable so as not to interfere with pennant baseball."[35] Such precautions were prudent, as the Pirates concluded their first season at Forbes Field in storybook fashion with a World Series victory over the Detroit Tigers. The series created a national showcase for Forbes Field and the city of Pittsburgh. According to one reporter, the series added luster to Pittsburgh because "in every city and town throughout the United States, an army of fans await[ed] the result of each contest."[36]

Barney Dreyfuss' plan to create a ballpark that would attract a more upscale audience was intensely visionary. His success was so profound that Giants' legend Christy Mathewson joked that players could easily "lose a fly ball in the glint of diamonds in the stands." By adding various luxurious amenities, Dreyfuss was able to attract a greater number of women and families to the ballpark than was the case at Exposition Park. The result was a more civilized atmosphere for all. Pirates shortstop Honus Wagner confessed this new clientele changed the attitude of ballplayers, forcing them to "stop cussin'" during games.[37]

The unintended consequences of this cultural shift may have been media coverage that was more inclined to support professional sports as an integral part of a community's culture. In such a scenario, sports gradually became a key "quality of life" issue in many major metropolitan areas, including Pittsburgh. Venues such as Forbes Field established the ballpark as a source of community pride. With the construction of Forbes Field, sports fans became less tolerant of rickety structures that seemed acceptable before 1909. As this new facility opened, Pittsburgh's citizens may have interpreted their visit to the ballpark in a variety of ways, but the ballpark's modernity was probably appreciated by all fans of that era. Forbes Field was a thoroughly modern structure that gave fans a feeling that baseball was not afraid to embrace new technologies. As a result, it is ironic that we tend to regard stadiums designed to emulate the intimacy of Forbes Field as a nostalgic reflection of a simpler time. It is more likely that the citizens of Pittsburgh visiting Forbes Field for the first time shared similar feelings of awe and amazement that more closely paralleled what those entering the Astrodome in the 1960s felt than what a typical fan feels now when entering a ballpark carefully designed to recreate memories of yesteryear.

The main entrance at Sennott and Boquet streets decorated for the 1909 World Series (Library of Congress, Prints and Photographs Division, Detroit Publishing Company Collection).

When Officer Mike Carney patrolled Forbes Field on June 30, 1909, he was probably overwhelmed by modern amenities that seemed out of place in a typical major league ballpark. A few decades later, those amenities had become expected standards in ballparks around the league. In one example, Philadelphia sports historian Rich Westcott indicates that telephones were installed in Shibe Park in 1910, the season after Forbes Field included them in the original design.[38] Civic pride had entered the ballpark construction business, and the citizens from Philadelphia were not going to be outdone on the technology front by their heavily industrialized rivals in western Pennsylvania. Without the luxury of Forbes Field, professional sports in America may have developed in a very different manner.

When the twentieth century opened, man had never flown a plane, the light bulb was an impractical luxury because of filament limitations, and foods that we take for granted today, such as the ice cream cone, hamburgers, and pizza, were unknown to most Americans. After a single decade, all these items were on their way to becoming popular parts of the American cultural landscape. Forbes Field may not have radically transformed America culture as profoundly as the light bulb or the airplane, but it had a remarkable impact on what spectators came to expect when attending a baseball game in twentieth-century America.

## Notes

1. Gene Carney, "Notes from the Shadows of Cooperstown." March 17, 1996. Available: http://www.baseball1.com/carney/index.php?storyid=65. "The Stickpin" first appeared in *Fan* magazine #7 in 1991.

2. The author attended the first game at PNC Park, a pre-season exhibition event on March 31, 2001, and spoke with various attendees during the unveiling of this new ballpark.

3. Claude Fisher, "'Touch Someone': The Telephone Industry Discovers Sociability," *Technology and Culture* (January 1988): 32–61.

4. Rich Westcott, *Philadelphia's Old Ballparks* (Philadelphia: Temple University Press, 1996), 103–107.

5. John Bodnar, "Families Enter America" in Leon Fink, ed., *Major Problems in the Gilded Age and the Progressive Era* (Lexington, MA: D.C. Heath and Company, 1993), 281.

6. "Pittsburgh 150 Years Old and Still Smoky," *Pittsburgh Post*, November 28, 1908, p. 9.

7. Although reasonably clean now, Pittsburgh's air quality in the Progressive Era was truly horrid. See Lewis Mumford, *The City in History* (New York: Harcourt Brace, 1961), 472. Mumford rails against the long-standing tradition of acrid smoke in Pittsburgh. In a December 21, 1999, speech addressing clean air legislation, U.S. President William Clinton cited Pittsburgh's Progressive Era pollution problems as a vivid example of a worst-case scenario. Available www.pub.whitehouse.gov/uri-res/I2R?urn:pdi://oma.eop.gov.us/1999/12/21/9.text.1.

8. Bayrd Still, *Urban America: A History with Documents* (Boston: Little Brown, 1974), 210–211. After World War II, Pittsburgh struggled to retain its declining population base. By 1990 Pittsburgh's population was 369,879.

9. An abbreviated history of the influence of sports reporting on commercial development of media enterprises is available at Robert McChesney, "Media Made Sport: A History of Sports Coverage in the United States," in Lawrence Wenner, ed., *Media, Sports, and Society* (Newbury Park, CA: Sage, 1989), 49–69.

10. See Stephen Meyer, *The Five Dollar Day: Labor Management and Social Control in the Ford Motor Company* (Albany, NY: State University of New York Press, 1981), 149–162.

11. Francis Couvares, *The Remaking of Pittsburgh: Class and Culture in an Industrializing City* (Albany, NY: State University of New York Press, 1984), 105. The author provides a highly detailed narrative of the hegemonic battle to control working-class leisure.

12. Roy Lubove, *Twentieth Century Pittsburgh: Government, Business, and Environmental Change* (New York: John Wiley & Sons, 1969), 51.

13. "Playgrounds," *Pittsburgh Post*, March 13, 1909, p. 6. For two examples of coverage afforded park-related endeavors, see "Public School Pupils Join in Playfest," *Pittsburgh Post*, May 15, 1909, p. 1; "Ormsby Park — A Playground for the People of To-Morrow [*sic*]," *Pittsburgh Post*, April 25, 1909, p. 6.

14. Olmstead briefly visited Pittsburgh, preparing a 12-page plan to improve Pittsburgh's parks in 1910. His most sweeping ideas were not considered until after 1945.

15. Ironically, Kennywood was the product of ultra-rich Andrew Mellon's desire to attract more customers to his Monongahela Street Railway Company. In 1906, the railway company fully exited day-to-day amusement park management, leasing the park to A. S. McSwiggin and Fredrick Henninger. See Kennywood website, http://www.kennywood.com/park_info/history.php.

16. David Koskoff, *The Mellons: A Chronicle of America's Richest Family* (New York: Thomas Y. Crowell & Company, 1953), 85.

17. Couvares, 120.

18. For more detail on boxing and bachelor subcultures, see Elliot Gorn, *The Manly Art of Bare Knuckle Prize Fighting in America* (Ithaca, NY: Cornell University Press, 1986). By 1909, boxing in Pittsburgh was increasingly controlled by wealthier fans. Working-class boxers frequently became pugilistic cannon-fodder for these moneyed individuals.

19. Theodore Roosevelt's call for a strenuous life represented the essence of this response to a very real fear that young men of privilege could be feminized if not challenged by rigorous competition. In addition to a number of texts on Roosevelt's philosophy, two recent scholars provide a detailed account of how Progressive Era elites coped with these fears. See Gail Bederman, *Manliness and Civilization* (Chicago: University of Chicago Press, 1995); Michael Kimmel, *Manhood in America* (New York: Free Press, 1996).

20. Perusal of a typical sports section will reveal coverage of some of these affluent activities, which are described in Donald Mrozek, *Sport and the American Mentality: 1880–1910* (Knoxville, TN: University of Tennessee Press, 1983), 103–135.

21. Some teams were partially owned by newspaper practitioners. See Bruce Kuckilick, *To Everything a Season: Shibe Park and Urban Philadelphia, 1909–1970* (Princeton, NJ: Princeton University Press, 1991), 14–15.

22. For editorial examples, see *Pittsburgh Post*, December 11, 1908, p. 4; March 8, 1909, p. 4; June 1, 1909, p. 6; June 21, 1909, p. 4; October 9, 1909, p. 4.

23. *Pittsburgh Post*, February 23, 1909, p. 12; February 28, 1909, sec. 3, p. 1; March 7, 1909, p. 1; March 28, 1909, sec. 3, p. 1; May 1, 1909, p. 10; May 9, 1909, sec. 3, p. 1; June 11, 1909, p. 8; June 19, 1909, p. 6; June 27, 1909, p. 6. Shibe Park also used turnstiles in 1909.

24. "Baseball Games by Electric Light Are Planned for Pirate Park," *Pittsburgh Post*, April 4, 1909, sec. 3, p. 1. Electric lights of sufficient power to allow for night baseball were not installed in Forbes Field until June 4, 1940, almost 31 years after Opening Day at this park. Major league baseball did not permit an official night game until the 1930s. See David Pietrusza, *Lights On! The Wild Century-Long Saga of Night Baseball* (Lanham, MD: Scarecrow Press, 1997), 135.

25. "Forbes Field World's Finest Baseball Park Ready for Opening Day," *Pittsburg Press*, June 27, 1909, Summer Resort Section, p. 6. The spelling of Pittsburgh was not yet standardized in 1909. As a result, Pittsburgh was spelled without an *h* in editions of the *Pittsburg Press*, but the currently accepted spelling was used throughout the *Pittsburgh Post*.

26. "Forbes Field the World's Finest Baseball Grounds." *Pittsburgh Post*, June 27, 1909, p. 6. Claims that the ballpark would be the finest in the world were routinely repeated in a host of shorter articles.

27. "Shower Prevents Baseball Game; Overworked Pirates Enjoy Rest," *Pittsburgh Post*, June 2, 1909, p. 9.

28. "Warm Tribute Is Paid to Steel City by Nation's Chief Executive," *Pittsburgh Post*, May 30, 1909, p. 1. Taft's brother was a part owner of the Cubs.

29. "President Harry C. Pulliam Visits Pirates New Baseball Park," *Pittsburgh Post*, June 14, 1909, p. 10.

30. "World's Greatest Ballpark to be Dedicated This Afternoon," *Pittsburgh Post*, June 30, 1909, p. 9.

31. Shibe Park, which opened to the public on April 12, 1909, received limited front-page coverage and much less column space and photos on its Opening Day. *Philadelphia Inquirer*, April 12, 1909, p. 1; April 13, 1909, pp. 1, 10. On April 12, 1909, the *Pittsburgh Post* described Shibe Park as "the largest and most ornate monument to sports in this country." Pittsburgh reporters knew that Forbes Field was a significantly larger project, reporting on February 28, 1909 (*Post*, sec. 3, p. 1) that almost three times more steel would be utilized in construction.

32. "Baseball" [Editorial], *Pittsburgh Post*, July 1, 1909, p. 6.

33. The fireworks show took place on Monday, July 5, 1909, and was heavily advertised in the newspapers on Sunday, July 4, 1909.

34. "Audience of 15,000 Sees Hippodrome Open," *Pittsburgh Post*, July 27, 1909, p. 2. The Hippodrome included an array of acts, including animal trainers, human cannonballs, marksmen, and dramatic acts. Many of the props and stage settings were highly elaborate. It was exceedingly well publicized, with newspaper stories throughout July and August.

35. "Turn First Dirt To-Day [*sic*] for New Hippodrome," *Pittsburgh Post*, July 19, 1909, p. 2.

36. "World's Championship Ball Games Have Boosted National Sport," *Pittsburgh Post*, October 4, 1909, p. 10.

37. Dennis DeValeria and Jeanne Burke DeValeria, *Honus Wagner: A Biography* (New York: Henry Holt & Company, 1996), 213. The authors paraphrase Mathewson in the first quotation.

38. Westcott, 111.

# The Pirates at Forbes:
# 62 Memorable Games for 62 Seasons

## David Cicotello and Angelo J. Louisa

*Games are listed in chronological order, and all records cited are current as of April 1, 2005. Box scores were copied as closely as possible from the originals and are therefore somewhat inconsistent in content and style.*

**June 30, 1909:** Frank Chance's Cub Machine spoiled the park's opener by defeating the Bucs, 3–2, but the Pirates would eventually get their revenge on the Cubs by beating out Chicago for the pennant by six and a half games.

### June 30, 1909: The Birth of a Classic

| CHICAGO | AB | R | H | PO | A | PITTSBURG | AB | R | H | PO | A |
|---|---|---|---|---|---|---|---|---|---|---|---|
| Evers, 2b | 3 | 2 | 2 | 1 | 2 | B'beau, 3b | 3 | 0 | 0 | 2 | 0 |
| Sh'kard, lf | 1 | 1 | 0 | 1 | 0 | Leach, cf | 5 | 0 | 0 | 2 | 1 |
| Hofman, cf | 2 | 0 | 1 | 4 | 0 | Clarke, lf | 4 | 1 | 0 | 1 | 0 |
| Chance, 1b | 4 | 0 | 1 | 13 | 0 | Wagner, ss | 4 | 1 | 2 | 1 | 2 |
| St'nf'dt, 3b | 2 | 0 | 0 | 1 | 4 | Abst'n, 1b | 2 | 0 | 0 | 13 | 0 |
| Schulte, rf | 4 | 0 | 0 | 1 | 0 | Miller, 2b | 4 | 0 | 2 | 0 | 3 |
| Tinker, ss | 4 | 0 | 0 | 0 | 1 | Wilson, rf | 2 | 0 | 0 | 2 | 0 |
| Archer, c | 4 | 0 | 0 | 6 | 0 | Hyatt, rf | 1 | 0 | 0 | 0 | 0 |
| R'lbach, p | 4 | 0 | 0 | 0 | 4 | Gibson, c | 2 | 0 | 1 | 6 | 1 |
| **Total** | **28** | **3** | **4** | **27** | **11** | *Durbin | 0 | 0 | 0 | 0 | 0 |
| | | | | | | Willis, p | 3 | 0 | 0 | 0 | 5 |
| | | | | | | †Storke | 0 | 0 | 0 | 0 | 0 |
| | | | | | | **Total** | **30** | **2** | **5** | **27** | **12** |

Errors— Barbeau, Evers (2).

*Durbin ran for Gibson in ninth inning.
†Batted for Willis in ninth inning.

| Pittsburg | 0 0 0 | 0 0 1 | 0 1 0—2 |
|---|---|---|---|
| Chicago | 1 0 0 | 0 0 0 | 0 2 0—3 |

Two-base hit — Miller. Sacrifice hits— Abstein (2), Storke, Sheckard (2), Hofman, Steinfeldt. Stolen base — Hofman. Double play — Steinfeldt and Chance. Left on bases— Pittsburg, 10; Chicago, 6. First base on balls— Off Reulbach, 6; off Willis, 3. First base on errors— Pittsburg, 2; Chicago, 1. Hit by pitched ball — Evers. Struck out — By Reulbach, 6; by Willis, 5. Time of game — One hour and fifty minutes. Umpires— Messrs. Emslie and O'Day.

Editors' Note: At this time, "Pittsburgh" was spelled without the "h."

June 30, 1909: Play ball! (Pittsburgh Photographic Library Collection of Carnegie Library of Pittsburgh).

**August 16, 1909:** Facing Christy Mathewson and the hated New York Giants with runners on first and third, two out, the scored tied at two in the eighth inning, and a thunderstorm beginning, Dots Miller hit a shot to deep right center field, which should have won the game for the Pirates. But Red Murray, the Giants' right fielder, made a spectacular barehanded catch of the ball just as a bolt of lightning flashed behind him, illuminating his figure in the surrounding darkness. Honus Wagner said that this was the greatest play he had ever seen.

### August 16, 1909: What a Catch!

| PITTSBURG | AB | R | H | PO | A | NEW YORK | AB | R | H | PO | A |
|---|---|---|---|---|---|---|---|---|---|---|---|
| Barbeau, 3b | 3 | 0 | 1 | 1 | 0 | Doyle, 2b | 4 | 0 | 2 | 1 | 1 |
| Leach, cf | 4 | 0 | 1 | 1 | 0 | Seymour, cf | 3 | 0 | 0 | 2 | 0 |
| Clarke, lf | 4 | 0 | 0 | 3 | 0 | McC'm'k, lf | 4 | 0 | 1 | 3 | 0 |
| Wagner, ss | 3 | 0 | 1 | 5 | 0 | Murray, rf | 4 | 1 | 0 | 2 | 1 |
| Miller, 2b | 4 | 0 | 1 | 2 | 4 | Devlin, 3b | 3 | 1 | 0 | 0 | 1 |
| Abstein, 1b | 2 | 0 | 0 | 8 | 2 | B'dwell, ss | 2 | 0 | 2 | 2 | 1 |
| Wilson, rf | 3 | 0 | 0 | 1 | 0 | Merkle, 1b | 2 | 0 | 1 | 13 | 0 |
| Gibson, c | 3 | 1 | 2 | 2 | 5 | Meyers, c | 2 | 0 | 0 | 1 | 1 |
| Willis, p | 2 | 0 | 0 | 1 | 4 | M'th'son, p | 3 | 0 | 0 | 0 | 6 |
| *Hyatt | 1 | 0 | 1 | 0 | 0 | Total | 27 | 2 | 6 | 24 | 11 |
| †Abbat'o | 0 | 1 | 0 | 0 | 0 | | | | | | |
| Total | 29 | 2 | 7 | 24 | 15 | | | | | | |

*Batted for Willis in the eighth inning.
†Ran for Hyatt in the eighth inning.
Errors— Barbeau, Clarke, Abstein.

Pittsburg    0 0 1  0 0 0  0 1—2
New York    0 2 0  0 0 0  0 0—2

Two-base hit — Leach. Three-base hits— Gibson, Hyatt. Sacrifice fly — Barbeau. Sacrifice hits— Seymour, Bridwell, and Merkle. Double play — Murray and Merkle. Left on bases— Pittsburgh, 6; New York, 5. First base on balls— Off Willis, 1; off Mathewson, 2. First base on errors— New York, 3. Struck out — By Willis, 1; by Mathewson, 1. Time of game — One hour and thirty minutes. Umpires— Messrs. Klem and Kane.

Editors' Note: Pittsburgh was the home team, but was cited first in the box score.

**October 8, 1909:** The strong pitching of Babe Adams and Fred Clarke's home run powered the Pirates to a 4–1 victory over the Detroit Tigers in the first game of the World Series.

**October 13, 1909:** Fred Clarke pounded out a pair of hits, one of them a home run, drove

New Base Ball Stadium and Park, "Forbes Field," Pittsburg, Pa.

Postcard sent October 15, 1909, from Pittsburgh to Lincoln, Nebraska: "Saw a big World Series game Wed. Pittsburgh 8, Detroit 4. 35,000 rooters there. More noise than when we beat Wesleyan. It was great" (collection of David Cicotello).

in three runs, and scored twice to lead the Pirates to an 8–4 victory over the Tigers in the last game of the '09 World Series played at Forbes. The Pirates would clinch the World Series championship in Detroit on October 16.

**August 23, 1910:**  Fred Clarke showed off his arm by gunning down four Philadelphia runners in a 6–2 Pirate loss. Clarke's performance tied a major league record, which still exists. And when Chief Wilson's single assist is added to Clarke's four, the Pirates set a major league team record, which has since been tied twice, for the most assists by an outfield in one game.

## August 23, 1910: Clarke's Arm

| | *PHILADELPHIA* | | | | | | *PITTSBURG* | | | | |
| | *AB* | *R* | *H* | *PO* | *A* | | *AB* | *R* | *H* | *PO* | *A* |
|---|---|---|---|---|---|---|---|---|---|---|---|
| Titus, rf | 4 | 1 | 1 | 1 | 0 | Byrne, 3b | 5 | 1 | 1 | 1 | 4 |
| Knabe, 2b | 3 | 0 | 0 | 2 | 4 | Leach, cf | 4 | 0 | 2 | 0 | 0 |
| Bates, cf | 4 | 1 | 1 | 4 | 0 | Clarke, lf | 4 | 0 | 1 | 4 | 4 |
| Magee, lf | 4 | 2 | 3 | 3 | 0 | Wagner, ss | 4 | 0 | 1 | 0 | 3 |
| Grant, 3b | 3 | 0 | 0 | 1 | 1 | Miller, 2b | 3 | 0 | 0 | 3 | 0 |
| Bransf'd, 1b | 4 | 0 | 2 | 8 | 1 | Flynn, 1b | 4 | 0 | 2 | 10 | 1 |
| Doolan, ss | 3 | 1 | 1 | 3 | 2 | Wilson, rf | 4 | 1 | 2 | 3 | 1 |
| Moran, c | 4 | 1 | 1 | 5 | 0 | Gibson, c | 4 | 0 | 2 | 5 | 1 |
| Moore, p | 2 | 0 | 1 | 0 | 3 | Leifield, p | 0 | 0 | 0 | 0 | 1 |
| **Total** | **31** | **6** | **10** | **27** | **11** | Phillippe, p | 2 | 0 | 0 | 1 | 0 |
| | | | | | | •Hyatt | 0 | 0 | 0 | 0 | 0 |
| | | | | | | Maddox, p | 0 | 0 | 0 | 0 | 1 |
| | | | | | | †Campbell | 1 | 0 | 0 | 0 | 0 |
| | | | | | | **Total** | **35** | **2** | **11** | **27** | **16** |

The 1909 World Series Champion Pittsburgh Pirates. Left to right: Ed LaForce, trainer; Tommy Leach; Bobby Byrne; Howie Camnitz; Paddy O'Connor; Chick Brandom; Sam Leever; Ed Abbaticchio; Ham Hyatt; Nick Maddox; Chief Wilson; Bill Abstein; Vic Willis; Lefty Leifield; Bill Powell; Gene Moore; George Gibson; Sam Frock; Harry Camnitz; Babe Adams; Deacon Phillippe; Dots Miller; Mike Simon; Honus Wagner; Skeeter Shelton; Fred Clarke, player-manager (Library of Congress, Prints and Photographs Division [Pan Subject, Sports No. 159]).

•Batted for Phillippe in seventh inning.
†Batted for Maddox in ninth inning.
Errors— Knabe, Byrne, Wagner (2).

Philadelphia   3 2 0   0 0 0   0 0 1 — 6
Pittsburg      1 0 0   0 0 0   0 0 1 — 2

     Two-base hits— Wilson, Gibson, Magee, Moore. Three-base hit — Titus. Home run — Magee. Sacrifice hits— Knabe, Grant, Moore. Double plays— Clarke and Gibson; Wilson and Flynn; Clarke, Wagner, and Miller; Knabe and Bransfield; Doolan and Bransfield; Grant and Bransfield. First base on balls— Off Leifield, 1; off Moore, 2. Struck out — by Phillippe, 3; by Moore, 4. First base on errors— Philadelphia, 2. Left on bases— Pittsburg, 8; Philadelphia, 2. Hits— Off Leifield, 4 in one and one-third innings; off Phillippe, 3 in five and two-thirds innings; off Maddox, 3 in two innings. Time of game — One hour and forty-five minutes. Umpires— Messrs. Brennan and O'Day.

On-field action during Pittsburgh-Brooklyn game in 1911 (National Baseball Hall of Fame Library, Cooperstown, N.Y.).

**August 22, 1912:**  After going three for four in the first game of a doubleheader against the first-place New York Giants, Honus Wagner hit for the cycle in the second game. It would be the first time anyone hit for the cycle at Forbes and the only time that the Flying Dutchman would do it in his illustrious career.

**July 17, 1914:**  Rube Marquard outdueled Babe Adams as the New York Giants beat the Pirates, 3–1, in a 21-inning game. Both pitchers went the distance, with Adams not surrendering a single walk. Adams' feat set a major league record for pitching the most innings in a single game without giving up a base on balls.

**July 29, 1915:**  Forty-one-year-old Honus Wagner proved that age is not a factor when he hit an inside-the-park grand slam off Jeff Pfeffer to help the Pirates trounce the Brooklyn Dodgers, 8–2.

**September 23, 1915:**  Fred Clarke Day. The great player-manager of the Pirates, Fred Clarke, who would retire at the end of the season, was given an eight-day clock and a leather binder containing the names of thousands of fans. For his part, Clarke inserted himself in the lineup for the last time and went one for two (a line out to left and a single to right) before leaving the game in the fourth inning.

**April 29, 1916:**  Honus Wagner showed why most baseball historians consider him the greatest shortstop of all time when, at the age of 42, he secured a 2–1 Pirate victory by making a spectacular fielding play to gun down a Cincinnati runner attempting to score.

**October 2, 1920:**  The last major league tripleheader was played, with the Pirates losing two out of three times to the Cincinnati Reds.

**August 5, 1921:**  KDKA aired the first radio broadcast of a major league game. Harold Arlin was the announcer and the Pirates were the victors, defeating the Philadelphia Phillies, 8–5. The game lasted an hour and 57 minutes.

## August 5, 1921: KDKA, Pittsburgh ... First with the News

### PITTSBURGH (N.)

| | AB | R | H | PO | A |
|---|---|---|---|---|---|
| Bigbee, lf | 4 | 0 | 0 | 2 | 0 |
| Carey, cf | 4 | 0 | 0 | 0 | 0 |
| Maranv'le, ss | 3 | 0 | 0 | 1 | 2 |
| Wh'ted, rf, 1b | 3 | 3 | 2 | 4 | 1 |
| Barnhart, 3b | 3 | 2 | 1 | 0 | 2 |
| Tierney, 2b | 2 | 1 | 1 | 4 | 2 |
| Grimm, 1b | 2 | 0 | 1 | 9 | 0 |
| Rohwer, rf | 1 | 1 | 1 | 1 | 0 |
| Brotten, c | 4 | 1 | 2 | 6 | 3 |
| Carlson, p | 1 | 0 | 0 | 0 | 4 |
| Zinn, p | 3 | 0 | 2 | 0 | 0 |
| Total | 30 | 8 | 10 | 27 | 14 |

### PHILADELPHIA (N.)

| | AB | R | H | PO | A |
|---|---|---|---|---|---|
| Rapp, 3b | 4 | 0 | 0 | 0 | 1 |
| J. Smith, 2b | 4 | 1 | 1 | 4 | 2 |
| Leb'veau, lf | 3 | 3 | 2 | 2 | 0 |
| Walker, rf | 2 | 0 | 1 | 1 | 0 |
| Konetchy, 1b | 4 | 0 | 2 | 8 | 2 |
| Williams, cf | 4 | 1 | 2 | 2 | 0 |
| Parkinson, ss | 4 | 0 | 1 | 2 | 5 |
| Peters, c | 3 | 0 | 2 | 5 | 1 |
| Ring, p | 3 | 0 | 0 | 0 | 1 |
| a Monroe | 1 | 0 | 0 | 0 | 0 |
| Total | 32 | 5 | 11 | 24 | 12 |

a Batted for Ring in ninth.
Error — Rohmer [sic].

| | | | | | | | | |
|---|---|---|---|---|---|---|---|---|
| Pittsburgh | 0 2 0 | 0 1 2 | 0 3 X — 8 |
| Philadelphia | 1 0 3 | 0 0 0 | 0 1 0 — 5 |

Two-base hits — Whitted, Zinn. Three-base hit — Barnhart. Home runs — Williams. Stolen bases — Le Bourveau, Konetchy. Sacrifices — Walker (2), Peters, Bigbee, Tierney. Double play — Maranville, Tierney and Grimm. Left on bases — Philadelphia 6, Pittsburgh, 5. Base on balls — Off Ring 4, Carlson 2, Zinn 1. Hits — Off Carlson 5 in 3, Zinn 6 in 6. Hit by pitcher — By Ring (Grimm). Struck out — By Ring 3, Carlson 1, Zinn 3. Wild pitch — Ring. Winning pitcher — Zinn. Losing pitcher — Ring. Umpires — Rigler and Moran. Time of game — 1:57.

Editors' Note: Pittsburgh was the home team, but was cited first in the box score.

The sixth game of the 1925 World Series, October 13, 1925 (Bettmann/Corbis).

**July 7, 1922:** Max Carey demonstrated his versatility by getting six hits (five singles and a double), three walks, and three stolen bases—including one of home—and making seven putouts in an 18-inning, 9–8 loss to the New York Giants. Carey's offensive performance set a major league record that hasn't been broken for the most times reaching base in an extra-inning game.

**May 7, 1925:** Glenn Wright dazzled the Pirate fans by pulling off an unassisted triple play against the St. Louis Cardinals.

**October 13, 1925:** After having been down three games to one and then three games to two against the Washington Senators in the second World Series played at Forbes Field, Pittsburgh evened matters when Eddie Moore hit a home run in the fifth inning of the sixth game to give the Bucs a 3–2 lead and the victory.

**October 15, 1925:** With the bases loaded in the bottom of the eighth inning of the seventh game of the World Series, the scored tied at seven, and Walter Johnson on the mound for the Washington Senators, Kiki Cuyler doubled to right on a rain-soaked field to drive in two runs and win the game for the Corsairs, 9–7.

## October 15, 1925: Cuyler's Clutch Hit

| WASH'TON (A.L.) | AB | R | H | O | A | E | PITTSBURGH (N.L.) | AB | R | H | O | A | E |
|---|---|---|---|---|---|---|---|---|---|---|---|---|---|
| Rice, cf | 5 | 2 | 2 | 3 | 0 | 0 | Moore, 2b | 4 | 3 | 1 | 2 | 0 | 1 |
| S. Harris, 2b | 5 | 0 | 0 | 6 | 3 | 0 | Carey, cf | 5 | 3 | 4 | 4 | 0 | 0 |
| Goslin, lf | 4 | 2 | 1 | 2 | 0 | 0 | Cuyler, rf | 4 | 0 | 2 | 4 | 0 | 1 |
| J. Harris, rf | 3 | 1 | 1 | 1 | 1 | 0 | Barnhart, lf | 5 | 0 | 1 | 2 | 0 | 0 |
| Judge, 1b | 3 | 1 | 1 | 6 | 0 | 0 | Oldham, p | 0 | 0 | 0 | 0 | 0 | 0 |

| WASH'TON (A.L.) | AB | R | H | O | A | E |
|---|---|---|---|---|---|---|
| Bluege, 3b | 4 | 0 | 1 | 0 | 0 | 0 |
| a Peckinpaugh, ss | 3 | 1 | 1 | 0 | 2 | 2 |
| Ruel, c | 4 | 0 | 0 | 6 | 0 | 0 |
| Johnson, p | 4 | 0 | 0 | 0 | 3 | 0 |
| Totals | 35 | 7 | 7 | 24 | 9 | 2 |

| PITTSBURGH (N.L.) | AB | R | H | O | A | E |
|---|---|---|---|---|---|---|
| Traynor, 3b | 4 | 0 | 1 | 1 | 3 | 0 |
| Wright, ss | 4 | 0 | 1 | 1 | 3 | 0 |
| McInnis, 1b | 4 | 0 | 2 | 7 | 0 | 0 |
| Smith, c | 4 | 0 | 1 | 4 | 0 | 0 |
| c Yde | 0 | 1 | 0 | 0 | 0 | 0 |
| Gooch, c | 0 | 0 | 0 | 2 | 0 | 0 |
| Aldridge, p | 0 | 0 | 0 | 0 | 0 | 0 |
| Morrison, p | 1 | 1 | 1 | 0 | 0 | 0 |
| b Grantham | 1 | 0 | 0 | 0 | 0 | 0 |
| Kremer, p | 1 | 0 | 0 | 0 | 1 | 0 |
| d Bigbee, lf | 1 | 1 | 1 | 0 | 0 | 0 |
| Totals | 38 | 9 | 15 | 27 | 7 | 2 |

a Peckinpaugh given base in first inning on Smith's interference.
b Flied out for Morrison in fourth.
c Ran for Smith in eighth.
d Doubled for Kremer in eighth.

Washington    4 0 0    2 0 0    0 1 0 — 7
Pittsburgh     0 0 3    0 1 0    2 3 * — 9

Runs batted in — Barnhart, Moore, Cuyler 3, Carey 2, Traynor, Bluege, Ruel, J. Harris 2, Bigbee, Peckinpaugh 2. Two-base hits — Carey 3, Moore, J. Harris, Cuyler 2, Smith, Bigbee. Three-base hit — Traynor. Home run — Peckinpaugh. Sacrifice hit — Cuyler. Stolen base — Carey. Double play — S. Harris and Judge. Left on bases — Pittsburgh 7, Washington 5. Earned runs — Washington 7, Pittsburgh 5. Struck out — By Morrison 2, by Kremer 1, by Oldham 2, by Johnson 3. Bases on balls — Off Aldridge 3, off Johnson 1. Wild pitches — Aldridge 2. Hits — Off Aldridge 2 in ⅓ inning, off Morrison 4 in 3⅔ innings, off Kremer 1 in 4 innings, off Oldham 0 in 1 inning. Winning pitcher — Kremer. Umpires — McCormick (N.L.), Moriarty (A.L.), Rigler (N.L.) and Owens (A.L.). Time — 2:31. Attendance — 42,856.

**August 26, 1926:** In a day full of sixes, Paul Waner got six hits in six at bats with six different bats as the Bucs outscored the New York Giants, 15–7.

**May 30, 1927:** What goes around comes around. In the first game of a doubleheader, Jimmy Cooney, who was one of the Cardinal runners erased from the base paths during Glenn Wright's unassisted triple play, performed his own unassisted triple play against the Pirates while playing for the Chicago Cubs.

**October 5, 1927:** The first encounter with the great '27 New York Yankees almost produced a Pirate victory, but the Bucs beat themselves with fielding mistakes and lost, 5–4.

**August 30, 1929:** Pie Traynor went five for five as the Pirates destroyed the league-leading, and eventual pennant-winning, Chicago Cubs, 15–0.

**September 22, 1931:** Hal Finney, the Pirate catcher, had no putouts in a 13-inning, 3–2 Pirate victory over Philadelphia. In the same game, Paul Waner walked five times.

**May 7, 1932:** In an unusual Pittsburgh-Philadelphia doubleheader, the Pirates played the Philadelphia Phillies in the first game, and the Homestead Grays played the Philadelphia Hilldales in the second game.

**June 30, 1932:** The Pirates celebrated the first Ladies Day at Forbes by defeating the defending World Series champion St. Louis Cardinals, 9–6. It was the Pirates' seventh victory in a row.

**April 29, 1934:** In the first major league baseball game played in Pittsburgh on a Sunday, the Pirates downed the Cincinnati Reds, 9–5.

**May 25, 1935:** Babe Ruth, now in a Boston Braves' uniform, showed a final burst of power by hitting three home runs at Forbes Field — the last three of his career. The third of the three went over the right field roof, making Ruth the first ballplayer to ever accomplish that feat. However, the Pirates won the game, 11–7.

Part of the first Ladies Day crowd at Forbes Field, June 30, 1932 (Pittsburgh Pirates Baseball Club).

## May 25, 1935: The Babe

| BOSTON (N). | AB | R | H | PO | A | E |
|---|---|---|---|---|---|---|
| Urbanski, ss | 3 | 1 | 0 | 1 | 1 | 0 |
| Mallon, 2b | 4 | 2 | 1 | 4 | 4 | 1 |
| Mowry, rf | 1 | 0 | 1 | 0 | 0 | 0 |
| Ruth, rf | 4 | 3 | 4 | 3 | 0 | 0 |
| Berger, cf | 5 | 1 | 3 | 4 | 0 | 0 |
| Moore, 1b | 4 | 0 | 2 | 6 | 0 | 0 |
| Lee, lf | 5 | 0 | 0 | 3 | 1 | 0 |
| Coscarart, 3b | 4 | 0 | 2 | 0 | 3 | 0 |
| Spohrer, c | 4 | 0 | 0 | 3 | 0 | 0 |
| Betts, p | 2 | 0 | 0 | 0 | 1 | 0 |
| Cantwell, p | 1 | 0 | 0 | 0 | 1 | 0 |
| a Whitney | 1 | 0 | 0 | 0 | 0 | 0 |
| Benton, p | 0 | 0 | 0 | 0 | 0 | 0 |
| Total | 38 | 7 | 13 | 24 | 11 | 1 |

| PITTSBURGH (N). | AB | R | H | PO | A | E |
|---|---|---|---|---|---|---|
| L. Waner, cf | 5 | 2 | 3 | 3 | 0 | 0 |
| Jensen, lf | 4 | 1 | 2 | 1 | 0 | 0 |
| P. Waner, rf | 4 | 2 | 2 | 5 | 0 | 0 |
| Vaughan, ss | 4 | 2 | 2 | 1 | 2 | 0 |
| Young, 2b | 3 | 1 | 1 | 3 | 3 | 0 |
| Suhr, 1b | 3 | 2 | 2 | 11 | 0 | 0 |
| Thevenow, 3b | 4 | 1 | 2 | 0 | 4 | 0 |
| Grace, c | 4 | 0 | 0 | 3 | 0 | 0 |
| Lucas, p | 0 | 0 | 0 | 0 | 0 | 0 |
| Bush, p | 3 | 0 | 0 | 0 | 3 | 0 |
| Hoyt, p | 1 | 0 | 0 | 0 | 1 | 0 |
| Total | 35 | 11 | 14 | 27 | 13 | 0 |

a Batted for Cantwell in eighth.

```
Boston       2 0 2  0 1 0  2 0 0 — 7
Pittsburgh   0 0 0  4 3 0  3 1 .. — 11
```

Runs batted in — Ruth 6, Suhr, Thevenow 5, Young 3, Grace, Lee, Vaughan. Two-base hits— Mallon, Thevenow. Three-base hits— Thevenow, Suhr, L. Waner. Home runs— Ruth 3, Young. Sacrifices— Mallon, Young, Jensen. Double plays— Vauhan [sic], Young and Suhr; Urbanski, Mallon and Moore. Left on bases— Boston 8, Pittsburgh 5. Bases on balls— Off Lucas 1, Betts 1, Bush 2, Cantwell 2. Struck out — By Betts 1, Hoyt 2. Hits— Off Lucas 3 in 1–3 inning, Betts 9 in 4 2–3, Hoyt 2 in 2 2–3, Bush 8 in 6, Cantwell 3 in 2 1–3, Benton 2 in 1. Winning pitcher — Hoyt. Losing pitcher — Cantwell. Umpires— Reardon, Magerkurth and Moran. Time of game — 2:14.

**July 10, 1936:** Chuck Klein of the Philadelphia Phillies put on an awesome display of slugging by blasting four home runs (in the first, fifth, seventh, and tenth innings) and a deep fly out (to the right field wall in the second inning) in five at bats during a 10-inning 9–6 victory over the Pirates.

## July 10, 1936: Klein's Clouts

| PHILADELPHIA (N). | AB | R | H | PO | A | E | PITTSBURGH (N). | AB | R | H | PO | A | E |
|---|---|---|---|---|---|---|---|---|---|---|---|---|---|
| Sulik, cf | 5 | 1 | 1 | 5 | 0 | 0 | Jensen, lf | 4 | 1 | 1 | 3 | 0 | 0 |
| J. Moore, lf | 5 | 1 | 1 | 1 | 0 | 0 | L. Waner, cf | 4 | 1 | 1 | 4 | 0 | 1 |
| Klein, rf | 5 | 4 | 4 | 5 | 0 | 0 | P. Waner, rf | 4 | 2 | 2 | 1 | 0 | 0 |
| Camilli, 1b | 4 | 2 | 1 | 10 | 1 | 0 | Vaughan, ss | 5 | 0 | 1 | 2 | 2 | 2 |
| Atwood, c | 4 | 0 | 1 | 2 | 0 | 0 | Suhr, 1b | 4 | 0 | 2 | 13 | 1 | 0 |
| Wilson, c | 0 | 1 | 0 | 0 | 0 | 0 | B'baker, 3b | 5 | 0 | 0 | 1 | 1 | 0 |
| Chiozza, 3b | 5 | 0 | 2 | 1 | 1 | 0 | Young, 2b | 3 | 0 | 1 | 1 | 5 | 1 |
| Norris, ss | 4 | 0 | 1 | 3 | 4 | 2 | Lavag'to, 2b | 1 | 1 | 0 | 1 | 1 | 0 |
| Gomez, 2b | 5 | 0 | 0 | 3 | 2 | 0 | Todd, c | 2 | 0 | 0 | 3 | 0 | 0 |
| Passeau, p | 4 | 0 | 1 | 0 | 0 | 0 | Padden, c | 2 | 1 | 0 | 1 | 0 | 0 |
| Walter, p | 0 | 0 | 0 | 0 | 1 | 0 | Weaver, p | 1 | 0 | 0 | 0 | 2 | 0 |
| Total | 41 | 9 | 12 | 30 | 9 | 2 | a Lucas | 1 | 0 | 0 | 0 | 0 | 0 |
| | | | | | | | Brown, p | 1 | 0 | 0 | 0 | 2 | 0 |
| | | | | | | | b Schultze [sic] | 1 | 0 | 1 | 0 | 0 | 0 |
| | | | | | | | c Finney | 0 | 0 | 0 | 0 | 0 | 0 |
| | | | | | | | Swift, p | 0 | 0 | 0 | 0 | 0 | 0 |
| | | | | | | | Total | 38 | 6 | 9 | 30 | 14 | 4 |

a Batted for Weaver in fifth.
b Batted for Brown in ninth.
c Ran for Schulte in ninth.

Philadelphia  4 0 0  0 1 0  1 0 0  3 — 9
Pittsburgh    0 0 0  1 0 3  0 0 2  0 — 6

Runs batted in — Klein 6, Norris 2, Suhr, P. Waner, Vaughan, Schulte, L. Waner, Chiozza. Two-base hit — Camilli. Three-base hit — Suhr. Home runs — Klein 4. Sacrifices — Atwood, Norris. Double plays — Chiozza, Gomez and Camilli; Camilli, Norris and Camilli; Vaughan, Lavagetto and Suhr; Walter, Gomez and Camilli. Left on bases — Philadelphia 5, Pittsburgh 7. Bases on balls — Off Weaver 1, Passeau 2. Walter 3. Struck out — By Weaver 2, Passeau 1, Brown 1. Hits — Off Weaver 6 in 5 innings, Brown 2 in 4, Swift 4 in 1, Passeau 8 in 8 2–3, Walter 1 in 1 1–3. Winning pitcher — Walter. Losing pitcher — Swift. Umpires — Sears, Klem and Ballanfant. Time of game — 2:15.

**June 4, 1940:** The Pirates destroyed the Boston Braves, 14–2, in the first major league night game played at Forbes Field.

**September 21, 1940:** After going hitless in the first game of a doubleheader against the Cincinnati Reds, Debs Garms got five hits in six at bats, including the game winner, in the second game to clinch the National League batting championship.

**July 11, 1944:** Forbes hosted the Major League All-Star Game for the first time. The National League easily handled the American League by a score of 7–1, but the highlight of the game for Pirate fans was the appearance of Rip Sewell, who pitched three no-hit, scoreless innings, and displayed his famous "eephus" pitch. Sewell threw the pitch three times, but no American League batter could successfully put it in play.

**May 15, 1947:** Jackie Robinson played his first game at Forbes. Robinson went two for five,

The first night game at Forbes Field, June 4, 1940 (Pittsburgh Photographic Library Collection of Carnegie Library of Pittsburgh).

with two runs driven in, but the Pirates beat the eventual pennant-winning Brooklyn Dodgers, 7–3.

**September 12, 1947:** Dale Long would later have his place in the sun when he hit eight home runs in eight games, but on this date, Ralph Kiner one-upped him by hitting his eighth home run in four games as the Pirates bested the Boston Braves, 4–3. Kiner's second round tripper of the game broke Tony Lazzeri's record of seven homers in four games in 1936.

**September 30, 1949:** Ralph Kiner bashed his 54th home run of the season and his 16th during the month of September — a shot over the clock in left field — as the Pirates defeated Cincinnati, 3–2. This is still a National League record for September.

**June 22, 1951:** Patience is a virtue: Ten thousand loyal fans out of a total attendance of 24,966 remained to watch the latest single game to end at Forbes Field, an 8–4 loss to the Brooklyn Dodgers. A power failure delayed the game for two hours and 14 minutes, and then rain stopped the game for another 36 minutes. So, by the time the final out was recorded, it was 1:56 A.M.

**May 25, 1953:** Ralph Kiner joined an elite group of sluggers on the 18th anniversary of Babe Ruth's triple-home-run barrage when he hit his 300th career homer in a 6–3 Pirate loss to the New York Giants.

**April 13, 1954:** Curt Roberts, the first African American to wear a Pirate uniform, played his first game at Forbes Field, a 4–2 Pittsburgh victory over the Philadelphia Phillies. Roberts went one for three (a triple) and recorded three putouts and five assists before being pinch-hit for in the eighth inning.

## April 13, 1954: The Pirates' Jackie Robinson

| PHILADELPHIA (N.) | AB | R | H | PO | A | PITTSBURGH (N.) | AB | R | H | PO | A |
|---|---|---|---|---|---|---|---|---|---|---|---|
| Kazanski, ss | 5 | 0 | 0 | 3 | 4 | Abrams, cf | 3 | 1 | 1 | 0 | 0 |
| Ashburn, cf | 4 | 0 | 0 | 3 | 0 | C. Rob'ts, 2b | 3 | 0 | 1 | 3 | 5 |
| Torgeson, 1b | 4 | 0 | 0 | 3 | 0 | c Skinner | 1 | 1 | 1 | 0 | 0 |
| Ennis, lf | 3 | 0 | 1 | 3 | 0 | Rice, lf | 4 | 0 | 1 | 3 | 1 |
| Hamner, 2b | 4 | 0 | 2 | 5 | 1 | Gordon, 3b | 3 | 0 | 0 | 0 | 2 |
| Wyrostek, rf | 3 | 0 | 0 | 1 | 0 | Thomas, cf | 3 | 0 | 0 | 4 | 0 |
| Jones, 3b | 1 | 0 | 1 | 1 | 1 | Ward, 1b | 4 | 0 | 1 | 12 | 0 |
| d Schell | 1 | 0 | 0 | 0 | 0 | Allie, ss | 2 | 1 | 0 | 1 | 4 |
| Lopata, c | 4 | 1 | 3 | 5 | 1 | Atwell, c | 3 | 1 | 2 | 4 | 0 |
| R. Rob'ts, p | 2 | 1 | 0 | 0 | 0 | Friend, p | 1 | 0 | 0 | 0 | 1 |
| K'stanty, p | 0 | 0 | 0 | 0 | 0 | a Henley | 1 | 0 | 0 | 0 | 0 |
| e Jok | 1 | 0 | 0 | 0 | 0 | Law, p | 0 | 0 | 0 | 0 | 0 |
| Total | 32 | 2 | 7 | 24 | 7 | b Pel'grini | 0 | 0 | 0 | 0 | 0 |
| | | | | | | Hetki, p | 0 | 0 | 0 | 0 | 0 |
| | | | | | | Total | 28 | 4 | 7 | 27 | 13 |

a Grounded out for Friend in sixth.
b Sacrificed for Law in eighth.
c Singled for C. Roberts in eighth.
d Flied out for Jones in ninth.
e Flied out for Konstanty in ninth.

Philadelphia  0 0 0   0 2 0   0 0 0 — 2
Pittsburgh    0 0 0   0 0 0   0 4 ..— 4

Error — Lopata. Runs batted in — Ashburn, Abrams, Skinner, Rice, Thomas. Two-base hit — Rice. Three-base hits — Lopata, C. Roberts. Stolen bases — Wyrostek, Pellagrini. Sacrifice fly — Thomas. Double plays — Hamner, Kazanski and Torgeson; Roberts, Allie and Ward. Left on bases — Philadelphia 7, Pittsburgh 5. Bases on balls — Off Roberts 2, Konstanty, Friend, 4. Struck out — By Roberts 4, Friend 3. Hits — Off Roberts 6 in 7½ innings, Konstanty 1 in 2–3, Friend 6 in 6, Law 0 in 2, Hetki 1 in 1. Runs and earned runs — Off Roberts 2 and 2, Konstanty 2 and 2, Friend 2 and 2. Balk — Friend. Winning pitcher — Law (1–0). Losing pitcher [—] Roberts (0–1). Umpires — Goetz, Dascoli, Gorman and Dixon. Time of game — 2:15. Attendance — 32,294.

**April 17, 1955:** Roberto Clemente made his major league debut in the first game of a doubleheader against the Brooklyn Dodgers. In his first at bat, he beat out an infield single off Johnny Podres and then scored a run after Frank Thomas (The Original One) tripled.

**May 19, 1956:** Dale Long began his eight-home-runs-in-eight-games hitting spree by smashing a Jim Davis pitch into the upper deck of right field to help the Pirates defeat the Chicago Cubs, 7–4.

**May 28, 1956:** Dale Long delighted the Pirate faithful by socking his eighth home run in eight games, a shot off Carl Erskine as the Pirates beat the Brooklyn Dodgers, 3–2. Lost in the hoopla over Long's spectacular performance — still a National League record — was the fact that Bob Friend pitched a two-hitter.

## May 28, 1956: Eight in Eight

| BROOKLYN (N.) | AB | R | H | PO | A | PITTSBURGH (N.) | AB | R | H | PO | A |
|---|---|---|---|---|---|---|---|---|---|---|---|
| Gilliam, 2b | 3 | 1 | 1 | 1 | 1 | Virdon, cf | 4 | 0 | 1 | 3 | 0 |
| Reese, ss | 3 | 0 | 0 | 3 | 4 | Groat, ss | 4 | 0 | 0 | 1 | 7 |
| Snider, cf | 3 | 1 | 1 | 3 | 1 | Long, 1b | 4 | 1 | 1 | 14 | 0 |
| C'mp'nella, c | 4 | 0 | 0 | 5 | 0 | Thomas, lf | 4 | 0 | 2 | 1 | 0 |
| Hodges, 1b | 3 | 0 | 0 | 9 | 2 | c Clem'nte, lf | 0 | 0 | 0 | 0 | 0 |
| Robinson, 3b | 1 | 0 | 0 | 1 | 1 | Walls, rf | 4 | 1 | 1 | 1 | 0 |
| Amoros, lf | 3 | 0 | 0 | 0 | 0 | Freese, 3b | 3 | 0 | 0 | 0 | 3 |
| Furillo, rf | 3 | 0 | 0 | 1 | 0 | Foiles, c | 2 | 1 | 1 | 5 | 1 |
| Erskine, p | 2 | 0 | 0 | 1 | 3 | J. O'Brien, 2b | 1 | 0 | 0 | 1 | 2 |
| b Jackson | 1 | 0 | 0 | 0 | 0 | a Skinner | 1 | 0 | 1 | 0 | 0 |
| Labine, p | 0 | 0 | 0 | 0 | 1 | Roberts, 2b | 1 | 0 | 1 | 1 | 2 |
| Total | 26 | 2 | 2 | 24 | 13 | Friend, p | 2 | 0 | 0 | 0 | 1 |
| | | | | | | Total | 30 | 3 | 8 | 27 | 16 |

a Singled for J. O'Brien in fifth.
b Grounded out for Erskine in eighth.
c Ran for Thomas in eighth.

| Brooklyn | 2 0 0 | 0 0 0 | 0 0 0 — 2 |
|---|---|---|---|
| Pittsburgh | 0 1 0 | 1 1 0 | 0 0 .. — 3 |

Error — Gilliam. Runs batted in — Snider 2, Freese, Long, Skinner. Two-base hit — Roberts. Three-base hits — Walls, Foiles. Home runs — Snider, Long. Sacrifice — Friend. Sacrifice fly — Freese. Double plays — Erskine, Reese and Hodges; Groat, J. O'Brien and Long; Groat, Roberts and Long. Left on bases — Brooklyn 3, Pittsburgh 6. Bases on balls — Off Erskine 1, Friend 6. Struck out — By Erskine 3, Labine 1, Friend 3. Hits — Off Erskine 7 in 7 innings, Labine 1 in 1. Runs and earned runs — Off Erskine 3 and 3, Friend 2 and 2. Winning pitcher — Friend (8–2). Losing pitcher — Erskine (2–4). Umpires — Ballanfant, Gore, Jackowski and Crawford. Time of game — 2:13. Attendance — 32,221.

**July 25, 1956:** With the bases loaded, no one out, and the Pirates trailing the Chicago Cubs 8–5 in the bottom of the ninth, Roberto Clemente hit an inside-the-park grand slam off Jim Brosnan to give Pittsburgh the victory. Interestingly enough, Clemente ran through Bobby Bragan's hold sign to narrowly score the winning run.

**July 18, 1957:** Ernie Banks and Chuck Tanner each accounted for an inside-the-park home run for the Chicago Cubs, but the Pirates still squeaked out a victory, 6–5. Tanner later managed the Buccos for nine seasons and led them to the 1979 World Series championship.

**September 8, 1958:** Roberto Clemente hit three triples as the Pirates beat Cincinnati, 4–1.

**June 5, 1959:** Dr. Strangeglove — Dick Stuart — became the first and only major leaguer to slug a home run over the 457 mark with a blast during a 10–5 loss to the Chicago Cubs.

**July 7, 1959:** Forbes hosted the Major League All-Star Game for the second time, the first of two such exhibitions held that season. This one was an exciting contest, with the National League rallying for two runs in the bottom of the eighth to win by a score of 5–4.

**August 30, 1959:** ElRoy Face won his 17th game in a row in relief for the season, still a major league record for relievers, and recorded his 22nd consecutive relief victory, a streak dat-

Forbes Field was the site of the first of two All-Star games in 1959 in which the National League defeated the American League, 5–4 (copyright, *Pittsburgh Post-Gazette*, 2005, all rights reserved. Reprinted with permission).

ing back to the '58 season. And in doing so, Face helped the Pirates edge the Philadelphia Phillies, 7–6, in the second game of a doubleheader sweep. Trailing 5–0 at one point, the Pirates rallied to tie the game at five at the end of nine innings. Face then gave up a home run to Ed Bouchee in the top of the 10th, but Pittsburgh scored twice in the bottom of the 10th to pull out the victory.

**September 11, 1959:** Roy Face's consecutive win streak ended at 22 as the Los Angeles Dodgers beat the Pirates, 5–4.

**June 30, 1960:** Dick Stuart once again demonstrated his hitting prowess by belting three home runs and driving in seven runs as the Pirates took the second game of a doubleheader against the San Francisco Giants, 11–6, after getting shut out in the first game.

**October 5, 1960:** The Pirates, behind Bill Mazeroski's bat and glove, stunned the heavily favored New York Yankees in the first game of the 1960 World Series, 6–4.

**October 13, 1960:** In storybook fashion, Bill Mazeroski hit a homer off Ralph Terry in the bottom of the ninth inning to upset the powerful New York Yankees and clinch the World Series for the Pirates. As during the 1909 and 1925 World Series, October 13 proved to be a lucky day once again for the Pirates.

## October 13, 1960: We Had 'Em All the Way!

| NEW YORK YANKEES | AB | R | H | RBI | PO | A | PITTSBURGH PIRATES | AB | R | H | RBI | PO | A |
|---|---|---|---|---|---|---|---|---|---|---|---|---|---|
| Richardson, b | 5 | 2 | 2 | 0 | 2 | 5 | Virdon, cf | 4 | 1 | 2 | 2 | 3 | 0 |
| Kubek, ss | 3 | 1 | 0 | 0 | 3 | 2 | Groat, ss | 4 | 1 | 1 | 1 | 3 | 2 |
| DeMaestri, ss | 0 | 0 | 0 | 0 | 0 | 0 | Skinner, lf | 2 | 1 | 0 | 0 | 1 | 0 |
| d Long | 1 | 0 | 1 | 0 | 0 | 0 | Nelson, 1b | 3 | 1 | 1 | 2 | 7 | 0 |
| e McD'gald, 3b | 0 | 1 | 0 | 0 | 0 | 0 | Clemente, rf | 4 | 1 | 1 | 1 | 4 | 0 |
| Maris, rf | 5 | 0 | 0 | 0 | 2 | 0 | Burgess, c | 3 | 0 | 2 | 0 | 0 | 0 |
| Mantle, cf | 5 | 1 | 3 | 2 | 0 | 0 | d Christopher | 0 | 0 | 0 | 0 | 0 | 0 |
| Berra, lf | 4 | 2 | 1 | 4 | 3 | 0 | Smith, c | 1 | 1 | 1 | 3 | 1 | 0 |

(continued on page 51)

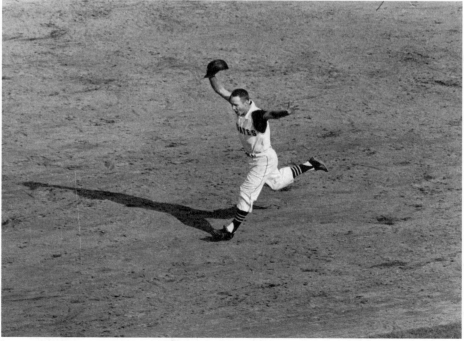

*Top:* Bill Mazeroski launches his World Series–winning home run that beat the New York Yankees, 10–9, on October 13, 1960 (Marvin E. Newman, *Sports Illustrated*). *Bottom:* Mazeroski triumphantly passing second base (copyright, *Pittsburgh Post-Gazette*, 2005, all rights reserved. Reprinted with permission).

*Left:* Coach Frank Oceak and two unidentified young fans greet Mazeroski as he rounds the third base and heads for home (copyright, *Pittsburgh Post-Gazette*, 2005, all rights reserved. Reprinted with permission). *Bottom:* Mazeroski nears home plate where teammates and fans wait to celebrate the Pirates' victory. In the foreground, New York Yankee manager Casey Stengel (32), looking ahead, walks off in defeat (copyright, *Pittsburgh Post-Gazette*, 2005, all rights reserved. Reprinted with permission).

|  | AB | R | H | RBI | PO | A |
|---|---|---|---|---|---|---|
| **NEW YORK YANKEES** | | | | | | |
| Skowron, 1b | 5 | 2 | 2 | 1 | 10 | 2 |
| Blanchard, c | 4 | 0 | 1 | 1 | 1 | 1 |
| Boyer, 3b, ss | 4 | 0 | 1 | 1 | 0 | 3 |
| Turley, p | 0 | 0 | 0 | 0 | 0 | 0 |
| Stafford, p | 0 | 0 | 0 | 0 | 0 | 1 |
| a Lopez | 1 | 0 | 1 | 0 | 0 | 0 |
| Shantz, p | 3 | 0 | 1 | 0 | 3 | 1 |
| Coates, p | 0 | 0 | 0 | 0 | 0 | 0 |
| Terry, p | 0 | 0 | 0 | 0 | 0 | 0 |
| **Total** | 40 | 9 | 13 | 9 | 24 | 15 |

|  | AB | R | H | RBI | PO | A |
|---|---|---|---|---|---|---|
| **PITTSBURGH PIRATES** | | | | | | |
| Hoak, 3b | 3 | 1 | 0 | 0 | 3 | 2 |
| Mazeroski, 2b | 4 | 2 | 2 | 1 | 5 | 0 |
| Law, p | 2 | 0 | 0 | 0 | 0 | 1 |
| Face, p | 0 | 0 | 0 | 0 | 0 | 1 |
| c Cimoli | 1 | 1 | 1 | 0 | 0 | 0 |
| Friend, p | 0 | 0 | 0 | 0 | 0 | 0 |
| Haddix, p | 0 | 0 | 0 | 0 | 0 | 0 |
| **Total** | 31 | 10 | 11 | 10 | 27 | 6 |

a Singled for Stafford in third.
b Ran for Burgess in seventh.
c Singled for Face in eighth.
d Singled for DeMaestri in ninth.
e Ran for Long in ninth.

```
New York      0 0 0   0 1 4   0 2 2 — 9
Pittsburgh    2 2 0   0 0 0   0 5 1 — 10
```

None out when winning run was scored. Error—Maris. Double plays—Stafford, Blanchard and Skowron; Richardson, Kubek and Skowron; Kubek, Richardson and Skowron, Left on bases—New York 6, Pittsburgh 1. Two-base hit—Boyer. Home runs—Nelson, Skowrun [*sic*], Berra, Smith, Mazeroski. Sacrifice—Skinner.

|  | IP | H | R | ER |
|---|---|---|---|---|
| † Law | 5 | 4 | 3 | 3 |
| Face | 3 | 6 | 4 | 4 |
| ¶ Friend | 0 | 2 | 2 | 2 |
| Haddix (W.) | 1 | 1 | 0 | 0 |
| • Turley | 1 | 2 | 3 | 3 |
| Stafford | 1 | 2 | 1 | 1 |
| ◊ Shantz | 5 | 4 | 3 | 3 |
| Coates | ⅔ | 2 | 2 | 2 |
| § Terry (L.) | ⅓ | 1 | 1 | 1 |

• Faced 1 batter in second.
† Faced 2 batters in sixth.
◊ Faced 3 batters in eighth.
¶ Faced 2 batters in ninth.
§ Faced 1 batter in ninth.

Bases on balls—Law 1 (Kubek), Face 1 (Berra), Turley 1 (Skinner), Stafford 1 (Hoak), Shantz 1 (Nelson). Umpires—Jackowski (N.), plate; Chylak (A.), first base; Boggess (N.), second base; Stevens (A.), third base; Landes (N.), left field; Honochick (A.), right field. Time of game—2:36.

Editors' Notes: Richardson's position should have been listed as "2b" and the letter before Christopher's name should have been a "b."

**June 18, 1961:** Don Leppert hit a home run in his first major league at bat as the Pirates defeated the St. Louis Cardinals, 5–3.

**September 26, 1961:** Joe Gibbon came close to breaking the Forbes Field jinx on no-hitters by giving up only one hit to the Los Angeles Dodgers in the second game of a twilight doubleheader. The Dodgers had won the first game, 5–3, but the Pirates took the nightcap, 8–0, with the one hit being a single to left by pinch hitter Bob Aspromonte to lead off the sixth inning. Aspromonte advanced to second on a fielder's choice, but was then picked off by Gibbon on a throw to Dick Groat. The Pirate win clinched the National League championship for Cincinnati by eliminating Los Angeles from the pennant race.

**April 22, 1962:** The Bucs downed the New York Mets, 4–3, to win their 10th consecutive game since the start of the season — still a Pirate record for the team's best start — and to give the winless Mets their ninth straight loss.

**April 23, 1962:** Behind the five-hit pitching of Jay Hook, the New York Mets stopped the Pirates' winning streak and won the first game of their young franchise's history. Bob Prince would later say that he would rather face a 10–0 team than an 0–9 team any day of the week.

**April 9, 1963:** In the home opener, Roberto Clemente's great defensive play in the top of the ninth inning helped to preserve a 2–2 tie with Milwaukee and set the stage for the Pirates to edge the Braves, 3–2, in the bottom of the ninth. Perhaps the best description of the play was provided by the famous Pittsburgh sportswriter and, at that time, sports editor of *The Pittsburgh Press*, Chet Smith, when he wrote:

> As the stage was set, the Braves had a run in to tie the score at 2–2, and the bases filled.... Del Crandall bumped a short fly to right, which Clemente dived for at an angle, caught, did a complete flip-flop and came up with arm cocked to throw.... Eddie Mathews, on third, showed so much respect for the Senor's whip that he made nary a move toward the plate.... Mack Jones, on second, had tagged up and was off with the catch, but quickly sized up what was going on, and returned.... He escaped being doubled on Clemente's snap to Dick Schofield by a split second miss of the necessary tag.
>
> In the press box, a voice exclaimed, "Maybe there's another outfielder in the league who could have made that catch, recovery and throw the way Bob did it, but he'd have to show me. And that goes for them all, Willie Mays included.["]
>
> No one gave the speaker an argument.... He was so right [*The Pittsburgh Press*, April 14, 1963, sec. 4, p. 2].

**August 9, 1963:** Thank God that it was a Friday evening! Pittsburgh and Houston played the longest doubleheader in Forbes Field history. Houston won the first game, a rain-delayed 15-inning marathon, by the score of 7–6. Pittsburgh retaliated by winning the second game, a relatively shorter marathon, by the same score. Only 400 or 500 fans remained by the time the second contest ended at 2:30 A.M. the next morning. Interestingly enough, just a few hours earlier, Warren Giles, the president of the National League, suspended the curfew rules for night games, except for those played on Saturday nights in New York, Philadelphia, and Pittsburgh.

**September 15, 1963:** The Three Hermanos. The Alou brothers — Felipe, Matteo, and Jesus — made baseball history by appearing together in the outfield for the San Francisco Giants. Felipe played center field, Matty played left, and Jesus played right during the eighth and ninth innings of a 13–5 Giant victory over the Bucs.

**June 1, 1965:** Bob Veale set a Pirate record by striking out 16 Philadelphia Phillies in a 12-inning game that suffered from three rain delays.

**September 2, 1966:** Roberto Clemente got his 2,000th hit, a three-run homer off Ferguson Jenkins, to help defeat the Chicago Cubs, 7–3, and give the Pirates sole possession of first place.

**July 9, 1967:** In the bottom of the ninth, with the Pirates and the Cincinnati Reds tied at one, Willie Stargell blasted the first of his seven career home runs over the right field roof to give the Bucs a 2–1 victory.

**June 14, 1968:** Pirate rookie Bob Moose got the closest to throwing a no-hitter in Forbes when he pitched hitless ball against the Houston Astros for seven and two-thirds innings until the former Pirate, Julio Gotay, singled in the eighth. Moose gave up another single in the ninth — this time to Ron Davis — before the Pirates won the game, 3–0.

## June 14, 1968: So Close, Yet So Far Away

| HOUSTON (N.) | AB | R | H | BI | | PITTSBURGH (N.) | AB | R | H | BI |
|---|---|---|---|---|---|---|---|---|---|---|
| Davis, cf | 4 | 0 | 1 | 0 | | Willis, 3b | 4 | 0 | 1 | 0 |
| Torres, ss | 4 | 0 | 0 | 0 | | Pagan, lf | 3 | 0 | 0 | 0 |

| HOUSTON (N.) | AB | R | H | BI |
|---|---|---|---|---|
| Staub, 1b | 3 | 0 | 0 | 0 |
| Thomas, rf | 3 | 0 | 0 | 0 |
| Wynn, lf | 3 | 0 | 0 | 0 |
| Aspr'm'te, 3b | 3 | 0 | 0 | 0 |
| Gotay, 2b | 3 | 0 | 1 | 0 |
| Bateman, c | 3 | 0 | 0 | 0 |
| Lemaster, p | 2 | 0 | 0 | 0 |
| Murrell, ph | 1 | 0 | 0 | 0 |
| Total | 29 | 0 | 2 | 0 |

| PITTSBURGH (N.) | AB | R | H | BI |
|---|---|---|---|---|
| Alou, cf | 0 | 0 | 0 | 0 |
| Clemente, rf | 4 | 1 | 3 | 0 |
| Mota, cf | 2 | 0 | 0 | 1 |
| Clendenon, 1b | 4 | 1 | 1 | 1 |
| Mazeroski, 2b | 4 | 0 | 2 | 0 |
| Patek, ss | 4 | 1 | 1 | 0 |
| May, c | 3 | 0 | 1 | 1 |
| Moose, p | 2 | 0 | 0 | 0 |
| Total | 30 | 3 | 9 | 3 |

```
Houston      0 0 0   0 0 0   0 0 0 — 0
Pittsburgh   0 1 0   0 0 1   0 1 X — 3
```

E — Bateman 2. LOB — Houston 3, Pittsburgh 7. 2B — Clemente. 3B — Clemente. HR — Clendenon (5). SB — Patek, Mazeroski. S — Moose. SF — Mota.

| | IP | H | R | ER | BB | SO |
|---|---|---|---|---|---|---|
| Lemaster (L, 5–6) | 8 | 9 | 3 | 3 | 2 | 9 |
| Moose (W, 2–4) | 9 | 2 | 0 | 0 | 1 | 5 |

T — 1:59. A — 8,600.

**April 7, 1970:** The Pirates lost their last home opener at Forbes, 5–3, to the defending World Series champion New York Mets. Honus Wagner's widow threw out the first ball to start the game.

**April 25, 1970:** Willie Stargell became the last batter to launch a home run over the right field roof as the Pirates outscored the Atlanta Braves, 8–7.

**June 28, 1970:** Al Oliver belted the last home run ever hit at Forbes Field as the Pirates defeated the Chicago Cubs, 4–1, in the last game played at Forbes.

## June 28, 1970: Goodbye, Lady Forbes

| CHICAGO (N.) | AB | R | H | BI |
|---|---|---|---|---|
| Kessinger, ss | 5 | 1 | 2 | 0 |
| Popovich, 2b | 3 | 0 | 1 | 0 |
| Williams, lf | 4 | 0 | 3 | 1 |
| Hickman, 1b | 3 | 0 | 0 | 0 |
| Santo, 3b | 3 | 0 | 0 | 0 |
| Callison, rf | 3 | 0 | 0 | 0 |
| James, cf | 3 | 0 | 0 | 0 |
| Martin, c | 3 | 0 | 0 | 0 |
| Pappas, p | 2 | 0 | 0 | 0 |
| Beckert, ph | 1 | 0 | 0 | 0 |
| Gura, p | 0 | 0 | 0 | 0 |
| Smith, ph | 1 | 0 | 1 | 0 |
| Total | 31 | 1 | 7 | 1 |

| PITTSBURGH (N.) | AB | R | H | BI |
|---|---|---|---|---|
| Alou, cf | 4 | 0 | 1 | 2 |
| Hebner, 3b | 4 | 0 | 0 | 0 |
| Oliver, rf | 4 | 2 | 2 | 1 |
| Stargell, lf | 4 | 0 | 0 | 0 |
| Robertson, 1b | 2 | 1 | 1 | 1 |
| Alley, ss | 3 | 0 | 0 | 0 |
| May, c | 3 | 0 | 0 | 0 |
| Mazeroski [sic], 2b | 2 | 1 | 1 | 0 |
| Nelson, p | 3 | 0 | 0 | 0 |
| Giusti, p | 0 | 0 | 0 | 0 |
| Total | 29 | 4 | 5 | 4 |

```
Chicago      1 0 0   0 0 0   0 0 0 — 1
Pittsburgh   1 0 0   0 2 1   0 0 X — 4
```

E — Hickman. DP — Pittsburgh 2. LOB — Chicago 9, Pittsburgh 3. 2B — Williams, Oliver, Mazeroski. HR — Oliver (6). SB — Robertson. SF — Robertson.

| | IP | H | R | ER | BB | SO |
|---|---|---|---|---|---|---|
| Pappas (L, 2–3) | 6 | 4 | 4 | 2 | 1 | 3 |
| Gura | 2 | 1 | 0 | 0 | 0 | 0 |

|                | IP | H | R | ER | BB | SO |
|----------------|----|---|---|----|----|----|
| Nelson (W, 3–0)| 8  | 6 | 1 | 1  | 5  | 2  |
| Giusti         | 1  | 1 | 0 | 0  | 0  | 0  |

Save — Giusti. HBP — by Nelson (James). T — 2:14. A — 40,918.

# 4

# BLACK BASEBALL AT FORBES FIELD

## David C. Ogden

In mid–May 1947, an African American infielder took his position at Forbes Field, to the delight of thousands of African American fans. Black players had competed at Forbes Field before, but never with a white major league team. That day marked the first time the Brooklyn Dodgers, with Jackie Robinson, played the Pittsburgh Pirates, and that day was one of the first signs that all-black baseball was ending at Forbes.

In the ensuing years, few games, at least recorded ones, between Negro League teams would be held at Forbes.[1] Forbes lost its decades-long role as one of the home fields for black baseball in Pittsburgh. But "Dreyfuss' Folly" was more than just a stadium for black ballclubs. It also at times served as a stage on which the aspirations of two Negro League icons competed and played out. Those icons— Cumberland Posey and Gus Greenlee — battled on and off the field for black baseball supremacy, and Forbes Field was the scene of many epic skirmishes.

Among black teams, Homestead was most closely associated with Forbes Field. A group of steelworkers in the mill town of Homestead formed the Grays in 1910 and played weekends at their town park. Posey, who was better known in Pittsburgh as a basketball star, joined the club in 1911 and assumed leadership of the team in 1912. Ten years later, as part of an effort to establish the team as a financial and on-field success, Posey began booking the Grays' games at Forbes Field.[2] Barney Dreyfuss and Bill Benswanger, owners of the Pirates, befriended Posey and rented the field to the Grays, and occasionally to Pittsburgh's other great Negro League team, the Crawfords, when the Pirates were on the road. According to Pittsburgh baseball historian Rob Ruck, those were the only black teams to be consistently booked at Forbes.[3]

Forbes was used by the Grays more out of necessity than out of design. Ammon Field was the only other viable baseball venue in Pittsburgh, and that was used primarily by Greenlee's Crawfords (until Greenlee built his own stadium). While Forbes could accommodate large crowds, it "was not conveniently located near the black communities on the Hill or in Homestead."[4] Additionally, Pittsburgh's African American population grew very little during the 1930s, compared with other eastern cities,[5] so gate receipts for games between black teams left much to be desired. But Posey, not having the capital to build a baseball facility for the Grays, made Forbes its exclusive home field for 17 years (1922–1939). In doing so, the Grays became an important part of the legacy of Forbes and put Forbes in the center of some of the game's richest moments of history, albeit a history that lacks precision. As with black baseball in general, the contexts and contents of some of those games and events suffer from the dependence on oral history, only some of which was chronicled at the time by newspapers. As a result, Forbes Field is a study in the deconstruction of black ball history. While various accounts of games and certain historic on-field feats bear a strong resemblance, the authors of those accounts often don't agree on dates or in which games those feats took place.

Jackie Robinson at Forbes Field, ca. 1947 (Charles "Teenie" Harris, Carnegie Museum of Art, Pittsburgh: Heinz Family Fund).

A crowd watching a Negro League baseball game, ca. 1945 (Charles "Teenie" Harris, Carnegie Museum of Art, Pittsburgh: Heinz Family Fund).

Such ambiguity tinges some of Forbes historical highlights, such as the first night game at Forbes Field, almost five years before the first night game in the major leagues (at Cincinnati's Crosley Field). Robert Peterson[6] and William Brashler[7] state the game between the Grays and Kansas City Monarchs took place July 25, 1930, and an article in the July 19, 1930, issue of *The Pittsburgh Courier* infers that date.[8] But the summary of the game in the July 26 *Courier* indicates the night game was played July 18,[9] and articles in the *Pittsburgh Post-Gazette* and *The Pittsburgh Press* confirm that July 18 was indeed the correct date.[10] The date is not the only issue at question in modern accounts of that game. There is much debate over an incident during that July 18 contest between the Grays and Monarchs that became part of Negro League mythology. The game was the third in a series between the teams, with the first played in Cleveland and the second in Akron. The series continued through July, with the teams facing each other in Forbes and in Ohio and Pennsylvania towns. The teams' caravan included 12 trucks, which transported a portable lighting system. The system consisted of a 250-horsepower engine used as a generator and long poles on which hung clusters of lights that were placed around the playing field.

The trucks accompanied the Monarchs on barnstorming tours and the Monarchs' owner, J. L. Wilkinson, rented the system out to other teams.

It was by no means a piece of lighting perfection, for the poles were not very tall and the lights capable only of putting out illumination which in the minds of the players was just better than candles.

Added to that was a generator that coughed and sputtered, causing the lights to dim annoyingly. It was also easy to hit a ball above the lights into the pitch blackness of the night sky, and when this happened, the fielders wandered around like bugs trying to figure out when and where the ball would come back into sight.[11]

The poor lighting, some players say, was partly responsible for the Grays' acquisition of black baseball's greatest home run hitter. Had it not been for the Homestead pitcher's inability to read the catcher's signals, the entrance of Josh Gibson into Negro League lore might have been different, or at least the accounts of it. According to historian Robert Peterson, more than 30,000 attended the game and witnessed, not only the first night baseball game at Forbes, but also the professional debut of Gibson. Gibson had played for two Pittsburgh-area sandlot teams the three years before that season. As Grays' manager and Negro League great Judy Johnson related the story to Peterson, Joe Williams was pitching that night and got his signals crossed with his catcher, Buck Ewing. Because of the poor lighting, Williams misread Ewing's sign for the curve and instead threw a fastball to the unsuspecting catcher. The ball caught Ewing on the bare hand and split a finger. Johnson continued with the story:

> Well, my other catcher was Vic Harris and he was playing the outfield and wouldn't catch. So Josh was sitting in the grandstand, and I asked the Grays' owner, Cum Posey, to get him to finish the game. So Cum asked Josh would he catch, and Josh said, "Yeah, oh yeah!" We had to hold the game up until he went into the clubhouse and got a uniform. And that's what started him out with the Homestead Grays.[12]

Johnson told historian Jim Bankes the same story.[13] Supposedly, Gibson was hitless that night. Gibson biographer William Brashler has heard the story, but claims it is a part of the fiction surrounding the Hall of Famer.

> The situation arose not in the midst of a crucial night game before thousands of fans, as the popular story holds, but in a twilight doubleheader against Dormont, a white semipro team. Buck Ewing did split a finger, and Posey put Vic Harris in to catch until Josh could be brought over. Posey then sent Vic's brother by taxi over to Ammon Center, where Josh was playing with the Crawford Giants. The two returned a few innings later, and Josh was unceremoniously put into the Grays' lineup.[14]

Posey had indicated his interest in Gibson before that night, according to Brashler, who acknowledges that Gibson later shared catching duties with Ewing, including the first Forbes night game against the Monarchs. But there was no injury to Ewing forcing Gibson into the game, and the Grays' pitcher was not Smokey Joe Williams, but Charles "Lefty" Williams, said Brashler.[15] Furthermore, the box scores found in the Pittsburgh papers show that Ewing was the lone Grays catcher in the July 18 game.[16] Also, sports editor Chester Washington of *The Pittsburgh Courier* did not refer in his column to Gibson's involvement in the game.[17]

Regardless of the actual date of Gibson's recruitment by the Grays, the summer of 1930 marked the beginning of a long, illustrious, and stormy relationship between Pittsburgh black baseball teams and Gibson. Gibson embodied the power struggle between Posey and Pittsburgh numbers racketeer, Gus Greenlee, whose involvement in black baseball was rooted in a Crawford team that Gibson had left to join the Grays. Accounts vary as to when Greenlee took control of the Crawfords, and as to the dates of the historic battles between the two teams. According to Peterson, Greenlee formed the professional version of the Crawfords in 1931,[18] although historians Jim Bankes and Rob Ruck claim that Greenlee put the Crawford players on salary during the 1930 season.[19]

Many historians agree that the first meeting at Forbes Field between the Grays and Crawfords was in 1930 and that the Grays beat the Crawfords, 3–2. That is where the consistency among accounts ends. Mark Ribowsky claims the game occurred on July 14, which was four days before the mythical Monarchs-Grays game under the lights.[20] But according to *The Pittsburgh Courier*, the first on-field clash between the teams occurred on August 23. The game included "some fielding feats which rivaled anything ever seen on the turf of spike-scuffed Forbes Field."[21] The player responsible for these feats, according to modern accounts, was outfielder Vic Harris, who made a spectacular catch of a line drive by the Crawfords' Charlie Hughes in the ninth inning.[22] However, Bankes says Harris made his "diving catch" in the eighth inning, and the game was then called because of darkness.[23] An account of the game in *The Pittsburgh Courier* one week after it was played also indicated that the game went only eight innings. That account does not mention the fielding of Harris, but does credit two "circus catches" to right fielder Still (with no first game given by *The Courier*). That account also heralded the pitching of the Crawford's Harry Kincannon (but misspelled his name as "Tincannon" throughout the article) and the Grays' Oscar Owens, who had a no-hitter through six innings.[24]

Bankes claims the Grays beat the Crawfords at Forbes a second time that summer,[25] although Ruck and Ribowsky note that the second meeting between the two teams did not happen until the following year (1931).[26] That second meeting occurred on June 19. The Grays led 1–0 after five innings when the Crawford infield and outfield fell apart and the Grays scored eight more runs while blanking the Crawfords. The blow-out of his team "made Gus Greenlee maniacal about cutting Cum Posey down to size." Greenlee "fancied himself the greatest sports promoter in Pittsburgh" and was determined not to share the spotlight with Posey.[27]

The Grays and Crawfords met for a third time on July 18, 1931. According to Ruck and Ribowsky, Satchel Paige made his first appearance in a Crawford's uniform at Forbes,[28] but according to accounts by *The Pittsburgh Courier*, Sam Streeter pitched that game for the Crawfords, who again lost to the Grays 3–1.[29] Paige faced the Grays for the first time about two weeks later, when the teams squared off at Cycler Park in McKeesport, Pennsylvania. Paige relieved Harry Kincannon in the fifth inning during that August 1 contest, and the Crawfords won 10–7. Four days later, Paige made his debut at Forbes Field, but not against the Grays. The Indianapolis ABCs opposed the Crawfords during that August 5 game and lost 6–1 due to the "baffling slants" of Paige's pitches. According to *The Courier*, "Paige hurled sensational ball, striking out 11 and keeping the Naptownmen's hits well scattered."[30]

By the 1931 season, the Crawfords were under the full command and payroll of Gus Greenlee. Greenlee used his influence and money to lure Josh Gibson away from Homestead in 1932, although Gibson had already signed a contract with Posey and the Grays. Gibson and Paige remained teammates in the early 1930s. That relationship was sporadic, with Paige's occasional contract jumping to play for baseball teams in the Midwest. After 1937, both players made their rounds of teams in Mexico and Latin America. Eventually, both returned to the Negro Leagues and fulfilled a prophecy by Paige. While they were Crawford teammates, Paige predicted to Gibson that both would meet on the field some day as opponents instead of teammates.[31] That meeting purportedly took place in Forbes Field in 1942, when Paige was pitching for the Kansas City Monarchs and Gibson was playing for the Grays. In his book on the Negro Leagues, Donn Rogosin cites the date of the game as July 21, which corresponds to accounts in *The Pittsburgh Courier*.[32] But Ribowsky claims they faced each other several times, the first being in Griffith Stadium on June 18 and the second on July 21. They met again in early September at Forbes Field during the second game of the newly revived Negro League World Series.[33] Rogosin's and Ribowsky's accounts of what transpired seem to be a hybrid of those games.

Rogosin claims that in Paige and Gibson's July 21 meeting Satchel started and had thrown six shut-out innings with the Monarchs ahead 4–0,[34] as witnessed by what one newspaper called the largest crowd ever at a black baseball game in Pittsburgh.[35] According to some accounts, Gibson came to the plate with two outs in the seventh and following a hit by the Grays' Jerry Benjamin. Paige then summoned Monarchs first baseman Buck O'Neil to the mound. Paige said he planned to intentionally walk the next two batters, Howard Easterling and Buck Leonard, to load the bases and to bring Gibson to the plate. O'Neil recalls that the first two pitches to Gibson were strikes.

A team portrait of the 1942 Homestead Grays at Forbes Field. Standing (left to right): Jerry Benjamin; Roy Partlow; Josh Gibson; Johnny Wright; Chester Williams; Ray Brown; John Leftwich; J. C. Hamilton; Roy Gaston; Buck Leonard. Kneeling (left to right); David Whatley; Jud Wilson; Matt Carlisle; Frank Williams; Sam Bankhead; Roy Welmaker; Howard Easterling; Vic Harris (Charles "Teenie" Harris, Carnegie Museum of Art, Pittsburgh: Heinz Family Fund).

Now everybody's standin' and goin' crazy. And Satch looks in at Josh and says, "Okay, now I got you oh and two, and in this league I'm supposed to knock you down. But I'm not gonna throw smoke at yo' yolk — I'm gonna throw a pea at yo' knee" — and, *boom*, strike three; Josh didn't move the bat. And Satch walks off the mound and the crowd is yellin' and screamin' and he walks by me and he says real slow, "You know what, Buck? Nobody hits Satchel's fastball."[36]

Ribowsky later attributed that incident to the Negro League World Series game in September and amended his story of the July 21 game to correspond with the accounts in the July 22, 1942, issues of the *Pittsburgh Post-Gazette* and *The Pittsburgh Press*. Indeed, Paige did purposely walk Easterling to get to Gibson, but not with the bases loaded. Easterling was walked after the Grays' right fielder, Whatley, hit a one-out single and was sacrificed to second. According to the *Post-Gazette*, "the vaunted slugger of the Homesteaders, and the big catcher flied weakly to left to end the frame,"[37] and *The Pittsburgh Press* account agrees.[38] The Grays eventually won 5–4 in 11 innings. *The Pittsburgh Courier* gave little play-by-play coverage of the game, but sports editor Chester L. Washington did praise Paige's performance in his column on August 1, 1942.

[T]o top the evening off, he held the mighty jolter, Joshua Gibson, hitless, fanning him at one particular time when the chips were really down and after he had walked Easterling, another good hitter, to get to Josh.... He fanned Joshua twice, made him pop up once and fly out to center field twice.[39]

Josh Gibson, ca. 1942 (Charles "Teenie" Harris, Carnegie Museum of Art, Pittsburgh: Heinz Family Fund).

The bases were loaded when Gibson faced Paige during Josh's last at-bat during the September 10 game. There may have been more at stake in that encounter since it took place in the second game of the Negro League World Series. As in Ribowsky's account, Paige relieved Hilton Smith in the sixth inning with the Monarchs leading 2–0, which agrees with what was reported in the September 11, 1942, issues of the *Pittsburgh Post-Gazette* and *The Pittsburgh Press*.[40] But Ribowsky contends that Paige's intentional walks of Vic Harris and Easterling and the subsequent meeting on the mound with O'Neil were a part of that World Series game,[41] although newspaper coverage of the game told a different story. According to *The Pittsburgh Press*, Paige indeed faced Gibson in the seventh inning with the bases loaded, but not as a result of intentional walks. The bases were loaded as a result of singles by Lefty Partlow, Harris, and Easterling.[42] *Pittsburgh Post-Gazette* sportswriter, Jack Sell confirms that Gibson struck out on three pitches, but not in the fashion described by O'Neil. "While Homestead fans groaned, Josh fouled off the first two tosses weakly, then fanned on the third."[43] And *The Pittsburgh Press* account stated that Paige "toyed with Gibson" and then struck him out.[44]

That would not be the only occasion where Paige and Gibson used Forbes Field as a stage for their on-field dramatics. Gibson became known for his mammoth home runs at Forbes, one of which was claimed by Posey to be the longest ever hit at that park.[45] Paige appeared at Forbes several times, not only on Negro League teams, but also with barnstorming teams. In one exhibition game in 1935, Paige, who was with a team of Negro League all-stars, took the mound against Dizzy Dean, who had his own team of major league all-stars. Paige beat Dean 3–0 with the help of a home run by Boojum Wilson.[46]

During the early 1940s, black baseball in Pittsburgh boomed, with War World II workers serving as a substantial pool of patrons for Forbes Field. More than three million fans clicked the turnstiles of black games in 1942, and Cum Posey called baseball "the largest black enterprise in the world except for the insurance companies."[47] The only major threats to the black teams were the draft and player raids by teams in the Mexican League. Posey and his business partner, Rufus "Sonnyman" Jackson, were on the lookout for any attempts to steal Gray players, and such vigilance got Jackson thrown in jail. As Ruck relates the incident that happened in July 1943 at Forbes Field, Mexican Consul A. J. Guina arrived at Forbes looking for Grays' players Howard Easterling and Sam Bankhead, who had agreed to play for a team in Mexico, but never showed up. Guina was in Pittsburgh with the approval of the U.S. government, but not with the approval of Posey or Jackson.

> When he [Guina] got to the park, he made the mistake of asking Jackson where he could find Easterling and Bankhead. Hearing Guina's accent and suspicious of anyone inquiring about his players, Jackson asked Guina if he was Mexican. The startled Guina, not realizing who Jackson was, explained that he was a representative of the Mexican government, at which point he was forcefully ejected from the ballpark. Jackson was arrested for his part in the altercation, and he later declared, "I don't care if they send Pancho Villa, they're not going to get my ballplayers."[48]

Posey was just as protective of his control over the use of Forbes Field by black teams. Newspaper columnist Joe Ward complained that Posey "stipulated in his bookings of certain games that his club will not play there if another colored club is booked."[49] When Tom Brown scheduled his All-Stars for a Sunday game with Syd Pollock's Cuban Stars and billed it as the first to be played in Pennsylvania by the Cubans, Posey arranged a game with the Cubans for Saturday. "Brown went to court to attach the proceeds from the Saturday game but was unable to win legal relief." Brown charged "that Posey monopolized" black baseball in Pittsburgh.[50]

Even so, keeping rosters intact was a continual struggle for Posey and Jackson. The threat of player raids came not only from teams south of the border and Caribbean countries, but also from across town. Gus Greenlee had the financial resources to lure players like Josh Gibson away from the Grays, and Greenlee offered playing accommodations that were upscale, compared with Forbes Field. In 1932, Greenlee spent $100,000 to build the 6,000-seat Greenlee Field on Bedford Avenue in Pittsburgh.[51] Greenlee reasoned that a new stadium was necessary, since Forbes Field was not located near Pittsburgh's African American community and presented a "relative disadvantage" for the blacks who wanted to see baseball.[52] Greenlee Field presented other advantages over Forbes Field, especially for players. The field "included fine locker room facilities for both home and visiting clubs. No longer did black players have to dress and shower in the dingy surroundings of the YMCA because the white owners of Ammon Field and Forbes Field refused the use of their accommodations."[53] Cool Papa Bell, who joined the Crawfords the year after Greenlee Field opened, described the facility as "beautiful. It had lots of grass, and you felt like you were playing in a major-league park. The best thing for me was the big outfield. Plenty of room to run."[54] According to Ruck, Greenlee Field became known as Pittsburgh's "Sports Center"[55] and served as the base from which Greenlee launched a second version of the Negro National League (with the first Negro National League folding in 1931 shortly after the death of its creator, Rube Foster). The Great Depression, however, stifled Greenlee's venture, and the Crawfords were not able to turn a profit. The stadium was torn down in 1938, making Forbes the only viable venue once again for black baseball. But Posey was also having trouble making ends meet for his team, the Grays. He believed, like Gus Greenlee, that success at the gate meant playing somewhere else besides Forbes. Greenlee Field was no longer an option.

According to historian Brad Snyder, "The demise of the Crawfords and the demolition of Greenlee Field left the Grays without a home ballpark and without a convenient rival."[56]

In the July 8, 1939, issue of *The Pittsburgh Courier*, the Grays announced their intentions to begin negotiations with Clark Griffith, owner of the Washington Senators, to play in Griffith Stadium. Grays co-owner Rufus Jackson told the newspaper that he and Posey were "[d]isappointed over the lack of support in Pittsburgh" and had "failed to make money in their hometown."[57] Jackson and Posey reasoned that Washington, D.C.'s racial makeup was more conducive to supporting a black baseball team. The black population in the nation's capitol was almost 190,000 in 1940, compared with a little more than 62,000 in Pittsburgh.[58] Late in 1939, the Grays began playing Sunday games at Griffith Stadium and Saturday games at Forbes[59] (although Snyder, in *Beyond the Shadow of the Senators*, his book on the Grays and Griffith Stadium, says the Grays did not begin playing games there until 1940). The Grays were the only black team that made its home field at two major league parks.[60] Many in Pittsburgh voiced concern over the Grays splitting time between Washington and Pittsburgh. Ruck and Snyder refer to one letter sent to a Pittsburgh newspaper by a vexed fan: "It is the duty of every colored baseball fan of Pittsburgh to give the Homestead Grays his whole-hearted support.... The Grays belong to this city. It is a great team and a credit to our community. Let us, as a race, give this great team our full measure of appreciation and support."[61]

While Snyder contends that "[t]he Grays failed to catch on in Washington in 1940 and 1941," Ruck writes about Sonnyman Jackson's claim that the Grays turned a profit for the first time in 1941 because of the Griffith Stadium connection. In 1942, says Ruck, the Grays drew between 25,000 and 30,000 spectators to each game in Washington and played at Griffith throughout the years of World War II.[62] Meanwhile, Gus Greenlee was involved in a new venture, along with Branch Rickey. It was the United States Negro Baseball League, and Greenlee used the league to revive his Crawfords, who became additional tenants of Forbes Field in 1945 and 1946.[63] But black baseball at Forbes was in its twilight. Posey died in a Pittsburgh hospital in 1946 of lung cancer,[64] and the Grays ceased to be members of the Negro National League after the 1948 season,[65] playing their last game at Forbes Field supposedly on August 9, 1948. They won, beating Indianapolis, 4–1.[66]

The main attraction for fans of black players by that time was Jackie Robinson. In that first mid-May series in 1947 between the Brooklyn Dodgers and Pittsburgh Pirates at Forbes Field, Pittsburgh businessman Sam Jackson organized a group of 5,000 fans to attend the game to support Robinson (although Ruck says Jackson recruited 500, not 5,000, fans to attend).[67] Still, the climate of segregation that had kept Gray players and other Negro leaguers from using the showers and lockers at Forbes became evident again. In Robinson's first game at Forbes, "some of the Pirates appeared to balk at taking the field against Robinson and the Dodgers, but quickly came to their senses."[68] During that game Robinson, in trying to beat a throw, collided with Pirate first baseman Hank Greenberg, who was the first Jewish player and, because of that, the object of derision from players and fans. Biographer Arnold Rampersad describes their post-collision chat at the bag as amiable. "'Stick in there,' Jack remembered Greenberg telling him. 'You're doing fine. Keep your chin up.'"[69] Robinson didn't fare as well from his next clash at Forbes. That came the following year, and this time with home plate umpire Butch Henline. On August 31, 1948, Henline ejected Robinson from a game for the first time in the second baseman's career. Robinson was tossed from the game after he protested from the bench the ejection of his teammate, catcher Bruce Edwards. According to *The Courier* account, "Henline jerked off his mask, turned a scarlet crimson, faced the Dodger dugout and motioned for Jackie to leave the bench. Jackie came rushing out of the dugout as if he were possessed with the very devil itself and proceeded to give Henline a verbal lacing down that had all the characteristics of a three-ring circus." Robinson was fined $25 for the episode.[70]

Almost six years after Robinson's first ejection as a major leaguer at Forbes, Curt Roberts

**Three unidentified players of the Pittsburgh Crawfords of the United States Negro Baseball League at Forbes Field, ca. 1945 (Charles "Teenie" Harris, Carnegie Museum of Art, Pittsburgh: Heinz Family Fund).**

became the first black to don a Pirates uniform. The Pirates released him two years later. When Roberts was signed in 1954, Branch Rickey had been general manager of the Pirates for three years. Ruck wonders why it took so long for Rickey, who ended segregation in the major leagues, to sign the first black player to Pittsburgh.[71]

The Pittsburgh Baseball Club had flirted with the possibility of showcasing black players and breaking the color barrier. The Pirates shared a twin-bill with the Grays at Forbes on May 7, 1932, with the Pirates playing the Philadelphia Phillies and the Grays facing the Philadelphia Hilldales in the second game.[72] Pirate owners Bill Benswanger and Barney Dreyfuss maintained a close relationship with Cum Posey. Mourning the death of Dreyfuss in his column in *The Courier*, Posey wrote: "Dreyfuss seldom missed a Homestead Gray game and always paid to get it. The favors he did the Homestead Grays are too numerous to mention."[73]

Ten years after Dreyfuss' death and bowing to pressure from players and sportswriters, including *The Courier*'s Wendell Smith, Benswanger agreed to hold tryouts for several Negro leaguers, four of whom (Josh Gibson, Willie Wells, Sam Bankhead and Leon Day) were nominated by *The Courier*. The Pirates later backed out, or "chickened out" as described by another player, Dave Barnhill, who was promised a tryout.[74] Until the signing of Roberts in 1954, the Pirates avoided building a relationship with the Negro Leagues other than renting Forbes Field to black teams.

> [L]ike the rest of organized white ball, the Pirates showed little interest in helping black baseball. The Pirate owners were painfully aware of the talent to be had beyond the racial boundary that divided

black and white ball, but they made no attempt to tap it. Instead, they sat in their box seats and wondered what it would be like to have Martin Dihigo, Cool Papa Bell, or Smokey Joe Williams in their lineup.[75]

Said former Homestead Gray and Pittsburgh Crawford player Maurice Peatros: "Bill Benswanger ... did not want to be in the vanguard. He was just like [Clark] Griffith in Washington, D.C. The Senators could've been the most powerful ballclub for a decade in major league baseball because they had first choice of all the Homestead Grays. That was one of our home fields. When we played in the South, we were known as the Washington Homestead Grays. He could've had Josh, he could've had Buck, he could've had Bankhead...."[76]

A "picture album" published on the 60th anniversary of Forbes Field devotes only one sentence to the Homestead Grays.[77] But the Grays and other teams etched their legacies and left their memories with those in the stands at Forbes Field. Of the 18 Negro leaguers who have been inducted into the National Baseball Hall of Fame, nine wore Homestead uniforms at some point in their careers.[78] As Josh Gibson biographer William Brashler notes, "The Grays were undisputed masters of Pennsylvania baseball, and their many games in Forbes Field were exciting attractions in Pittsburgh, events witnessed by thousands and which never failed to light up the skies in the minds of the little black boys who watched."[79]

## Notes

1. Rich Emert, "Pittsburgh Was a Special Place in the History of Negro Leagues Baseball," *Pittsburgh Post-Gazette*, July 8, 2001, pp. 1–5 (retrieved from www.post-gazette.com/sports/page 3, May 26, 2003).

2. James A. Riley, *The Biographical Encyclopedia of the Negro Baseball Leagues* (New York: Carroll & Graf Publishers, 1994), 637.

3. Rob Ruck, *Sandlot Seasons: Sport in Black Pittsburgh* (Urbana, IL: University of Illinois Press, 1987), 186.

4. Brad Snyder, *Beyond the Shadow of the Senators: The Untold Story of the Homestead Grays and the Integration of Baseball* (Chicago: Contemporary Books, 2003), 53.

5. Ibid.

6. Robert Peterson, *Only the Ball Was White: A History of Legendary Black Players and All-Black Professional Teams* (Englewood Cliffs, NJ: Prentice-Hall, Inc., 1970), 163.

7. William Brashler, *Josh Gibson: A Life in the Negro Leagues* (New York: Harper & Row, Publishers, Inc., 1978), 23.

8. "Westerners to Test Grays Strength at Forbes Field Friday," *The Pittsburgh Courier*, July 19, 1930, sec. 2, p. 4.

9. "Nite Games Here Bring Thrills," *The Pittsburgh Courier*, July 26, 1930, sec. 2, p. 5; Chester L. Washington, "Sez 'Ches,'" *The Pittsburgh Courier*, July 26, 1930, sec. 2, p. 5.

10. "Grays Win Night Game in 12th, 5 to 4," *Pittsburgh Post-Gazette*, July 19, 1930, p. 18; "Grays Cop Thriller, 5–4," *The Pittsburgh Press*, July 19, 1930, sec. 2, p. 9.

11. Brashler, 22.

12. Peterson, 163.

13. Jim Bankes, *The Pittsburgh Crawfords* (Jefferson, NC: McFarland & Company, 2001), 38–39.

14. Brashler, 23.

15. Ibid. According to the box score in the July 26, 1930, issue of the *The Pittsburgh Courier*, George Britt

pitched for the Grays and Chet Brewer for the Monarchs ("Nite Games Here Bring Thrills," sec. 2, p. 5.).

16. Compare the *Pittsburgh Post-Gazette*, July 19, 1930, p. 18; *The Pittsburgh Press*, July 19, 1930, sec. 2, p. 9; and *The Pittsburgh Courier*, July 26, 1930, sec. 2, p. 5.

17. "Sez 'Ches,'" *The Pittsburgh Courier*, July 26, 1930, sec. 2, p. 5.

18. Peterson, 92.

19. Bankes, 20, and Ruck, 152.

20. Mark Ribowsky, *A Complete History of the Negro Leagues: 1884 to 1955* (New York: Birch Lane Press, 1995), 161. In his biography of Gibson (*The Power and the Darkness: The Life of Josh Gibson in the Shadows of the Game*, New York: Simon & Schuster, 1996), Ribowsky cites a different date for the first Crawford-Gray match-up: August 27, p. 55.

21. "Crawfords Beaten by Grays 3–2 in Classic," *The Pittsburgh Courier*, August 30, 1930, sec. 2, p. 5.

22. Ruck, 62.

23. Bankes, 17.

24. "Crawfords Beaten by Grays 3–2 in Classic," sec. 2, p. 5.

25. Bankes, 21.

26. Ruck, 153, and Ribowsky, *A Complete History of the Negro Leagues*, 161.

27. Ribowsky, *A Complete History of the Negro Leagues*, 161.

28. Ruck, 154. Mark Ribowsky, *The Power and the Darkness*, 78 and 79. Ribowsky claims that the third meeting of the Grays and Crawfords took place August 6, 1931.

29. "Crawfords Lose to Grays, 3–1," *The Pittsburgh Courier*, July 25, 1931, sec. 2, p. 4.

30. "Crawfords Cop, 6–1; Second Tilt Thurs.," *The Pittsburgh Courier*, August 8, 1931, sec. 2, p. 5.

31. Ribowsky, *A Complete History of the Negro Leagues*, 260–261.

32. Donn Rogosin, *Invisible Men: Life in Baseball's Negro Leagues* (New York: Atheneum, 1983), 97; "Returning Home," *The Pittsburgh Courier*, July 18,

1942, p. 16; Cum Posey, "Posey's Points," *The Pittsburgh Courier*, September 5, 1942, p. 16.

33. Ribowsky, *The Power and the Darkness*, 238–246. Ribowsky notes that Gibson and Paige also squared off during the 1942 East-West Game at Comiskey Park. During that contest, Paige intentionally walked Gibson.

34. Rogosin, 97.

35. Ribowsky, *The Power and the Darkness*, 240.

36. Ribowsky, *A Complete History of the Negro Leagues*, 261.

37. Jack Sell, "Grays Defeat Paige In 11 Innings, 5–4," *Pittsburgh Post-Gazette*, July 22, 1942, p. 15.

38. Paul Kurtz, "Paige Bits," *The Pittsburgh Press*, July 22, 1942, p. 19.

39. Chester L. Washington, "Sez 'Ches,'" *The Pittsburgh Courier*, August 1, 1942, p. 16.

40. Jack Sell, "Late Spurt by Monarchs Beats Grays," *Pittsburgh Post-Gazette*, September 11, 1942, p. 16; "Grays Laced by Monarchs," *The Pittsburgh Press*, September 11, 1942, p. 38.

41. Ribowsky, *The Power and the Darkness*, 246.

42. "Grays Laced by Monarchs," p. 38.

43. Jack Sell, "Late Spurt by Monarchs Beats Grays," p. 16.

44. "Grays Laced by Monarchs," p. 38. [Editors' Note: Angelo Louisa, who has studied both the July 21 and September 10 games, believes that the legendary encounter of Paige walking two men to load the bases so that he could pitch to Gibson and eventually strike him out on three called strikes was either a combination of the July and September matchups, which was then embellished to create another Paige myth, or occurred in some other game.]

45. Brashler, 46.

46. Ribowsky, *A Complete History of the Negro Leagues*, 198.

47. Ruck, 173.

48. Ibid., 174.

49. Ibid., 133.

50. Ibid., 133–134.

51. Brashler, 59, and Ruck, 156.

52. Larry Lester, *Black Baseball's National Showcase: The East-West All-Star Game, 1933–1953* (Lincoln, NE: University of Nebraska Press, 2001), 13.

53. Bankes, 23.

54. Ibid., 49.

55. Ruck, 156.

56. Snyder, 53.

57. "Grays May Shift Home Park to D.C.," *The Pittsburgh Courier*, July 8, 1939, p. 17.

58. Snyder, 331, 107n.

59. Ruck, 173.

60. Ribowsky, *A Complete History of the Negro Leagues*, 211.

61. Snyder, 53, and Ruck, 173.

62. Ruck, 173.

63. Leslie A. Heaphy, *The Negro Leagues, 1869–1960* (Jefferson, NC: McFarland & Company, 2003), 200.

64. Riley, 638.

65. Peterson, 202.

66. Emert, p. 5. It is not certain when the last game between Negro league teams was played at Forbes Field. Henry "Doc" Horn, an outfielder for the Kansas City Monarchs in the 1950s, claims he played three games at Forbes during the summer of 1954 against the Indianapolis Clowns. Horn, a left-handed hitter, remembers Forbes as a hitter-friendly park. "Forbes had a short porch in right field. I think it was 297 [feet] to right field and I was a pull hitter. Until the guys found out what kind of hitter I was, I hit eight home runs during that series" (personal communication, July 23, 2003).

67. Ribowsky, *A Complete History of the Negro Leagues*, 302, and Ruck, 184.

68. Arnold Rampersad, *Jackie Robinson: A Biography* (New York: Alfred A. Knopf, 1997), 177.

69. Ibid.

70. Bill Nunn, Jr., "Robinson Ejected from His First Major League Game," *The Pittsburgh Courier*, September 4, 1948, p. 12.

71. Ruck, 189.

72. Larry Lester and Sammy J. Miller, *Black Baseball in Pittsburgh* (Charleston, SC: Arcadia Publishing, 2001), 37.

73. Cumberland Posey, "'Cum' Posey's Pointed Paragraphs," *The Pittsburgh Courier*, February 13, 1932, sec. 2, p. 5.

74. John B. Holway, *Black Diamonds: Life in the Negro Leagues from the Men Who Lived It* (Westport, CT: Meckler Books, 1989), 135.

75. Ruck, 187.

76. Brent Kelley, *The Negro Leagues Revisited: Conversations with 66 More Baseball Heroes* (Jefferson, NC: McFarland & Company, 2000), 184–185.

77. *Forbes Field 60th Birthday, 1909–1969: Pittsburgh Pirates Picture Album* (Pittsburgh: Century Printing Co., n.d.), 1.

78. Snyder, 35.

79. Brashler, 11.

# 5

# FORBES (MORE THAN JUST A BASEBALL) FIELD

## David Rocchi

### More than Mazeroski's Home Run

The score was 9–9 in the bottom of the ninth inning of the 1960 World Series at Pittsburgh's Forbes Field. With Ralph Terry pitching for the heavily favored New York Yankees, Bill Mazeroski stepped to the plate for the Pittsburgh Pirates. The first pitch was a ball. The second was a high fastball that Mazeroski sent over the left field wall for a home run, and the Pirates had won the World Series for the first time since 1925.

Forbes Field opened June 30, 1909, another year in which Pittsburgh won the World Series. Barney Dreyfuss, the owner of the Pirates, had moved the team from Exposition Park in Allegheny City to Forbes Field in the Oakland section of Pittsburgh. Many were skeptical of the location and what they believed to be its overly large seating capacity. Critics thought that fans would never travel to Oakland and the stadium would never be filled. But 30,338 spectators attended the first game, proving the skeptics wrong.

Forbes Field was a cozy, friendly ballpark and the home of the Pirates for 61 years. Famous players such as Honus Wagner, Ralph Kiner, Roberto Clemente, Bill Mazeroski, and Willie Stargell graced the field. In 1970, the Pirates moved to Three Rivers Stadium, and the University of Pittsburgh purchased Forbes for demolition. In the intervening years, the structure had become obsolete and its public facilities cramped. Ironically, the Pirates also considered Forbes Field's seating capacity of 35,000 too small. Dreyfuss' critics would never have believed that the ballpark would be abandoned for that reason.

Pittsburghers pass by a few remnants of Forbes Field every day, preserved in and around the University of Pittsburgh's Wesley W. Posvar Hall and Forbes Quadrangle. Inside, one can see home plate, where teammates and fans greeted Mazeroski after his home run. A portion of the ivy-covered outfield wall still stands, too, some 400 feet away from home plate. These remnants serve as reminders of Pittsburgh's rich sports legacy. Historically passionate about their teams and athletic heroes, Pittsburghers also have been closely identified with the city's persona.

For a number of decades, Pittsburgh was the epitome of a blue-collar town, and though it has changed over the years, it still has the connotation of a city forged out of steel, literally and figuratively. The steel industry, along with the steelworker, defined Pittsburgh's image. Steelworkers labored long, arduous hours producing the materials that helped build a nation. Mostly immigrant Germans, Irish, Italians, Poles, and Slavs worked in the steel mills. Their jobs demanded strength, skill, discipline, and a sense of fearlessness because their work was frequently dangerous. Though there was little chance of improving their fortunes, they found ways to enjoy their lives. Among their pursuits were sports and a passion for Pittsburgh's athletic teams. These steelworkers expected their sports heroes to be as tough as they were, to have high standards, and to perform on the athletic field as they performed in the steel mills.

Some of the greatest athletes in all of sports played in Pittsburgh or had roots there. Baseball stars from the Pittsburgh Pirates and football standouts from the University of Pittsburgh and the Pittsburgh Steelers make up most of the city's sports history. Boxers such as Harry Greb, Fritzie Zivic, and Billy Conn also contributed to local sports lore. All these teams and individuals would eventually be successful. For some, it would be immediate; for others, it would take longer. The Pitt Panthers enjoyed early success, winning several national championships in the first half of the 20th century. The Pirates won the World Series in 1909 and 1925, lost in 1927 to Babe Ruth, Lou Gehrig, and the New York Yankees, and won again in 1960 on Mazeroski's home run. Each of the boxers would go on to win individual titles in their weight divisions. The Steelers struggled for quite a few years and would not be successful until the decade of the '70s. This was a turning point for the city and its sports teams. Pittsburgh became the City of Champions in the 1970s with the dominance of the Steelers and their four Super Bowl victories, the Pirates winning the World Series in 1971 and 1979, and even the Pittsburgh Triangles, the Steel City's professional tennis team, winning the World Team Tennis championship in 1975. Also, Pitt added another national championship in 1976 and a Heisman Trophy winner in Tony Dorsett. These collective achievements showcased the city of Pittsburgh to the rest of the country and furthered the image of Pittsburgh teams and athletes as being hard-nosed and hardworking.

More than anything else, Forbes Field is remembered as a baseball park and for the baseball players who played there. Also, Mazeroski's dramatic World Series home run may be the most enduring memory of this stadium. But Forbes Field was much more than just a baseball park and its history is replete with numerous tales of other legendary athletes and coaches, unbelievable games, and athletic innovations.

Forbes Field was the home of the Pitt Panthers from 1909 through 1924. The Pittsburgh Steelers played there, too, from 1933 through 1962. Boxing matches, as well as various other sporting events, were also held there from 1909 to 1970. During these overlapping timelines, every moment, every game, every player, every pass, and every punch created a vibrant (other than baseball) history at Forbes Field.

## The Panthers and Others Grace the Gridiron

While Pittsburgh fans did not always see great football games from the Steelers, the opposite was true of the Pitt Panthers' football program. Pitt's 1910 squad went undefeated and did not surrender a single point. During its time at Forbes Field, Pitt won its first national championship in 1915, followed by two more in 1916 and 1918. The 1916 squad is arguably the best team in the school's football history.[1] Pitt had a number of outstanding players such as Robert "Tex" Richards, Bob Peck, Jimmy DeHart, Tommy Davies, John "Jock" Sutherland, and George McLaren. Many of these athletes would earn All-America status at Pitt.

Legendary coaches also graced the sidelines of Forbes Field. Pitt's Colonel Joe Thompson started coaching in 1908 and "later would become one of the most decorated American soldiers in World War I."[2] In 1915, Glenn "Pop" Warner would take over as the Pitt coach. After finishing a stint coaching Jim Thorpe at Carlisle, he would lead Pitt to three national championships and produce several All-Americas. Warner, a coaching genius and legend, is often credited with many innovations of modern football that are still used today. Jock Sutherland, one of Warner's former players, would succeed him as coach. Sutherland, who was perhaps a more successful

**Jimmy DeHart, pictured here, was a star half back on the University of Pittsburgh football teams during the 1914–1916 and 1919 seasons (Pittsburgh Photographic Library Collection of Carnegie Library of Pittsburgh).**

coach than Warner, would lead Pitt in its final season at Forbes Field in 1924. The following year the Panthers moved into Pitt Stadium. Whether it was Pitt's football dynasty or the evolvement of the modern game of football by its players, the history occurred at Forbes Field.

The University of Pittsburgh played its first ever football game at Forbes Field on Saturday, October 16, 1909. Pitt faced a foe from eastern Pennsylvania, Bucknell University. Kickoff was at 3:00 P.M., but a preliminary game between Pittsburgh High School and Sharon High School was scheduled at 1:15 P.M. so that the fans could enjoy even more football. For these games, the playing field was set up to run parallel to the bleachers, providing excellent opportunities for the fans to see the action from their seats.[3] The players would also be wearing numbers on the backs of their uniforms similar to athletes in track meets.[4] Forbes Field looked spectacular: "The field is in splendid shape and after being carefully surveyed and marked out, gives the blue and gold a stadium of which they may well be proud."[5]

On game day, Pitt was ready and beat Bucknell 18–6. The Panthers looked strong in victory, dominating the line of scrimmage. Tex Richards led the way on the ground, but Bill Bud was the star, controlling the offense at quarterback and returning punts. Bucknell managed to score one touchdown on a controversial kicking play. Apparently, the ball bounced over the bleachers and the Pitt players did not field it, thinking it was out of play. However, when the ball bounced back into play, Bucknell recovered it and ran it over Pitt's goal line. Referee Knox conferred with the other officials and ruled a touchdown. After the game was over, Knox admitted he had made a mistake. But despite this fluke play, it was Pitt's game, and the team's supporters had high hopes that Coach Joe Thompson would provide a winning season.[6] Thompson did not disappoint them, as the Panthers finished the year with a 6–2–1 record.

It was a monumental day for Pitt and Forbes Field — a day on which Pitt's football dynasty may have started. Pitt teams would go on to win many more games at Forbes Field and the university would have one of the most successful college football programs while playing there.

In the friendly confines of Forbes Field, the Panthers generally played well in front of their home fans. One such game occurred on October 18, 1913. Pitt faced a tough adversary in Carlisle and its coach, Pop Warner. Joe Duff, Pitt's coach, thought the Panthers had a legitimate chance to beat this quality team.[7]

The undefeated, untied, and unscored upon 1910 University of Pittsburgh football team at Forbes Field (courtesy University Archives, University of Pittsburgh).

At the 3:00 P.M. kickoff, a large crowd had arrived at Forbes Field to witness the game. Most of the fans had been in attendance the previous year as the great Jim Thorpe and Carlisle crushed Pitt 45–8. The rematch turned out to be much more competitive and thrilling. In a back-and-forth contest that was not decided until late in the fourth quarter, Pitt was victorious, winning 12–6. Coach Duff devised a solid game plan to attack Carlisle and received credit for outcoaching Warner.

Pitt fielded the opening kickoff and did not have much success on its first drive. Carlisle attempted a field goal in the same quarter, but it was blocked. There was not much action until the second quarter. Both teams traded possessions, but Carlisle was starting to control the game. An excellent running team under Warner's tutelage, the Indians successfully ran the ball off tackle and between the guard and tackle. Eventually, Carlisle wore the Pitt players down and scored a touchdown before halftime. The Indians were winning 6–0.

Pitt kicked off to start the third quarter. Again, the teams went back and forth until Pitt mounted a drive at the close of the period. At the start of the fourth quarter, the Panthers were five yards from the end zone. A running play on first down failed to produce a score. On second down, Red Smith ran a route with perfect execution to the end zone and caught a touchdown pass. Pitt missed the point after, and the score was tied 6–6. After Pitt's touchdown, both teams traded possessions. Forced to punt, the Panthers' fortunes changed quickly as a Carlisle player bobbled the ball, and Pitt recovered on Indians' five-yard line. The Panthers would have four chances to score from the five and needed all four downs to do it. Earl Ammons carried on first down for a gain of two. On second down, Philip Dillon carried to the one-yard line. Dillon carried again for Pitt on third down and was stopped inches short of the goal line. It was now fourth down, and the game's outcome rested on the upcoming play. Roy Heil, Pitt's quar-

**During Pop Warner's first season, the University of Pittsburgh beat Washington and Jefferson 19–0 at Forbes Field on November 6, 1915 (Library of Congress, Prints and Photographs Division [LC-USZ62–127596 DLC]).**

terback, took the snap and plunged into the end zone as the Panthers gained the lead, 12–6. The conversion was missed, but Pitt was close to victory with little time remaining in the game. Both teams would exchange interceptions before the final gun sounded.

The fans at Forbes Field went crazy over the victory. It was a classic game with a dramatic finish.[8]

In 1915, Pop Warner would arrive to coach the Panthers. While at Forbes Field, Pitt won 81 percent of its games with Warner at the helm and would claim three national championships during his tenure.

One of Warner's legendary games occurred on November 23, 1918. On that day, Pitt was scheduled to meet the vaunted Georgia Tech Golden Tornado at Forbes Field. It was "the game of the century" before such marquee advertising was invented. Georgia Tech was considered the champion of the South and had not lost a game in over three years. However, despite Tech's impressive status, Pitt, which had also not lost a game in over three years, was favored to win that day. Newspapers and news services from around the country were at Forbes to cover the contest. Even the famous football authority, Walter Camp, was on hand as a spectator. A large crowd of Pitt fans was expected, and special police protection was added to patrol outside Forbes Field and maintain order inside the stadium. The Panthers had a light workout the day before the game, as Warner's team went over the game plan and prepared to face the Golden Tornado. The Georgia Tech players came in confident, predicting that they would score at least three touchdowns against Pitt. John Heisman, Tech's coach, was also confident his team would win and declared, "Pitt will have to beat us in the first quarter if it is to be done at all."[9]

Kickoff was at 2:30 P.M. on game day, and the Panthers, expertly prepared by Warner, rolled to a 32–0 victory. Not only was the outcome lopsided, but also Pitt thoroughly outplayed Georgia Tech, handing the Tornado its first loss since November 7, 1914. Pitt scored on big plays, and Tommy Davies was the hero, returning two punts for touchdowns. Approximately 30,000 people were at Forbes Field to witness Pitt's victory as "[t]he Old Gold and White of Georgia Tech was trampled in the dust at Forbes Field yesterday afternoon in the most important gridiron struggle of the season."[10]

Warner knew he would have to use numerous strategies and plays to beat the Tornado. To stop Tech's famous "jump shift" play, Warner devised a wide defensive spread which the Panthers executed with impressive results. Armed with the scheme, Pitt's defense was stifling, so much so that Tech would find it futile to use its signature play after the first half. In fact, "Atlanta newspapermen in the press box stated that it was the first time in their memory that the shift had been successfully stopped."[11]

The game began slowly. Nervous at the start, both teams were called for penalties. As the first quarter progressed, neither offense was productive running the ball. On a punt by Tech, Roy Easterday had a nifty return all the way to Tech's 37-yard line that provided a spark for the Panthers. Pitt started to drive, made a first down, and was headed toward the end zone. Warner,

Tommy Davies, an outstanding half back for the University of Pittsburgh football teams during the 1918–1921 seasons, dazzles the opposition (Pittsburgh Photographic Library Collection of Carnegie Library of Pittsburgh).

mixing his plays, called for a pass. Tommy Davies threw to Easterday for a touchdown and then converted the point after. Pitt was up 7–0.

Georgia Tech would fumble on the next couple of series; however, Pitt was unable to capitalize on the Tornado's mistakes. In the second quarter, Tech was forced to punt again, and Davies was set to receive and work his magic. He fielded the punt, slashed through Tech's kicking team, and raced 50 yards for a touchdown. Davies also converted the extra point to put Pitt up 14–0. The Golden Tornado tried to mount a comeback before the half ended, but Pitt's defense held.

The Panthers received the kickoff to start the second half and mounted an impressive drive toward Tech's end zone. Again in scoring position, Warner would call another pass play. This time, it was a double–forward pass from George McLaren to Davies to Easterday that yielded a third touchdown for Pitt. That made the score 20–0 in favor of the Panthers. As the game continued, Tech's offense still could not get on track. Pitt, on the other hand, was able to drive against Tech's defense. Long runs by Davies and Easterday had the Panthers in position to put more points on the board. This time, McLaren would carry the ball for a touchdown. Pitt was leading 26–0 at the end of the third quarter.

As the fourth quarter arrived, the game's outcome had already been determined. With the Panthers thoroughly in control, Davies returned another punt for a touchdown, which increased Pitt's lead to 32 points and sealed Georgia Tech's fate.

Davies, a Pitt freshman, was the star that day, while Easterday was a close second. Starting at left halfback, Davies was incredible throughout the game and electrified the crowd with his punt returns. He would be selected as an All-America in 1918, and Pitt would also be crowned national champion that same year.[12]

Another classic game that Warner coached at Forbes Field occurred on November 29,

J.J. Tressel of Washington and Jefferson College leaps to make a catch during a game against the University of Pittsburgh at Forbes Field, ca. 1916–1918 (Pittsburgh Photographic Library Collection of Carnegie Library of Pittsburgh).

1923 — the Panthers' final contest of the year. The opponent was Pitt's in-state rival, Penn State, and it was an important game for two reasons. Having suffered four losses during the year, the Panthers knew a win against Penn State would salvage their season. The Panthers could say, "Well, we beat the teams we wanted to and what more could be asked?"[13] though, it would not be an easy task because the Nittany Lions had a solid running attack and the edge in that facet of the game. But in addition to knowing they would have to play well to win, the Pitt players had something else on their minds. This would be the last game Pop Warner ever coached for the Panthers. He was headed west to be the coach of Stanford, and his players desperately wanted him to finish his career at Pitt with a win.

Kickoff was at 2:00 P.M. Pitt outplayed Penn State and won 20–3 in a rainy, muddy contest. Pitt walked off triumphant but hardly recognizable as the players were caked with mud. The Panthers stopped State's running game, and along the way, showed more heart, character, and determination to salvage their season and bring Warner a final victory. All of the players had a part in Pitt's win, but Karl Bohren was the true star as he led them by running, passing, and playing exceptional defense.

Penn State took an early 3–0 lead after converting a field goal. But following that score, it was all Pitt as the Panthers moved the ball effectively, running and passing on a muddy field. The drive culminated in a touchdown and the crowd went wild. Pitt was up 7–3. Notwithstanding the field conditions, the Panthers took no chances, even though the lead was probably secure. While mounting a drive later in the half, the Nittany Lions decided to call a pass play. However, Bohren intercepted the pass on Pitt's 30-yard line. He broke two tackles and headed towards the open, muddy field. No one from State could catch him as he pulled away for a touchdown. Pitt was ahead 14–3 at halftime.

In the second half, the Panthers would score again by blocking a Penn State punt and recovering it for a touchdown. That concluded the scoring and made Pitt victorious in a romp over Penn State.[14] However, the real story of the game was Pop Warner.

Warner walked off Forbes Field for the last time as Pitt's coach, victorious. His players knew what he meant to them and their football program. He was the brains of the team and a true innovator of the game. In a presentation before the kickoff to honor him, his players pitched in to buy him a watch and ring to show their gratitude. It was a momentous occasion for Pitt's players and fans to witness Warner, a truly outstanding coach, as he departed on that dreary November day: "Some few minutes later a venerable old coach, with mud nowhere but on his shoes, but no cobwebs in his brain, made that same march for the last time. No round of cheers greeted his exit, because the crowd knew only too well that his great duty had been performed and they seemed awe stricken as they watched him make his way out of the picture."[15]

Pop Warner was a coaching legend, and modern football evolved from his concepts and imagination. He used both the single wing and double wing formations and ran a variety of plays such as reverses, fakes, and screens. Warner was also thought of as a genuine, caring man, hence the nickname "Pop." His players loved to play for him and were quite successful under his tutelage. Warner's legacy survives in the Pitt football program that he built and in the game that he helped to create on the gridiron at Forbes Field.

November 27, 1924, would add another chapter to the storied rivalry between Pitt and Penn State. It was Thanksgiving Day, and again, the game was held at Forbes Field. The scenario of the game was practically the same. Pitt was having a mediocre season and wanted to finish positively with a win over Penn State. The year before was Pop Warner's last game at Forbes Field as Pitt's coach, and John "Jock" Sutherland, who had played for Warner, had succeeded him as the team's head man. But this year's Pitt–Penn State matchup had just as much significance as last year's because Pitt would be moving into its own stadium in 1925. The players, coaches, and fans all wanted to see Pitt victorious in its final game at Forbes Field.[16]

The outcome of the game was virtually the same, too. Crushing Penn State 24–3, Pitt outplayed, outclassed, and dominated the Nittany Lions. The Panthers salvaged their season and proved that Jock Sutherland had the ability to win important games and be another outstanding coach.

It was an afternoon contest and some 34,000 people had come to Forbes Field to watch the historic event. Penn State received the kickoff to start the game. Both teams exchanged punts on their initial drives. On its second drive following Pitt's short punt, State gained a few yards and moved into scoring position. Reminiscent of the year before, the Lions kicked a field goal to take an early 3–0 lead over the Panthers. The first quarter ended with no further scoring. The rest of the game, like the one the year before, would belong to Pitt.

During the second quarter, Pitt capitalized on a Penn State fumble. The Panthers drove down the field and Andy Gustafson ran for a touchdown. Pitt missed the point after and was leading 6–3. The score would remain the same as the teams traded possessions until halftime.

Following the intermission, Pitt was ready to seize the game from Penn State. The Panthers mounted an impressive drive in the third quarter by running the ball, controlling the line of scrimmage, and using double-pass plays to keep the Nittany Lions off balance. State did not have an answer as Pitt moved the ball at will. Near the goal line, Jesse Brown carried for a touchdown. The Panthers missed the extra point, and the score was 12–3 in Pitt's favor. Pitt's offensive juggernaut would continue to attack Penn State and add another touchdown in the third frame.

On this scoring drive, Pitt caught State off guard with a "double pass and then a forward to Brown and then a forward to [Milo] Gwosden [which] took the State team by utter surprise and they permitted Gwosden to cross the goal line for another touchdown."[17] After failing again to convert, the Panthers had an 18–3 lead. Dominant to the end, Pitt added a final touchdown in the fourth quarter that put the game beyond any hope of a Penn State comeback.

For one of the few times during the year, the Panthers excelled on both sides of the line. The offense displayed versatility by running the ball, mixing formations, and throwing double passes, triple passes, and forward passes, which resulted in 11 first downs and four touchdowns. The stalwart defense limited the opposition to a field goal. It was the second year that Pitt embarrassed Penn State. The 24–3 victory salvaged the Panthers' season and was a fitting way for Pitt to close out its history at Forbes Field.[18]

Pitt's football legacy at Forbes Field was quite an impressive one. But other universities played there, too. In fact, on November 1, 1929, in the first major sporting event played outside in Pittsburgh with an evening starting time, Duquesne University defeated Geneva, 27–7. Carnegie Tech, now Carnegie Mellon University, also played there and faced one of the finest college teams ever.

November 29, 1924, marked the day Forbes Field was invaded by Knute Rockne and the Four Horsemen of Notre Dame. Rockne's squad was in Pittsburgh to play Carnegie Tech as the game was billed as the Scotch against the Irish. It was an unforgettable college football weekend at Forbes Field. Pitt had already beaten Penn State two days earlier, and now fans had the opportunity to see a legendary squad play at Forbes Field. Billed as the Four Horsemen of Notre Dame, Harry Stuhldreher, Jim Crowley, Don Miller, and Elmer Layden fueled Notre Dame's formidable attack. Wally Steffen was the coach of Carnegie Tech, and despite Notre Dame's reputation, he believed his team had a legitimate chance to beat the Irish. Now at the end of a long, tough season, Steffen hoped the Irish would underestimate the Scotch, but he also knew that his team would have to play a near-perfect game to beat Notre Dame. Rockne, like the great coach that he was, made sure his team was taking this game seriously. He warned his squad, "You fellows are not going to run into anything soft at Pittsburgh next Saturday"[19] as he went over the scouting report for Tech. And it was true that the Scotch were not scared of the Irish. After personally scouting Notre Dame, Steffen prepared his team for the game by removing some of his old plays and creating new ones with trick formations. Carnegie Tech was ready for a fight.

This game marked the end of college football in the Pittsburgh area for the year. It was also the last time people in the East had an opportunity to see the celebrated Four Horsemen because they would be graduating in the near future. Football coaches from all over the country had requested field passes so they could witness this legendary quartet play one more time. Entering the contest, Notre Dame was undefeated with victories over Army, Princeton, Georgia Tech, Wisconsin, Nebraska, and Northwestern. Propelling the Irish to a perfect record, the Four Horsemen wanted to leave their mark on Carnegie Tech and on Forbes Field.

Carnegie Tech kicked off to start the game. Notre Dame mounted an opening drive, but the Scotch held. However, Tech could not do much either and also had to punt. The Irish got the ball and again could go nowhere. So far, the game was a stalemate, but as Notre Dame attempted to punt, Carnegie Tech broke through the line and was able to block the ball. Benedict Kristof jumped on the loose ball and returned it for a Tech touchdown. The Scotch missed the extra point, but had a 6–0 lead against this legendary Notre Dame team. At the end of the first quarter, Carnegie Tech was still in the lead.

During the second quarter, Notre Dame's superb Four Horsemen started to make their mark. Layden was hurting and did not see much action, but Crowley, Miller, and Stuhldreher displayed their excellence. Crowley passed to Miller, who caught the ball and ran for a 25-yard touchdown. Crowley then converted the extra point and the Irish had a 7–6 lead over Tech. The action continued and Notre Dame scored again. Bill Cerney, who was filling in for Layden, scored a touchdown for the Irish. Tech blocked the point after, and the score was now 13–6 in favor of Notre Dame. Despite being down, Carnegie Tech would not quit and continued to fight. The Scotch mounted a drive, and Dwight Beede scored a touchdown for Tech. Following the extra point, the score was 13–13 at halftime. So far, this was the most points Notre Dame had surrendered all season.

It was in the third quarter that Notre Dame took control of the game. Crowley, Miller, and Stuhldreher spearheaded the Irish attack and made one play after another. Cerney and Bernie Livergood also got into the action for the Irish. Stuhldreher threw to Livergood, who made the score 19–13. Crowley converted the extra point to give Notre Dame a 20–13 lead. Notre Dame would continue to dominate as Stuhldreher threw another touchdown pass and Crowley added another extra point. Notre Dame now had the upper hand, 27–13.

In the fourth quarter, Livergood and Stuhldreher scored consecutive touchdowns, and Crowley added an extra point. The Irish were in command, 40–13. But despite the onslaught, Tech never gave up. The Scotch, determined to fight to the final whistle, began an offensive drive. Mixing the run and the pass, Beede carried the load. Nearing the end of the drive, Tech lined up in spread formation, and Notre Dame reacted by moving out wide to stop what appeared to be an obvious passing play. Instead, Beede surprised the Irish as he dashed through the defense for a touchdown. The Scotch missed the extra point and the score was Notre Dame 40, Carnegie Tech 19. There would be no further scoring.

Though outmatched, Carnegie Tech put up a valiant effort against Notre Dame. An impressed Rockne praised the Scotch after the game. The fans at Forbes Field that day witnessed a memorable sporting event, for Carnegie Tech had played the best it could but lost to an incredible Notre Dame team with legendary players.[20]

## Of Fights and Fighters

During the first half of the 20th century, Pittsburgh was synonymous with great boxing and great boxers— a fight town so good and passionate that it rivaled New York City. In Pittsburgh, Forbes Field was a prime venue for boxing matches that were just as common as the baseball and football games played there. Of course, Pittsburghers loved their own boxing heroes the most. Men such as Harry Greb, Billy Conn, Fritzie Zivic, and Teddy Yarosz thrilled local fight fans at Forbes Field for decades. In addition, Jersey Joe Walcott and Ezzard Charles, though not from Pittsburgh, fought a heavyweight championship there in 1951.

Boxing, as it is known today, is a much different sport than it used to be. Modern boxers, who are groomed to be successful and have impressive win totals, usually fight lesser opponents on their way up the ladder and go into title bouts undefeated. However, the pugilists of the 1920s, 1930s, and 1940s fought constantly. It was a job to them. They would fight a couple of times a month because the purses were often small and this helped them earn extra money. In part because they fought so frequently, some boxers did not have outstanding records. This was especially true of fighters who were just starting their careers. Modern boxers are well-conditioned athletes who train constantly. In the early era, training was not as advanced as it is now, so the pugilists, who were always fighting, had to be extremely durable with unflagging stamina.[21]

Also, fights then were vastly different from fights now. Today, boxing matches are events usually held in glamorous places with celebrities sitting at ringside. Decades earlier, fights were not spectacles, especially in the 1930s during the Depression, when the atmosphere and opponents were quite different. Boxers would often travel to other boxers' hometowns to fight. Many times, a hostile crowd waited, along with a boxer who would do anything to provide his loyal fans with a victory. During this period, most pugilists were thought of as dirty fighters.[22] Boxers had to bite, punch below the belt, grab, and do whatever they could to survive. Fighters could not back down from each other or the violent crowds, and that is how they got tough.

This was the nature of boxing all over the country, and it was especially true in Pittsburgh, a fight town with its share of top-notch fighters. Men such as Harry Greb, Fritzie Zivic, and Billy Conn were as good, as tough, and as successful as any boxers in their day.

It was June 23, 1919, and it was a fight night at Forbes Field. Harry Greb was scheduled to face Mike Gibbons in an evening bout. It was expected to be a competitive fight. Both men were considered to be excellent boxers in their weight class, and both were in superb condition for the fight. Greb was an endurance fighter. He was young, strong, and aggressive. Greb was also persistent, would always attack his opponent, and thought he could fight 20 rounds if he had to. On the other hand, Gibbons was a clever boxer with speed and quickness. He was older than Greb, a stronger puncher and more calculating, with the ability to use his head inside the ring. Ed Smith was the referee for the fight, and the fans at Forbes Field would be rooting hard for a Greb victory.[23]

Harry Greb was born in Pittsburgh and was a typical Pittsburgh fighter. He was tough, smart, and a little dirty. He was nicknamed "The Human Windmill" or "The Pittsburgh Windmill" because of his style of throwing a constant barrage of punches and keeping a fast pace throughout his fights. During his career, he was the middleweight champion from 1923 to 1926 and the American light heavyweight champion from 1922 to 1923. He is officially credited with 299 professional fights, but probably fought more times than that. He was also the only man to ever beat the great Gene Tunney.

On the day of the fight, 12,000 fans came to Forbes Field to watch what proved to be an entertaining bout that held true to form. Greb threw punch after punch at Gibbons, while Gibbons fought cleverly, which kept him from being seriously hurt. Greb was wide open and landed punches from long range with his windmill style. Gibbons fought defensively and did his best work inside to Greb's body and head when the two got locked up with each other.

The fight started with Gibbons landing a right to Greb's chin. Then Greb went to work with a combination and a punch to Gibbons' body. Greb delivered another shot to the body, and Gibbons countered with a punch to Greb's cheek. It was a fast, even first round.

Greb came out fighting in the second and attacked Gibbons with a flurry of punches. At this point, Gibbons was up against the ropes and started to fight back. Greb continued to keep him off balance and landed a right to his ear. It was Greb's round as Gibbons spit blood in his corner.

Round three was a little slower as both fighters clutched and grabbed. It was Greb's round by a close call. The action increased in rounds four, five, and six. Gibbons landed a left to Greb's face and then a right as he continued to protect himself, making it difficult for Greb to deliver punches. But this did not deter Greb as he pressed forward, throwing a lot of punches to Gibbons' body. He was starting to control the fight. Gibbons had a cut nose and was bleeding. Greb was winning.

Gibbons would make a comeback in rounds seven and eight. He was more aggressive, landing punches to Greb's chin and face and keeping Greb off balance with his jab. Greb now had a cut under his eye. The last two rounds would be pivotal.

At the start of the ninth round, Greb attacked and tried for a knockout. He had Gibbons up against the ropes and landed a left and a right to his face. Then both fighters got tied up again, and Greb connected with a hook to Gibbons' stomach. Greb took the ninth and was ready for the final round. The combatants shook hands at the start of round 10 and the action resumed. They both threw punches to each other's face and body and then got tied up again. Greb landed another shot to Gibbons' face and then attacked his body. Gibbons countered with a right to Greb's face. Greb then followed with a left and a right to Gibbons' chin before the bell rang. It was Greb's round and fight. Harry Greb was victorious—a popular decision that delighted the crowd at Forbes Field.[24]

Another of Pittsburgh's outstanding fighters was Fritzie Zivic. Zivic was the fifth and youngest son of a Croatian immigrant. He lived in Lawrenceville and he, along with all of his brothers, learned to box. He worked at the Black Diamond Steel Mill and had a pleasing personality outside of the ring. He was witty and easygoing, and his distinctive physical trait was a bashed-in nose. Credited with 233 fights, Zivic lost 65 and had 10 ties. He was sometimes an enigma. One night he could beat the best fighter in the world, and the next night he could lose to a bum. Zivic also had a reputation for being "unquestionably the dirtiest fighter ever to scrape his laces across another fighter's cut eye."[25]

It was August 29, 1940. Zivic was scheduled to fight Sammy Angott at Forbes Field in a 10-round bout. The winner would get a title shot against Henry Armstrong. Both fighters were from the Pittsburgh area. Angott, from nearby Washington, Pennsylvania, was the favorite to win the fight; however, he was giving about 10 pounds away to Zivic. More of a local boy and hero than his opponent, Zivic would have plenty of supporters in the Forbes Field stands. In addition, Angott's style of fighting definitely favored Zivic. Angott rushed at his opponents and liked to trade punches standing toe to toe. Zivic liked to mix it up, too, and this would allow him to counter-punch Angott. Pittsburgh boxing fans were excited about the match and expected an entertaining bout. They hoped to see one of the best fights ever at Forbes Field and thought a knockout was possible.[26] Zivic was unruffled that Angott was favored to win. Actually, it motivated him as he predicted to a reporter that he would knock Angott out of the ring before the fight was over: "Well, I hope you're sitting close enough, and if you are I'll plant him [Angott] right in your lap around the ninth round."[27]

A crowd of over 10,700 attended the fight that night at Forbes. The gross gate was $20,596, and the net gate was $17,531.[28] And the fans got what they paid for and expected. The bell rang to start the first round. Each fighter got tangled up, and then they exchanged blows to the body. Zivic followed with three shots to Angott's jaw and an uppercut. Zivic landed a left to Angott's jaw to win the round.

Both men sparred at the center of the ring at the beginning of the second round. Zivic blocked Angott's punches and delivered a shot to Angott's jaw. Angott answered with a punch to Zivic's jaw, but Zivic countered with a left and a right of his own to Angott's jaw. It was another round for Zivic.

The third round was even and filled with a lot of clutching and grabbing from both fighters. The fourth provided more action. Angott landed a short left, then a right, and then another left to Zivic's jaw. Zivic countered with an uppercut and a hook. They then exchanged lefts and rights at close range, and Zivic scored with a few combinations. Tempers flared at the end of the round as Angott hit Zivic after the bell. It was a competitive round, but Zivic won it.

Each fighter blocked lefts to start the fifth round and then traded lefts to the face. Zivic caught Angott with a right and followed it with two others. Angott scored with a solid left to Zivic's body. Zivic answered with a left to Angott's body and won another round.

Zivic had a good round in the sixth. Following a tie-up, he pounded Angott's body and then landed a shot to Angott's jaw. Angott countered with two left hooks. Zivic threw a left hook, followed by a right cross to Angott's jaw. Then Zivic unleashed a strong right uppercut, then a second uppercut to win another round. He would also take the seventh using his left and throwing uppercuts. Zivic was in total control of the fight.

It was now the eighth round, and it would be Zivic's best. Both fighters exchanged punches, but could not land them, as each fought defensively. They got tangled up and the referee stepped in to separate the two. Then Zivic connected with a left jab to Angott's jaw and followed it with three lefts to his stomach. He proceeded with a series of rights and lefts to Angott's jaw, causing Angott to stagger a little and the crowd to clamor for a knockout.

Angott danced and retreated to start the ninth. Each fighter missed shots and then they got tied up. Zivic landed a left hook to the jaw before Angott tied him up again. Once free, he followed with a left and then a right. The bell sounded after Zivic hit Angott in the face to take another round. There was not much action in the 10th and final round. Zivic did not try for a knockout because he knew he had won the fight.

Zivic fought extremely well. He took an early lead and, never looking back, won eight rounds. He was defensive when he needed to be and kept Angott off balance with his left jab and by mixing it up with a powerful left and right uppercut. Zivic's best round was the eighth when he staggered Angott and almost got the knockout he predicted. He was just too much for Angott. When the fight was over, Angott admitted to Bert Taggart of the *Pittsburgh Post-Gazette* that Zivic "was too big and strong, and a little too rough ... I haven't any alibi. It was just a case of being up against a bigger and stronger opponent."[29] Zivic also saw Taggart after the fight and said, "I told you I'd lick him."[30] That Zivic did and, in the process, earned a title shot against Henry Armstrong.[31]

The following October, Zivic defeated Armstrong in a 15-round decision to win the World Welterweight Title, and he would continue to fight for several more years and be involved in some other memorable matches.

One of those legendary bouts occurred on Monday, July 12, 1943, when Zivic met Jake LaMotta under the lights at Forbes Field. A large crowd was expected to attend. The gates opened at 5:00 P.M. and an excellent lineup of preliminary fights was scheduled with local Pittsburgh fighters on the undercard. The railway company even added several extra cars to help with transportation. In a patriotic gesture amid World War II, service men and women were admitted through the box-holders' gate and seated in sections 14 and 15 of the grandstand's first floor.[32]

The fighters weighed in at noon at Forbes Field. LaMotta weighed 157½ pounds, while Zivic weighed 151 pounds. The two had faced each other before in a 10-round event that LaMotta won, but a majority of observers actually thought that Zivic should have been the winner. LaMotta was a 7–5 favorite to beat Zivic, mainly because this fight was scheduled for 15 rounds. LaMotta, younger and stronger, was expected to have more endurance. He had tried to box with Zivic during the last fight, and that almost cost him. LaMotta liked to move in and go after his opponents, and this would be his strategy against Zivic. The confident Zivic, on the other hand, was not worried about the 15 rounds and planned to knock out LaMotta: "He's made to order for me. I'm going to shoot for a knockout this time, so don't worry about the 15 rounds."[33] But not many people believed Zivic could deliver. LaMotta was a tough fighter and was able to take a beating, if necessary; however, a technical knockout was possible. In their previous fight, Zivic cut LaMotta around the eyes, and he would try to do that again. Clearly, the two fighters disliked each other. LaMotta claimed that Zivic had fought dirty the last time and used his elbows, laces, and thumbs, as well as head butts, against him. During that same fight, LaMotta retaliated in kind, as he almost choked Zivic when they were up against the ropes. The antagonists would not disappoint fight fans this time either.

The stage was set for an outstanding match. That night, a crowd of 15,462 was on hand at Forbes Field to watch the bout. The gross gate was $46,018; the net was $39,392. The action was much closer in this fight, and the 15 rounds almost cost Zivic the victory, as LaMotta dominated the later rounds. LaMotta started out fast in round one, but Zivic would control rounds two through six. Zivic made LaMotta fight his fight. Using his left jab to keep LaMotta off balance, Zivic prevented LaMotta from attacking him. The action was so intense that both fighters suffered cuts over their eyes. The seventh round was even and Zivic took rounds eight and nine. LaMotta made his move in the 10th. He staggered Zivic with a hard left to his jaw, and Zivic's knees buckled as he absorbed the shot. LaMotta won the 11th, too, while Zivic managed to regain his composure and win the 12th. The last three rounds would determine the outcome of the fight. LaMotta, the "Bronx Bull," furiously attacked Zivic in these rounds. He knew Zivic was in control and had to get to him. LaMotta took the 13th and 14th rounds as momentum swung in his favor. Round 15 would be crucial. LaMotta came out attacking to start the round, but Zivic still had enough energy left to deliver a strong final round. Zivic caught LaMotta with a left and then a right to his jaw, staggering LaMotta. Then both fighters boxed feverishly, exchanging punches, until the final bell rang to end the fight.

It was an entertaining match as both men put on a memorable display of boxing. Because the fight was so close, it was left to the judges to determine the outcome. Judge Buck McTiernan voted eight rounds to Zivic and seven to LaMotta. Judge Alvin J. "Vic" Williams voted seven rounds to LaMotta, five rounds to Zivic, with three rounds even. Referee Ernie Sesto voted eight rounds to Zivic, five rounds to LaMotta, with two rounds even. Zivic was the winner in a split decision. It was a close, competitive fight. Though some thought LaMotta had won, Zivic's gutsy performance in the 15th round may have given him an edge and the victory. That night, the fans at Forbes Field witnessed an extraordinary performance from these two fighters. It was yet another historic Forbes Field moment.[34]

Probably the most popular boxer to come out of the city of Pittsburgh was Billy Conn, from East Liberty, who staged a memorable bout with another local boxer, Teddy Yarosz, from Monaca, Pennsylvania. Before a large crowd at Forbes Field, Conn and Yarosz met each other in a 12-round bout on June 30, 1937. Both of these fighters were well-known in Pittsburgh and considered nice guys. Yarosz, a former middleweight champion of the world, was making a comeback after he injured his leg in a previous fight against Babe Risko. Yarosz was older, an exceptional defensive boxer who had become a better puncher than he used to be, and who was favored to beat Conn. Conn was a heavy underdog for the fight. He was 19, young, fearless, aggressive, and an average defensive fighter who was not expected to do much against the cagey Yarosz. Both fighters weighed in at 161 pounds.[35]

A crowd of 13,874 was in attendance to see the match, which yielded a gross gate of $26,178, and a net gate of $24,869. Tickets sold for one to three dollars. Yarosz got 30 percent of the net, or $7,461, while Conn got 25 percent, or $6,217.

The fight's action went through certain stages. It started out fast, slowed down as the two men just boxed, and then ended with a fury as Yarosz and Conn stood toe-to-toe exchanging punches. Rounds one through five were entertaining and full of action. Yarosz came out strong in the first round as he consistently pounded Conn with powerful blows to his head and body. Conn started off slowly and was taking a beating. He could not do much fighting because he was too busy trying to evade Yarosz's volleys of lefts, right crosses, and left hooks to the head. Yarosz knew he could not keep up this frenetic pace, so he slowed down in the fourth round and began to fight defensively. Conn took advantage of this and started to attack, connecting with left hooks to Yarosz's body. Conn mixed in left jabs to Yarosz's head and an occasional right. This was an important round for Conn. He had taken some big shots from Yarosz in the previous rounds and was not fazed. From this point on, Conn would be the aggressor throughout the remainder of the fight.

The action slowed down between the sixth and the 10th round. Yarosz knew he could not slug it out with Conn and had to box. He fought defensively and scored lightly. Conn realized that Yarosz could not hurt him and continued to attack. At times, Yarosz tied up Conn, preventing him from landing shots. This seemed to tire Yarosz out, as Conn was the fresher of the two fighters. As the fight progressed, there was not much to distinguish one fighter from the other. It was a close fight. Conn's best weapons were a right cross to the jaw and a left hook to Yarosz's body. Yarosz countered with a left of his own to Conn's body and with a hook to the jaw.

The action then reached a crescendo in the final two rounds. Both fighters slugged it out, trying to score a knockout and win the fight. Neither could do this as the final bell rang. The fight shifted from Yarosz to Conn, and the decision was now in the judges' hands.

The crowd anxiously awaited the verdict. In an upset, Billy Conn was declared the victor and proclaimed the State Middleweight Champion. When Conn was announced the winner, the Pittsburgh fight fans at Forbes Field went crazy. They pelted the ring with newspapers and pillows in disgust over the split decision. Some fans even threw chairs, which caused damage at ringside, but fortunately no one was hurt. It was a close, competitive fight over 12 rounds, and Conn may have won because he was the more aggressive fighter. Judge George MacBeth voted for Yarosz. Referee Al Grayber and Judge Jap Williams voted for Conn.[36]

Considering Yarosz's experience, Conn fought an excellent fight and won a major victory. Asked if Yarosz had hurt him during the bout, Conn replied, "No, he didn't hurt me at all, but he was a hard man to fight. He does more infighting than I do, and that is where he got in his hardest blows, but still they did not hurt me."[37] Conn was not impressed with Yarosz's punching power either. Conn said, "He is the third former champion I have fought and he did not give me as much trouble as Dundee and Risko. Both of them, [sic] hit harder than Teddy, but Teddy is a better boxer than either."[38]

It was a tough loss for Yarosz. A win would have led to another title shot against Freddy Steel. Yarosz objected to the decision: "Billy is a good boy, but I was certain I beat him. If we meet again, and I would be glad to do so, I am sure I would be able to make it so decisive the officials wouldn't rule against me."[39]

September 25, 1939, marked another fight night in Forbes Field history. This time the stakes were a bit higher as the light heavyweight title was on the line. Billy Conn, now the light heavyweight champion, would be defending his title against Melio Bettina. The two had fought a few months earlier, with Conn the victor. The title bout was scheduled for 15 rounds and Conn was a 3-to-1 favorite to beat Bettina. Both fighters weighed 175 pounds, were in excellent condition, and confident of their abilities. Conn stated, "I'll whip Bettina again ... I know I'm the better man; I proved that the first time we met and I'll make more certain tonight."[40] Bettina thought he was better prepared for this fight and declared, "I just loaned that title to Billy for a few weeks, now I'm going to reclaim my property."[41]

Seventeen thousand fans were at Forbes Field to watch the evening bout. The gross gate was $67,892 and the net gate was $58,118. Celebrities—including Pie Traynor, the manager of the Pirates, and Art Rooney, the owner of the football Pirates—were among those in attendance.

Both fighters came out for the first round. They sparred and jabbed and there was not much action. Both were trying to get a feel for each other. The second round went the same as the first. In rounds three, four, and five, Bettina was the aggressor. He attacked Conn and landed punches to Conn's body and jaw. Conn just could not get on track as Bettina easily won these rounds.

It was now round six, and Conn desperately needed to start boxing. He delivered solid shots to Bettina's body and jaw and won the round, thereby gaining some momentum. Conn and Bettina exchanged punches to start the seventh. Then Conn unleashed a vicious two-hand attack. He threw a flurry of punches and Bettina was taking a beating. The crowd got into the action and wanted a knockout. Conn threw more rights and lefts to Bettina's body to close the round and win his second in a row.

Conn took round eight, as well, and was now fighting the way he wanted to. He came out strong in the ninth, charging Bettina and landing two powerful shots to Bettina's head. Bettina was in trouble. Conn then attacked Bettina's body and scored with one punch after another to his stomach. Conn finished the round with another flurry of lefts and rights to Bettina's head. Bettina tried to rally in rounds 10 and 11, but he could not slow Conn down. Round 12 was basically even.

In the 13th round, Conn pounded Bettina, but Bettina counterpunched. He landed a right to Conn's jaw, then a left to his head. Conn responded with a left hook to Bettina's jaw. Both fighters tied each other up. Conn finished the round with a left hook to Bettina's jaw and a right hook to Bettina's stomach, which won Conn another round.

Conn went on the offensive again in the 14th. It was another furious two-handed attack to Bettina's body and face. Bettina was looking for cover, but there was nowhere to hide. Conn then landed two sharp right uppercuts to his body, which Bettina could not answer as his hands were down at his sides. Conn finished the round with a left hook, followed by a right to Bettina's stomach.

Both fighters came out for the 15th and final round. As the action started, Bettina moved Conn toward the ropes and tried to hold him. Conn pounded Bettina's stomach. Bettina had nothing left, and Conn was doing whatever he wanted. Conn delivered lefts to Bettina's body and jaw, then rights to his stomach. Next, Conn unleashed a barrage of lefts and rights to Bettina's head. Conn landed shots at will and finished with a left to Bettina's jaw. The final bell rang, and it was Conn's round and fight.[42]

Conn won the match by a large margin and retained his light heavyweight title. Bettina won some earlier rounds, but Conn dominated rounds six through 15 and was never in trouble. Judges Johnny Fundy and Irish Chick Rodgers, together with Referee Red Robinson, awarded Conn the unanimous decision. Bettina took a pounding and was tired and sore after the fight with cuts over his eyes. He had no complaints, though, because he knew the better fighter had won. Hoping for a rematch, Bettina said, "Yes, I'd like to fight him again. I'll admit he's a pretty good fighter, and a hard man to fight but I'd like to get another crack at him."[43]

It was a jubilant atmosphere in Conn's dressing room after the fight. Family and friends crowded around the champion as he answered questions and received congratulations. Conn had some swelling on his nose and an abrasion on his left temple, but was otherwise unmarked. He also took pictures with his dad and his manager, Johnny Ray. Describing the fight, Conn remarked, "It was a tougher fight than my first one.... I just couldn't get started in the first six rounds; after the lucky seventh began, however, I was back in form and never worried about the result. Bettina never hurt me with any of his punches, but he certainly did a lot of butting that had my nose bleeding so much."[44]

It was an impressive victory and another classic Conn fight at Forbes Field. In the 1930s and 1940s, when boxing was extremely popular in Pittsburgh, Conn became the most liked and recognizable of all the local fighters: He "was the No. 1 guy here. He wasn't just a boxer, he was a star. He looked like a matinee idol."[45] Conn had God-given talent, and it was evident at an early age. He began his pro career in 1934 and never fought as an amateur. He fought in an upright style and was technically perfect. Conn won the light heavyweight title at 21 and "[b]y age 23, [he] had been up against nine world champions in three weight divisions and had beaten them all."[46] Then, on June 18, 1941, Billy Conn fought Joe Louis for the heavyweight title in a scheduled 15-round bout at the Polo Grounds in New York. On the verge of becoming heavyweight champion of the world, Conn was beating Louis, and all he had to do was avoid a knockout. But if Conn had a weakness, it was his stubbornness. He went after Louis and tried to knock him out, a move that doomed Conn as Louis kayoed him instead.

While Conn was fighting Louis, an interesting scenario occurred during the Pirates' game at Forbes Field: "The night Conn came close to beating Joe Louis in New York, a crowd of 24,738 was in the stands at Forbes Field for a game between the Pirates and Giants. Minutes before the fight, the umpires called time. Both teams retired to their dugouts, and for almost an hour, while Conn won and lost the heavyweight championship, everyone sat and listened to the amplified radio broadcast."[47] This showed how much Pittsburgh loved Billy Conn, and he loved her right back. Conn's career record was 64–12–1, which included 15 knockouts. Billy Conn was one of the best fighters ever, and his talent was on display at Forbes Field.

July 18, 1951, was a significant night in Forbes Field lore. For the first time in history, Pittsburgh hosted a heavyweight championship bout. Ezzard Charles would face Jersey Joe Walcott in a 15-round main event. The city was excited about the fight and the national attention it would receive. Twenty-five thousand people were expected to attend the fight. The gates opened

Jersey Joe Walcott (left) and Ezzard Charles pose during the weigh-in prior to their heavyweight championship fight, July 18, 1951 (copyright, *Pittsburgh Post-Gazette*, 2005, all rights reserved. Reprinted with permission).

at 6:00 P.M. and ticket prices ranged from $2.95 to $25. Celebrities, public officials, and some 60 national boxing writers from across the country would be in the crowd. Hoping for a title shot against the winner, Joe Louis, the former heavyweight champion, would also be there. Because a large crowd was anticipated, 130 police officers were assigned to Forbes Field for the fight, with special officers guarding Charles and Walcott on their way to and from their dressing rooms.

Ezzard Charles was 30 years old and weighed 183 pounds. Jersey Joe Walcott was 37 and weighed 194. He was the father of six children and was a 10–1 underdog going into the fight, which was his fifth attempt to win the heavyweight title.[48]

The atmosphere at Forbes Field was electric. The city and fight fans were thrilled to host this bout and hoped for an entertaining match. A record crowd for a fight — 28,272 — was on hand to witness the occasion. It surpassed the Billy Conn–Buddy Knox fight in 1941. An estimated 60 million people were watching the fight via television, as well. The gross gate was $245,004 and the net was $176,568. TV and radio receipts were $100,000. Ezzard Charles got 40 percent, or $99,564, and Walcott got 20 percent, or $49,782.

The bell rang for round one, and both fighters came out cautiously. They exchanged jabs and danced around the ring, allowing for little action.

There was more action in round two. The fighters met in the center of the ring and traded punches. Charles landed a right to Walcott's body. Walcott responded with two rights to Charles' body. Walcott then threw a left and a right to Charles' body again, and won the round.

The tempo of the fight increased in round three. Walcott led with his jab. Charles countered with a left and a right to Walcott's body. Charles then scored with a left and a right to Walcott's head. Walcott landed two rights to Charles' head. Near the end of the round, Walcott staggered Charles with a right to the head, followed by a flurry of lefts and rights to his head and body. The crowd loved the action as roars for a knockout echoed throughout Forbes Field.

Walcott led with his jab again to start the fourth round. The crowd wanted Walcott to go after Charles. Walcott delivered a hard left jab to Charles' head. Charles was bleeding from his mouth. Walcott then landed a powerful left to Charles' body, followed by a right. Charles countered with a right uppercut to Walcott's jaw.

Charles attacked Walcott to start round five. He realized he was behind and needed to win some rounds. Charles landed a left and a right at close range. Then he connected with a hard right to Walcott's body and followed it with a left to his head. The crowd enjoyed the action. Before the bell rang, Walcott landed a powerful right to Charles' head that staggered the champion and split his lip. Charles was bleeding as he went to his corner.

Charles had a strong sixth round and started to regain his form. He delivered powerful shots to Walcott's body and head. When round seven started, Charles was on the attack again. He threw a left and a right to Walcott's head. Walcott retreated from the trouble as the two moved to the center of the ring. Then Walcott faked with a right and connected with a powerful left hook that sent Charles to the canvas. Charles was badly hurt and dazed. He tried to get up as the referee counted, but fell back down, still shaken and hurt. Walcott scored a knockout 55 seconds into round seven and won the heavyweight title on his fifth attempt. The knockout stunned the Forbes Field crowd.[49]

A mob of family, friends, and reporters waited to see Walcott after the fight. Walcott did not have a scratch on him and talked about his knockout punch. "It was a left hook that did it … I feinted with my right to set him up and then let him have it. I never was hurt at any time."[50]

Charles had cuts under his right eye and lower left lip. He was shocked that Walcott knocked him out. He asked after the fight, "Did they really count me out … I kinda remember trying to get up at the count of five or six but that's all I remember."[51]

It was a spectacular moment in Forbes Field history that perhaps was best summed up this way: "The greatest Cinderella story in fistic history was written at Forbes Field last night when 37-year-old Jersey Joe Walcott of Camden, N.J., won the world heavyweight championship by knocking out Ezzard Charles in 55 seconds of the seventh round of a scheduled 15-round title battle."[52]

## Thirty Years of Steeler Football

Professional football came to Pittsburgh in 1933 when Art Rooney bought for a franchise for $2,500 with money that he had accumulated from his racetrack winnings. The team was originally called the Pirates; Rooney changed the name to the Steelers in 1941. Losers in the 1930s and 1940s, the team was slightly better in the 1950s and 1960s, and had some winning seasons during those decades. Rooney was the leader of the Steelers from the team's inception until he died. Both the Steelers and Rooney started out from humble beginnings: "He had offices in hotels, first the Fort Pitt, later the Roosevelt, but he ran the club out of a little book he kept in his jacket pocket, held together with rubber bands."[53] While it took a few decades for the Steelers to become successful, there were a number of individual players who achieved stardom. Hall of Famers Bill Dudley, John Henry Johnson, Walt Kiesling, Bobby Layne, Johnny "Blood" McNally, and Ernie Stautner all played at Forbes Field.[54] Art Rooney and co-owner Bert Bell would be inducted into the Hall of Fame, too. Byron "Whizzer" White is also famous in Steelers' lore. In 1938, he led the league in rushing yards and was its highest paid player, earning $15,800. However, after only one year, White departed to pursue a Rhodes scholarship at Oxford University. Later in White's life, President John F. Kennedy would appoint him to serve as an associate justice of the United States Supreme Court.

The Pittsburgh Pirates made their professional debut at Forbes Field on Wednesday, September 20, 1933, against the New York Giants. It was the inaugural season of professional football in Pittsburgh and an important year in the city's sports history. Local fans would be treated to watching various former college football stars in action, such as Harry Newman, Ken Strong, Angelo Brovelli, and Elmer Schwartz. Pirate coach Jap Douds thought his team would make a strong showing and have a solid first season: "We have boys just out of college who are strong and fast and are imbued with confidence and desire to win."[55] But obviously, the Pirates were underdogs due to their lack of experience.

Kickoff was scheduled for 8:30 P.M., but the game, played under floodlights, started late because fans were still filing into their seats. Some 25,000 were in attendance to witness the debut of the Pirates. However, professional football at Forbes Field began inauspiciously as New York defeated Pittsburgh 23–2. Clearly outmanned, the Pirates put up a valiant effort, but lacked enough players with professional experience. The game was close until the fourth quarter, when the Giants scored 16 points in that frame. Harry Newman, the star for the Giants, ran for a touchdown, threw for a touchdown, returned punts, and directed his club to victory. Pittsburgh simply did not have a player as good as Newman. Angelo Brovelli was supposed to be the Pirates' star, but the Giants smothered him every time he touched the ball. The rest of the offense was so inept that the Pirates could only manage to score a safety on a blocked punt.[56]

Different than the atmosphere of the college games, professional football had neither cheerleaders nor bands to promote enthusiasm that fans were used to. The crowd warmed up slowly and got excited at times, but also grew impatient with the frequent penalties and timeouts, and occasional injuries. In addition, the game was played on a Wednesday night because blue laws, intended to keep the Sabbath holy, were still in effect in Pittsburgh. But no matter what the score of the game, it was a monumental moment because it introduced professional football to Pittsburgh, and it happened at Forbes Field.

History was made again that same year at Forbes Field in a game matching the Pirates against the football Brooklyn Dodgers. But instead of a Wednesday night game, the contest was scheduled on a Sunday afternoon with a 2:30 P.M. kickoff. It marked the end of the antiquated blue laws and ushered in the first professional sporting event ever held in Pittsburgh on a Sunday.

On November 12, 1933, approximately 12,000 fans at Forbes Field welcomed the end of the blue laws and made up the first legal Sunday sports crowd in Pittsburgh history. The Pirates sported new uniforms, including black and gold striped jerseys. The fans anticipated a competitive game; however, after the kickoff, their hopes were dashed. The Dodgers crushed the Pirates 32–0, scoring points in every quarter and leaving the Pittsburgh fans disappointed. The Dodgers' Shipwreck Kelly stole the show. He scored three touchdowns and also added an extra point. Outmatched by the Dodgers, the Pirates continued to struggle throughout their first season.[57]

Fans of the 1933 Pirates' football club did not have much to cheer about. But more significant than the action and the final score was that all of the games, especially these two, provided a foundation on which the team could grow. Over time, the Pirates would become the Steelers. After a tradition of losing, the team's fortunes would change, and though distant memories, the Steelers' rich history can be traced back to a Wednesday night and Sunday afternoon at Forbes Field in 1933.

As professional football grew in popularity in Pittsburgh, the Steelers managed to improve, as well. At Forbes Field on Sunday, October 19, 1947, the Steelers faced their intrastate rivals, the Philadelphia Eagles, who were six-point favorites. The Steelers' coach was Jock Sutherland, and this game held importance. If the Steelers won and the Washington Redskins lost, Pittsburgh would be in first place in the Eastern Division of the National Football League. The game would feature a duel between running backs: Steve Van Buren of the Eagles and Johnny Clement of the Steelers were the leading two rushers in the league, respectively.[58]

Kickoff was at 2:00 P.M., and 33,538 people were at Forbes Field to watch the game. Pittsburgh scored first. The Eagles fumbled and the Steelers recovered on the Eagles' 38-yard line. Clement carried and was stopped. On the next play, he threw a pass to Tony Compagno who raced 39 yards for a touchdown. Joe Giamp added the point after. The Steelers were winning 7–0. The Eagles answered with a touchdown on the next possession, as Pete Pihos scored and Philadelphia made the extra point. The game was now tied 7–7. The Steelers mounted a drive and missed a field goal. The Eagles got the ball back and Van Buren carried for a 45-yard gain. Pittsburgh held and the Eagles settled for a field goal. The score was now 10–7 in favor of Philadelphia, but the action and the scoring chances would continue. The Steelers missed another field goal and the Eagles would capitalize again. This time Tommy Thompson threw a pass to Bosh Pritchard that resulted in a 69-yard touchdown that added to the Philadelphia lead. The Eagles were up 17–7 with time winding down in the second quarter. The Steelers were not deterred, though, driving the ball 82 yards in five plays. Johnny Clement scored on a five-yard touchdown run and Giamp added the extra point. The Eagles still led 17–14. Although the first half was almost over, Philadelphia tried to score once more and moved the ball down the field. Then it happened — a controversial call from the referee. Bryant Meeks, a Steeler, collided with Gil Steinke, an Eagle, and was called for interference, though it looked like Steinke caused the contact. The Pittsburgh fans protested the call and booed the official. Nevertheless, the ruling went in the Eagles' favor, and the next play turned out even worse for the Steelers. Thompson threw another touchdown pass to Pihos with 25 seconds left in the second quarter. The Eagles added the extra point and were up 24–14 at the half.

There was no scoring in the third quarter, but the fourth was filled with plenty of action. The Steelers intercepted a pass to halt a Philadelphia drive. With momentum from that play, Pittsburgh then mounted a drive and finished it when Clement threw a touchdown pass to Bill Garnaas. Again, Giamp added the extra point and the score was now 24–21. The Eagles still led, but Pittsburgh's defense forced a punt on Philadelphia's next drive and got the ball back. Immediately, the Steeler offense went to work and moved the ball. Johnny Clement dropped back to pass. He scrambled, and seeing an opening down the left sideline, he took off to score a 24-yard touchdown. Giamp made the extra point and the Steelers were now winning 28–24. Pittsburgh was dominating the game and put together a final scoring drive which propelled them to the one-foot line. From there, Steve Lach plunged into the end zone for another touchdown, and Giamp converted his fifth extra point of the day to make the score 35–24 in favor of the Steelers.

That proved to be the final tally, as the Steelers scored 21 points in a dramatic fourth-quarter comeback at Forbes Field. With its third win of the year, Pittsburgh moved into first place in its division because Washington lost its game. Johnny Clement was the hero. Although Van Buren won the rushing duel that day, Clement was on the field for every offensive play, threw

14 passes, and scored two touchdowns. The Steelers' five touchdowns and five conversions tied an all-time club record for points in a home game. Sutherland had the Steelers moving in the right direction.[59]

Another classic Steeler game occurred in 1952. It was November 30, and the New York Giants were in town to play the Steelers at Forbes Field. The Giants were favored by seven and a half points and were 6–3 on the season. The Steelers were 3–6. New York had a formidable running attack led by Eddie Price, the National Football League's leading rusher, and Kyle Rote.[60]

Kickoff was at 2:00 P.M. It was a frozen, snowy turf at Forbes, but in attendance were 15,140 hearty fans. The teams were headed in opposite directions, and the Steelers, coached by Joe Bach, were not expected to do much. But what happened that day turned out to be something special. Pittsburgh crushed the Giants by a score of 63–7 and broke several team records in the process.

Lynn Chandois returned the opening kickoff 91 yards for a touchdown. He ran straight up the middle and broke through to daylight. Seventeen seconds into the game, Gary Kerkorian added the extra point, and the Steelers were leading 7–0. Pittsburgh then scored on an eight-play drive, culminated by a Chandois five-yard sweep around left end for his second touchdown of the game. Kerkorian converted the kick, and it was 14–0 at the end of the first quarter.

In the second quarter, Jim Finks, the Steeler quarterback, threw a 21-yard touchdown pass to Elbie Nickel. The point after was good and the Steelers led 21–0. Finks threw his second touchdown pass minutes later — a 42-yard toss to Ray Mathews— and Pittsburgh led 28–0 at halftime.

The Steelers went right back to work in the third quarter. Finks added a third touchdown pass to his statistics. This one covered 25 yards to Dick Hensley. Kerkorian kicked the extra point to make it 35–0. The Giants finally scored in the third on a fluke play that involved a double lateral. Tom Landry threw a pass to Bill Stribling who lateraled to Joe Scott who lateraled back to Stribling who ran for a touchdown. It was 35–7 at the end of the third quarter.

But there would be no New York comeback on this day, as the Steelers continued to dismantle the Giants' defense. Finks threw a 60-yard touchdown pass to Hensley. It was his fourth touchdown pass of the day. Kerkorian added the extra point to make it 42–7. The Giants were forced to punt, as they had to do several times that day. Dale Dodrill blocked Landry's kick and George Hays picked it up and walked a couple of yards into the end zone. This time Mathews converted the extra point, and the Steelers were winning 49–7. Kerkorian took over at quarterback for Finks, whose day was done. He was 12 of 24 for 254 yards and four touchdowns. Kerkorian then got into the action. He threw a 20-yard touchdown pass to Jack Butler and also kicked the point after to make it 56–7. Fullback Ed Modzelewski capped the scoring for the Steelers, as he carried three yards around the right tackle for a touchdown. Kerkorian added another extra point. It was the end of the game or the Steelers might have scored again. The final score read Pittsburgh 63, New York 7.

The Steelers set several team records that day: seven pass interceptions (the previous record was six set in 1950); five touchdown passes in one game (the old mark was four set earlier in the season); nine touchdowns in one game (the highest total was five set in 1948); and 63 points, the most for a game. This eclipsed the old scoring record of 38 that had been accomplished on three different occasions. The Steeler fans were so excited by this astounding display of offensive prowess that they tore down the uprights to the goalpost, but they could not get them completely out of the ground before the police arrived.[61]

For some reason, the Steelers were an offensive juggernaut that day in 1952. Their performance rivals other great offensive feats throughout NFL history. It was one of the Steelers' best games ever, and it happened at Forbes Field.

Any meaningful portrayal of professional football history in Pittsburgh must include an account of a game against the Steelers' hated rival, the Cleveland Browns. This one occurred

**Second quarter action, Pittsburgh Steelers versus New York Giants, September 27, 1949 (Raymond N. Baum, Jr., courtesy of Matthew Baum).**

on Sunday, November 20, 1960, at Forbes Field. The Steelers, coached by Buddy Parker, were 2–5–1 on the season while the Browns, coached by Paul Brown, were 5–2. Pittsburgh was out to avenge a 28–20 loss suffered against Cleveland earlier in the year. Leading the Browns' impressive offense were quarterback Milt Plum, one of the league's best, and Jim Brown, the outstanding runner. The Steelers' hopes rested on the arm and shoulders of Bobby Layne. He would have to control the ball, command the offense, and match Plum in order for Pittsburgh to win.

Kickoff was at 2:05 P.M. Pete Rozelle, the commissioner of the NFL and successor to the late Bert Bell, was at Forbes Field to witness another chapter in the storied rivalry between Pittsburgh and Cleveland.[62] But Rozelle was not alone, as 35,215 fans were also there to watch the game.

The fans were not disappointed, for they saw an unforgettable game comprised of two strong defenses, exciting plays, and a thrilling finish. The Steelers scored first, engineering a drive to Cleveland's 1-yard line. There, John Henry Johnson got the call and plunged over the right guard for a touchdown. Layne converted the extra point to give the Steelers a 7–0 lead. That would be all the scoring until the third quarter, but the game did not lack excitement. The offenses made plays and there were scoring opportunities, but neither team could convert when it counted. This was partially due to both defenses. The Steelers held Jim Brown in check, but Cleveland eventually got on the scoreboard. With fifteen seconds left in the third quarter, the Browns kicked a 19-yard field goal to make it 7–3. Cleveland kept moving in the fourth quarter and manufactured another scoring drive. Taking control of the Browns' offense, Milt Plum dropped back to pass and found an open Cleveland receiver. The pass went down the sideline and the Browns were in scoring position again on Pittsburgh's 25-yard line. A few plays later, Plum pumped right and threw left to Rich Kreitling for a touchdown. The Browns led 10–7 and set the stage for a dramatic finish.

**The Steelers drive for a second touchdown on their way to a 28–7 victory over the Giants (Raymond N. Baum, Jr., courtesy of Matthew Baum).**

It was now Bobby Layne's turn to work his magic. The Steelers were 75 yards away from Cleveland's end zone. Layne started the drive with a 17-yard completion and followed it with an 11-yard gain on a screen pass. Next, he completed another pass that moved the Steelers to Cleveland's 12-yard line. John Henry Johnson then carried the ball for seven yards. Layne threw an incomplete pass on the following play. Tom "The Bomb" Tracy ran the ball on the next play for a short gain. It was now fourth down. Pittsburgh needed three yards for a first down and four for a touchdown. Layne took the snap and handed off to Tracy, who ran right. Mike Sandusky cleared the way and Tracy followed him into the end zone. Layne converted the point after to give the Steelers a 14–10 lead.

The Browns were not deterred, though. With two minutes left in the game, Plum went back to work, completing passes at will and picking apart the Steelers' secondary. He threw down-and-outs to his receivers so that they could catch the ball and get out of bounds. Cleveland drove the ball to the 11-yard line and called timeout with 36 seconds left to play. Once time resumed, Plum threw an incomplete pass. On the next play, under intense Steeler pressure, he had to throw the ball away and took an intentional grounding penalty that sent his team back to the 25-yard line. Plum then completed a pass to Leon Clarke.

The Browns were now on the 10-yard line as the seconds ticked away. With time for one final play, Cleveland rushed to the line. Plum called his signals and just managed to get the play off. He dropped back to pass and spotted Clarke in the end zone. He threw and Clarke dove to catch the ball as 35,215 fans anxiously awaited the outcome of the play. Clarke got up and began to celebrate his touchdown as another victory had eluded the Steelers. But wait! The official ruled that Clarke had trapped the ball and it was an incomplete pass. The game was over, as the Steelers won 14–10 in a fantastic finish! The Steelers fans rushed onto Forbes Field in jubilation.[63]

The Steelers were led by John Henry Johnson, Tom Tracy and, of course, Bobby Layne. Plum threw for more yards, but Layne scored points when he needed to and controlled the Steelers' offense by mixing his running and aerial attacks. The Steelers defense also played well and limited Jim Brown to 86 yards on 17 carries. It was another memorable moment at Forbes Field as reported in the *Pittsburgh Post-Gazette*: "Pro football at its most exciting, heart-thumping best was presented to 35,215 boosters and critics yesterday afternoon as the Pittsburgh Steelers, a team going no place, knocked off the Cleveland Browns, a top contender for honors, by the score of 14 to 10. They carried this one down to the very last second before it was decided."[64]

December 12, 1962, was the final home game of the season for the Steelers at Forbes Field. Their opponent was the St. Louis Cardinals. The Steelers were 6–5 on the season under Coach Buddy Parker. The Cardinals, coached by Wally Lemm, were 2–8–1 and had not won at Forbes Field in their last 11 games. The Steelers were six-point favorites and still had a chance to finish in first place. A more likely scenario would be a second-place finish and a trip to the Playoff Bowl in Miami on January 6. Pittsburgh's quarterback was Ed Brown instead of Bobby Layne. John Henry Johnson, the Steelers' running back, needed 82 yards to eclipse 1,000 yards rushing on the season.[65]

Kickoff was at 2:05 P.M. and 17,265 were in attendance. The Steelers got on the board first, thanks to an outstanding defensive play. Willie Daniel, a defensive back, made a twisting interception on a Charley Johnson pass, then proceeded to make a great return to the end zone for a touchdown. Lou Michaels added the extra point to give Pittsburgh a 7–0 lead. Throughout the first two quarters, the Steelers moved the ball but failed to score. Michaels missed two field goals in the second quarter: he was short on a 44-yarder and wide right on a 30-yarder. John Henry Johnson was having his trouble as well. He had only 24 yards rushing at halftime.

The Steelers received the kickoff to start the third quarter and mounted a long drive to the Cardinals 11-yard line. After losing yardage on the next few plays, Pittsburgh was forced to try a field goal. This time, Michaels' effort was true, and he gave the Steelers a 10–0 lead. After stopping the Cardinals' next drive, Pittsburgh moved into scoring position and Michaels kicked a 37-yard field goal to put the Steelers up 13–0. The score remained that way until the fourth quarter.

The Cardinals, now desperate, drove the ball to midfield and faced a crucial fourth-down-and-one play. The Steelers stuffed the Cardinal rusher for no gain. Pittsburgh took over at midfield and was quickly in field goal range. Michaels made a 23-yard field goal to give the Steelers a 16–0 lead. But St. Louis answered and engineered a scoring drive to make it 16–7. From that point on, however, it was all Pittsburgh and John Henry Johnson. The powerful Johnson took over the game, ran down the clock on his bruising carries, and in the process, shredded the Cardinals' defense en route to a 1,000-yard rushing season. Now in scoring range after Johnson's efforts, Michaels booted his fourth field goal of the day to make it 19–7 in favor of Pittsburgh.

The Steelers dominated the game on both sides of the ball. Though accumulating 23 first downs and 412 yards of offense, Pittsburgh managed only one touchdown which came from the defense. Lou Michaels had 13 points on the day. That gave him 87 total points for the year, which broke Bobby Layne's record of 77 points set in 1960. John Henry Johnson, with a strong second half, finished with 98 yards rushing in the game and 1,016 on the year to date. As a result of the Steelers' methodical victory, Pittsburgh moved into second place in the Eastern Conference and was a favorite to be in the Playoff Bowl in Miami.[66]

Much more significant, the victory marked the last time the Steelers would play at Forbes Field. Despite a checkered history of losing and winning there, the franchise closed out its stay in splendid fashion. In some games and seasons, the blueprint for success was clearly evident; however, the Steelers' crowning glory was still ahead of them. Reaching the pinnacle in the 1970s, the Pittsburgh franchise was considered one of the best in football. Art Rooney, beloved in Pittsburgh, was a generous man and was able to unite a city through the Steelers. And it all started at Forbes Field, where the Pirates became the Steelers and Rooney's dreams and visions began.

## The Sum of the Parts

Mazeroski's World Series home run is certainly the single most memorable sporting event associated with Forbes Field. But to remember only that occurrence would be a grave injustice to this venue and to the thousands of other spectacular moments that transpired there. A kickoff return, an interception, a crushing tackle, a fumble, or a screen pass calls forth countless memories, as does a jab, a combination to the body, a low blow, or a knockout punch. The athletic competition on the gridiron and in the ring at Forbes Field made sports history and created a treasure of recollections other than baseball ones.

During the era of Forbes Field, sports were pure. Athletes played the game because they loved it. Forbes Field was able to unite an entire city of different races, nationalities, and creeds. People would congregate there for one simple reason: to cheer on their home team or local fighter. More than just a ballpark, Forbes Field brought together fathers and sons, mothers and daughters, and friends to witness a sporting event. That is why Forbes Field is important, why it matters.[67]

## Notes

1. Jim O'Brien, "Pop Warner's Teams Won Three National Titles in Four Years," in *Hail to Pitt: A Sports History of the University of Pittsburgh*, Jim O'Brien, ed. (Pittsburgh: Wolfson Publishing Co., 1982), 71. The college football national championship has always been a muddled picture. According to its website, the National Collegiate Athletic Association (NCAA) does not conduct or participate in the selection process of the college football national champion (see http://www.ncaa.org/champadminJia football past champs.html). However, this site does provide a list of previous national champions and the organizations, foundations, and people who selected the winners. It also provides an explanation of who or what these organizations, foundations, and people are and how they selected their national champions.

In accordance with the NCAA website, the National Championship Foundation selected Pitt as the national champion for 1910. For that same year, the Billingsley Report crowned Michigan national champion and the Helms Athletic Foundation, the Houlgate System, and the National Championship Foundation selected Harvard to share the title. It should be noted that certain groups or people select multiple winners each year. For 1915, Parke Davis crowned Pitt as the national champion. For that same year, the Helms Athletic Founda-tion, the Houlgate System, the National Championship Foundation, and Parke Davis, who split his vote, selected Cornell as their national champion. The Billingsley Report considers Nebraska as the champion that year. For 1916, Parke Davis chose Army as a national champion. He also selected Pitt as did the Billingsley Report, the Helms Athletic Foundation, the Houlgate System, and the National Championship Foundation. For 1918, the National Championship Foundation, the Helms Athletic Foundation, and the Houlgate System crowned Pitt as the national champion. For that same year, the National Championship Foundation and the Billingsley Report selected Michigan as the national champion.

For a different perspective, HickockSports.com (see http://www.hickocksports.com/history/cfchamps.shtml/) provides another look at the college football national championship picture. According to this site, Pitt was crowned as a national champion in 1910, 1916, and 1918 while playing at Forbes Field. For 1910, the National Championship Foundation selected Pitt as its national champion. But the College Football Researchers Association and the Helms Athletic Foundation selected Harvard as champion. In 1915, HickockSports.com lists Cornell as the consensus national champion. In 1916, under Pop Warner, Pitt was the unanimous national champion. For 1918, Pitt was selected as the national champion by the College Football Researchers

Association and the Helms Athletic Foundation, while Michigan shared the national championship that same year and was chosen by the National Championship Foundation.

2. Mike Bynum, Larry Eldridge, Jr., and Sam Sciullo, Jr., eds., *Greatest Moments in Pitt Football History* (Nashville: Athlon Sports Communications, 1994), 4.

3. *Pittsburgh Post,* October 16, 1909, p. 9.

4. Ibid. Football was a different game in this era. Players played multiple positions on offense and defense and not every team had numbers on their uniforms.

5. Ibid.

6. The source for the details of the Pitt-Bucknell game is the *Pittsburgh Post,* October 17, 1909, sec. 3, p. 1.

7. The source for the pregame information for the Pitt-Carlisle game is the *Pittsburgh Post,* October 18, 1913, Sporting News Section, p. 1.

8. The source for the details of the Pitt-Carlisle game is the *Pittsburgh Post,* October 19, 1913, Sporting News Section, pp. 1–2.

9. *Pittsburgh Post,* November 22, 1918, p. 11.

10. *Pittsburgh Post,* November 24, 1918, sec. 3, p. 2.

11. Ibid.

12. The sources for the details of the Pitt-Georgia Tech game are the *Pittsburgh Post,* November 24, 1918, sec. 3, pp. 2–3, and Bynum et al., 29–32.

13. *Pittsburgh Post,* November 29, 1923, p. 21.

14. The source for the details of the Pitt-Penn State game is the *Pittsburgh Post,* November 30, 1923, p. 17.

15. *Pittsburgh Post,* November 30, 1923, p. 1.

16. The source for the pregame information for the Pitt-Penn State game is the *Pittsburgh Post,* November 27, 1924, p. 31.

17. *Pittsburgh Post,* November 28, 1924, p. 12.

18. The source for the details of the Pitt-Penn State game is the *Pittsburgh Post,* November 28, 1924, p. 11.

19. Ibid.

20. The source for the details of the Carnegie Tech–Notre Dame game is the *Pittsburgh Post,* November 30, 1924, sec. 3, p. 2.

21. Randy Roberts, "Between the Whale and Death," *Pittsburgh Sports: Stories from the Steel City,* Randy Roberts, ed. (Pittsburgh: University of Pittsburgh Press, 2000), 20–22. In these pages, Roberts describes boxing of yesteryear and uses Fritzie Zivic to explain Depression era boxing and dirty fighting.

22. Ibid.

23. The source for the details on Greb is the *Pittsburgh Post,* June 23, 1919, p. 9.

24. The source for the details of the Greb-Gibbons fight is the *Pittsburgh Post,* June 24, 1919, pp. 14–15.

25. Roberts, 19. Zivic might have been a dirty fighter, but he was also a champion. He did what he had to do, and his opponents were also dirty.

26. The source for the details of the prefight publicity for the Zivic-Angott fight is the *Pittsburgh Post-Gazette,* August 28, 1940, p. 105, and August 29, 1940, pp. 107–108.

27. *Pittsburgh Post-Gazette,* August 28, 1940, p. 16.

28. *Pittsburgh Post-Gazette,* August 30, 1940, p. 14.

29. *Pittsburgh Post-Gazette,* August 30, 1940, p. 15.

30. Ibid.

31. The source for the details of the Zivic-Angott fight is the *Pittsburgh Post-Gazette,* August 30, 1940, p. 15.

32. *Pittsburgh Post-Gazette,* July 12, 1943, p. 15.

33. Ibid., p. 14.

34. The source for the details of the Zivic-LaMotta fight is the *Pittsburgh Post-Gazette,* July 13, 1943, pp. 14–15.

35. The source for the details on Yarosz and Conn is the *Pittsburgh Post-Gazette,* June 30, 1937, pp. 18–19.

36. The source for the details of the Conn-Yarosz fight is the *Pittsburgh Post-Gazette,* July 1, 1937, pp. 17, 20.

37. *Pittsburgh Post-Gazette,* July 1, 1937, p. 20.

38. Ibid.

39. Ibid., p. 17.

40. *Pittsburgh Post-Gazette,* September 25, 1939, p. 15.

41. Ibid.

42. The source for the details of the Conn-Bettina fight is the *Pittsburgh Post-Gazette,* September 26, 1939, pp. 1, 15, 17.

43. *Pittsburgh Post-Gazette,* September 26, 1939, p. 15.

44. Ibid.

45. Jim O'Brien, *Hometown Heroes: Profiles in Sports and Spirit* (Pittsburgh: James P. O'Brien Publishing, 1999), 81.

46. See http://www.post-gazette.com/sports_head lines/19991128mchugh4.asp.

47. Ibid.

48. The source for the details on Charles and Walcott is the *Pittsburgh Post-Gazette,* July 18, 1951, pp. 1, 18.

49. The source for the details of the Charles-Walcott fight is the *Pittsburgh Post-Gazette,* July 19, 1951, pp. 1, 14–15, 17.

50. *Pittsburgh Post-Gazette,* July 19, 1951, p. 15.

51. Ibid.

52. Ibid., p. 1.

53. Abby Mendelson, *The Pittsburgh Steelers: The Official Team History* (Dallas: Taylor Publishing Company, 1996), 22.

54. Ibid., 211–212.

55. *Pittsburgh Post-Gazette,* September 20, 1933, p. 18.

56. The source for the details of the Pirate-Giant game is the *Pittsburgh Post-Gazette,* September 21, 1933, pp. 14–15.

57. The source for the details of the Pirate-Dodger game is the *Pittsburgh Post-Gazette,* November 13, 1933, p. 16.

58. The source for the pregame information for the Steeler-Eagle game is the *Pittsburgh Post-Gazette,* October 18, 1947, p. 8.

59. The source for the details of the Steeler-Eagle game is the *Pittsburgh Post-Gazette,* October 20, 1947, pp. 18, 20.

60. The source for the pregame information for the Steeler-Giant game is the *Pittsburgh Post-Gazette,* November 29, 1952, p. 10.

61. The source for the details of the Steeler-Giant game is the *Pittsburgh Post-Gazette,* December 1, 1952, pp. 22, 24.

62. The source for the pregame information for the Steeler-Brown game is the *Pittsburgh Post-Gazette,* November 20, 1960, sec. 3, p. 4.

63. The source for the details of the Steeler-Brown game is the *Pittsburgh Post-Gazette,* November 21, 1960, pp. 24, 27.

64. *Pittsburgh Post-Gazette,* November 21, 1960, p. 24.

65. The source for the pregame information for the Steeler-Cardinal game is the *Pittsburgh Post-Gazette*, December 1, 1962, pp. 11–12.

66. The source for the details of the Steeler-Cardinal game is the *Pittsburgh Post-Gazette*, December 3, 1962, pp. 29, 31.

67. My father tells me stories of when his father took him to see games at Forbes Field. Personally, I never got to see a game at Forbes Field. I missed so much history—I guess I was born too late.

# 6

# JUNE 28, 1970: A PLAY-BY-PLAY ACCOUNT OF THE FINAL PIRATE GAME AT FORBES FIELD

*Editors' Note: This transcript of the last game played at Forbes Field has been produced from an audio recording of the KDKA broadcast hosted by Bob Prince, Nellie King, and Gene Osborn. Prior to the game, Nellie King conducted an interview with Pirate right fielder, Roberto Clemente. The contents of the interview and the play-by-play of the final game have been minimally edited.*

*The editors wish to acknowledge the Infinity Broadcasting Corporation and Station KDKA who granted us permission to use their recording.*

NELLIE KING: How do you feel physically? How many more years do you think you can play? How many more years do you want to play baseball in the major league?

ROBERTO CLEMENTE: Well, Nellie, I, I am very funny person because I think that I would like to play as long as I can play, help a ballclub. And sometimes, like year before last — last year, I play with a very bad left shoulder; it was very, very tough for me. I don't wanna play like that because I hurt myself. I hurt also the players and I hurt the Pittsburgh organization. So I would like to ... I would like to play until I get 3,000 hits. I think that's for sure. I think that that is something that not too many fellows accomplish. In fact, not too many fellows goin' ... they are [not] going to accomplish in the future, either. So, I would say, I would like to play until I break the 3,000 hits.

NELLIE KING: Well, you're going to manage this year in San Juan in the winter league. Would you like to continue in baseball in that category in the future?

ROBERTO CLEMENTE: Well, Nellie, I manage one time in Puerto Rico, and did it a second time that I went to manage down there. I will be managing the San Juan Baseball Club in San Juan. I would like to stay in baseball in some capacity. Right now, I cannot tell you which capacity, but I would like to stay in baseball in some capacity 'cuz I love baseball too much and I will ... it will be a completely loss for myself just to stay away from baseball. I don't think I could never stay away as long as I got life. I cannot stay away from baseball. So it might be that I might continue because I like to work with players, I really enjoy to be in the ballpark.

NELLIE KING: And I know the ball players enjoy having you around, and one guy in particular who is favorably impressed with you, who [is] meeting with you for the first time personally this year, was Dave Giusti. And I might mention, too, that your judgment of pitchers is pretty good. I think you made a recommendation on Giusti, didn't you?

ROBERTO CLEMENTE: Well, Nellie, Mr. Joe Brown called me in the wintertime, and he asked me what I thought of Giusti, and I give him my opinion, and I probably ... I don't know ...

probably he sign, he was going to sign him anyhow, but he called me, and he asked me what I thought of Giusti to help the ballclub. So I gave my opinion: I sign him. So we went to Kansas City, and I knew that we was weak in the bullpen for a while, and I recommend Orlando Peña, which I think was really, really gonna help this ballclub because this fellow know how to pitch, and this fellow is a tough competitor. So I will say that Peña also wanna help this ballclub.

NELLIE KING: Roberto, I want to thank you on behalf of Bob Prince and Gene Osborn, too, for the very warm and sincere gift you gave us of an autographed baseball. You're a quite a deep sort of a person as far as emotion and warmth, and it's been my pleasure to know you for many years. And you told me one time you had ... you kinda had a philosophy on life. That was one of getting up and doing the best you can everyday, and when you meet people, try and be as nice as you can to them. Did you suddenly come across that, or is that just a recent philosophy in life for you?

ROBERTO CLEMENTE: Well, Nellie, all my life ... all my life I, I come from very, very sentimental family, and my mother, she's very, very religious. And all my life, I'm very, very close to my mother, and I will say that a lots of times through playing baseball, I am [one] person as a ballplayer probably and as a human being another person. I really love people, and all my life, I never have any problem with people outside the ballpark. Sometime I have to say something to some of the writers because I feel that they are ... they are not right, you know, sometime, but I love people. I will say that I love all kind of people, so I say before, I never have any hate for any human being in my life, thanks ... thanks to God, and I will say that I love everybody. So this is the way I always feel and I think that I am glad because I took after my mother.

NELLIE KING: Roberto, we'll end with that, and it's been a pleasure talking to you, and I know it's a joy to be here to wind up Forbes Field and see this great crowd, isn't it?

ROBERTO CLEMENTE: Oh, this is great, Nellie. This is a big emotion for me because this will mean a great deal to me because I've been here 16 years, almost half of my life. I've been here 16 years in this ballpark and this ballpark been great for me right here, and the fans have been great for me here, too. So it's like I was telling some of the fellows today: You've been married to your wife for 16 years and so all of a sudden something happen, and you gonna be hurt about it. But, it's like a new ballpark. It's like you might find another wife or somethin' like that; you have to wait and see. So now we have to wait and see how the other ballpark gonna be good to me or not like Forbes Field was.

NELLIE KING: And I'm sure you'll be good to it. Roberto, nice talking to you.

ROBERTO CLEMENTE: Okay, thank you, Nellie.

NELLIE KING: Very quickly, scores in the National League after six innings, it's 4 to 2, St. Louis leading Philadelphia. That's the first of two. Montreal and New York tied 1–1 after six. San Francisco leads Atlanta 1 to nothing after two and a half, and Houston and Cincinnati — the Reds leading 2 to 1 after three and a half. San Diego and Los Angeles. Roberts against Foster. That winds it up on our Dugout Show. Stay tuned for the second game of the Pirates' doubleheader.

GENE OSBORN: It's time for Pirate baseball. Hello everyone, with Bob Prince and Nellie King, this is Gene Osborn speaking to you from Forbes Field in Pittsburgh, where we've set up our microphones to bring to you the second game of the doubleheader between the Pirates and the Cubs in the final professional Pittsburgh Pirate baseball game to be played in Forbes Field after 61 years.

Both clubs have come back to the dugout. The batting order for the Chicago Cubs: the battery, Milt Pappas on the mound and J. C. Martin behind the plate. For the Chicago Cubs, leading off and playing at shortstop will be Don Kessinger. Kessinger at short. Hitting second and playing at second base will be Paul Popovich. Popovich at second. Batting third and in left field, Billy Williams. Williams in left. Batting fourth and at first base, Jim Hickman. Hickman at first. Hitting fifth and at third base, Ron Santo. Santo at third. Batting sixth and in right field, Johnny

The 1970 National League Eastern Division Champion Pittsburgh Pirates, the last Pirate team to play at Forbes Field. Back row (left to right): Bill Mazeroski; Lou Marone; Bob Veale; Bob Moose; Dock Ellis; Jerry May; John Jeter; Luke Walker; Bruce Dal Canton; Joe Gibbon. Middle row: Dr. Joseph Finegold, team physician; Tony Bartirome, trainer; Roberto Clemente; Gene Garber; Chuck Hartenstein; Dave Giusti; Richie Hebner; Dave Ricketts; Bob Robertson; Willie Stargell; Gene Alley; Steve Blass; John Hallahan, equipment manager; John Fitzpatrick, traveling secretary. Front row: Jose Pagan; Matty Alou; Jose Martinez; Bill Virdon, coach; Frank Oceak, coach; Danny Murtaugh, manager; Don Osborn, coach; Don Leppert, coach; Al Oliver; Fred Patek; Manny Sanguillen. Seated on ground: Tommy Hallahan and Dave Patrisko, batboys (Pittsburgh Pirates Baseball Club).

Callison. Callison in right. Hitting seventh and playing in center field will be Cleo James. Cleo James in center. Hitting eighth and doing the catching will be J. C. Martin. Martin catching. And batting ninth and doing the pitching will be the veteran right-hander, Milt Pappas. He will be making his first start since coming to Chicago from Atlanta.

And for the Bucs, who get a fine ovation now as they come out of the dugout and head onto the field. Leading off and playing in center field will be Matty Alou. Batting second, the third baseman, Richie Hebner. Hitting third and in right field will be Al Oliver. Batting fourth and in left field, Willie Stargell. Batting fifth at first base, Bobby Robertson. Hitting sixth, the shortstop will be Gene Alley. Batting seventh and doing the catching will be Jerry May. Hitting eighth, the second baseman will be Bill Mazeroski. And batting ninth and doing the pitching will be Jim Nelson. Nelson comes into the ballgame with a record of two and nothing.

By virtue of the victory in the first game of a doubleheader, a real thriller here, the Chicago Cubs and the Pittsburgh Pirates are divided by another full game, which means that as of right now, the Cubs lead 'em by a game and a half. So, that victory string was a big one. It's extended to six. That's the longest winning streak for the Bucs this year. For the Cubbies now, they have lost nine in a row. Nelson, who has turned everything around last Monday night in the second game in the doubleheader, will toe the pitching rubber of this one this afternoon, Nellie.

NELLIE KING: Well, he sure did in a real gutty performance. This is a kind of a fella that has the same attitude as Bob Moose. I don't think he's overwhelmed with victory, and he's not saddened by any kind of defeat or bad performance. He's kind of even-tempered. Steve Blass put it pretty well last night. We were out at Greengate Mall and he's talking about Jim Nelson. He said he's the kind of a guy that you can hit with everything you got. You knock him down, he just keeps coming back. He doesn't know when he's whipped. And it's a kind of intangible, you cannot scout for it, but really great pitchers, and I think great athletes, have, and I think this guy can be one of them. He doesn't have an overpowering fastball, but he's got that good palm ball that sets up the fastball good. And he challenges hitters from the time he walks on the mound until he gets out.

GENE OSBORN: Bob, we have nine innings to go, and hopefully the Cubs will bow again to the Pittsburgh Pirates. But as you come onto the start of this game, there must be a little sadness in one Robert Prince after all these years.

BOB PRINCE: Thank you, Gene. Nellie. Hello again, everybody. There's more than a little sadness; it's a tremendous overpowering amount of grief in a sense. It's one of the real tough things to do because I realize this is where I received my start from the late Rosey Rowswell. I've seen so many wonderful and great thrills, and I know now that I have approached the final — absolutely, totally, final end of this ballpark. It's something. It's like losing a dear loved one, not quite as bad, when you expect them to pass away, and when it does happen, you still are grief ridden.

All right, Kessinger in at .289, one homer and 18 runs batted in. Coaching at third is Peanuts Lowrey. Over to first, Joey Amalfitano. Jimmy Nelson, 2 and 0 on the year. Now Nelson works, and the palm ball is hit foul. Wide at first. 0 and 2. Buccos won the front game, 3 to 2, and that's now history. Bat is broken and Kessinger needs a new wedge.

I just had the pleasure of being on television in the Chicago area with Jack Brickhouse, the veteran Chicago 'caster, with whom I've had the pleasure of working several All-Star games, and the veteran voice of the Cubs. And we got kinda nostalgic because he and I both had some fine memories of this ballpark and working here in an All-Star game together and elsewhere. But that's somethin'. This is the end of the Old Lady.

Ball outside. 1 and 2. And "Horse" Czarnecki, who is the groundskeeper par excellence, of course, from Pittsburgh, and every[one] will sometime be over here watching it go. There's a base hit to the left by Kessinger. Scooped up by Stargell. He goes to opposite field off Nelson's palm ball. Significantly, Chicago's Cubs, who opened here, close here, but their opening victory, Nineteen Hundred and Nine, was by a score of 3 to 2.

GENE OSBORN: We've had two close games in the series, yesterday afternoon and the first one today, Bob.

BOB PRINCE: Yup. And the score in game one was 3 to 2 our way, so we paid them back. I'd like to do it again 3 to 2 and let them know we really meant it. So, over to first base where Bobby Robertson grabs the ball. Kessinger is back. Batter is Paul Popovich, the second baseman, at .263, three homers, and 10 runs batted in. Stargell, Alou, and Oliver, the outfield. Hebner, Alley, Mazeroski, Robertson, the infield. The throw to first and Kessinger just does scramble back. Left-hand batting Paul Popovich. Jim Nelson checks at first, delivers. Swing and a foul tip, strike one. In behind the plate, Jerry May. He walked to drive in a big run. In the late stages of the ballgame. And then Giusti got into some trouble, and Luke Walker came in, striking out Banks and grounding out a batter, and it was all over, 3–2, with the bases loaded.

There's a ball hit out the right side, diving. Maz can't get it. It's gonna be on him for a base hit into right center. Kessinger's on his way into third, and so we now have runners at first and third with nobody out. And the batter will be the left fielder, Billy Williams, at .290, 19 homers, and 61 runs batted in.

Straight away in the outfield here now to Billy Williams. Billy in the front game, 1 for 4. Popovich is playing in this game. Did not appear in the first game. There's a drive into the gap in right center. They're after Nelson in a hurry. That'll drive in one run. Alou fires the ball into Mazeroski, first and third occupied, and we're up with action in our bullpen, Orlando Peña.

Now the batter is Jim Hickman who is 1 for 3 in the first game. He's batting .331, 18 homers, 51 runs batted in. So the Cubs take a lead here and threaten to pop it open, if they can. Orlando Peña shouldn't take a lot of loosening up, as he was up several times in the first game, but you'll have to stop Chicago here, if they possibly can, without further damage. First and third occupied and nobody out. The pitch. Palm ball up high, one ball and no strikes. Kessinger opened up with a two-strike single through the gap in left. Popovich then singled into right center and Williams did likewise, driving Kessinger home and putting Paul Popovich to third. Palm ball, strike is called, 1 and 1, Hickman checking off.

One ball and one strike. Fastball into the dirt blocked down nicely by Jerry May. 1 ... 2 and 1. 2 balls and 1 strike. Jimmy Nelson in trouble. The right-hand hitting Hickman. The pitch. Just inside, and it's 3 and 1. Chicago leading here 1 to nothing in the second and the final game between these two teams, or Pirates, or anybody at Forbes. 3 balls and a strike. Right-hand batting Jim Hickman. Now a throw over to first base and the batter or the runner there, Williams, is back. 3 balls, 1 strike. Outfield around to the left on Hickman. Now the look by Nelson. 3–1 pitch, and it's driven deep to left, hooking, and it's going to be foul. So, we have a 3–2 count, and we'll watch Williams now. Popovich at third and Williams at first. Cubs lead 1–0. We're in the top half of the first of game two. Pirates won the first game 3 to 2 before a sellout throng, standing room only crowd.

And the pitch. There's the palm ball. Hits towards third, Hebner gets it, holds the runner there, they come to the plate now, and they got the runner hung up as Nelson interferes. Now Hebner tags him. They got a double play. Now Durocher is gonna argue for interference on the part of Nelson. I called an interference on the part of Nelson, but I don't know whether or not the umpire feels that had anything to do with the double play. We'll have to wait and see. Now what happened was the ball was hit by Hickman down to Hebner. Hebner came up with it and held the runner Popovich for a moment. Then he threw to second base. That forced Williams, 5–4. Maz came home with the ball, and as Popovich was comin' down the line at third, he was thumped by Nelson coming across to cover on a play. And then they got him in a rundown. And it looks as though they're gonna overrule Durocher, but there was definitely thumping around on the part of Jimmy Nelson. As I called it for you when it occurred. The ruling will stand, and it'll be a double play, and Hickman will be at first base on what is a forced play, and Williams will be out 5 to 4, and Popovich will be out 4 to Hebner. With a 2 in there, a catcher, 4–2–5. They have a very unusual double play, and they do not rule interference. Brother. Unusual. 2 outs. Throw over to first. Hickman is back. So put Hickman on first on a forced play. Erase Williams 5 to 4. And as Maz comes to the plate. Swing and a miss by Santo. And then he throws to Hebner, who puts out Popovich who claimed he was interfered with as Nelson ran into him coming over to cover up halfway between third and home. Ron Santo 0 for 3 in the first game, batting at .230. No balls, a strike. Palm ball inside, 1 and 1. I have to go on the assumption that the umpires that ... I know they saw the bumping around. There ain't any doubt about that bumping around business. The question is whether or not, in their opinion, the runner was obstructed in such a way that he could not either get home or go back to third, and it's obviously a rule that he could not do either. That's why I'm sure Al Barlick and third base umpire or plate umpire Vargo felt there was nothing to it. Two balls and a strike. He was so far down the line that there wasn't any way you could get him either way. That he could get back either way, but there was definite bumping. All right. Two balls and a strike.

Santo the batter. Now the 2–1 pitch. Over the plate for a strike, 2 and 2. So, to Eddie Vargo of Butler, Pennsylvania, who as a youngster saw many a game here at Forbes, goes the honor of calling the last game in the major leagues to be performed at Forbes Field. 2 balls, 2 strikes. And it won't make one wit of difference to him behind that plate. He just knows it's two teams goin', and that's as far as he knows. From that time on, it's a ball or a strike, you're safe or you're out, period. 2 balls, 2 strikes.

The look at first, the pitch to Santo, ball outside, 3 and 2, Hickman will be up and goin'. It's opened up with a single by Kessinger; single, Popovich; single, Williams; and Peña warming up. Now he's just lobbing. With two down and Hickman the runner at first. This represents right here, I would think, for Nelson a very key out. 3 balls, 2 strikes. Hickman takes off. Palm ball, pops him up, and Hebner and Alley and it's Alley saying, "I got it." And he's there for the out. 1 run on 3 hits, no errors, and 1 left, and we go to the bottom of the first, Chicago leading one to nothing.

BOB PRINCE: Milt Pappas, the right-hander, 2 and 2 on the hill. Matty Alou batting. Here's the pitch and Alou [inaudible] a foul on the play. Alou 1 for 4 in the first game, batting at .276. Rusty Staub hit his 11th for Montreal in the eighth with one on. They lead 3 to 2. They're leading the Mets 3–2 and still batting. Now the 0 and 1. Ball inside and a count of one ball and one strike. Sorry to learn of the passing of Jim Spots [assumed spelling of last name], the manager of WLEM on our Pirate Radio Network, and pass our dear sympathies along to his family. Curveball for a strike. 1 and 2. At the end of eight innings, in Montreal, the Montreal Expos lead the New York Mets, 3 to 2.

One ball, 2 strikes. The pitch. Ball outside. 2 and 2. Carl Morton and Sadecki are hooked up there, and Morton has three outs to go to help the Buccos gain a game. Hear the crowd roar. 2 balls, 2 strikes. Alou hits a high fly ball down the right field line. Callison running very hard, running, running, running. It's a foul ball as Callison can't get to it.

Funny thing, I was just talking with Jack Brickhouse. We were going around the park looking at things that I'm going to sorely miss just in the way of views, and we showed the scoreboard and said when we take this down, you'll have the only one left in the major leagues where you see the inning by inning. And see the charm of that with that crowd roaring when they see Montreal get 2 up there. Because the folks are cognizant of what we did in the first game that are here; they're aware of what we're doing in this game.

A foul up along third. There may be a play for Santo this time. The ball drifting on him and he snatches it. Beautiful play by Ron Santo. And when you saw the two come up here, you heard that crowd roar. Now when you'll really hear the roar is if they just start taking down the numbers and putting up Montreal 3 and New York Mets 2. The way this race is going, we need all the help we can get, but we can't do anything about what's going on in Montreal. What's going on right here we gotta worry about.

Hebner, who is 1 for 3 in the first game, hitting at .309. Here's the pitch. Swing and a miss, strike 1. Cubs lead 1 to nothing. Pirates won the first game 3 to 2. No balls, 1 strike. The outfield around to the right for Hebner. Al Oliver on deck. Pappas, a right-hander, works. And there's a high fly ball out into center field. Cleo James drifting over to the left. He's there and it's 2 outs. Cubs 1 and the Pirates nothing. The right fielder, Al Oliver, at .250, 5 homers and 31 runs batted in.

One thing I'm gonna request to you, Nellie, and I'm gonna want, I know you can prepare it in due time. I'd like a scorecard signed by everybody that played in this last game. We'll get Chicago when we get to Chicago. And then make me up a little plaque, if you will. Ball outside. I'd like to have a plaque, if you don't mind, of the last game I ever called here with the scoring of the game for both clubs signing in their proper position. Would you do that for me?

NELLIE KING: Be happy to, Bob.

BOB PRINCE: You're making money hand over fist with these firsts. A foul. Out of play, 1 and 1. But, it's all right, old buddy.

NELLIE KING: Selling them all at cost, too.

BOB PRINCE: I don't want you to do that. Take your markup. It's hard to get.

NELLIE KING: He's looking for a no-hitter every game, Bob.

BOB PRINCE: He better not get one here. I won't speak to either of you guys if you throw up a no-hitter in this game. 2 and 1. I wanna walk out of here saying I never saw a no-hitter in this ballpark. You join me in that Arthur? We don't want this ba..., we don't want Lady Forbes to give up a no-hitter here, do we? 2 balls and a strike. Not this far, not after 61 years, no way. 2–1, pitch. And a swing, and it's 2 and 2. Well, we've already lost our chance to get one. Now the first hit we get, we can breathe easy. Come on, Al. Get it over with. 2 balls, 2 strikes, 2 outs, the pitch. Turned it over outside, 3 and 2. I remember when I asked Hank Bauer one day what Pappas threw. He said [imitating Bauer's gravelly voice] 'Fastball, slider. Gets it up, it's out of the park.' I'd like to see him get a slider up if he still throws it. 3 balls, 2 strikes. Milt Pappas working to Al Oliver. The pitch. And there she goes! High drive, kiss it good bye!

NELLIE KING: Got anything good in the second race in The Meadows tomorrow night?

BOB PRINCE: Want me to come over? I haven't missed so far today. I've been pretty fortunate. A slider up. Here's Willie the Starge at .245. High fly ball, deep left field. Billy Williams back. Will have a play. And that will retire the side. There will *never* be a no-hitter at Forbes Field. 1 run on 1 hit and get a homer by Oliver. At the end of one, we're tied up 1–1.

BOB PRINCE: All right, here we go now into the second inning. Tied up 1 to 1. Johnny Callison batting in. Johnny had a 0 for 3 day in the front game. He's batting at .247, 8 homers, 34 runs batted in. A swing and miss. Strike one. Those of you who might have missed it earlier, Roberto Clemente, who is just ... made a magnificent gesture. He autographed baseballs for Art McKennan, Gene, and Nellie, and me, and I'm quite sure for several other members around here. And he sent 'em up to us, personally autographed baseballs with a message for each one of us for what, what either one of us, and any one of us, particularly meant to him. To Gene one thing, and of course he's only known Gene a little bit, but Nellie a long time, and me for the things I've been involved with him, and it's just a treasured thing, and we'll really treasure it. And that's just the word for it: treasure. Callison, foul away. What a thoughtful individual. The Great One — Arriba, Arriba Clemente. Vera just walked in with the youngsters. I would sort of suspect, somehow or other, Roberto will play in the last game at Forbes Field, wouldn't you, Nellie?

NELLIE KING: I imagine he's gonna make some sort of appearance. If it's if we're out in front, you can bet he's gonna be defensively in the outfield, and if we're behind, he's gonna be doing some pinch hitting. I hope it's the first rather than the latter.

BOB PRINCE: You've got to think positively, my boy, positively. 1 ball, 2 strikes to John Callison. Sails it all the way to the backstop. 2 and 2. Well, in the first game, we had a problem with regard to the greasy kid stuff and umpire Al Barlick went out and ran his hands through the hair and the cap of Regan. There's a strikeout swinging by Callison. First strikeout for Nelson.

So we're moving along here right now. And the batter is gonna be Cleo James, batting at .198. He had 2 hits. He was the fellow really with Pittsburgh 3 and Cleo James 2 in the first game. He scored a run and drove in a run, so that he was responsible for 2 tallies. Billy Hands lost a tough ball game. But the Bucs won a big one when they held them off in the ninth. Cleo, a right-hand batter. Bunts the ball. It's off to the right foul. Strike 1.

NELLIE KING: There's a sign out there. Somebody's not gonna give it up. Bed sheet hanging down looks like Shea Stadium. It says "Forbes Field Forever."

BOB PRINCE: Well, I tell you, it's been great for 61 years, but it's not gonna be forever. Nothing ever is. Progress will prevail. But this will be a beautiful scene that we'll remember forever. 1 and 1, and the fans that have been here will value and enjoy tremendously Three Rivers Stadium, and believe me you will, it's an awe-inspiring thing. Here's the 1–1. Foul ball went right down the left side. 1 and 2. There has never been a ballpark ... [cheering in background] ... never been a ballpark ... [now booing] ... with the background of the center field that we have here. The fans are upset, the bat slipped out, and one of the fans got it, but for Cleo James, could be his gamer [booing]. Let me ask you folks something. This could be his game bat, this could be the one that he had the two hits with and they're gonna give him another bat. Leo Durocher's sending it down to him. That's all he wanted, was his own bat back. Leo Durocher sends it back down. See, just wait awhile, you'll find him happy.

I'll tell you, one of the tragic things would be if somebody were somehow or other able to take Billy Mazeroski's game glove. The one he's kept with him for years. They don't make them like that anymore. There don't even, don't ... sonny, get down. Nellie, escort him off there, will you? Here's the 2–2 pitch, just underneath 3 and 2. I'll say that would be a great souvenir, but let me tell you what it does. It belongs to the nation. When the Maz is finished with it, it'll go to Cooperstown, and that's where it belongs. Where they can all see it. Foul to the right, out of play. And I'm quite confident that Bill will send that glove to Cooperstown. It belongs up there. It looks like a glove used in 1909. I've never seen a smaller glove in my life on a major league ball player. 3 balls, 2 strikes, 1 out, we're in the second inning tied up 1–1. Pirates won the first game 3 to 2. On deck is J. C. Martin. Jimmy Nelson working. 3–2 pitch to Cleo James. Foul ball to the right side, out of play. Cleo's choking up just a little bit on his bat. He's not trying for pumpsville; he's just trying to make contact. Man, you don't think we're gonna be in the middle of a hornet's nest when we come flying around into New York next Monday, tomorrow night. 3–2 pitch, a fly ball toward left. Coming up for it Will Stargell—has it.

I can't wait for Jane Jarvis and that magnificent organ music of Shea Stadium, and 55,000 people going wild. And that'll be about how many will be there when we play the Mets tomorrow night and Tuesday night and then again on Wednesday afternoon. But what if everything goes the way it's going right now? We'll be for the lead in the Eastern Division. Cardinals beat the Phillies, 5–4. Pitch to J. C. Martin, batting at .149. 1 ball, no strike. Sawed him off inside, 2 and 0.

Ladies and gentlemen, Montreal has beaten the Mets. That's 2 out of 3 for them over the Mets. They win it 3–6–0, 2–12 and 1. Morton beats Sadecki, 27,000, in Parc Jarry. There's a high fly to left field. Starge will get it. And our folks think we're on fire. 3 up and 3 down, and we go to the bottom of the second, 1 and 1.

BOB PRINCE: Here's Bobby Robertson, didn't play in the first game, at .296, 10 homers, and 35 runs batted in. The Pirates now right in behind the New York Mets. Be interesting to hear the total announcement of attendance here today as sent up by John Fitzpatrick, our traveling secretary. We know that it's a sellout, and in effect, it's standing room only. And such being the case as standing room only, it's hard to tell how many people are actually here. There really is no aisle way in the upper deck or lower deck, they're just packed in there. Pitch is low for a ball. 1 and 0. And then in behind the lower deck, it's just packed in there, to witness the final two games at Forbes Field, of which the Pirates won the first game. Now the pitch. A swing by Robertson and a count of 1 and 1. Robbie at .296, 10 homers and 35 runs batted in. They're very deep in the outfield and a little bit around to the left. Pappas is working. The 1–1 pitch. Strike 2. The slider to the outside corner. 1 ball and 2 strikes. Milt Pappas, the right-hander, kicks, delivers. He's low and away, into the dirt for a ball. 2–2. Jack Brand visiting, watching the ball game and, of course, very much up to his ears in the Arnold Palmer festivities for July 21 at the Hilton Hotel, which will benefit the Caddie Scholarship. And a shot at four-ball at Laurel. Robertson hits a towering fly to left field and Billy Williams comes jogging up. 1 out. The Arnold Palmer get-together is open to the public on the 21st of July and all the net proceeds will be going towards the benefit of Caddie's Scholarship sponsored by the Ham-Am and the Western Pennsylvania Golf Association. If you'd like to come on to the dinner dance and see all the greats of golf and honor Arnie Palmer, you can get your tickets through Jim Potts at the Western Pennsylvania Golf Association.

Alley swings and misses, batting at .240, 4 homers and 13 runs batted in. Geno in the first game went 0 for 3. No balls and a strike. Pappas into the windup and the pitch. There's a fly ball coming rather deep into the right center. James, sunglasses down, borders against the sun. 2 outs. And the batter now will be Jerry May. Jerry walked in the first game with the bases loaded and thus drove in what proved to be the winning run. And so, he will receive credit for a game-winning hit in a way. After all, he had a game-winning hit before or two, and bases on balls with the sacks loaded is a RBI. Jerry at .207. Slider on the corner for a strike. Minnesota beat the White Sox 9 to 1. A lot of doubleheaders today. No balls, 1 strike. Now the 0 and 1. Fly ball out into right center. Callison going over. Drifting now, turning to his right, and under for the out. 3 up and 3 down and at the end of two innings of play, the Pirates and the Cubs are tied at 1 and 1.

GENE OSBORN: The Pirates won the first game of the doubleheader 3–2 to extend their winning streak to six straight. At the same time, handed the Cubs their ninth consecutive loss. Now at the end of two complete innings in the second game of the doubleheader, the game is all tied at 1.

As we go to the top of the third, Milt Pappas will lead it off. The first pitch from Nelson is outside for a ball. 1 and nothing. Nobody on and nobody out. The young right-hander delivers, Pappas swings, broken bat blooper on the edge of the outfield grass, the shortstop makes the catch. Looking right into the brilliant sunshine, Alley flipped those glasses from under the visor down very quickly and caught the ball for the first out of the inning.

Here's Don Kessinger. Kessinger led off the ballgame with a base hit into left field. He has scored the Chicago run. Kessinger in the first game went nothing for 4. He has 2 hits now in 9 trips to the plate in the series. He leads the Chicago Cubs in three-base hits with seven. Kessinger, the batter. Third baseman Hebner will play him up on the grass. The right side of the infield playing about straightaway. The outfield, however, playing for him to hit the ball late and into left. Palm ball is fouled over here to our left. 1 strike to Kessinger. Lowrey coaching at third base and Amalfitano at first. Bucs are set up defensively: Stargell in left, Alou in center, and Oliver in right.

40,918. That's the attendance here. On a drive hit to right ... scooped by the "Scoop." Al Oliver on a fine play. He came charging in to catch that sinking smash off the bat of Kessinger. He scooped it right up into that big trapper's mitt of his for the second out of the inning. 2 up and 2 down, and the batter now is Paul Popovich. The largest crowd since 1956 looking on this afternoon.

Batter now is Paul Popovich. The pitch is a strike called. Here's the fellow who turned it all around for the Bucs last Monday night. Palm ball is low to the left-handed batter. Ball 1 and strike 1. 2 out, nobody on, in the top of third. Cubs have outhit the Bucs 3 to 1, but the game is tied at 1. And here's the 1–1 pitch. Strike, palm ball, beauty that time over the outside part of the plate. 1 ball and 2 strikes. Outfield straight away for Popovich, who did not play in the first game. Backs away from a breaking ball in close. Ball 2, strike 2, 2 out and nobody on. Popovich batting at .263. Singled into right center field his first time up against Nelson. The 2–2 pitch. Backs him out of the batter's box in a hurry. 3 and 2. Nelson had little zip to that fast ball of his on that delivery. Ninth meeting of the season between the two teams. Series is tied at four. Nelson reads the sign. The 3–2 pitch. Low into the dirt. Popovich tosses the bat away and heads toward first. That's the first walk given up by Nelson in this ball game. A 2-out Annie Oakley to Popovich. Here's Billy Williams. Williams singled into center field in the first inning to drive in the Chicago run. Playing in his 1,052nd consecutive game. Nelson will work with a runner at first. Robertson will hold the inside corner against him. The pitch to Williams is outside for a ball. 1 and nothing. Outfield shaded toward right and right center. Runner leads at first. Nelson looks over the shoulder, draws the arms in. Here's the pitch. The ball is swung on and hit into right. It's in the field of play as Oliver, in the brilliant sunshine, hauls it in to retire the Cubs. In the third: no runs, no hits, no errors, 1 walk, one man left on. We go to the home half in the third at Forbes Field in the second game of a doubleheader, and our game is tied at 1.

GENE OSBORN: The crowd now hearing the announcement from the P.A. announcer, Art McKennan, that the crowd is 40,918. It's the fourth largest regular season crowd. If you count World Series, it's the fifth largest in the history of Forbes Field. Here's Mazeroski. He's played before them all. Pitch is cut at and missed for a strike, and it's nothing and 1. 1 for 4 in the first game, Maz is 1 out of 6 on the series. Pappas throws in close for a ball. 1 and 1. Santo at third, Kessinger the shortstop, Popovich at second with Hickman at first. Williams, James, and Callison around the infield. Martin gives the sign and Milt Pappas gets ready to go to work. 1–1 to the batter. That's a breaking ball outside. 2 balls and a strike. Frank Oceak coaching at third. Don Leppert at first. Maz waves that bat back and forth a couple of times. Now holds it steady as Pappas works 2–1. Ball is tapped foul. 2 and 2 to Mazeroski. Nelson in the on-deck circle will be up next, and then Matty Alou in the hole. Cubs scored in the top of the first. Three consecutive hits, and Oliver tied it up with one swing of the bat in the home half of the first for his sixth home run of the season and his 32nd run batted in. Low for a ball. Swing runs out on Mazeroski. 3 and 2. This crowd had a lot to cheer about in the first game, and they're ready to let it all out here in this encounter. Here's the 3–2 pitch. Swing and a foul. It will come back onto the screen. Still 3 and 2 on the batter. Calling balls and strikes for the second game and the final game in the history of Forbes Field, Vargo behind the plate, Pryor at first, Stello at second, Barlick at third. Milt Pappas leans from the waist, picks up the sign, kicks and throws. And Maz strikes out. Went for the breaking ball that time, didn't get it. That's the first strikeout for Pappas. One out in the home half of the third and the batter is the pitcher, Jim Nelson. Nelson 2 for 6 at the plate. Batting .333. As a pitcher, he has won 2 and lost none. Fastball pops in for a strike, and it's nothing and 1. Nelson chokes up a bit on the handle of the bat. Outfield looking at him for the first time, they're playing shallow toward right. Fastball. He had a great cut at that one. No balls, 2 strikes. Steps out for a moment and then digs back in. Pappas works 0–2 to the batter. Ball is hit slight to the right side and foul. Rolls just beyond the first base dugout.

Tony Perez has just hit his 27th home run of the season for Cincinnati in the ninth inning. Nobody on. 3–2 Cincinnati. The game is being played in Houston. The strike-2 pitch. A ball outside. Teased him with a curve ball that time. Down around the knees. It just missed. 1 ball, 2 strikes. Rhythmic applause beginning to generate now through the stadium as Nelson swings and misses. He's out on strikes as we pause for station identification on the Pittsburgh Pirate Radio Network.

Here is Matty Alou. Two out and nobody on in the last half of the third. Tied at one. Swinging on the first pitch. He pops it up into short center. The shortstop going out, center fielder coming on, and the center fielder comes on to make the catch to retire the Cubs. In the third, 3 up, 3 down, no runs, no hits, no errors, nobody left on. At the end of three innings of play in the second game of the doubleheader, Chicago 1, Pittsburgh 1.

GENE OSBORN: The first three innings were brought to you by Atlantic Richfield Company and your local Atlantic dealer. These next three innings are brought to you by Iron City Beer. Have an Iron City right now.

The batter is Hickman here in the top of the fourth inning. Pitch is a strike called. That was a fastball, knee high. Outfield is shaded toward left to left center. The gap is in right center field and down the right field line. Swing and a foul back. Nelson picks up the sign from catcher Jerry May. The pitch to Hickman. Outside, off the corner. A ball. The count on Hickman, ball 2 and strike 2. Nelson very deliberate. Delivers. The ball is swung on and broken bat fly ball into right, left center field. And Alou has to angle away. Turn his left shoulder into the bright sun and then sort of catch it going away. One out. The batter will be Ron Santo. Santo popped to the shortstop in the first inning. He is nothing for 1 against Nelson. He has 1 hit in 8 trips to the plate in this series after being shut out in 3 tries in the first game. Swing and a miss. Nelson gave him a fastball. Nothing and 1. California has edged Kansas City 2 to 1. Murphy the winner, Rooker the loser. The pitch to Santo. Fast ball is low. Ball 1 and strike 1. A light breeze now blowing the American flag out toward right center, coming across the scoreboard and out toward the seats. All the folks jammed in the double deck right field area. Swing and a foul onto the screen. One ball and two strikes. Home plate umpire looking over that baseball, and he'll throw it out of the game. A new one has gone to the mound.

Cubs are 21 and 16 at home court, 14–17 on the road for a 35–33 record. Palm ball fouled away to the right side. Ball is into the third deck and we'll give that fan an error because it dropped all the way down below. Still 1 and 2 on the batter. Now digging in and waiting, Nelson kicks and throws. Curve is low. 2 and 2. One out, nobody on as the Cubs bat in the fourth inning, and the game is tied at one. The 2–2 pitch. Curve, way outside, May had to slide out in a hurry that time. But there isn't anybody on so there's no damage done. Full count of 3 and 2. With two out in the third inning, Nelson walked his first and only batter thus far in the ball game. He gave a walk to Popovich on a 3–2 pitch. Now for the second time he has gone 3–2 on a Chicago batter. Right-hander delivers, the ball is swung on and hit towards right. Going back is Oliver. Still back peddling, he's there. He made a karate-type catch right in front of his body about belt high after he got to the warning track. 2 up and 2 down. And the batter will be Johnny Callison.

NELLIE KING: Oliver giving the impression that he's startin' to like playing the outfield. Made a great play on that one. Just kind of routine.

GENE OSBORN: I kind of had that feeling because he seemed to be a little more freer when he's playing out in left field, too.

Callison struck out in the second inning. Nelson has but one strikeout and it was against this left-handed batter. This is outside and a little high and off the corner for a ball. 1 and nothing. Montreal defeated New York 3 to 2. St. Louis downed Philadelphia 5 to 4. The pitch, swing and a miss! That's a fastball right up around his shoulders that time. He didn't get it. Bucs won the first game, 3 to 2. Picked up a full game now that New York has lost. Swing and a miss. One ball and 2 strikes to the batter. Callison was shut out in three tries in the first game. He's now 1 for 8 against Pirate pitching in this series, which started yesterday afternoon with a Pirate victory. The pitch is low. Ball 2 and strike 2 on Callison. Bucs have won six in a row, four from the Cardinals, and yesterday and the first game this afternoon from Chicago. Fastball is way over the batter's head. And he has gone to 3 and 2 now to Callison. On a 3–2 pitch to Santo, Santo hit a fly ball caught by Oliver in right. Now the 3–2 pitch to Callison. He takes ball 4 in close. Second walk issued in the ball game by Nelson and it brings up Cleo James. 2 for 3 in the front game. Fly to the left fielder his first time around against Nelson. Boston defeated New York 5 to 3 in the American League. Minnesota 9, Chicago 1. California 2, Kansas City 1, as we mentioned. Nelson will be working with a runner at first. Callison takes a short lead. Robertson holding the inside corner against him. Step by Jimmy, and the pitch. Low for a ball. One and nothing. Stargell in straightaway left field. Alou has moved *way* over to his right or toward left center field. There's a tremendous gap over second base into straightaway center and into right center field. Oliver all alone out there in right. Here's the step by Nelson. The pitch. Breaking ball off the corner. Ball 2 and no strikes. Nelson looks over the left shoulder as the runner takes a short lead. He stays. The ball is ripped foul, through the third base coaching box, off the railing, and into fair territory. Time will be held up while Stargell gets the ball. He flicks it into the Chicago bullpen down the left field line. 2 balls and a strike to Cleo James. Big series beginning tomorrow night in New York between the Pittsburgh Pirates and the New York Mets. Monday night, Tuesday night, and Wednesday afternoon. The throw to first, the runner is back. Thursday will be an open day, and then next weekend in Chicago and then on to Philadelphia.

Closing out before the All-Star break in St. Louis. Pitch is tipped right at the batter. He ducked underneath it, turned his head, and it hit him on his batting helmet and he is all right. He'll go to first. He couldn't seem to get away from that delivery at all. So now we have Johnny Callison in scoring position at second, Cleo James, hit on the batting helmet, the runner at first. Two men on, 2 outs. May has called time and he has gone to the mound to talk to Nelson.

Outfield will play straight away for J. C. Martin making his first appearance in the series. Batting at .149, one home run, four runs batted in. Hiatt has been catching in the series. Yesterday afternoon and in the first game of the doubleheader today. Orlando Peña walking around in the Pirate bullpen. Ricketts, the catcher, also loosening up, and believe, Joe Gibbon will go to work. It is Joe Gibbon loosening up for Pittsburgh. Pitch from Nelson is outside for a ball. 1 and nothing. Fans, fans are getting a bit anxious now and time has been called as the pitching coach, Don Osborn, will go to the mound to talk to the young right-hander. Nell, this is the first time that he has been in a situation like that since he has been called up from Columbus.

NELLIE KING: He's been able to throw strikes and that is the thing that has really pleased Danny Murtaugh and, of course, Osborn, too, but the ability to stay out in front of the hitters. He's traveling with control. You're gonna run into those kinds of games. You don't pitch shutouts every time. He's gonna find that out himself.

GENE OSBORN: Right now it's a 1–1 ball game with the Cubs batting in the top of the fourth. The first 2 men were retired, Hickman and Santo. Then a walk to Callison, and James was hit by a pitch. Runners lead at first and second. Time about to be resumed. J. C. Martin waiting on a 1–0 pitch. Here it comes. It's low, into the dirt. 2 balls, no strikes. In the first game, Moose started, then Giusti, and then Walker. Now Joe Gibbon begins to loosen up. Set by Nelson, and the pitch. Fastball is high and outside. Three balls, no strikes. Another wide one would load 'em up and then bring up the pitcher, Milt Pappas. Down through the years, as I remember Milt from Baltimore, in the American League, he is an excellent hitting pitcher. He's been around in the major league baseball for some 14 seasons now. There's a strike called, and it's 3 and 1. He was involved in a trade between Baltimore and Cincinnati, he going to Cincinnati and Frank Robinson going from the Reds to the Baltimore Orioles. Runners lead at first and second. The pitch. Swing and a ground ball foul. Something will have to give now. A runner at first. A runner at second. There are 2 outs and ball 3-strike-2-count to the left-handed hitting J. C. Martin. Time held up momentarily as that ball came off the wall, rolled down into the playing area. Retrieved by Luke Walker. So Nelson goes to the back part of the mound, goes to the "razzle tack" [rosin bag], squeezes it a couple of times. Now steps back atop the pitching rubber. Runners lead at first and second. J. C. Martin waiting on a ball-3-strike-2 pitch. The look to second. Here's the pitch. The runners go! He almost threw it away. Fastball was high and away, and Jerry May was lucky to even get it. The bases are loaded. Callison at third, Cleo James at second, and J. C. Martin on a 3–2 pitch is at first. And the batter is Milt Pappas.

Pappas, just acquired from Atlanta, stepped in. The game is tied at 1. Runners lead at first, second, and third. Nelson has the windup restored, and he will use the windup. Coming down the line a good distance is Callison. Swing! And a miss. Callison, a veteran performer, figuring that maybe by darting toward the plate, then putting on the brakes and heading back toward third he could force Nelson into committing a balk. This fella has a lot of poise. Now he steps off the pitching rubber and looks over there so Callison goes back. He'll probably get the message that this kid has a lot of know-how. A fly ball into center. Should end the inning without any trouble. Alou is coming in. He's got it! And it retires the side. So Nelson gets out of a tough spot in the fourth inning. No runs, no hits, no errors. And three men left on the bases. We go to the last half of the fourth inning. The game is tied at 1.

GENE OSBORN: In the last of the fourth inning Hebner, Oliver, and Stargell will be the first three men to go against Milt Pappas. If you haven't heard, you just dialed across, the Pirates won the first game 3 to 2. And are tied in this game at 1. Here is Hebner and the folks would like to get something started now with that rhythmic applause. 40,000 plus. There's a foul back to the screen. One strike on Hebner. Hebner flied to the center fielder in the first inning. He had 1 for 3 in the first game and 3 out of 8 now against Cub pitching in the series. For the year, Richie is hitting at .309. He leads the team in doubles with 16. The strike-1 pitch. Curve bends in a little close to the left-handed batter. Ball 1 and strike 1. Cincinnati has defeated Houston 3 to 2. The difference in the ball game — Perez's 27th home run in the season. He leads the major leagues in home runs. Change up is popped into the air down the third base line. Coming down the line is Santo, and he makes the catch. 1 out. It will bring up now Oliver. Oliver tied the game in the home half of the first inning with his sixth home run of the season. And his 32nd run batted in. Oliver now with 2 hits in 8 trips to the plate in the series. Left handed batter batting .240, .250 for the year — 2–5–0. Oooo-eeee! He is just able to get away from a pitch that backed him off the plate after stepping up to [the] delivery in a hurry. He moved into the pitch and was real lucky to get out of there. He's still out of the batter's box, leaning on the bat, and Pappas off the skin part of the mound, walking to the grass, roughing up the baseball. Outfield around toward right and right center. The pitch to Oliver. Swing and a foul off to the left. Ball was in on his hands that time. I don't imagine, Nellie, that he'll see anything outside from Pappas for the rest of the afternoon.

NELLIE KING: I don't know. He's been pitched tight before and a lot of guys try to brush him off the plate. He doesn't back up on anybody. A very aggressive hitter.

GENE OSBORN: Pappas works, and it's outside for a ball. 2 and 1.

NELLIE KING: I think that first pitch may have been a retaliation from the front of the set when Cleo James got hit. Those things have been known to happen in baseball before.

GENE OSBORN: Yes! The pitch. Swing and a foul, over here to the left and out of play. Ball 2, strike 2 to the batter, Al Oliver. One out, nobody on in the last half of the fourth inning. Oliver waiting on a 2–2 pitch. Pappas winds and delivers. Swing and a foul back to the screen. It's still 2 and 2 on the batter. Milt Pappas picks up the sign. The right-hander delivers. Swing and a foul tip. Pitch was down around the knees. Sinking away that time and Oliver was able to get just a piece of it. Still ball 2 and strike 2. Willie Stargell on the on-deck circle to the right will be up next. And in a final, Cleveland over Detroit 8 to 2. McDowell won his 11th ball game against 4 defeats, and he's from Pittsburgh. Wilson the loser, 4 and 5. Ball is pulled foul into the seats just atop the first base dugout. Still 2 and 2 on the batter. 40,918 looking on this afternoon. Fourth largest crowd during a regular season. Fifth largest if you count the World Series. Pappas works 2–2 to the batter. Pops it up into left. Coming hard is Williams, Santo, and Kessinger going out. Kessinger, the shortstop, cuts across and makes the catch. 2 up, 2 down in the last half of the fourth inning and the batter now is Willie Stargell. Big Will is way overdue. He leads the team in home runs with 14. He has 37 runs batted in. He flied to the left field earlier in the first inning. So he is looking for his first hit in this series. Strike to Big Will. Nothing and 1. Outfield around toward right and very deep. The pitch. Tried for the outside corner. Didn't get it. Ball 1 and strike 1. In winning six in a row the Bucs are four over .500 now. They've won 39 and lost 35. They've won more games in the Eastern Division than any other team. The 1–1 pitch. Swing and a miss. Outside about letter high. 1 ball and 2 strikes to Stargell. Willie digs back in. Pappas reads the sign. Kicks and throws 1–2 to the batter. Let up and he strikes him out on a called strike. Third strikeout for Pappas. Changed up on him completely that time in the inning. 3 up, 3 down, no runs, no errors, nobody left on. Through four innings of the second game of the doubleheader, Chicago 1, Pittsburgh 1.

NELLIE KING: Second game of a doubleheader. The final game at Forbes Field, 61-year history, and the Pirates winning the front game of a double header, 3–2. We're tied 1–1 into the top of the fifth. And the leadoff batter, Don Kessinger, will step in for the third time in this game. Singled and scored the lone run for the Cubs in the first inning and was robbed of a possible base hit in the third inning on a good grab by Al Oliver's shoestring catch in the third. Kessinger has made himself into a very fine major league ball player. Always had the good defensive tools, but went to switch hitting and has become very effective from the left side. Proves it with a looping single into center field. And he is 2 for 3. It's the first hit that Jim Nelson has given up since the first inning.

Paul Popovich from neighboring West Virginia steps in. He singled in the first inning and he was out on the tail end of a disputed double play. He walked back in the third. Tim Toomey [assumed spelling of last name] and his son taking in the final game at Forbes. Palm ball by Nelson is down low. Ball 1. Jimmy's only had one 1–2-3 inning and that was back in the second. Callison, James, and Martin went out. Strikeout and 2 fly balls to left. And as Rob likes to say, he's been kinda runnin' through the rain drops here. Throw to first. Kessinger back safely. Bobby Moose, Dave Giusti, and Luke Walker. In that order. And Walker with a great clutch performance, nailed down the first win. Throw to first and a good play by Robertson. Thrown behind the runner. Bobby had to backhand the ball to prevent it from going into the box seats. Cubs by nature are not a good running ball club. They don't have any abundance of speed. Ball chopped off the first base side. It's going to curl foul. And Kessinger at second will come back to first. The Giants a couple of years ago, the kind of ball club that very seldom did any running, but they've picked up some speed with Bobby Bonds in the lineup now. A little bit of a change in theirs, but the Cubs so far have had only 12 stolen bases. Pirates have had 28. Ball looped to shallow left. Stargell coming on quickly. Has time to get there, and he's got it for the first out. One out. The score tied 1–1. We're in the top of the fifth of the second game of a doubleheader at Forbes. The runner at first, Kessinger, and the batter, Billy Williams. Williams singled, drove in Kessinger with the first run.

BOB PRINCE: I want you to know, son, I know how smart you feel, Chancellor Wesley Posvar of the University of Pittsburgh. I said, "What are you putting in here?" He said, "You're sittin' in the middle of our law school right now, so if you feel more learned, go right ahead, Nellie" [chuckle].

NELLIE KING: Rob should know all about law school. Billy Williams takes the pitch down low. One ball and no strikes. Chancellor Wesley Posvar here to take in the final game. Of course, this is the property of the University of Pittsburgh. And this is gonna be a law school I understand. Starting this fall, they are gonna do some construction. Fly ball, deep to left. Going back is Stargell. Still going, and he's near the wall. He makes the grab. No! He drops the ball! Holding at second is Kessinger. He'll come to third. The long throw. It is not in time. He slides ahead of the tag. Hebner arguing now with Barlick and he's jaw to jaw with him. He said he came off the bag. Now Barlick is right on top of him. Hebner is really fuming with Al Barlick at third base. Stargell had the ball in his glove, and as we mentioned before, the sun has become a very serious problem for outfielders right now. 5:30 or close to it here. Alou had troubles earlier, and Stargell that time caught the ball over his shoulder like a football player going for a touchdown. The ball bobbled out of his glove. He was about 3 or 4 feet from the wall. Picked it up, hustled the throw to third base. It was a strong throw. Almost got Kessinger. It's gonna be ruled a double. Kessinger goes to third base. Williams moves on into second base. The batter coming up is Jimmy Hickman. He's 0 for 2, but they're going to intentionally walk him to take their shot with Ronnie Santo. Stargell had room, had the ball in his glove, but dropped it. The walk will be the fourth of the ball game given up by Jimmy Nelson. This is the first intentional walk. And that'll do it. Ball 4. So they're loaded up. Hickman at first base, Billy Williams at second, and Don Kessinger has moved to third. Ron Santo, who is 0 for 2 in this ball game, flied to right field his last time up. Well, the Pitts came back with some football last year to finish respectable under Carl DePasqua. They're looking for good things in '70. The Penguins had a great year. And we're hoping this is the start of something big for the Bucs right now. The Mets lost this afternoon in Montreal 3 to 2. Here's the pitch to Santo. Off the fist. Foul, back out of play. Only

1 out. The Pirates are hoping for the strikeout here by Nelson, or possibly the ground ball double play. Not a whole lot of speed with Hickman at third base or Santo at the plate. But there's an awful lot of power at the plate with Santo who's only hit seven this year. Palm ball just inside. 1 ball and 1 strike. Rick Reichardt has hit his ninth in the twelfth with one on. Washington wins that ball game in 12 innings, 4 to 3. Thinking positive for a 6 to 4 to 3. Here's a 1–1. Change up to just a little bit high. Oy! Santo just checked off that pitch. Almost into the lane. Two balls and a strike. A lot of the people you haven't seen in a while dropping by to see this game. Chuck Boyle, former cameraman with KDKA and now with NBC was here. Chopping ball to short. Alley on two hops to Mazeroski to throw to first. It is in time for two. Nelson took us out of it. A 6 to 4 to 3 double play. Listen to the crowd.

Fifth inning for the Chicago. No runs, 2 hits, no errors. They strand a pair. We go to the bottom of the fifth. It's still tied 1–1.

NELLIE KING: 40,918 present here at Forbes Field. The final game at Lady Forbes. We'll close her down today. And boy, they sure are enjoying a whale of a ball game in the second game, much like they did in the front one. Pirates won the front game, 3–2. Six in a row we've won. Robertson leads it off. Curveball by Pappas is outside. Ball 1. Fans trying to get something started with some rhythmic applause. And don't think that a rooting crowd doesn't help a ballclub. 1–0 pitch. Wide to the hole down to the left field. Base hit for Robertson. That's only the second hit off Milt Pappas. The other one left the ballpark as Bob described on a home run by Al Oliver. Two down in the first. Pappas has been tough. Mixing the pitches effectively. Slider, fastball. And a pitch we haven't seen him use a whole lot, the changeup that has a screwball type of effect. Gene Alley, who can do a lot of things with the bat. He's bunting this time. Pops a first base out, it's going to curve foul, picked up by Jimmy Hickman. Yeah, Alley is bunting. He's had a look at third base coach, Frank Oceak. Bob Robertson surprisingly for his size, 200 pounds, just little bit over, can pick 'em up and put 'em down pretty good. And Alley's ability to punch the ball to right field is something that Murtaugh might be thinking about. Cubs are finding it that way in the outfield. Cleo James about 10 feet to right center. He's going, the pitch is foul tip. Held by the catcher. Throw to second, not in time. He steals it. The hit and run was on. Robertson beat the throw at second by J. C. Martin. It was a foul tip held by Martin, but he didn't get Robertson at second. Bobby'll surprise ya. You recall in a recent home stand he went from first to third on a wild pitch. Now the go-ahead run at second base. Nobody out. Bottom half of the fifth. Tie ball game 1–1. Alley now will try to get him to third. Here's the pitch. Swung on and missed. Foul tip not held by Martin. Now the count holds at nothing and 2. Bob remarked we'll be in New York tomorrow at Shea Stadium. Gene was checking the won and loss percentages. The Mets now with a loss here at .535. If we're gonna win this second ball game, we'll be at .532. Here's the pitch. Off the fist. Pops up on the first base side giving chase with Hickman in foul territory, and he's got it. So Robertson forced to hold at second base as Alley pops out to the first baseman, Jim Hickman.

Jerry May, the batter, takes the pitch by Pappas down low. Ball 1. Jerry May's walk in the front ball game in the eighth inning with the bases loaded off Phil Regan produced the winning run in that one 3 to 2. Cuts on a slider, doesn't get it. Evens the count at 1 ball and 1 strike. I tell ya, Pappas has had excellent control in this ball game. Has not walked anybody and, for the most part, has been out in front of everybody. Checked Robertson at second, the fastball. Hit foul off the first base side. Hickman might have a play. Now he can't get to it. About five rows back in the box seats. People were out early to try to get into Forbes Field this morning. Boy, that was a welcomed sign. Bob remarked they're gonna be late tryin' to get out, too. And no place to go 'til seven o'clock tomorrow morning, I guess. That's the time to ring in at the old time clock. I remember I used to do that. Carry that lunch pail in the off-season. 75 cents an hour wasn't bad. Curveball just misses outside. Count even. 2 balls, 2 strikes.

BOB PRINCE: What were ya? A riveter?

NELLIE KING: Just a good old, common ordinary laborer. Used a shovel to take it off.

BOB PRINCE: I been there, buddy. Anytime you go by the locks at Rochester, remember, I lived under that like a sandhog all one summer, with a jackhammer trying to burrow out of there and get up alive.

NELLIE KING: 2–2 pitch. Checked off by Jerry. Now he goes around, says the first base umpire. Paul Pryor. Tried to save the swing, but couldn't do it. And he'll be strikeout victim number four. And Bobby Robertson opened with a single, got to second on a steal, is still there. Pappas trying to pitch out of it. They will intentionally walk Bill Mazeroski to go to Jimmy Nelson. This is the first walk issued by Pappas.

Scores around the National League: Houston was knocked off by Cincinnati. Tony Perez hit his 27th in the ninth. 3 to 2. Winning pitcher there was Clay Carroll in relief of Nolan. Wilson lost. Los Angeles leads San Diego 2 to nothing after five and a half. Roberts against Alan Foster. And in a complete ball game up at Montreal, the one you're interested in, the New York Mets were knocked off 3 to 2. Sadecki lost it. Carl Morton picked up the win. Marshall homered for New York. Bateman and Staub, and Staub's home run in the eighth with one on, won that one for Montreal. And it gives the Bucs a chance to finish just two percentage points after today's activity from first place in the Eastern Division.

Maz is at first, Robertson at second. Check swing is fouled off the front foot of the pitcher, Jimmy Nelson. And the count nothing and 1. Nelson not a bad hitting pitcher by any means. Had a pretty good debut in the major leagues. Hasn't had a too bad of performance after that either. Opened up with a strikeout on Mays, got McCovey on a double play, and he got up and banged a single. [Inaudible] [used] to be a shortstop and catcher. He's become a pretty good pitcher. Chopper hit to third base weakly. Santo has the short hop, throws, and it is in time! Got the first break. Hickman dropped the ball. They're safe all around. Robertson at third, Maz at second, and Nelson safe at first on the error on Jimmy Hickman. Boy, that was a big break for the Bucs. Santo threw it at the knees. But Hickman lost the ball, and the Pirates have 'em loaded up. Robertson at third, Bill Mazeroski at second, Jimmy Nelson at first. And a pesky guy, Matty Alou at the plate. He's 0 for 2 in this ball game. Had a hit in 4 times at bat in the front. Pappas in the windup. The pitch to Matty. Pulled foul off the first base side, out of play. Strike 1.

BOB PRINCE: You know, Nellie, sometimes when that infielder this time of night throws off that left side of the diamond, you're throwing out of the scoreboard numbers and all those white shirts, and that guy at first base is looking for a ball out of a lot of white.

NELLIE KING: It very well happens. As the sun starting to set down there, it's reflecting off the box seats right back Santo and where he was coming from. C'mon Matty, the 0–1 pitch. Inside. A good save by J. C. Martin prevented a wild pitch. Looks like a hard platter. Martin made a great play to prevent a wild pitch on that one. Had to go way to his right. I don't know how Alou kept from getting hit. The count is even at a ball and a strike. We're tied 1–1, but a base hit could end that very quickly. 2 down. The windup. The 1–1 pitch. Down low, blocked by Martin. Can't find it, but it stays right in front of the plate. Another good save by Martin. Two balls and a strike on Matty Alou. Pirates took advantage of wildness in the front ball game to win that one as Phil Regan came on. Walked the bases loaded and then walked in the winning run with Jerry May at bat.

ElRoy Face, the greatest reliever in Pirate history, and maybe in all of major league baseball, drops into the booth, viewing the final game, of course. 2–1 pitch. Chopped in the hole. On through, base hit. Robertson scores. Mazeroski is coming to the plate. The throw not in time. Alou goes to second and the Pirates lead it 3 to 1.

BOB PRINCE: You know, I wanna win, but I have to feel sorry for Jim Hickman out there at first base. That guy is going through torture right now, Nellie.

NELLIE KING: He sure is, but I'll tell ya, if there is any reason why the Cubs have been in the spot they are, you gotta put it right on his shoulders. He's carried that ball club offensively. Hebner first-ball hitting, and he fouls it off the third base side. Strike 1.

Here's a guy that's made himself into a very fine hitter. He was not known for anything but striking out a lot and hitting the ground-ball double plays. But last year, he suddenly came alive. Very good money player. Came up with a very costly error and the Pirates have taken advantage of it on a big single by Matty Alou. 3 to 1 we lead. The crowd enjoying it all. The 0–1 changeup moves outside on Richie. Turned over the fastball. 1 ball and 1 strike. It's been a very effective pitch for Pappas in this ball game. Well, these 2 runs will be unearned tallies. But it doesn't matter. We have 'em. Fly ball to right. It's going to curve, foul. Richie hit a shot, right down the right field line, curved. Not 10 feet to the right of the foul pole.

Larry Gura, who worked in the front ball game, the left-hander is up and popping down the Chicago bullpen. Jim Nelson at third base, Matty Alou at second. Lead away, the windup, the 1–2 pitch. Fly ball left field. Giving chase is Williams, spotting the sun and near the scoreboard. He got it. A pretty well hit ball in the opposite field by Richie Hebner. The Pirates take the lead 2 runs on 2 hits, 1 error. We strand a pair, and after five innings of play in the second and final game at Forbes Field, the Pirates now lead it 3 to 1.

BOB PRINCE: Well, let's see, here in the sixth, Chancellor Wesley Posvar just went to call Nellie to say, "I think I better stay for a while, I'll be a little late for dinner." And I said, "Why, she's gotta be listening to the game."

A fairly good group of cadets came out of West Point when Chancellor was there. A fellow named Bill Powers, a great athlete in gymnastics and now a financial wizard around here. Roland Catarinella and there were three other fellows that were rather well known: Blanchard, Davis, and Tucker. They never knew a losing season.

All right, we have now Johnny Callison who struck out and walked standing in. Jim Nelson leading 3 to 1 in the top of the sixth. Outfield around to the right. 40,918 and nobody leaving. Strike! The early part of this game, Nelson's palm ball, he might as well have put it on a shelf, or let's not throw it for strikes, just show it. But he was trying to throw it for strikes and it got him in trouble. Let's see if he can bring it back. He bunted through it for strike 2. A lot of times a good pitch for him. Wasn't his best pitch right now. Here's a palm ball. But if it isn't coming for you, you just waste it, and go to your other stuff. And then if it comes back, then you go to it. And Jerry May is the type of a catcher that'll bring it back in there for him, if it's at all possible.

The 0–2 pitch. There's the palm ball pulled down to Mazeroski. The Glove has him. On to Robertson. One out. John Callison retired 4 to 3. The batter now will be Cleo James. He lined to left and was hit by a pitch. Well, in this game we'll have everything going for the fans here. And I know, of course, that nobody will get out of line because we're just going to have a few things given away. All baseball caps have been autographed, and they'll be awarded. There'll be some 50 prizes. Bricks some of them and bases and what have you. But this time of the year belongs to the University of Pittsburgh. And there's a strike. And the Jehovah's Witnesses will be in here for a big conclave. That fine group will be in here, and there will be other things going on. And the University — strike 2 — has other plans. Ultimately, of course, this ballpark will be dismantled, and School of Law and other schools involved in the University program will be in here in the next three to six years. No balls, 2 strikes here to Cleo James. There's a fast ball outside all the way to the backstop.

They're warming down the left field line for the Cubbies. A left-hander, we'll pick him up in a moment. Right now, if they want to get anything going, they want to be ready to hit for Pappas. Gura. Swing, strikeout. And that's the second. Now here's J. C. Martin. He flied to left and he drew a walk. Pirates leading 3 to 1. Won the first game 3 to 2. First game ever played here in this park — Chicago won it 3–2 in Nineteen Hundred and Nine. And Honus Wagner in that year set an all-time high for stolen bases in the World Series against the Detroit Tigers and

Contrary to what Bob Prince thought would happen after the final game, the fans did "get out of line" as they stormed the field in search of souvenirs (Bettmann/Corbis).

Ty Cobb. Foul back. The Pirates played in the first World Series, but not here. They were the game sponsors in 1903 in the first World Series ever played. My memory is they went 9 games. That is, it was a 9-game series. I don't know how long it went, but they would have gone best of 9. Here's the 0 and 1 to Martin. Foul ball off the sinker. 0 and 2. That would have been then Exposition Park for the games that were played here in Pittsburgh between the Bosox and the Pirates. Then Mr. Dreyfuss built this ballpark and his son-in-law, Bill Benswanger, kept the rich tradition going. Bill wanted to be here today but couldn't be. And he's one of the great pioneers in the game of baseball. Bill Benswanger, and he's not to be forgotten by all who are dear to baseball in this area. 1 ball, 2 strikes. Popped him up and Hebner is looking for it. Alley bird dogging in behind him and he'll take it. Alley takes it. That'll retire the side. 3 up and 3 down and we go now to the bottom of the sixth leading 3 to 1.

BOB PRINCE: All right, ready now to move into the bottom of the sixth, and Al Oliver who hit his sixth homer of the year to tie up the game back in the first inning will be the leadoff batter. Then Stargell and Bobby Robertson against Milt Pappas. If we can take what Durocher was doing in the sixth inning as an indication, this will be the last inning for Milt. They were warming Gura, G-u-r-a. Oliver hits a drive deep right side. Way back she goes annnnnnd off the wall. Callison comes up firing and it's a double standing up for Oliver.

That's the fourth hit. He has 2 of them for 6 bases. And the batter's now gonna be Willie Stargell who is 0 for 2. Flied to left and was called out on strikes. Now Gura getting up again. And they indicate they're now pitching, of course, to Stargell. Milt Pappas with runner at second in Al Oliver. Stargell tossed a foul down the right field line. And our bullpen scattered like a covey of quail.

GENE OSBORN: You know, Bob, if this keeps up, Gura may be in the ball game a little earlier than Leo would like to have him in there.

BOB PRINCE: Yeah, but he's gonna try to get three outs, and he can't [inaudible] Pappas, as you and I both know, because he doesn't want to have to put him in there and then bring out another hitter.

There's a drive hit very deep to center. James jogged in. Now drifting back, way out toward the monument. And he makes a strong throw, but Oliver is tagged and comes over safely to third.

That'll bring up Bobby Robertson who singled to lead the Buccos into a rally in the fifth inning. While but 2 runs that scored in that inning were unearned due to an error, the Bucs, nonetheless, accept those. Now they bring the infield up and Bobby taking a long look to Frank Oceak. They switched off Gura to a right-hander. Bobby Rodriguez. Outfield around to the left, infield is up. The pitch from Pappas, and there's a foul down the left field line way out of play. And that brought J. C. Martin out quickly to say something to Milt.

The Cubs don't want to make 10 the hard way, I'll tell ya that. I think the black line on that's two and a half. But we're gonna try to make it that way for 'em. As we've won 6 in a row and they've lost 9 in a row, and that's their season high. Make no mistake about it, though, Chicago is anything but out of this pennant race. Anybody has it locked up. It's gonna be a bubble job right down to the very end. It's gonna bubble your blood for ya. Wait 'til we come home to Three Rivers and we meet those Cincinnati Reds. Wowie! Pitch to Robertson — inside. 1 and 1. I think I'd be getting my tickets for that one — the 16th of July. Window 100 is going to remain open. You won't be able to get your tickets at Three Rivers Stadium. You'll get them at the regular outlets. Remember that, ladies and gentlemen. Don't write to Three Rivers. Write to Forbes Field. Come to Window 100. G. C. Murphy Store downtown ticket office. Ticketron. Any of those outlets. 1–1 pitch to Robertson. Ball inside.

Two balls and a strike. And the pitch. There's a fly ball hit deep toward left. Williams coming up. The tag by Oliver. Here's a strong high throw. Oliver scores. So it's 4 to 1.

Dave Fay of the *Pennsylvania Mirror*, State College. I haven't said we may never lose another game for so long it isn't even funny. But he seemed to think I'd been saying it. He said if we win this one, he wants me, he said, "to shut your mouth." All right, David, you button up your typewriter and we'll be even. [Nellie King and Gene Osborn can be heard laughing at Prince's comments.]

Alley up. He's 0 for 2. Ball inside. 1 and 0. Now have either of you heard me say we may never lose a game. How long has it been?

NELLIE KING: I know the first time I heard you say it and I think the last this year was down in Bradenton.

BOB PRINCE: That's right. I did it as a gag. Ball inside. 2 and 0. Well, I know Davy, he's a good writer, but he's right. We're not counting any chickens that haven't been roosted. Lots of ways to go, but this is just great to be in the thick of things. 2–0 pitch now to Alley. High ball 3. 3 and 0. This game here is not over. But we know one thing, it's the last game that WILL be played here. And I can say we may never lose another game in this park and be right. 3 and 1. I believe I can say that. Three balls and a strike. Outfield around to the right on Gene Alley. Pappas into the windup. The 3–1 pitch. Punched it foul back up on the net. Oliver opened up with a double off the right field wall. Stargell flashed deep to center and Oliver came over after the catch. And then Robertson scored him on a rope to deep left. 3–2 pitch. Fly ball to right field chasing Callison back. Looking up in that murderous sun. Nice catch by John, right on the wall on the warning track out there. A run on 1 hit, no errors, and nobody left at the end of 6. The Pirates lead it 4 to 1.

NELLIE KING: The last 3 innings were sent your way by Iron City Beer. Innings 7, 8, and 9 will be brought to you by Colorful Pittsburgh Paint. A product of PPG Industries. Well, before we go to the seventh inning, the Pirates leading 4 to 1, let's pause for station identification on the Pirates Baseball Network.

GENE OSBORN: Glenn Beckert will bat for Pappas here as the top of the seventh inning is about to get underway at Forbes Field before 40,918. In the first game of the doubleheader, Pittsburgh 3 and Chicago 2, as the Pirates extended their winning streak to 6 straight, and the Cubs losing streak to 9 in a row. Now through 6 innings of play, the Bucs have 4 runs and 4 hits, and the Cubs 1 run and 5 hits. Beckert, a right-handed batter. Heading out the second game of the doubleheader. Takes the first pitch low for a ball. 1 and nothing. Beckert batting at .268. He has a couple of home runs, 18 runs batted in. Curve across. Ball 1 and strike 1. Larry Gura, who saw action in the first game of this doubleheader, continues to keep warm in the bullpen down the line. There's a foul ball that fooled Beckert. Boy, he stepped to the front part of the box that time, and he was leaning and then tried to hold up. Then leaned again, and about that time, it was a little too late. Beautiful pitch. Here's the 1–2 delivery. Fastball for the last strike. It's all the way back to the screen. 2 and 2 on Glenn Beckert. Don Kessinger in the on-deck circle to the left. And then Paul Popovich. Buc outfield playing straight away. Stargell, Alou, and Oliver. Around the infield Hebner, Alley, Mazeroski, and Robertson. May catching and Nelson on the mound. He has won 2 and lost none since coming up from Columbus. Curve is fouled back onto the screen. It gets over the screen, so the folks down below have a lot of fun fighting for that souvenir. Now remember, there will be a lot of souvenirs to be given away at the conclusion of this game. Here's the 2–2 pitch. It is lined to the shortstop. 1 out. We go to the top of the Cub batting order and the left-handed hitting Don Kessinger. Singled and scored in the first inning, flied to right in the third, and singled in the fifth inning.

BOB PRINCE: In addition to this being the final game, this would be a wonderful 36th wedding anniversary for Jane and Tom Johnson. So congratulations to them. One of our Pirate owners and secretary and vice-president of the baseball club, and it would be a great going away. Not going away, going away from Forbes Field, but an anniversary present to Jane and Tom.

GENE OSBORN: And many happy years to come, too, to the Johnson family. As the pitch is outside for a ball. 1 and nothing. Kessinger 2 out of 3 in this ball game. He was shut out in the first game. Nothing for 4. So he is 3 for 11 in the series. Swing and a foul tip! Here's the pitch. A little high for a ball. Kessinger the batter. A slugfest underway in Chicago in the second game of a doubleheader. Wow! Tell you about it in a moment. There's a strike called! 2 and 2 on the batter. Minnesota got 4 in the top of the first, Chicago came back with 6 in the last of the first. 4 to 1 in favor of Pittsburgh here. Ball is hit down the left field line. Coming hard is Stargell. He can't get it. It's into the bull pen just out of his reach. Still 2 and 2 on the batter. Joe Gibbon who was loosening up a couple of innings back in this ball game, is again ready, should they need him. And Bruce Dal Canton, the right-hander, is now throwing also. And Larry Gura, a left-hander, in the bullpen for the Chicago Cubs. He's been joined by Rodriguez. Here's the 2–2 delivery. Swing and a foul back. It's still 2 and 2 on the batter. 1 out and nobody on. Boy, the folks are having a great time here this afternoon. Nelson works 2–2 to the batter. Ground ball to the right side. Mazeroski to his glove side comes up with it, throws on to first in time. Kessinger is an easy out. 2 up and 2 down in the top of the seventh inning, and the batter will be the second baseman, Paul Popovich. San Francisco and Atlanta are tied at 4 through 9 innings of play. The game is being played at Candlestick. Popovich singled into right center field in the first inning, walked on a 3–2 pitch in the third, and then flied to left. So he's 1 for 2 against Nelson. The pitch. Outside, just off the corner for a ball. It's 1 and nothing. Just after 6:00 here in Pittsburgh. Swing and a high pop up. May coming down the line. So is Hebner in foul territory. Richie stays with it, looking into that brilliant sunshine, and he made a one-hand stab on the ball to retire the side. Nothing across in the Chicago half of the seventh inning. The Bucs coming into bat in the stretch half of inning number 7. Last time they'll do this tradition in this park. Leading 4 to 1.

GENE OSBORN: 40,918 looking on as the Chicago Cubs and Pittsburgh Pirates do battle in a doubleheader at Forbes Field in Pittsburgh. The Cubs won the first game 3 to—check that—

the Pirates won that first game 3 to 2 over the Cubs and we lead in this game 4 to 1. And Nellie, we got a new left-hander.

NELLIE KING: Possibly Steve Barber. First time he had a chance to pitch.

GENE OSBORN: And May will lead it off in the home half of the seventh inning. Crowd beginning to settle back into their seats now. The left-hander ready to go to work. Curve ball picked up the outside corner. Started it way out wide that time. Broke it in on the corner, and it is nothing and 1 to Jerry May. May has flied to the right fielder and struck out in 2 trips against Pappas in this ball game. Milt worked the first 6 innings. There's a curve across. No balls, 2 strikes. Continuing to have action in the bullpen for Chicago. Jim Colborn now throwing. Ball got away from the bullpen catcher and the home plate umpire spotted it and called time. In the outfield for the Cubs in the second game, we're looking at Williams, James, and Callison with Santo, Kessinger, Popovich, and Hickman on the inner defense. Pitch in close to May. 1 ball and 2 strikes. Hiatt caught the game yesterday and the first game of the double-header. J. C. Martin working behind the plate this afternoon.

Here's the 1–2 pitch. In close for a ball and it's 2 and 2 now. Mazeroski in the on-deck circle to the right due up next. And the third man up in the inning will be the pitcher, Jim Nelson. May waiting on a ball-2-strike-2 delivery. Here it comes. He takes low for a ball. So after getting ahead of the right-handed batter, no balls, 2 strikes, the string has run out. Home plate umpire Vargo looking over the left shoulder. May waiting on a 3–2 delivery. With a flick of the glove, Gura is shaking off a sign. Now he comes back and strikes him out. That's Jerry, that time on a breaking pitch. Second time May has gone down via the strikeout route in this ball game. First strikeout for Larry Gura, and it brings up Mazeroski. The New York Yankees have knocked off Boston 8 to 2. Bahnsen the winner, Culp the loser. Maz has struck out and drawn an intentional walk. The pitch is a strike called and it's nothing and 1. The pitch. Ground ball down the line. It's a fair ball. Headed toward the bullpen. Maz is gonna try for 2. He cuts the inside corner of the bag and he'll go into second standing up with a double. Maz has doubled down the line. Runner in scoring position. 1 out, and it brings up the pitcher, Jim Nelson. It's a ground ball between third base and the third baseman, Santo. That is the third extra base hit in the ball game. Oliver had the other two. A home run and a double. And now Maz has doubled off the left-hander, Gura. Hits are even at 5 for each club, but the Bucs lead in the payoff department, 4 to 1, after winning the first game 3 to 2.

And remember, after this ball game, then the club will go on the road and tango with the New York Mets beginning a three-game series tomorrow night at Shea Stadium in New York. The look at second, the pitch. Curve low into the dirt. Ball 1, no strikes. Colborn continues to throw in the bullpen. The bullpen catcher is wearing a mask. No activity in the Pirate bullpen. Jim Nelson waiting on a ball one, no strike pitch. The look to second. Here it comes. It's a ball outside. 2 and 2. Frank Oceak is looking into Nelson, and Nelson steps out of the batter's box for a moment to be sure he has that sign correct. Checks again, now steps in. Don Leppert coaching at first. Shadows are beginning to lengthen here at the stadium. Reaching the home plate area now. Fastball was over from the left-hander. 2 balls and a strike. Bucs scored a run in the first, 2 in the fifth, and 1 in the sixth for four. The Chicago Cubs scored a run on 3 consecutive hits to get the ball game underway. It's been Nelson, and the Pirates have been in command. The 2–1 pitch. Swing and a foul. Ball will get back into the seats over here to the right. San Francisco winning their ball game on a home run by Gallagher. His second of the year in the tenth inning with one man on. Jim "Mudcat" Grant? Is that right? No, he's not with San Francisco. Giants win 6–4. Here's a ground ball to the right side. It'll get the runner onto third. Beckert backs up, gets it on the short hop and throws on to first. And Mazeroski goes to third. Play going 4–3.

Here is Alou, and a fine hand for Mateo Alou, who with the bases loaded, singled into right field in the fifth inning to drive in a couple of runs. Since then, the Bucs have added another run. Alou was 1 for 3 in the ball game. Now 3 out of 11 in the series. He has 88 hits. He leads the Bucs in that department. He now has 27 runs batted in. Chokes up quite a bit on the handle of the bat. Oh, there's a ball behind his head! That ball slipped from the left-hander, Gura, and it went behind Matty, and the catcher, Martin, had to move quickly to the right to get to that ball. Ball 1, no strikes. The left-hander's pitch. Low into the dirt. Alou was ready to offer, and I don't know whether he went around or not. Foul tipped the ball. He got down on it just like hitting it off a golf tee that time and then tried checking, looped his swing back, and tipped the ball. It's ruled 1 and 1 on Alou. Outfield toward left and not very deep. The 1–1 pitch. He's gonna strike it. He's gonna try to squeeze him home. The throw is inside. That brought the pitcher off the mound. And the throw to first nipped Alou. The play going 1–3 to retire the side. In the inning, no runs, 1 hit, no errors, 1 man left. At the end of seven, Pittsburgh 4, Chicago 1.

NELLIE KING: 40,918 at Forbes Field for the final game. And Bob, there's a guy sitting down here that made history here, and this ballpark is synonymous with his name, isn't it?

BOB PRINCE: Yeah, he made it as easy as Pie. His last name, I guess, has to be Traynor, doesn't it? Sure good to see him up and around and know that he's hale and hearty. I think it's quite an honor that this field that produced 2 players, didn't, didn't produce, but saw 2 players that were unanimously selected as the all-time greatest players in their positions. Traynor, who is here now, played third, and of course, the late Honus Wagner, who played short and is adjudged by many as the greatest player of all time.

NELLIE KING: Yes, it's good to see Pie out at the ballpark again. He's recovering from an illness. Billy Williams, who has had 2 hits in 3 times at bats, steps in. Fastball by Jimmy Nelson is just outside. Ball 1. Pirates leading 4 to 1. We won the front game of the doubleheader, 3–2. 6 more outs to go in this ballpark. Line drive center field. And Alou will play it on about the second hop. Holding at first base is Billy Williams. Another well hit ball by Williams.

Stepping in, Jim Hickman. He and Williams have been about it offensively for the Cubs in this series, and I guess for almost a week, too, although Williams had some sort of a slump prior to coming in here. The big guy was on, on a force play, flied to center, intentionally walked back in the fifth when Nelson pitched out of a tough jam. With the bases loaded, got Santo to hit into a double play. Curveball way outside. 1 ball and no strikes. Activity now in the Pirate bullpen. Left-hander Luke Walker, who got a save in the front game, getting the final 2 outs after the bases were loaded, and right-hander, Dave Giusti, who picked up the win in the front game.

Nelson, with that stare at first base, takes the sign. Here's the palm ball in, taken by Hickman. 1 ball, 1 strike. Jimmy Hickman has to be an All-Star player this year for the first time in his major league career. Having a great year. Hitting at .330. Leading the club in RBIs. Palm ball, taken, foul tip. Tried to get the bat out of there, couldn't make it. And the count now a ball and 2 strikes. Nelson started this winning streak for the Bucs when he shut out the Cardinals in 10 innings, 1–0. You can pardon the trite cliché, but it has been a pretty good team effort all around. 1–2 pitch. Curveball is outside. Count even, 2 balls and 2 strikes.

Hebner deep at third. About 5 feet off the line. 2–2 pitch. Bounced to shortstop, Alley over to Mazeroski, the throw to first ... double play! That's the third double play in this ball game. That's the second that Alley and Mazeroski have turned over. 1966 was a big year for Oop and Maz and the double play. Boy, it's good to see both of them back healthy and playing once again.

Santo 0 for 3. Bounced into a double play with the bases loaded the last time. Pirates leading 4 to 1. Breaking ball taken by Santo. Strike 1. Not too many people leaving their seats. 40,918. Boy, they've enjoyed a beautiful day for baseball and two good games. Curveball, backhanded by May in the dirt. The count even with a ball and a strike. Pirate pitching, which had been a question mark in the spring and the early weeks of the season, really starting to solidify now. Found another arm in this guy, Jimmy Nelson. The 1–1 pitch. Little bit high with a fastball. He's behind 2 balls and a strike. You've got to give Don Osborn a lot of credit for the confidence he has in the youngsters and installs in the youngsters. Or instills. Palm ball inside. 3 balls and a strike. 3–1 delivery just a little bit low, and that walks Santo. For Jimmy Nelson, that's walk number 5. Nelson would have to confess that this is not his best ball game, but they've only scored 1 run, Bob.

BOB PRINCE: That's right. He's been running through some rain drops. I had remarked a little earlier, Nellie, while you were out getting a sandwich, that I felt his palm ball wasn't doing what he wanted it to do. When he got Mays on the strikeout the first time he came into the biggies, and then got McCovey to go to the double play. And then the next time out against the Dodgers, it stayed with him and stayed him out the next time when he won the ball game. It seemed to me that so far, this early part of the game anyhow, his palm ball wasn't where he wanted it. Then he seemed to get it back for a while. Now it seems to have deserted him again.

NELLIE KING: The kind of a guy, though, we mentioned before that just doesn't know when to give up. He'll battle ya' right 'til the end. A very good competitor and that's something you have to have to be an outstanding pitcher just to make it to the big league. Robertson will play behind Santo at first base. 4 to 1 is the score, the Pirates leading the top of the eighth. Callison the batter. Fouls one back on the screen. Well, he had a good ball to hit that time. A little bit annoyed that he didn't poke it. Callison struck out, drew a walk, and bounced to Bill Mazeroski in 3 trips against Nelson. The Cubs were able to get only 6 hits in the front game. Chopping ball to second. Mazeroski on 2 hops, to first and that retires the Cubs. No runs, 1 hit, no errors, they strand 1. We go to the bottom half of the eighth. The Pirates lead it 4 to 1.

NELLIE KING: Well, the Pirates up here at bat for the final time in Forbes Field. Bottom half of the eighth. We lead 4 to 1. Richie Hebner, Al Oliver, and then Willie Stargell to go against left-hander Larry Gura. First-ball hitting. Fly ball to shallow left. Kessinger back. Williams on. Billy Williams has it for the first out.

And the way it stands right now, Al Oliver moving in. And what a hot bat he's had. He has hit the last home run in Forbes Field. Getting a fine hand, too. Much deservedly so. Boy, this guy's done a great job as we mentioned. Moved out of first base by Bob Robertson. He went into the outfield and what a job he's done. It's an off-speed pitch. Foul off the end of the bat down the third base side. Strike 1. The windup by Gura. Fastball. Fouled back out of play. Nothing and 2. Rob was talking about Dale Long's home run streak. And there's a gentleman who very seldom misses a Pirate game. From New Brighton, by the name of Smitty. And I recall going up to his place in 1956 with Dale Long. Fly ball to left, to right field. Back is Callison, near the wall, and he has got it for the out. That ball almost identically the same spot where the home run and the previous double went. Oliver has that spot pretty well lined up. Two up and two down. Like a gentleman, he had Dale Long and I down to his place in 1956. Gave us a toaster and that thing still works. And glad I am, too. Stargell off the pitch. Fly ball to left field. Drifting back is Billy Williams, and he runs it down. An easy inning for Larry Gura. 3 fly ball outs, no runs, no hits, no errors, and none left. We've completed 8 innings of play and the Pirates lead the second game, 4 to 1.

BOB PRINCE: Well, Dave Giusti has come on now, and Nelson has gone 8 innings for 1 run. He can win; he cannot lose. Giusti could pick up a save. He was the winner in the first game. No question, as we talked, he had been struggling. But he gave up 5 walks. He threw a lot of pitches, and Danny Murtaugh, you must remember one other thing, this boy had a history earlier of a sore arm. Danny Murtaugh doesn't want to horse around with that. We have Al Oliver in right field. And John Jeter has ... Jeter gone to left field. Giusti will go to Cleo James. So we're down to what the Pirates hope are the final three outs, before 40,918. Buccos won the first game, 3 to 2. Montreal beat New York, 3–2, to take 2 out of 3 from the Mets. And now we're here in the ninth inning leading 4 to 1. The outfield around to the left. Now the pitch. And he bounces it up the middle and over to the left is Alley up behind second, throws him out! Beautiful rang-ing play by Gene Alley. One away. Now J. C. Martin, 0 for 2. He flied to left, he walked, and he popped to short. Pirates leading 4 to 1. The outfield playing J. C. Martin straight away. Now the pitch. Ball high. Years ago, the gentleman that started me broadcasting baseball, the late Rosey Rowswell, opened Forbes Field broadcasting. And now, it looks like we're gonna close it down. 1 ball, 1 strike. And I'll be honest with you, it's gettin' to me. The 1–1 pitch. Palm ball popped to the left fielder. And Jeter waiting. 2 outs. Willie Smith coming up. 61 years, almost 5,000 baseball games. Lady Forbes is about to retire. The Cubs, who opened it 61 years ago, close it here with our Pirates. And just imagine, I doubt if maybe one man was livin' at the time that's on this field. It could have been Leo Durocher–about the only one. And he would been a baby. Strike is called. The left-hand batting Willie Smith. There isn't an umpire here that could say that. Foul back, strike 2. If I know Leo, he wouldn't leave, let his birthday get in that book. But I'd say Leo's at least 60. Here's the 0–2 pitch for Smith. High for a ball. 1 and 2. Les Worthington, the director of the club over here, just is beaming along general manager Joe Brown and his wife Cindy, and their guests, Thomas Johnson on the 36th wedding anniversary. 1–2 pitch, low. 1 and 2. 2 balls, 2 strikes. 2 out. 4–1 Pittsburgh, top half of the ninth. And the 2–2 pitch to Smith. Base hit, right up the middle. Number 7. Brings up Don Kessinger. He singled and scored the Cubs' lone run. He flied out to right field in the third, he looped a single to left in the fifth, he bounced out to second in the seventh. The outfield playing around to the left. To the left-hand batting Kessinger. Giusti, who won the first game, bidding for a save in the second game. Nelson, the pitcher of record. Now the pitch. Kessinger takes a strike. About 25 years from now, 300,000 people would have been here to this game. It always is that way. Pitch high. Ball 1, strike 1. Fitting that Al Barlick, the senior umpire of the National League, would call the balls and strikes in the first game, and Eddie Vargo, born and reared in Butler, Pennsylvania, who spent many a pleasurable hour here as a spectator, umpires the last game. 1 ball, 1 strike. A high chopper, over the mound, going over for it is Maz. He's got it! It's all over! It's all over! 61 years and the Bucs receive a standing ovation. They close it out. And the Cubs go down to defeat. No runs, 1 hit, no errors, and 1 left. Pittsburgh takes a double header 3–2 and 4 to 1.

GENE OSBORN: Before we summarize the doubleheader that has moved the Pittsburgh Pirates into a virtual tie for first place in the Eastern Division of the National League with the New York Mets, and the Mets coming up tomorrow night, let's pause for station identification along the Pittsburgh Pirates Radio Network.

In the first game of a doubleheader, the Pittsburgh Pirates, who have gone on to win 2 games, picked up a 3 to 2 victory to extend their winning streak to 6 in a row, and to move a half game at that stage of the day closer to the league-leading New York Mets. In the first game, the Pirates had 3 runs, 7 hits, and no errors, and for the Chicago Cubs 2 runs, 6 hits, and 1 error. The winning pitcher in relief was Dave Giusti. His record, 4 and nothing. The losing pitcher for the Chicago Cubs was Billy Hands, and his record dropped to 9 and 7. It was a great first game for the Bucs to win as they extended their winning streak to 6 straight and the Cubs losing streak to 9 in a row. And then in the second game of the doubleheader, the Chicago Cubs greeted the young right-hander, Nelson, with 3 consecutive hits. There was action in the Pirate bullpen and the Cubs had a 1-nothing lead. In the last of the first inning, Al Oliver hit his sixth home run of the season to tie the game at 1. Then, in the fifth inning, the Pirates went on top with a couple of runs, added another run in the sixth inning. 4 runs, 5 hits, and no errors for the victorious Pittsburgh Pirates. And for the Chicago Cubbies, 1 run, 7 hits, and 1 error. The winner in the second game, Nelson. His record is now 3 and nothing. And Giusti was credited with his 11th save of the season. The starter and loser for the Chicago Cubs was Pappas with a record of 2 and 2. 40,918 jammed Forbes Field for the final game to be played in the history of this park. It all began in Nineteen Hundred and Nine. And in that year, the Pirates went on to win the pennant, and to win the World Series. And now they close it out with a sweep of the 3-game series from the Chicago Cubs and move within a virtual tie of first place in the East-

**The last out at Forbes Field, June 28, 1970 (National Baseball Hall of Fame Library, Cooperstown, N.Y.).**

ern Division. New York lost today. Their record is 38 and 33. The Pirates, by winning 2, now 40 victories, more than any other team in the Eastern Division. They have lost 35 times. The percentage for New York is .535. The percentage for the Pittsburgh Pirates is .533. Nellie, this has been a grand and glorious day. I know how Bob has felt, beginning his broadcasting career here. Your pitching career was right out there on that mound. And before you do close it off, I'm sure there must be a goose bump or two along your arms and down your back. And maybe a, a sad note in your voice and a tear in your eye.

NELLIE KING: Well, not really. Not a tear in my eye, but I get a little nostalgic about these moments, I'm sure. And I got more goose bumps during the ball game because this ballclub had kinda attracted a lot of enthusiasm or brought some enthusiasm back to Pittsburgh and to sports, and I'm happy to see that. But as far as my pitching career, it was brief in the big leagues. I won my first ball game here, and that's something I'll always treasure. You can't take it away from me. It's something you dream when you're a little kid. A chance to play in the big league. And you always remember the first one you ever won. It was right here against the then Milwaukee Braves. "Auld Lang Syne" was being played, and players are now bringing their baseball caps out and they're getting a huge response, Eugene. It's a real heart-warming thing. The fans are enjoying it, and I think the players are too.

GENE OSBORN: And it's 7 in a row now for the Bucs.

NELLIE KING: That's right.

GENE OSBORN: Momentum is a wonderful thing.

I think Roberto's ovation would be something that the folks along our Pirate network would like to pick up as each player has autographed his baseball. [very *loud* applause].

NELLIE KING: That is Roberto Clemente. That was for Clemente. Bill Mazeroski will listen to a few pretty good cheers, too.

GENE OSBORN: Well, Nellie, along with everything that goes with the winning of a double-header and the closing of Forbes Field and all, you can't say, "Well, that's the season," because the players leave tomorrow morning. We go into New York, and they begin a road trip against the New York Mets Monday night, Tuesday night, Wednesday afternoon; Thursday afternoon and Thursday night will be a day off. Friday, Saturday, and Sunday in Chicago. Monday, Tuesday, and Wednesday along in Philadelphia. And then Thursday, Friday, Saturday, and Sunday in St. Louis. All before the All-Star break, so they have a lot of work cut out for them yet.

NELLIE KING: I tell ya, the next 6 days are gonna be real big ones for this ball club. In Shea Stadium and, of course, then the weekend series with the Cubs. They'll want to come back. This ball club is a good ball club, Chicago. They're not beaten. They're gonna bounce back. It's too early. Their pitching's a little bit hurtin' right now and they're not hitting. But every ball club goes through that. We've got momentum and they don't. But it's going to be a very interesting road trip and we'll be most happy to bring it to you.

Well, I guess we'll wind it up from Forbes Field. It's been my pleasure to sit along Bob Prince for 4 years and, this year, to sit along with Gene Osborn. And that winds up our final broadcast for the day and forever from Forbes Field. We'll be back on the air tomorrow at eight o'clock from Shea Stadium where we take on the New York Mets. Now speaking for Bob Prince, the Gunner; for Gene Osborn; the good old trusty engineer, George [inaudible]; and our loyal statistician, Radio Rich; Nellie King saying so long for your Colorful Pittsburgh Paint dealer, where you can select from a rainbow of colors. Pittsburgh Paint, a product of PPG Industries. For Iron City Beer. Next time your beer thirst comes up, wet it down with the number one beer around here, Iron City Beer. Once you get there, you'll never want to leave. And for Atlantic Richfield Company and your local Atlantic dealer. Drive in where you see the Red Ball sign. Red Ball service is your Atlantic dealer's way of assuring you good service every time you come in. This broadcast is authorized under broadcasting rights granted by the Pittsburgh Baseball Club solely for the entertainment of our listening audience. And any publication, rebroadcast, or other use of the description and accounts of this game without the expressed written consent of the Pittsburgh Baseball Club is prohibited.

Once again, the final scores ever from Forbes Field, the Pirates sweep a doubleheader. The Pirates winning the front ballgame, 3 to 2. They came back to win the nightcap, 4 to 1. "Auld Lang Syne" was sung, and we'll say it, too. This is the Pirate Baseball Network.

# 7

# INSIDE THE PARK: DIMENSIONS AND CONFIGURATIONS OF FORBES FIELD

*Ronald M. Selter*

## Hitters at Forbes Field

Forbes Field was one of the very first classic era ballparks to be built in America (only Philadelphia's Shibe Park preceded it). Home of the Pittsburgh Pirates for 62 seasons, it opened June 30, 1909. Forbes has been regarded as a spacious park and a poor one for hitters. Only during the 1947–1953 seasons, when the "Greenberg Gardens" reduced the left field foul line distance by 30 feet, was the park considered friendly to hitters.

The conventional wisdom about Forbes Field is illustrated by the following quotations taken from various ballpark books:

• "No no-hitter was ever pitched here. Given the fact that the Pirates, Grays, and Craws played here for 62 years, that is an incredible statistic."— Philip J. Lowry in *Green Cathedrals*.[1]

• "It was one of the most spacious parks in baseball, so much so that when slugger Hank Greenberg's contract was sold to the Pirates in 1947, he refused to report unless the team moved the fences in ... [and] the park remained a nightmare for many hitters, including the great Roberto Clemente...."— Eric Enders in *Ballparks Then and Now*.[2]

• "Strangely a no-hitter was never pitched in the entire history of Forbes Field."— Lawrence Ritter in *Lost Ballparks*.[3]

Much of this conventional wisdom reflects two facts: (1) Forbes Field was spacious, more so than the average National League park in the period from 1909 through 1946, and (2) during this period, the park was not conducive to the hitting of home runs. How spacious was Forbes relative to the other National League parks? When it opened in June 1909, only Redland Field in Cincinnati was larger. In the ensuing years, parks in other National League cities varied in size, but Forbes Field's overall size changed very little and was never less than 457 feet to centerfield. A comparison of the average outfield distances for Forbes Field and the entire National League (NL) is shown in Table 1.

## Table 1: Park Size, 1910–1946
## Average Outfield Distances in Feet

| Year | Forbes Field | NL Average |
|------|--------------|------------|
| 1910 | 395 | 380 |
| 1920 | 395 | 382 |
| 1925 | 388 | 383 |
| 1930 | 390 | 374 |
| 1935 | 390 | 373 |
| 1940 | 390 | 375 |
| 1946 | 390 | 373 |

The second item that leads to Forbes Field's reputation as a poor park for hitters is the undisputed evidence of relatively few home runs being hit there. The concept of a park home run factor has been developed to measure the number of home runs at a given park relative to the league average for that season. The determination of the park home run factor adjusts for the home team's hitters' and pitchers' proclivities for hitting and giving up home runs. By definition, the league average home run factor is equal to 100. Table 2 shows the home run factors for Forbes Field.

## Table 2: Home Run Factors for Forbes Field[4]

| Time Period | Forbes Field |
|-------------|--------------|
| 1910–1919 | 61 |
| 1920–1929 | 57 |
| 1930–1939 | 62 |
| 1940–1946 | 68 |
| 1909–1946 (Average) | 62 |

Compared to the average National League park, Forbes Field was about 40 percent below in home run production. By contrast, Forbes was always regarded as a good park for triples, but how much above the average National League park has not been known. Indirect evidence supporting the view of Forbes Field as a good triples park includes: (1) Owen Wilson of the 1912 Pirates setting the major league single-season record for triples (36) while playing half his games in Forbes Field, and (2) in 18 seasons (1921–1937), the Pirates led the National League in triples 14 times.

Except for the home run factors, all the above evidence consists of data that is either indirect or merely suggestive. Recent research into National League home/road batting by park has made available some direct evidence that bears on the question: Was Forbes Field a poor park for hitters?

## Deadball Era

For the last three years of the Deadball Era (1917–1919), park factors were computed for six batting categories based on the batting data for the Pirates and their opponents in games at Forbes Field versus data for Pirates games in all other National League parks.[5] The resulting park factors are shown in Table 3.

## Table 3: Forbes Field Park Factors, 1917–1919
(All categories are rate data; e.g., doubles are doubles per at bat)

| Category | Park Factor | NL Rank |
|---|---|---|
| Batting Average | 102 | 3 |
| On-Base Percentage | 100 | 4 |
| Slugging Percentage | 104 | 2 |
| Doubles | 95 | 4 |
| Triples | 157 | 1 |
| Home runs | 56 | 8 |

Thus, despite being dead last in home runs, Forbes Field was the second best park for slugging (behind Philadelphia's Baker Bowl). This result is due to the marked superiority of Forbes Field for triples— 50 percent better than the average National League park. In general, in the Deadball Era, triples had a greater effect on offense than home runs. For the three Deadball seasons studied, the National League seasonal average was 67 triples per team, nearly three times the average per team for home runs (23).

## Lively Ball Era

For the nine-year period from 1928 through 1936, park factors were computed for six batting categories based on the batting data for the Pirates and their opponents in games at Forbes Field versus data for Pirate games in all other National League parks.[6] The resulting park factors are shown in Table 4.

## Table 4: Forbes Field Park Factors, 1928–1936
(All categories are rate data; e.g., doubles are doubles per at bat)

| Category | Park Factor | NL Rank |
|---|---|---|
| Batting Average | 104 | 2 |
| On-Base Percentage | 102 | 2 |
| Slugging Percentage | 101 | 3 |
| Doubles | 94 | 5 |
| Triples | 161 | 1 |
| Home runs | 62 | 7 |

In this era of the lively ball, Forbes Field ranked second in batting average, on-base percentage, and again first in triples. Ranking first in triples was no surprise as the park had both a record and reputation for triples. What was more interesting is how a spacious park like Forbes Field ranked second in batting average and on-base percentage. Had other National League parks been modified to make them larger, and thus Forbes Field had become relatively smaller? The answer is *no*. The trend in the other National League parks in the 1920s and 1930s involved closer fences and smaller dimensions. In particular, Braves Field was in 1928 greatly reduced in size, and Redland Field in Cincinnati was downsized in 1927 by moving home plate 20 feet towards center field. In fact, despite Forbes Field being slightly smaller after 1925 (when right field was reduced by the extension of the grandstand into right field), the relative size of Forbes Field actually increased from the Deadball Era to the 1930s. Based on the data shown in Table 1, Forbes Field was 3.4 percent larger than the National League average park in 1920; by 1930–1935, it was 4.4 percent larger than the National League average.

Aerial view showing asymmetrical design of Forbes Field prior to the double-deck expansion in right field for the 1925 season (Library and Archives Division, Historical Society of Western Pennsylvania, Pittsburgh, PA).

## Batting and Forbes Field's Asymmetrical Configuration

Between 1925 and 1947, Forbes Field was a slightly asymmetrical park with an average right field distance that was 3 percent less than the average left field distance. A question arises: Did left-handed batters benefit from this configuration? Pittsburgh team batting data for left-handed (LH) and right-handed (RH) batters is available for 1927–1937 and 1940–1942. A comparison was made between the home and road batting data for both left-handers and right-handers.[7] A sample of this comparison — the 1929 season — is shown in Table 5.

## Table 5: Comparison of Home and Road Batting Data for Left-Handers (LH) and Right-Handers (RH) for 1929

|    |                 | *BA*  | *OBP* | *SP*  |
|----|-----------------|-------|-------|-------|
| LH | Home            | .334  | .417  | .511  |
|    | Road            | .329  | .399  | .486  |
|    | Home/Road Ratio | 1.017 | 1.044 | 1.051 |

|    |                 | *BA*  | *OBP* | *SP*  |
|----|-----------------|-------|-------|-------|
| RH | Home            | .311  | .360  | .430  |
|    | Road            | .265  | .323  | .359  |
|    | Home/Road Ratio | 1.175 | 1.116 | 1.199 |

As one can see from the above data, one inherent problem in comparing left-handed and right-handed batters' performances is that left-handed batters are generically better hitters— left-handers hit better than right-handers at home *and* on the road. The home/road ratio for left-handed and right-handed hitters was used in an attempt to compare how left-handed and right-handed batters performed relative to their production at other National League parks. The comparison for the years 1927–1937 and 1940–1942 was based on the three categories of batting average, on-base percentage, and slugging percentage and is shown in Table 6.

### Table 6: Forbes Field Left-Handed (LH)/Right-Handed (RH) Batting, 1927–1942 Home/Road (H/R) Ratios

| Category | LH H/R Ratio | RH H/R Ratio |
|---|---|---|
| Batting Average | 1.074 | 1.102 |
| On-Base Percentage | 1.060 | 1.088 |
| Slugging Percentage | 1.078 | 1.108 |

The above data clearly shows that left-handed batters had no advantage at Forbes Field relative to other National League parks in any of the three offensive categories. The average home/road ratio differential (RH-LH) was 2.9 points. However, there is a catch. The average National League ballpark during this period favored left-handed batters. Available data shows the average National League park in 1928–1936 had a right field average distance some 7 percent less than the average left field distance. Thus, right-handed Pittsburgh batters had a larger disadvantage in road games than at home. As a result, the right-handed batters hit relatively better (measured by the H/R ratio) at home when compared to left-handed batters. The data conforms to this difference — the differential RH-LH (2.9 points) is about the same as the relative left field/right field average distance relationship between the average National League park and Forbes Field (107 percent to 103 percent). The conclusion is that Forbes Field slightly favored left-handed batters, but to a lesser degree than the average National League park of this period.

## Notes

1. Philip J. Lowry, *Green Cathedrals*, rev. ed. (Reading, MA: Addison-Wesley Publishing Co., 1992), 218.
2. Eric Enders, *Ballparks Then and Now* (San Diego, CA: Thunder Bay Press, 2002), 128.
3. Lawrence S. Ritter, *Lost Ballparks* (New York: Penguin Group, 1992), 65.
4. *Total Baseball*, 4th ed., John Thorn and Pete Palmer, eds. (New York: Penguin Group, 1995), 2245-2246.

5. Research by the author using official National League day-by-day team batting records.
6. Ibid.
7. Research by the author using official National League day-by-day team and individual batting records.

Editors' Note: A similar version of this article first appeared in *The Baseball Research Journal* 31 (2003) and is reprinted here, with some modifications, by permission of the author.

## Forbes Field's Historical Configurations

Forbes Field opened on June 30, 1909. Sportsman's Park in St. Louis (Sportsman's III) had been largely rebuilt in steel and concrete before the 1909 season, but retained (from Sportsman's II) a substantial portion of the existing wooden stands. This made Forbes the first all steel and concrete ballpark in the National League. Described as "a gem when it opened,"[1] it had twice the seating capacity of the Pirates' former ballpark — Exposition Park — and was larger than the Polo Grounds in New York or the Cubs' West Side Park in Chicago.

On Opening Day, the park consisted of (1) a double-deck grandstand that extended a short distance beyond both first base and third base, (2) a large (43 rows of seating) steel and concrete set of bleachers (called a pavilion but not roofed) down the left field line, and (3) a set of temporary bleachers that extended from right center to almost dead center field. These temporary bleachers were replaced later in the season by a permanent set after the ground settled. There was no ballpark structure and thus no permanent seating between the first base end of the grandstand and the right field fence. For important games, temporary bleachers and standing room crowds were allowed in this area. When neither temporary bleachers nor standing room crowds were in place, there was a vast amount of in-play foul area down the right field line. Seating capacity was 25,000, of which 18,000 were in the grandstand.

## Original Configuration: June 30, 1909–May 25, 1911

The 1909 Opening Day configuration of the playing field was far different than in later years. Photos from the Library of Congress show the left field foul line intersecting the third base bleachers some 40 to 50 feet before the junction of the front of those third base bleachers with the left field wall.[2] Home plate was located a huge distance from the grandstand backstop (110 feet as listed in *Green Cathedrals*).[3] The home plate location and the alignment of the diamond that caused the intersection of the left field foul line with the third base bleachers meant the actual left field distance (300 to 305 feet) was a great deal less than the listed left field distance of 360 feet. As the foul line intersected the third base bleachers, the left field distance increased

Fans pack the left field bleachers and line up behind the ropes in center and left field during the 1909 World Series (Library of Congress, Prints and Photographs Division, Detroit Publishing Company Collection).

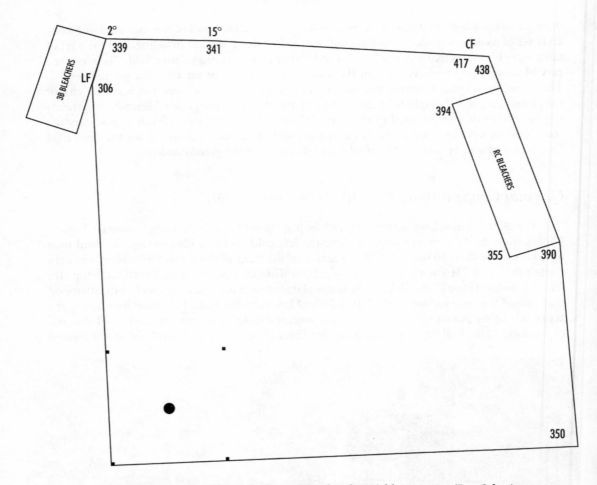

Diagram 1: Dimensions and configuration of Forbes Field, 1909–1911 (Ron Selter).

very rapidly until the junction with the left field fence. At this point (two degrees) the estimated distance was 339. Straightaway left field was about 340. This explains the 17 home runs hit over the left field fence in 1909, 1910, and early 1911. The Opening Day configuration with the location of home plate, 110 feet from the stands, made the actual right field distance (estimated at 353) less than the later well-known right field distance of 376 (as listed in *Green Cathedrals*). The dead center field distance was also less due to the location of home plate. In addition, the existence of the right center-center field bleachers (later removed in the 1925 expansion) reduced the distances to both right center (363) and the right side of center field (372 to 385). The deepest center field point (slightly to the left of the left end of the right center-center field bleachers) was estimated at 435 to 440.

Unlike most other major league parks of that era, the size and shape of the Forbes Field playing field was unconstrained by the pattern of the surrounding streets. Therefore, the outfield distances were as large or as small as the designer wished. The Forbes Field parcel or land plat was about seven acres in size — larger than most of the land plats of the preclassic major league ballparks. The fences were of wood until replaced with brick in 1946. When opened in mid-season 1909, Forbes Field (in terms of the fair territory of the playing field) was one of the smaller National League ballparks. Only Baker Bowl in Philadelphia was smaller. Exposition Park — where the Pirates had played from 1891 until late June of 1909 — was far larger than Forbes

Field, with an average outfield distance of 415 to 365 for Forbes. Table 7 lists the average outfield distances (in feet) for all National League parks for 1909.

## Table 7: National League 1909

| City | Park | Average Outfield Distance |
|------|------|---------------------------|
| BOS | South End Grounds | 375 |
| BRO | Washington Park | 378 |
| CHI | West Side Park | 394 |
| CIN | Palace of the Fans | 398 |
| NY | Polo Grounds III | 374 |
| PHL | Baker Bowl | 359 |
| PIT | Forbes Field | 365 |
| STL | Robison Field | 369 |
| | League Average | 377 |

The short down-the-line left field distance (estimated at 300 to 305 feet) resulted in an interesting home run. Bill Abstein of the Pirates hit a fair ball in a game on September 7, 1909, that landed far down the third base bleachers and bounced back into left field. Unsure of the situation, Abstein stopped at second. The umpires correctly ruled it a home run.

## Revised Configuration: May 26, 1911–1924

The Pirates reconfigured Forbes Field in May 1911. While the team was on a lengthy road trip, the Pirates management moved home plate back towards the grandstand an estimated distance of 26 feet and shifted the field slightly towards right field. These changes resulted in the left field foul line now ending in the left field corner at the junction of the third base bleachers and the left field fence. The new 1911 Forbes Field configuration can be seen in a photograph on page 128 of *Ballparks Then and Now*.[4] This photograph shows the left field foul line, foul pole, and corner. Of course, moving home plate altered all the dimensions of the ballpark. Left field was now 360, center field was 462, and right field was 376. The best description of the changed configuration and dimensions was provided by the *Cincinnati Enquirer* on the occasion of the Reds' first trip to Pittsburgh after the changed configuration:

> Since the team was here in April Forbes field [*sic*] has been greatly enlarged by moving back the left field wall, which is now so far from the plate that it will be very unusual for a ball to be driven over it, and a batter will get full value for his line drives to left center which was not true before.... Left field has been lengthened more than twenty feet in the foul line corner and more than fifty feet out toward center, and the field is now one of the largest in the league.[5]

How accurate was this description? The author's ballpark diagrams, drawn using the dimensions listed above for the original and revised configurations, show a 21-foot increase in the distance to the left field corner (defined in both configurations as the junction of the third base bleachers and the left field fence) and a 50-foot increase in the center field distance. The impact of this revised configuration changed the average outfield distances as shown in Table 8.

## Table 8: Average Outfield Distances in Feet

| Configurations | LF | CF | RF |
|----------------|----|----|----|
| Original Configuration (Opening Date 1909–May 25, 1911) | 344 | 385 | 367 |
| Revised Configuration (May 26, 1911–1924) | 373 | 407 | 382 |

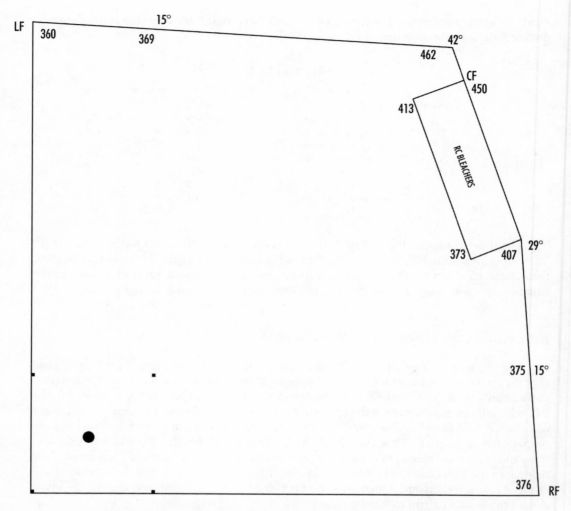

Diagram 2: Dimensions and configuration of Forbes Field, 1911–1924 (Ron Selter).

The shape of the playing field (fair territory) was now a trapezoid with the left field fence at 86 degrees to the foul line and the right field fence at 84 degrees to the foul line. In addition, there was a medium length center field fence section (at the back of the right center bleachers) running from right center to a short distance beyond dead center field (42 degrees). Forbes Field was now one of the larger ballparks in the National League. The opening of Ebbets Field in 1913 and Braves Field in 1915 made Forbes Field the fourth largest National League park by the end of the deadball era (1919). The comparison of the size of National League ballparks is shown in Table 9.

## Table 9: National League 1919

| City | Park | Average Outfield Distance |
|------|------|---------------------------|
| BOS | Braves Field | 419 |
| BRO | Ebbets Field | 394 |
| CHI | Cubs Park (later Wrigley Field) | 351 |
| CIN | Redland Field (later Crosley Field) | 403 |

## Table 9: continued

| City | Park | Average Outfield Distance |
|---|---|---|
| NY | Polo Grounds IV | 381 |
| PHL | Baker Bowl | 344 |
| PIT | Forbes Field | 387 |
| STL | Robison Field | 369 |
| | League Average | 381 |

## Impact on Home Runs

The revised configuration appears to have had only a small impact on the absolute number of home runs. Home runs at Forbes Field were 0.32 per game while in the original configuration and 0.37 per game in the immediately subsequent time period (most of the 1911 and all of the 1912 season) in the revised configuration. However, the mix of home runs was significantly altered, as shown in Table 10.

## Table 10: Home Runs by Type

| Configurations | Games | Total | OTF | Bounce | IP |
|---|---|---|---|---|---|
| Original Configuration (Opening Date 1909–May 25, 1911) | 137 | 44 | 22 | (1) | 22 |
| Revised Configuration (May 26, 1911–1924) | 145 | 53 | 8 | (3) | 45 |

OTF = over the fence. Bounce home runs are included in the OTF category. IP = inside-the-park home runs.

As 1911 was the first National League season with the use of the cork-center ball, home runs in the National League increased by 48 percent. In this context, the revised configuration of

A view of Forbes Field from beyond the outfield wall, prior to the double-deck expansion in right field for the 1925 season (John Gates Photograph Collection, Archives Service Center, University of Pittsburgh).

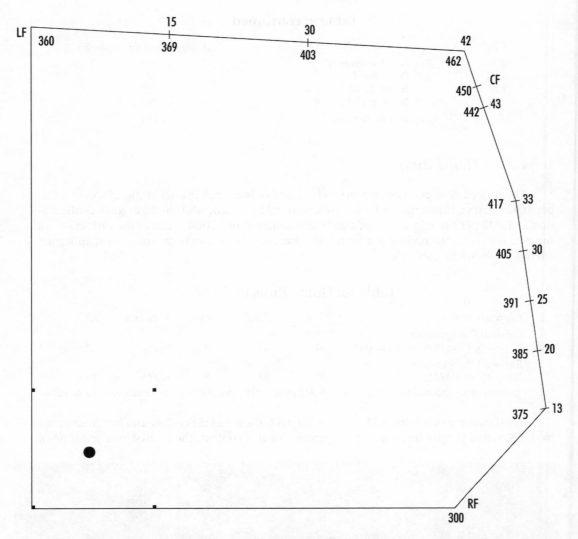

Diagram 3: Dimensions and configuration of Forbes Field, 1925–1929 (Ron Selter).

Forbes Field actually reduced the relative number of home runs as total home runs per game increased only 15 percent. As a result, the Pittsburgh home run park factor dropped from 125 in 1910 to 72 in 1911. Without a doubt, the larger playing area of the revised configuration decreased the number and the proportion of over-the-fence home runs and increased the number and the proportion of inside-the-park home runs. In the 135 games played (a bit less than two full seasons) in the original configuration 17 home runs cleared the Forbes Field left field fence. In the next nearly four full seasons, that feat was accomplished only four times.[6]

## 1925–1929

The listed dimension for left field, according to Philip Lowry in the sixth edition of *Total Baseball*, changed from 360 to 356.5 for 1921 and back to 360 in 1926. I believe there was no actual change in left field until 1930. For the 1925 season, the double-deck grandstand down the first base line was extended at an angle into the fair portion of right field. This made the right field distance 300, and this portion of the right field fence (i.e., the front of the extended stands) ran at 128 degrees to the right field foul line. Where the stands ended in right field, it was 375 feet from home plate, a point where the junction with the existing right field fence was. This point at 13 degrees was in nearly straight away right field. The second reported change for 1926, again according to Lowry in the sixth edition of *Total Baseball,* was that center field was listed for the first time at 442 and initially assumed to be dead center field. If the 1926 listed value of dead center field at 442 was correct, it would have made the center field corner (the corner at the flagpole slightly left of dead center at 42 degrees) less than the still listed distance of 462. It has been assumed that the 442 center field point was slightly to the right of dead center field and the center field corner was still 462.

Also, for the 1925 season, besides the extension of the double-deck stands into right field, additional field level seats were added near home plate, the backstop distance was reduced from its original incredible 110 feet to about 85 feet, as stated by Bill Shannon and George Kalinsky in *The Ball Parks,* and the right-center and center field bleachers that had been there since Opening Day 1909 were removed.[7]

## 1930–1946 and 1954–1970

Between the 1929 and 1930 seasons, two changes occurred in the Forbes Field configuration. Most noticeably, an in-play screen was installed in front of the lower deck of the right field stands. This screen (including the concrete base) varied in height from 27.7 feet at the foul pole to 24 feet at the end of the stands (at the 375 feet marker). Philip Lowry, in the second edition of *Green Cathedrals*, reports the installation of the screen in 1932. In an article found in the May 22, 1930, issue of *The Sporting News* that dealt with the proliferation of home run-reducing screens in the National League (the Baker Bowl in Philadelphia added one in right field in mid-season 1929 as did Sportsman's Park in St. Louis—also in right field), it was noted that a screen had been installed in front of part of the right field stands in Forbes Field. It appears that *The Sporting News* article is correct as to the date of the installation of the screen. However, unlike the implication of this article, the right field screen covered the entirety of the fair area of the right field stands.

The second change for the 1930 season occurred in the move of home plate five feet further from left field. This increased the left field distance from 360 to 365. To keep the right field distance at 300, it was necessary to shift the foul line one degree towards the third base stands. The left field fence now was at 86 degrees to the foul line, and the right field fence was now at 129 degrees to the foul line. At the same time, the listed center field distance (at the junction of the left field and center field fences) was changed from 462 to 457. For this to happen, a new alignment for the center field fence was required which moved the junction point in several feet towards home plate. These changes had very little effect on the overall size of the ballpark. The average left field distance did increase from 373 to 379, while center field increased from 429 to 430, and right field was unchanged. The right field screen did affect left-handed power hitters as the effective (adjusted for fence height) right field home run average distance increased from 365 to 376.

In time for the 1940 season, Forbes Field added lights. The only direct effect on the playing field was the location of the light towers in left center and right center. The light towers were built in front of the outfield fences and were in play to the top of a cage-like fence (16.5 feet in height) along the front and both sides of the towers. This change had very little impact on play.

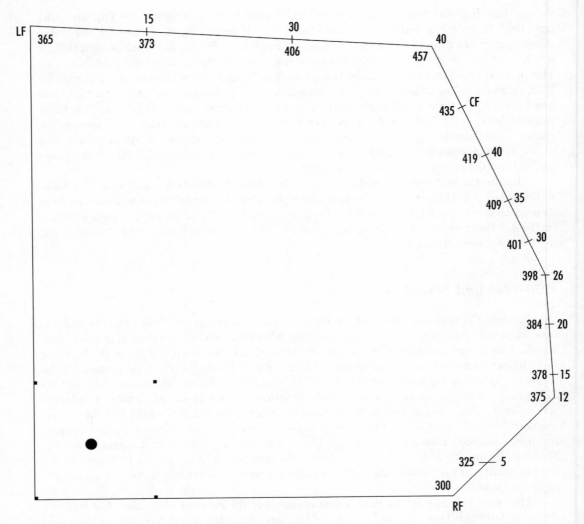

**Diagram 4: Dimensions and configuration of Forbes Field, 1930–1946 and 1954–1970 (Ron Selter).**

## 1947–1953

For the 1947 season, the Pirates acquired the American League slugger Hank Greenberg from Detroit. To increase the possible number of home runs, a change was made in left field. An interior fence was built in left field and was located 30 feet in front of the exterior fence at the foul line (335 from home plate). This area was known as "Greenberg Gardens." The Gardens' fence angled in towards left center more than the exterior fence. The right corner of the Gardens was 355 feet from home plate, and from the corner the fence angled back to the 406 mark in left center. This change reduced the average left field distance from 379 to 346. The effect was immediate. The Forbes Field home run factor went from 75 in 1946 to 130 in 1947 or an increase of 73 percent.[8]

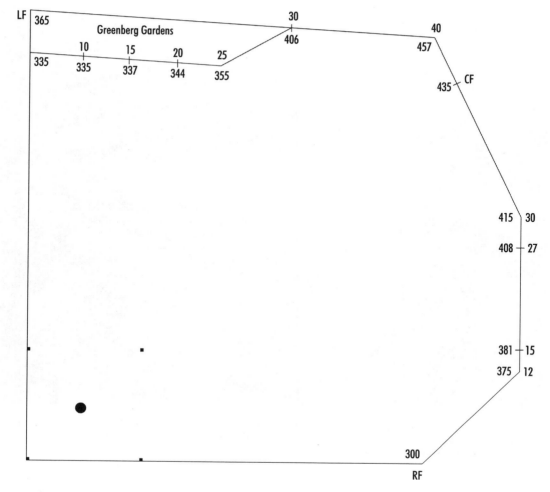

LF 365
Greenberg Gardens
30
406
40
457
435 CF
10 335
15 337
20 344
25 355
335
415 30
408 27
381 15
375 12
300
RF

**Diagram 5: Dimensions and configuration of Forbes Field, 1947–1953 (Ron Selter).**

## Notes

1. Donald G. Lancaster, "Forbes Field Praised as a Gem When It Opened," *The Baseball Research Journal* 15 (1986): 26–29.

2. The Forbes Field photographs are from the Library of Congress American Memory Collection. See page 125.

3. Philip J. Lowry, *Green Cathedrals*, rev. ed. (Reading, MA: Addison-Wesley Publishing Co., 1992), 216.

4. Eric Enders, *Ballparks Then and Now* (San Diego, CA: Thunder Bay Press, 2002), 128. See page 39.

5. *Cincinnati Enquirer*, May 27, 1911.

6. Home run research by the author using the *Pittsburgh Gazette Times*.

7. See page 41 of the 1925–29 configuration, though modified for the 1925 World Series with low temporary bleachers in right field in front of the double-deck and temporary bleachers in both center and left field.

8. When Hank Greenberg retired after the 1947 season, the area was renamed "Kiner's Korner" for the Pirates' young slugger, Ralph Kiner, who also benefited from the shorter distance. The interior fence was dismantled when Kiner was traded to Chicago in 1953.

The grandeur of Forbes Field as pictured on September 23, 1956, when the all-time single-game attendance record of 44,932 was set, though the Pirates lost that day to the Brooklyn Dodgers, 8–3 (courtesy University Archives, University of Pittsburgh).

# II

# *Memories of Forbes Field*

Among those in attendance for a doubleheader on July 4, 1951, were a throng of kids who watched the Pirates sweep both games from the Cincinnati Reds, 4–1 and 16–4 (Moods Image Archives).

# 8

# OLD FORBES FIELD

## *Rich Sestili*

It was an early Sunday morning in May 1958, about four weeks into the baseball season, when Mikey D'Andrea and I headed to Forbes Field to sell newspapers for the day. We had both served nine o'clock Mass and Mikey talked me into getting to the park early to be picked for the newspaper sales crew.

"If we sell ten papers before the gates open, then Muckles will get us in and we can see the game."

Muckles was the perennial newspaper distributor. A well-known figure in the Oakland area, he was a rotund fifty-year-old ex-marine who wore a barber shop leather strap as a belt. He was asked to leave the Marine Corps after the Korean War because his breath was so bad the other marines couldn't stand to have him around. Muckles stood there by the corner of the Home Plate Café and dished out the Sunday edition of the *Post-Gazette* to the youngsters who huddled around.

As a novice to the selling game, I had to take in all the instructions that Muckles decided to share. The veteran newsboys leaned against the cold concrete wall of the restaurant and traded stories about their best selling days. The rest of us had to listen as intently as if we were green freshmen on the campus lawn with stupid blue beanies on our heads.

"Let me sell today, Muckles," some of the young guys called out. The scene was reminiscent of *On the Waterfront* with Marlon Brando when the Brooklyn toughs fought to be picked for the day's work on the docks.

"No loafing today, guys, we gotta sell a lot of papers. Gotta make up for the lousy showing last week. With St. Louis here in town, we should have a big crowd. Remember, you put my money in your right pocket and your own money in your left pocket, so you don't go getting nothing mixed up. If you get it wrong, I kill you."

I wondered how I got myself into these things.

My mother had encouraged me to wear a sweatshirt, even though it was mid-May and starting to warm up. *Sissy boys wear sweatshirts,* I thought. *Can't be looked at as a sissy boy to Muckles. He wouldn't let me into the park.* I just wore a regular white t-shirt and jeans, and tried to look like a hardened veteran pulp pusher. Mikey hammered at me to wear something worn and tattered, emphasizing that the sympathy factor for the customers always works. *Slightly torn and tattered,* I thought. *My mother never would have let me out of the house with anything torn, not even a little hole in my white socks.*

"Get your paper, get your paper! Please, mister, buy a paper from me," I called out to the sparse crowd coming off the Forbes Avenue streetcars. I'd follow a clean-cut prospect for at least ten steps toward the main gate, prodding him along. "If I sell ten papers I can get in to see the game, mister."

The main entrance to Forbes Field at Sennott and Boquet streets (ca. 1956) which accurately represents the setting of "Old Forbes Field" and where the author and other boys would congregate to sell newspapers (Bettmann/Corbis).

Not too many fans were sympathetic to the innocent altar boy approach. *Try something else*, I thought. *Look for people you know and beg the daylights out of them. No can't do that, either. I sure don't want to hear somebody coming over to the house and banging on our kitchen door.*

"Hey, Pasqua. Are things so bad your kid gotta go begging at the ballpark?"

I don't know how, maybe by the miracle of Santo Roberto, the patron saint of ballplayers in San Juan, but somehow Muckles picked me to go into the ballpark and sell. This was a terrific honor. I was the new guy on the block, but I was still picked to get inside. Must have been the new marketing idea of having someone with polished shoes and pressed Levis that did it. I got into the game, almost half an hour before the first pitch, and started waving papers right away.

You can't see her anymore, the majestic old lady that was once Forbes Field. She was there and breathed life into everyone's soul she touched. She impressed me when I was a kid with her classic titanic size and style. Just being with her made me feel alive and important.

"Newspapers, get your newspapers here!"

"Not that loud!" Muckles instructed as we stood under the third base stands. "Do it with class," he said. He chomped at the big cigar in his over-sized mouth as he folded a newspaper in half lengthwise and waved it with the flair of an old bullfighter. "Like this, see?"

"Yeah, I got it, Mr. Muckles."

I felt like somebody. I had an arm full of *Post-Gazette*s, and although they might have seemed heavy, they were nothing compared to all the history books Sister Norbert made us take home each night: books we never read, just carried back and forth to make the nuns happy.

It was impressive, entering the Old Black Lady from the third base side, as the sun crackled over her right field roof and down onto the field. There was a massive difference between how dark the cave of the right field stands were and the flood of daylight that poured onto the field itself. The fresh cut grass looked like a farm full of green clover and had the smell that only Pittsburgh grass can have. Must be something with the red dust that comes from the steel mills that does it. Probably lots of vitamins that we don't know about. Somehow it makes the grass as green as shamrocks pasted on the front door of the school on St. Paddy's Day.

Was that Don Hoak in front of me who kept throwing the ball to the first baseman? I wanted to get closer and call out to him, to walk down those steps right into the dugout boxes and call out, "Newspapers! Get your newspapers!"

"Hey kid, over here. Gimme one of those."

"Sure, mister," I said as I fumbled my way over three old men perfectly dressed in Sunday suits with those floppy double-breasted lapels.

"I don't want none of those classifieds or funnies, kid. Just give me the sports page."

*I can't believe it, I'm selling papers in Forbes Field, and people are actually buying them. I have to be the coolest kid going.* I felt so alive. I belonged there. Grownups were talking to me as if I'd known them all my life. *Yes, this is it,* I thought. Everybody was somebody here.

"Hey, Don Hoak," I called out as I pocketed Muckles' money in my right pocket. "You gonna hit a homer today?"

He looked back toward me and wondered why a newspaper boy would even think of calling out his name.

"Yeah kid, sure, just for you. Maybe two homers."

The old guys sitting in the box seats with their black crooked cigars laughed at me for the stupid question.

"Hey, kid, don't bother the guy. Can't you see he's warming up?"

"Yeah, sorry about that."

The smell and sights inside the ballpark were hypnotizing. The boiling of hot dogs mixed with the mustard and onions fell down the concrete steps from the concession stands like the waterfall at Mellon Park and hit me in the face. *God, I should have listened to my mother and eaten those sandwiches she made for me before leaving the house. God, those hot dogs smelled good.*

I worked my way up to the concession stand and hoped for a miracle. Maybe some old guy would just be standing around with five or six hot dogs in his hand and holding them out for starving children from Dawson Street like me.

*Yeah, I'm sure that will happen. Let me just call out and beg for somebody to buy a newspaper and they'll notice me better. They'll see how hungry I am and just shove the dog in my hand. I'll have a Coke, too, please. Sure, the nuns taught us to always say "please."*

More people were coming in, a chance to sell more papers. I thought I'd hang around the counter there, but I didn't see anybody I knew. No Oaklanders, not even Greenfielders. These people must have been from Squirrel Hill or Shadyside, all dressed up.

"Excuse me, mister, but are those hot dogs any good?"

"Yeah, great, kid," he said as he munched half of one through his reddened face. Mustard and onions oozed over the side of the bun, over his fat fingers and down his chin. *Where's the fire?* I thought, as he inhaled that thing like a vacuum cleaner would a pile of dust. A huge wad of food was stuffed in his mouth, and his eyes were bulging. He could barely breathe.

"You gotta try one," came out, as a muffled mess of words and bun bits went flying toward me.

I held my hand out as if he was going to give me some money so I could also share in the delight, but all I got was a shaking of his head as to how good it was. He turned back toward the concession stand and waved a mustard stained hand to the vendor behind the steam table for one more.

I lit up. *It worked; he's going to order one for me.*

"I like it the same way you do," I sang out. "Mustard and onions. Not too many onions though. I gotta sell newspapers and the customers don't want any kid with bad breath calling out."

He shook his head again and again, grabbed the dog, slapped on the goodies, wrapped it in a large white paper napkin and headed off for his seat. His friend, another big guy, probably from North Side, was towed behind him with two dogs of his own and a large Coke.

As they pulled away talking and grunting and stuffing the food in their mouths I called out to them.

"Naw, I really can't have one, sir. You know why? Because I gotta save my appetite. My mother is cooking dinner and I gotta save room. She's making cheese ravioli with lots of sauce. That's how I like it, with lots of sauce. Not just a couple of raviolis, but lots of them piled high on the plate like pancakes or something. You see she makes them as big as a catcher's glove and as thick as your hand, and loads them up with that sweet ricotta cheese."

The men headed for their seats and I followed, continuing my diatribe of the culinary society. They kept looking at me as they shoved those funny looking skinny hot dogs farther into their mouths.

"Then she has these big bowls of baked, brown chicken covered with olive oil and garlic and then these giant boiled potatoes covered with Italian parsley, 'cause my grandmother likes them that way. Oh and you know what else?" I followed them down the steps back toward the seats on the third base side and into the bright sunlight.

"I know you aren't going to believe this," I continued. "But we also have pork every Sunday. Not little pieces, because you never know when somebody just might show up, but a huge pork roast sitting in a large pot of thick tomato sauce with rosemary and then big garden beans on the side, with lots of butter melted on top of them. It's a tradition. Yeah, I better not get filled up on no hot dogs. Hey, do you guys like dandelion salad? Bet you never had no dandelion salad. Those Italian people go crazy over it. I just better wait. Thanks for the offer, though. You know, you really need a newspaper for your lap so you don't get any mustard on those pants."

He shook his head and as he sat down I dropped a *Post Gazette* on his lap. I waited for the shifting of food from hand to hand, a hard shuffle to his pocket for some change and — zippo!— right into my right pocket for Muckles.

I gave them a quick, servant-like bow, and headed back for the center of the third base fans. The men were still forcing the American-made hot dogs and buns into their pouchy mouths, but made sure they followed my advice and covered their laps with the paper.

*Maybe I'll just sell all 10 of these papers, go back to Muckles underneath the stands, and get more papers, make a lot of money and buy one of those lousy hot dogs.*

I leaned against one of the huge black pillars around section 220 with the millions of rivets in them, and made sure none of those pigeons were overhead. I never did understand why they needed all those rivets, but it looked like the same metal girders on the Schenley Park Bridge. *I guess the people from Hazelwood who made a living putting rivets into steel beams were quite happy with the arrangement, though. Yeah, that's it, I'm sure.*

*Hey, who's that down there underneath the stands with Muckles? Is that Mikey? What's he doing there? He sold all his papers already? Can't be. God, what am I gonna do now? I'm way behind.* He was counting out his money and Mikey's, putting it in his left pocket. Right pocket for Muckles' money, left pocket for yourself. *How much is that?*

The stands started to get more crowded and I felt the seventy-five cents of Muckles' money burning in my pocket. How much of that was mine? I never asked and would have to wait for the end of the game to find out. I wondered if I could buy a couple hot dogs right then with the money I had and just make sure I sold enough to cover my costs by the eighth inning when we had to turn in our proceeds.

*Better not.* If I didn't make enough, then I'd be in real trouble. What was it about that place? I loved it. I walked down closer to home plate to see if any of those rich people wanted a paper. I belonged there. People weren't even ordering me out of the way.

"Hey, *Post-Gazette* here! Get your *Post-Gazette*! Throw away the funnies and just read the sports section. Tells all the statistics on the players, even the lineup. You don't even need a program."

A heavy-set, forty-year-old black guy with a red vendor hat and official apron gave me a nasty scowl.

"Program here," he said. "Get your official Pittsburgh Pirate program here." He got closer to me and bumped the newspapers out of my hand. I leaned down to pick them up and he followed me in my abject humble position.

"You better get out of my section boy, before I tear your head off," he said. His crappy teeth and day-old scraggly beard matched the mean look in his yellow-tinged eyes.

I looked at his huge arms with the tattoo on the right bicep that had *mother* scratched out with a knife-like scar, and I knew he meant business.

Interesting how a fourteen year old can learn in a hurry. They teach religion, reading, writing, arithmetic, and history in the schools, but somehow survival is never taught. It's a streetwise thing that came easy growing up in Oakland.

I was getting tired and my feet were killing me. I had to sit down. I figured I should go back to my assigned section on third base and work it. It was too cold in the shade. I didn't like it and wished I had my sweatshirt. But it was May, and was supposed to be warm. I thought about going back in the sun and maybe just watching the game for awhile.

"Hey, Richie. How many papers did you sell?" Muckles called out.

"Uhh... About three, but I've been working hard."

"What? That's not enough. What are you doing? Go on out there to right field and see if you can sell any out there. I got too many of you guys down here by home plate and third."

"But the people in right field don't have any money. That's the cheap seats, Mister Muckles," I said with my polite protest.

"Go on," he insisted. He placed his huge meat-hook hands on his barber shop strap and tugged on his faded green Marine Corps cap.

As I made my way along the concrete pathway from home plate to first, past the cyclone gate and into the right field stands, I kept feeling more like a rejected substitute banished to the bullpen for life. The game went on even though I was sent to right field. I was no longer in the limelight. No longer a star player, but banished to the cheap seats of right field. A dejected feeling came across my body. I felt colder inside now than ever before.

"Now batting for St. Louis, Stan Musial," the announcer blared out as the game continued. It could have been over for all I cared. There wasn't much left in life. I would simply protest being demoted, wouldn't sell any more papers for that damn meany Muckles, and would just watch the rest of the game in peace and quiet.

I continued my way toward right field and easily found plenty of available seats to plop down and rest my worn-out legs. There were seats even close to the wall. I headed on down there. "Hey, is anybody sitting in that seat, mister?"

"Hey thanks, mister, and thank you, Muckles," I said to myself. As soon as I sat down, the loud crack of the ball hitting the bat broke the murmur of the crowd. Musial smacked one deep to right and Clemente went back to the wall, my wall, right underneath me, jumped, and snagged the slugger's line drive right before it went out. Whoa, right in front of me! He stole a homer from Musial! It was terrific.

"Hey, kid. You ain't supposed to sit down when you're selling newspapers. That's the rule," the old grouchy, never-liked-nobody usher hollered to me.

"Ooooohhh. Sorry, I didn't know that," I said as I got up and started walking away from the wall. I was really getting hungry now. Should I just go over to the concession stand and beg them for a hot dog? My mother, the president of the Rosary Society, would be horrified. My dad, the head of the church improvement committee, would scold me for a week. I couldn't do that. It wouldn't be ethical. I walked along a bit further, a bit closer to those tasty swollen hot dogs sitting behind the tilted glass.

"Newspapers here, anybody want a newspaper? I'm a poor orphan trying to support myself. Please help. Newspapers here."

Editors' Note: "Old Forbes Field" first appeared online in *Strata Magazine* (Volume I, Issue 3, Spring 2002) and is reprinted with permission of the publisher, Elliot Strunk, and the author. The online magazine's website is http://www. fifth-letter.com/strata.

# 9

# AN USHER'S TALE:
# AN INTERVIEW WITH BOB SMITH

## Richard S. Morgan

*What was like growing up in the neighborhood near Forbes Field?*

Well, it was a wonderful neighborhood. I lived on Parkview Avenue. It was opposite Schenley Park. I went to Holmes Elementary School. We walked from Parkview Avenue to Schenley High School. It was when you started high school that you started to usher. Gus Miller had a magazine store in Oakland that is still there.[1] It was strictly a legitimate magazine store, and he used to sell papers. He was an uneducated man who was sort of self-made, and he turned out to be the usher boss. Back in 1929 and 1930, ushers certainly weren't in any union.

*So, they weren't unionized when you started?*

Oh, no. You sort of went into the store to get acquainted with Mr. Miller, so you could usher.

*It went through him, is that right?*

It went through him. If you lived in Oakland, ushering was the thing to do if you could make it. There was a little competition, but Gus Miller was the key in those days. That was 1929, and it was the Depression and you were hoping you would get what they called "getting on." That was the word they used.

*You mean getting on a list?*

Getting on the payroll. You could "get on" once you got a card from Gus Miller. He gave you some little membership card, and you didn't have to pay for it or anything. Then, you hoped he picked you. You know, you sat there, and you wanted to get picked. That was the key. You got 75 cents a game if you were an usher and a dollar if you were a director. Now the directors were not much more than ushers. They didn't usher people. They sort of told people where to go.

In 1936, Social Security came in. That created a problem. We're making seventy-five cents or a dollar a game. They gave you the dollar, but you had to give a penny back for your Social Security. You see, I worked for the Carnegie Museum, and they didn't have to have Social Security. Can you believe my first Social Security was ushering?

*How old were you when you first started ushering?*

Well, I was 15. I was a freshman in high school. I can always remember 1929.

*Were the usher's duties basically the same as now?*

Yeah. When customers arrived, you had to dust the seats.

Bob Smith (circled) and the ushers at Forbes Field (courtesy Dr. Stevie Smith).

*Describe a typical day as an usher.*
We would use our card and go through the press gate. We would sit in the stands and then you were picked.

*Was there a possibility when you went to the game you might not get picked?*
Oh, yeah.

*Who determined if you got picked for that day?*
Until they got the union, it was up to Gus Miller. That's why you sort of had to be his pal. The union, of course, changed everything. They had a list. I wasn't really real low on that list, but I was one of the older ushers. Near the end, it was all seniority.

*When you were ushering at Forbes Field, was there a specific seat for the general admission?*
In the grandstands, there was an usher in every section because the first seven rows were reserved. Then, from there on back was general admission.

*How did you do in tips?*
Now, if you made seventy-five cents a game, I'm talking about 1929, that was pretty good. Very good, in fact. We got paid by each game.

*So, when the game was over, you would go to cash out.*
Yes. They furnished the hat. It wasn't paramount. You just went in there and picked a hat. That was the only uniform.

*Did you have a permanent usher position that you went to every game, or were you assigned on a game-by-game basis?*
I didn't go very regularly. I just got potluck.

*Who were some of the players that you saw, some of the moments you might have experienced?*
Well, that's pretty hard. Paul Waner was my favorite. When you're a kid, you get almost an obsession for a ballplayer, and Paul Waner was mine. Why, if he had two hits, I felt better, and I was only a kid.

*If he was 0 for 3, it was a bad day, right?*
Yes, and also I liked Arky Vaughan.

*He won a batting championship.*
Yeah, they were the two who affected me by what they did. Sure, I liked Ralph Kiner, Bob Friend. I saw Willie Mays, Jackie Robinson, Carl Hubbell, and Dizzy Dean. I saw all those players.

*Did you see Babe Ruth?*

Well, I saw Babe Ruth. In fact, I went into that last game he played. He hit three home runs, and I was working at the museum, but I got off early enough. That was a day game and I walked in. I saw the last home run he hit.

*You began ushering in 1929 and wrapped it up in 1990. So you've been through Forbes Field and Three Rivers Stadium?*

Yes. Beginning in 1941, that was the key. If you were a '41 usher, you had a little more power with the union, and I was a '41 usher.

*Your daughter, Stevie, asked me to bring up the foul balls. What about the foul balls?*

During the Depression, we had to get the foul balls. If we turned a foul ball in, we would get on the next day. They wanted the ushers to grab those foul balls. Can you believe they were that hard up? And you got on the next day. Now, they wouldn't want an usher to get them.

*Nowadays, the players give them to the fans.*

Oh yeah, can you imagine how hard times were? Or maybe Barney Dreyfuss was tight.

*Why did the union come in?*

It was part of the times. Of course, we went from seventy-five cents a day to about eight dollars a game, and that is what the union did. I said we never could get eight dollars a game, and of course, when I left we were getting $33 a game. What do ushers get now?

*They get $16.00 an hour.*

They go by the hour now. I see.

*Was ushering merely a way to make some money, or was it some type of opportunity to see your favorite player?*

Well, I was like most of the young kids that worked as ushers. I was greedy enough to stay, because I liked the money.

*I understand from Stevie you used to take your girlfriends to Forbes Field.*

Oh, there was some librarian. She had a case on me. She came to the game as a fan. Can you imagine me treating her? Hey, I had her sitting there. Talk about mercenary, I was it.

*You ushered at the Forbes Field before night games.*

Yes.

*Would night games make any difference in the crowds?*

Well, I guess in some ways it did.

*How did the night baseball change things at Forbes Field and around Oakland?*

It certainly brought the attendance up. Of course, people would go the bars after the game. Frank Gustine had a restaurant. I liked to go in there a lot.

*On the average, how many games did you work a season?*

You had to work so many games or you would lose your seniority. Up until I retired, I got pretty good.

*Were you an usher for the boxing matches at Forbes Field?*

Yes. Ezzard Charles. It was pretty important.[2]

*Where was the boxing ring located at Forbes Field?*

Oh, I would say it was at second base or the pitching mound.

*The chairs were out on the field?*

Yes, for ringside. In fact, Forbes Field ushers didn't usher the ringside. The promoters more or less had their own ushers.

**Bill Mazeroski heads home, chased by usher Domenic "Woo" Varratti (Harry Harris, AP/World Wide Photos).**

*Could you talk about the 1960 World Series?*
It's funny. You have to realize that an usher is not really a fan.

*Or a spectator.*
It's almost like a job, but it's a fun job. I'm talking about the way I felt. I was glad when the game was over. I was part-time.

*What was it like when Mazeroski hit the home run to win the 1960 World Series?*
After the game, I went up to a restaurant in Oakland. Someone even bought my meal. I went in to sit with a bunch of guys from Oakland because I was waiting for the traffic. I didn't even have to pay for my meal. That's the way things were. When he hit that home run, I didn't realize what it was going to be. They tore the town up.

*I also was asked to mention "Woo" and Mazeroski.*
He was able to usher every game. He chased Maz into home, and he got into that picture.[3]

*When the season ended, would you find another job?*
I worked for the Duquesne Light. Ushering was only a hobby. It was a moneymaking hobby. The tips were really more important than the pay in the beginning.

*So, after a regular day of work for Duquesne Light, you would go work a ball game that night?*
Yes. You see, the night game saved the fellows who couldn't get off early. You had to be

over there two hours before the game started. The games started at seven o'clock and you had to be there at five o'clock.

*What other memories do you have of Forbes Field?*

You know, I'm going way back. This is 1927. The World Series was on. Do you realize you could stand in line and sell your place? Maybe the guy would give you 50 cents, and then you went back to the end of the line. Maybe you could make a buck. Now, you realize I was 15 and impressed. A buck was a lot of money.

*When the game was over, would you just leave with the crowd or did you have some responsibilities?*

You had to put the seats up.

*Did you have to clean around or just put the seats up?*

Just put the seats up. They were folding seats at Forbes Field.

*When I say "Forbes Field" to you, what comes to your mind?*

It's hard for me to give you an answer. I loved the place, and I hated it.

*What did you hate about it?*

Because it was a job. Really, I never hated it, but all the ushers worried about was getting out of there. That's bad. I liked it, or I was so hungry for money, I don't know. Why do any of us usher? The ushers are a different breed.

*What about some of the special promotion days at Forbes Field?*

One of the biggest messes was Kids Day. They used to put them all in left field, not the right field stands, and they had the big drums of water up there. You wouldn't believe it. They'd put an usher out there, or two. What a difficult time. It was almost like a riot. 'Cause the kids wanted the water, and they only had tin cups.

*So that section of the ballpark was strictly for kids on Kids Day.*

Yeah. It was Kids Day, and they were packed solid. I don't think they paid anything.

*How about Ladies Day?*

Ladies Day. That was another thing. They really flocked in there.

*Did you work doubleheaders? Did you get paid twice for doubleheaders?*

No, you got a little more money, but they used to have meal money, and we stayed right through. There was about a half hour. Now, of course, at one time they had a game in the morning and in the evening. They were two separate games.

*Did you get meal money for those, or did you go home and come back?*

I went home and came back.

*I take it you were a baseball fan before you were an usher?*

Oh, yeah. I played baseball. I played in high school.

*For Schenley?*

Yeah. In fact, I was captain of the team the last year.

*You played organized sandlot?*

I played organized sandlot. I played for the Ambassadors. They were a local group from Oakland, and they played in Frazier Field.

*Did you go to Forbes Field as a youngster?*

Yeah, my dad took me. I'm sure he did, especially the 50 cent bleachers. They were in left field. Part of it was seventy-five cents, and there was a little section for 50 cents. It was closer to the outfield.

You know, one of the joys I never got too often was working in the press box when I was an usher.

*Tell us about that.*

Well, I didn't work it often, but once in awhile I would get it when no one else did. I remember I met Roy McHugh when he first came to Pittsburgh. I was the first usher he talked to. We still talk.

*The press box was located right behind home plate?*
It was on the third level.

*Up on the top.*
Yeah.

*What was it like working the press box?*
That was good. They had food up there and the ushers would get their dibs in.

*Did you have any experience with Rosey Rowswell?*
No, but I went to high school with Bob Prince.

*You went to school with Bob Prince at Schenley High School. I imagine his high school days were just about like his broadcasting. He was quite a character.*

I've got a picture of the swimming team, and he's in a camel hair coat. He had a cold that day. Did you ever hear of the Fellows Club? They are a bunch of men who used to meet Saturday from noon to 2:00 P.M. and they still meet up at the Lamont. Bob Prince used to go there, and I used to see him there. Bob was a very good swimmer.

*What about people who would try to move down to a better seat? Would you have to chase them out?*

Oh, yeah. The trouble is if you would let them sit down there, they would give you a buck. You wouldn't sell the seat, but they would ask. But sometimes a guy would say, "Can I sit down there?" You'd say, "Okay," because it looked like the seat would be empty the whole game. One time a guy had tickets elsewhere, and there were four empty seats. He said, "Can I sit down there?" and he gave me $20. Now, I knew it was wrong to take the $20, but I never had to chase them.

*Did you see fans at every game, or every season, who you would know by their first name?*
Yes. In fact, the people seemed to like being close to you, it was a status symbol. Can you believe it having the ushers be real friendly to the fans? They seemed to like that.

*Did your assignment change year-to-year in terms of which section you ushered?*
Yeah, I never had a regular section.

*So, you ushered all over Forbes Field?*
I took whatever was available.

*How long did you work for Duquense Light?*
I had 34 years. I worked in the Carnegie Museum, and I went to the light company when the war came on in '41. They needed experienced operators, and I stayed until I retired.

*Were there any events during the war?*
The Homestead Grays played there.

*What about the Greenberg Gardens at Forbes Field?*[4]
Greenberg came there to more or less school Kiner. To have more home runs, they shortened left field. So they called it Greenberg Gardens. Of course, Forbes Field was really long. Shortening it only cheapened it. People called it cheap home runs. Thank goodness they got rid of it.

*There are some old pictures of people standing on the field.*
They had standing room only. They used to sell standing room. Can you imagine people

standing in the outfield to watch a ball game? I think when the place sells out, quit. Can you imagine standing on the field? You couldn't even enjoy the game.

*Photographers were also on the field.*
Oh, yes.

*Anything else?*
I saw more or less all of the right field bleachers being built.

*What is your current status with the ushers union?*
I'm still a member. I don't have to pay dues because of my age. I was paying dues up to age 84. I still get the notices of the meetings. In fact, I have two notices now about two meetings, and Stevie will get the $500.00 death benefit. But it's not costing me anything. I'm glad they sent me a baseball schedule, and I think it is very nice.

Editors' Note: W. Robert "Bob" Smith was born on May 26, 1914, in Pittsburgh. The interview was conducted at his home in Pittsburgh on March 6, 2002. Also present for the interview were Dr. Stevie Smith, Bob's daughter, and David Cicotello. Bob passed away on May 9, 2005.

## Notes

1. Gustave "Gus" Miller owned and operated a newsstand at the corner of Forbes and Oakland avenues. Opened in 1907, the store was situated one block from what would be the main entrance to Forbes Field. A neighborhood institution, Miller was both proprietor and chief usher. He worked games from Opening Day in 1909 through 1947. Miller died in 1967.

2. The match referred to was the World Heavyweight Title fight between Ezzard Charles and Jersey Joe Walcott held at Forbes Field on July 18, 1951.

3. Domenic "Woo" Varratti, an usher at Forbes Field, can be seen in numerous photographs and film footage running behind Mazeroski as he heads toward home plate.

4. Greenberg Gardens, also called Kiner's Korner, was the bullpen area between the left field scoreboard and a short fence that was built to increase home run production from 1947 to 1953. It was called Greenberg Gardens in 1947 and renamed Kiner's Korner from 1948 to 1953.

# 10

# AT THE WALL WITH SAUL

## Jim O'Brien

It all started with Saul Finkelstein.

Pirate loyalists gather each October 13th at what remains of the outfield wall of Forbes Field in Oakland to mark the anniversary of the team's 1960 World Series victory over the New York Yankees.

Once more, they go wild when Bill Mazeroski hits the ball out of the park as the lead-off batter in the bottom of the ninth inning, even if it's just on a taped broadcast of the most famous ball game in Pittsburgh history.

Some of them even want to get down bets that the Pirates will prevail.

Finkelstein started this baseball lovers' pilgrimage to the Pirates' old ballpark out where the University of Pittsburgh (Pitt) campus comes up against Schenley Park.

It's a beautiful scene. The ivy is still on the red-brick wall that runs up against the Katz Graduate School of Business on Roberto Clemente Drive. The foliage can be spectacular in October. One can still find a marker on the sidewalk showing where Maz's home run cleared the left field wall, right next to the scoreboard. Home plate is under Plexiglas in the hallway of Forbes Quadrangle, a Pitt building on the other side of Clemente Drive.

I've seen grown men, well, sportswriters anyway, visitors from Florida wearing blazers and slacks, run down that hallway and slide across home plate, just for the hell of it.

About 200 to 250 true baseball fans have flocked to the wall on October 13 the past eight years in what is regarded as one of the most unique expressions of a love of the game to be found in a major league city. In the eight years previous to 1993, Finkelstein sat alone at the base of the flagpole that remains at the 457-foot mark in center field. He did it the first time on October 13, 1985.

Back then, it was a one-man vigil. Finkelstein simply sat down shortly after one o'clock in the afternoon and turned on his tape recorder to listen to the original NBC radio broadcast of the seventh game of the 1960 World Series. That's the one where Chuck Thompson and Jack Quinlan describe the action in what is still regarded as one of the greatest World Series games in history.

In fact, that whole 1960 World Series is thought to be one of the all-time classics. It was certainly a zany affair. The mighty Yankees outscored the underdog Pirates, 55–27, in the seven games, yet came up short by one run in the deciding game, 10–9. The Yankees won their three games by lopsided scores of 16–3, 10–0, and 12–0.

"They set all the records, but we won the championship," shouted a gleeful Gino Cimoli, a Pirate outfielder, in the clubhouse after that last game.

Finkelstein has since come by two more taped versions of that seventh game, the NBC-TV broadcast by Mel Allen and Bob Prince, and a re-creation of the historic contest by Prince

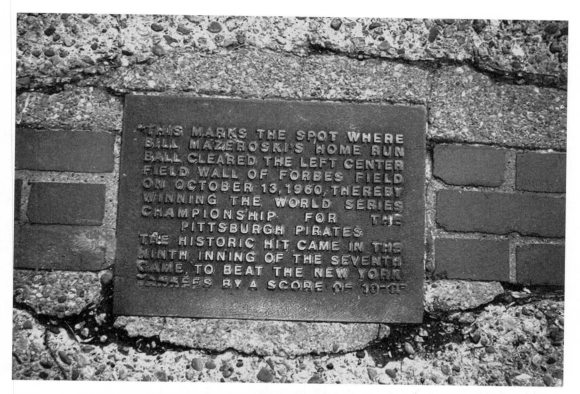

*Top:* Historical marker near Center Field Plaza on the University of Pittsburgh campus: "This marks the spot where Bill Mazeroski's home run ball cleared the left center field wall of Forbes Field on October 13, 1960, thereby winning the World Series championship for the Pittsburgh Pirates. The historic hit came in the ninth inning of the seventh game, to beat the New York Yankees by a score of 10–9" (David Finoli). *Bottom:* Section of the remaining wall in the deepest part of Forbes Field (David Finoli).

and his KDKA Radio sidekick, Jim Woods. The latter can still bring chills to a long-time Pirate fan.

Finkelstein is a soft-spoken little fellow, just a shade over five feet tall, who looks like a life-long college student. He lives in Squirrel Hill, just four or five miles from the Forbes Field site. He is a 52-year-old bachelor, a 1966 graduate of Taylor Allderdice High School, who provides office services in the downtown legal courts, and also does telemarketing and customer service work for the Pittsburgh Ballet Theater.

I first met Finkelstein and learned of his annual vigil back in January of 1992 at a Pirate-fest held at the Expomart in Monroeville. I had a table there at which I was soliciting stories and personal memories for a book I was writing called *Maz and the '60 Bucs*.

Finkelstein showed up and introduced himself. "I have a story I think you'll like," he said for openers.

After Finkelstein told me his story, I used it in the book. When word got out about the '60 Series anniversary gig, 30 or 40 other fans showed up at the wall of Forbes Field the next time around, October 13, 1993. Some of them have returned every year since. I spoke about this gathering on several radio and TV sports talk shows in Pittsburgh, and wrote about later gatherings in a book about Bob Prince called *We Had 'Em All the Way*.

Some of the visitors to the wall wore Pirate blouses and ball caps. Some brought their gloves and baseballs and played catch. Some brought ticket stubs from the 1960 World Series and other memorabilia. Some just brought their memories. Last year, the Pitt women's softball team took a break from practice at nearby Bill Mazeroski Field to join the festivities on the other side of the wall at Forbes Field.

One of the Forbes Field regulars, Ed Landolina, who also lives in Squirrel Hill, brought his son, Chris, to give him an idea of the team's rich history. "It's a day I always look forward to," allowed Landolina, "and for me, it's the unofficial last day of summer."

So the crowds grew in size. Some of the Pirates from that team started to show up, like pitchers Bob Friend and ElRoy, and then former Pirate pitcher and Prince sidekick Nellie King came out as well. Nellie Briles, a corporate sales executive with the Pirates and a former Pirate and Cardinal pitcher who looks after the Pirate Alumni, started to come and encourage other alumni to attend.

Briles was one of the key contributors to the Pirates' World Series triumph of 1971, in their second season at Three Rivers Stadium. He also has fond memories of Forbes Field. "That's where I had my 'break-out' game as a rookie pitcher with the Cardinals," recalled Briles. "We had a great left-handed pitcher named Curt Simmons who got knocked out in the second inning against the Pirates. I was pitching long relief at the time. I came in and stayed in, and we ended up winning the game. I got a lot more opportunities to pitch after that."

Forbes Field brings back interesting memories for Finkelstein as well. His was another story that he told me that day at the Piratefest at the Expomart.

"I wasn't able to go to the seventh game of the 1960 World Series, but I stayed home from school to watch it," Finkelstein said. "I was in seventh grade at the time. I gave up on the Pirates midway through the game, when they were behind by 6–4. My cat had died the night before, and I decided this was a good time to bury it. So I went out in my backyard and buried the cat under a tree. I go back to the game on TV about the eighth inning, and everything went crazy from thereon in."

A lot of fans have shared their personal experiences relating to the 1960 World Series, and where they were when Maz hit the home run, but none were quite as bizarre as Finkelstein's story.

He felt that the 1999 gathering was one of the best yet. The chemistry was just right. Those in attendance broke out into a spirited rendition of the song, "Take Me Out to the Ballgame" during the seventh inning stretch, the first time that has happened. It will, no doubt, be part of the program this time around.

The biggest crowd, however, turned out for the 2000 gathering. That was because it was the 40th anniversary of the 1960 World Series. Bill Mazeroski showed up for the first time ever, and he was overwhelmed by the reception he received from over 600 ball fans. He might have signed something for every one of them. It was a hot day, and he was sweating, but he signed everything that was handed to him and rejected offers to take a break.

He was joined at the wall by former teammates and friends such as ElRoy Face, Nellie Briles, Nellie King, and Ron Necciai. Later, he was joined at the Forbes Field Tavern on the South Side by Bob Purkey, Steve Blass, and Dave Giusti, among others.

Mazeroski never made it before because he was usually in Florida at that time, helping his son, Darren, who is the coach of the baseball team at Panama City College. If Maz ever showed up — rumors have always made the rounds that this would be the year — his biggest fans felt that it would have the same impact as the ballplayer appearing out of the cornfield in the movie *Field of Dreams*. And it did.

"This is something," he said. "I never thought there'd be something like this going on 40 years later."

His other son, David, during his graduate student days at Pitt, checked out the activity from a distance on October 13, 1993.

"I saw a man sitting by the flagpole listening to a tape of the game," David wrote to me. "I walked over to a picnic table and sat for a few minutes. I tried to visualize a guy about my age stepping up to the plate with nerves of steel and hitting the most memorable and unselfish home run ever.

"Then I thought about the same guy being my dad, and even though I wasn't alive to see him play, at least it is in my blood. Every time I drove down to school and winded my way around Roberto Clemente Drive, I pictured the infield of the old ballpark and would say to myself that this is where my dad worked. I am driving over my dad's footprints."

Rick Mitchell and S. P. Winovich, owners of the Forbes Field Tavern, hosted a post-game party at their place on Sarah Street on the South Side the past three years. In 2000, it was on an invitation-only basis. The Forbes Field Tavern is a neat place, three full floors of Pirates and Steelers photographs and memorabilia from the respective teams' Forbes Field days.

"Our place brings back a lot of great memories for fans," said Mitchell.

"It was great last year because we were all listening to the same broadcast," Finkelstein said. "That's better than when different people are listening to their own tapes. It's an interesting group. There are the curious, the people who were there that day, people who just remember it. Some who have no idea about the game but show up just because it's there."

Finkelstein said he has made many trips over to the North Side to check out PNC Park. He thought it was going to be even better than Forbes Field. "I think so," he said. "It's here. Forbes Field is gone. It'll be great to have real grass and dirt again. It gives you a better perspective of the game and what's going on. It will be a better stage."

Herb Soltman was also excited about the prospects of an old-fashioned ballpark as the Pirates' home field for next season. Soltman is a baseball fan forever. He still has his ticket stubs from the seventh game of the 1960 World Series. It cost him $7.70 for each of his first level reserved seats.

His seats were so close to the diamond at Forbes Field that he was among those who mobbed Mazeroski at home plate after the Pirates' 24-year-old second baseman hit a home run over the wall in left field to beat the Yankees, 10–9. It came at 3:36 P.M., as it does each year at the gathering at the wall.

Soltman is somewhere in the mob of a blurred photo he carries with him. When Mazeroski was at the Pirates' Fantasy Camp a couple of years ago, one of the attendees hit a home run, the first time that had ever happened at the Fantasy Camp. Maz met the man in the dugout after he rounded the bases and said, "I can give you some tips on how you can live off one home run for the rest of your life!"

**Section of the remaining wall near the spot of Mazeroski's home run (David Finoli).**

A resident of Virginia Manor Apartments in Scott Township, Soltman is a salesman for Babcor Packaging, in the paper bag business, working out of a building on the city's North Side. He bags his job responsibilities to come out to the wall on October 13 each year.

He said he had a grandmother who died at 105 years of age who had attended only one baseball game in her life and it was the seventh game of the 1960 World Series. And she lived at Webster Hall, just down Fifth Avenue from the ballpark. Soltman compiled his own pitch-by-pitch account of that seventh game on a yellow legal pad.

The fans make this annual pilgrimage to the wall from some faraway places: Illinois, New Jersey, Ohio, Tennessee, and Waynesburg and Franklin, Pennsylvania.

Doug Snyder used to come in from Schaumburg, Illinois, and now he comes from Bedminster, New Jersey. He schedules his business trips so he can be in Pittsburgh on this date every year.

A teacher from Waynesburg, Herb Carpenter, brought his teenage daughter, Leah, with him once when it coincided with Columbus Day. They brought a baseball board game and played it while everyone listened to a taped broadcast of the entire seventh game.

Renee and Enos Abel of Moon Township, who met each other at a post-game celebration of that World Series victory, returned once again. They had gotten engaged on October 13 a year after they met.

Those who gathered at the wall cheered at appropriate times and spoke aloud of their concern about the Pirates' chances when the Yankees would come back to take the lead in the wild battle.

They cheered like crazy when the Pirates scored five runs in the bottom of the eighth inning to regain the lead. Hal Smith hit a three-run shot over the wall in left-center in that inning, described by the broadcaster as "one of the most dramatic home runs of all time."

When Maz hit a 1-and-0 pitch by Ralph Terry out of the park, they were jumping up and down and cheering like it had just happened. Soltman shouted out, "We had 'em all the way!"

Editors' Note: A different version of this article first appeared in Jim O'Brien's *We Had 'Em All the Way: Bob Prince and His Pittsburgh Pirates* (Pittsburgh: James P. O'Brien Publishing, 1998).

# 11

# REMEMBRANCES OF THINGS PAST: PIRATES, FANS, AND MEDIA REMINISCE

## *The Pirates*

Ralph Leif Erickson, ca. 1930 (courtesy Barbara Bowman).

The older Pirate players initiated the rookies by distracting them and then spitting tobacco juice on their shoes! I made sure that didn't happen to me because I paid $12.00 for my shoes. I had two pairs, one to practice in and one to play in, and these were my good ones!

Paul Waner saved me once when he caught a long ball that someone hit off me (the bases were loaded). The manager would have yanked me from the game if he hadn't caught that ball (it was a slider that the batter shouldn't have hit).

Nearly everyone but me chewed tobacco. Sitting in the dugout during one game, a couple of the players talked me into chewing a piece. I was starting to get a little woozy when I heard, "Erickson, warm up—I'm sending you in!" I could hardly walk, and I staggered out of the bull pen to the mound. I couldn't read the signs from the catcher. Somehow, I managed to get through the inning.

Ralph Leif Erickson
Wichita, Kansas

*Hailing from Dubois, Idaho, Ralph Erickson made his major league debut with the Pirates on September 11, 1929, and remained on the Pittsburgh pitching staff for the 1930 season.*

*Editors' Note: Ralph Erickson dictated his memories to his daughter, Barbara Bowman, of Wichita, Kansas.*

It was one of the finest and cherished experiences of my life in addition to my professional medical experiences and one of my life's blessings that I played for the Pirates.

H. Hoffman Groskloss, M.D.
Vero Beach, Florida

*Dr. Howard "Howdy" Groskloss, a second baseman and shortstop, played his entire major league career with the Pirates from 1930 to 1932. On April 9, 2005, Dr. Groskloss turned 99, making him the oldest surviving ex–major leaguer.*

155

In 1931, after serving one year with the Bucs, I was playing first base at Forbes Field when I got hurt.

In 1935, Boston came to Pittsburgh, and they had the mighty Babe Ruth playing for them. I saw him hit three home runs off three different pitchers—the last one he hit was a beaut. But our club won the game, 11–8. The next day was a Sunday and the Babe stepped up to the plate, but in five times he didn't get a hit. He decided to retire.

In 1938, we went to Chicago (September 27–29) to play three games with the Cubs who were one and a half games back of us. They won the first game 2–1, the second game 6–5, and the third 10–1. The September 28, 1938, game was the "Homer in the Gloamin'," which took the Pirates essentially out of the playoffs.

Gus Suhr
Mesa, Arizona

*August "Gus" Suhr was a star first baseman with the Pirates during the 1930s. He drove in 100 or more runs three times and played in 822 consecutive games, the ninth longest streak in the history of the major leagues (as of April 1, 2005).*

Forbes Field was like a second home to me. In 1935, I was captain of the Westinghouse High School Baseball Team City Champions. As a reward, all team members received a pass to attend all Pirate games for the rest of the 1935 season. In 1938, I signed a Pirate minor league contract. After the minor league season was over, I came back to Pittsburgh and Forbes Field and caught Pirate batting practice under the watchful eye of coach Honus Wagner. In the 1950s, I was a member of a committee that started a program to erect a statue for Honus, which was placed just outside the left field fence. I was in the service from 1941 to 1946. During this period, I coached several Army teams.

In 1946, for a short period I managed the Pirates' minor league team in Oil City. In 1948, along with being baseball coach at Duquesne University, I became a part-time scout with the Pirates. In cooperation with Pie Traynor, I held tryout camps in Forbes Field and in the area around Pittsburgh. In three years, five players that I acquired for the Pirates made the major leagues. During this period, I assisted Ray Scott in broadcasting Duquesne University football games that were held at Forbes Field. In 1950, I was called back into the service, but in 1952, I resumed my job as a scout.

In March 1953, I was called into the office of Branch Rickey, the Pirate general manager, and was

The Honus Wagner Memorial Statue erected in 1955 and pictured in its first location outside the left field gate at Forbes Field. The statue was moved to Three Rivers Stadium and then to PNC Park (Pittsburgh Photographic Library Collection of Carnegie Library of Pittsburgh).

asked to take over a company that was experimenting with the development of a batting helmet. The company was owned by Mr. Rickey and some of his associates. I became general manager of the company and became prime developer of the batting helmet. My office and warehouse for a time were underneath the general admission seat area at Forbes Field. I was with the company for 11 years. In 1956, I watched as Dale Long set a record of hitting a home run in eight straight games. In 1960, I sat along the first base line at Forbes Field and watched Bill Mazeroski's home run ball go over the left field fence to win the 1960 World Series.

During the years 1958–1966, in a slow production period of the batting helmet, I was put in charge of the Little Pirates. This team was made up of outstanding high school players, and we played at Forbes Field and on area fields in the Pittsburgh district. This team became a scouting and publicity vehicle for the Pirates. In eight years, we won 416 games and lost only 102. Also during this period, I was made an executive of the Pittsburgh Pirates Foundation, which raised funds for amateur teams in the area. I did this by scheduling exhibition games between the Pirates and other major league teams. In 1966, I was made ticket manager of the Pirates. In 1968 to 1970, I became involved in making plans for the new Three Rivers Stadium. I started to sell tickets for both Forbes Field and Three Rivers Stadium, not knowing where we were playing on certain dates. It was finally resolved after two delays on the opening of Three Rivers on July 16, 1970.

I had a great plan for closing Forbes Field if the last game was at night, with former players introduced under a spotlight, marching bands, retiring the national flag with military personnel and the Pirate flag with Little League players, followed by fireworks. My plan was completely wiped out when it was decided to close the ballpark on a Sunday afternoon. Chaos reigned — after the last out, fans stormed onto the field. They tore up everything, including the pitcher's mound, home plate, turfs of grass, numbers from the scoreboard, seats— you name it. It was a nightmare to someone like me, who had spent many years in one of the finest ballparks in the majors, to see it demolished in this manner! I was somewhat relieved when I became part of the scene when the Pirates won the 1971 World Series with great games at Three Rivers Stadium.

Charles R. Muse
Sun City Center, Florida

*Known as "The Colonel," the multitalented Charles Muse was a valuable asset to the Pirate organization. Former Pirate manager Chuck Tanner called him "one of the greatest men I've ever known in my life."*

---

I only played a part of 1937, all of 1938, 1939, and part of 1940, so I do not speak with much authority. However, I was in the National League 11 years, so I visited the park frequently.

It was always a pleasure to play in Forbes Field with its good background and dimensions. The location was great, the field was always in good shape, the surroundings were pleasant, and the fans were wonderful. I wish I could have played there longer.

I am now 95 years of age. May I add that I spent 31 years in the majors and did not find any park I liked better than Forbes Field.

Ray Berres
Twin Lakes, Wisconsin

*Following two years with the Brooklyn Dodgers, Raymond "Ray" Berres came to Pittsburgh in 1937 and caught 144 games for the Pirates in four seasons. He later played for the Boston Braves and New York Giants.*

---

Mr. Branch Rickey, the greatest figure of professional baseball, hired me via telephone to be the manager of the Pirates in '56. By the time I arrived from home in Fort Worth, Texas, to Forbes Field, Pittsburgh, Mr. Rickey was fired, and I reported to Joe L. Brown — after a brief visit with Mr. Rickey at his home.

Joe L. Brown became a super general manager and did a wonderful job for the Pirates. I had known his father in Hollywood where I was player-manager for three years prior to coming to Pittsburgh.

Pittsburgh was a great experience for me, my first major league managerial job.

Forbes Field was the only field in the majors, or probably in all of baseball, where the ground crew would deposit the batting cage (huge) in left center field when practice ended. We had to have a ground rule in the event a batted ball lodged in it.

Dale Long's eight consecutive home runs in eight games occurred during my stint as manager. I made Dick Groat captain of the team in 1957.

We traded Bob Del Greco to St. Louis for Bill Virdon which was very beneficial. ElRoy Face became a fine pitcher as one of the first to use the split-finger pitch. Bob Friend, Vernon Law, Dick Hall, and Bob Purkey pitched well. Bill Mazeroski, 18 years of age, was installed at second base.

Myron O'Brisky ran the concessions for the teams and became a great friend of mine. One of the policemen who worked as a security man during games at Forbes Field was named Jim Laffey. We became friends, and he named his son Robert Bragan Laffey.

One of my greatest memories of Forbes Field came when I was playing for the Philadelphia Phillies from 1940 to 1942. We went to play Pittsburgh three times during the season (a three-game series each time). Honus Wagner was a coach for the Pirates. The "Immortal One" would hit grounders to the infielder prior to game time. It was a thrill to walk by him each day and greet him.

You see, both teams dressed on the first base side of the diamond, and since the visiting team occupied the third base dugout, we would have to enter the field from the first base side and walk to the third base dugout. That's where I would pass by the great Wagner. And each time I would say, "Hi ya, Honus," and he would respond, "Hi ya, kid. How's the weather?" That happened nine times during the season, and every time it was exactly the same exchange. "Hi ya, Honus," said I, and his answer still rings in my ears when I see his photo on my office wall — "Hi ya, kid. How's the weather?"

Frank Thomas was a member of the team when I managed the Pirates. He had great hands. He caught hit balls down the third base line with his bare right hand. Also, on one occasion he caught one in left field with his right hand. What I remember so vividly about him is this. We would be playing the Dodgers at Forbes Field, and Don Drysdale was the scheduled pitcher. After he had warmed up for 10 minutes or so, Frank would wander over to the bullpen, and after determining that Drysdale was about ready to pitch the game, he would ask John Roseboro or Norm Sherry — whoever was warming him up — if he could catch a couple of his fastballs. He would be handed the catcher's glove and obliged by the receiver to indeed catch a couple of fastballs. Thomas squatted down with the glove on his hand and received a pitch from the hard-throwing Drysdale. Then, when the pitcher fired the second pitch to him, he dropped the catcher's glove and caught the pitch *barehanded*. He loved to do that!

Roberto Clemente was easily the best defensive right fielder I ever saw. He did it all: catch, run, and throw with velocity and accuracy.

With the Dodgers, I was playing shortstop at Forbes Field and Johnny Allen was pitching for us in the late innings of a game, when George Barr, umpiring between the mound and second base, called a balk on Allen. Allen had a terrible temper. He ran immediately at Barr and actually ran over him, leaving him sprawling in the grass. Of course, he was suspended for the rest of the year by the president of the league.

Bob Skinner became a good hitter and an adequate left fielder at Forbes Field. Bob Prince was a Hall of Fame announcer and person, and was so recognized at Cooperstown.

The Brooklyn Dodgers were playing the Pirates at Forbes Field, and in the ninth inning, Hugh Casey, the closer for the Dodgers, was pitching with one or two outs (I don't recall which), and after throwing three balls to Ralph Kiner (I believe the bases were loaded), Casey called time out and went to our dugout and got a drink of water. He returned to the mound and proceeded to throw three strikes to Kiner, striking him out. We won the game. First time I'd ever seen a pitcher do that.

Robert "Bobby" Bragan
Fort Worth, Texas

*A native of Birmingham, Alabama, Robert "Bobby" Bragan was the field manager for Pittsburgh during the 1956 season and much of the following season. Before coming to the Pirates, he had a seven-year major league career with the Philadelphia Phillies and the Brooklyn Dodgers.*

What I remember about Forbes Field is:
1. The left field scoreboard with the clock on it and the Marine in the outfield.
2. In 1947, they created Greenberg Gardens.

Nick Strincevich
Portage, Indiana

*Nicholas "Nick" Strincevich joined the Pirates during the 1941 season and remained with them for six of the next seven seasons. His best years were 1944, when he was 14–7 with a 3.08 ERA, and 1945, when he was 16–10 with a 3.31 ERA.*

As with all young boys, we had dreams, dreams of being national baseball players. In my family, in 1942, sports were encouraged for enjoyment only, not as a way of making a living. The real goal in all families was survival. Get a steady job and make money! School was also important in my family and in our community. Many of our parents came from Italy and other European countries where education was only a luxury for the wealthy; here in America it was a door to opportunity for everyone!

It was my senior year at Schenley High School in Pittsburgh. The school was within walking distance of Forbes Field, the home of the Pittsburgh Pirates. My father and I didn't agree on many things, but the bond we did share was that we both loved baseball. In fact, my whole family loved baseball, and every chance my brothers and I had, we would go to Forbes Field hoping to sneak in without paying. In those days evening games were not prevalent, so we would play hooky from school and walk over to see if we could sneak into a game. This happened quite often, as it was very easy to do.

It was a humid spring day early in June, when my brother Carmen, two buddies, and I left school right before wood shop. We went running around the corner of the stadium entrance huffing and puffing as we saw a truant officer lurking around the field. We were standing around the entrance trying to look inconspicuous when a strange man walked toward us. "You guys want to make some money?" he asked. "Sure," we all eagerly yelled, "Doing what?" "We need some vendors inside, come with me." At first we were hesitant, thinking he might be a truant officer in disguise trying to trick us, but the thought of making money while watching a baseball game was a risk worth taking. After following him into Forbes Field, we each were given an official blue button-down shirt to wear, and instantly we became vendors. I couldn't believe it! No sneaking, and we also made some money.

We were asked to come back. Every time the Pirates played a home game, I was there. While working, I got to know a few people, and one of them was a tall African American whom I befriended. As we got to know each other, I found out his name was "Schoff." I didn't know what his job was, but he was there everyday. He would always buy something from me and give me a hefty tip. For a 17-year-old boy back in those days that 25-cent tip made my day!

I always went to work early, but one day I got there extra early to watch the players warm up. As I walked in under the stands, Schoff came up to me and said, "Kid, I need a batboy. Ya wanna be batboy today?" Oh gosh, I thought, I died and went to heaven. Do I want to be batboy? Was he kidding? Jumping for joy on the inside but dumbfounded on the outside, I said in a low voice, "Sure."

As I walked alongside him toward the field, he explained the situation to me. He was the Pirates' equipment manager and was in charge of the batboys. As he was explaining this, he opened a door, the door to the players' dressing room. In awe I walked in beside him. There I was among a group of half-naked ballplayers. What startled me more than their lack of clothes was their uniforms. On their uniforms was the word "Cincinnati." Totally confused, I looked at him and said, "This ain't the Pirates." He chuckled and said, "No boy, it ain't. I need you to be the visiting team's batboy. Still want the job?" A bit disappointed, but still excited, I said yes. He gave me a Cincinnati uniform and explained my duties. "The main duty of a batboy is to make sure when a batter drops his bat, you get that bat off the playing field immediately! You got that, son?" As serious as I could be with all that responsibility, I said, "Yes, sir."

The next day, it was the same: I was the visiting team's batboy. I didn't mind. I was having the time of my life; it couldn't be better, so I thought. After the two games with Cincinnati, Schoff gave me four dollars. He said I got two dollars a game and five dollars for doubleheaders, which were played every Sunday and on holidays.

As scheduled, the Pirates went on the road, and they'd be gone for one week. Schoff asked me if I'd come back when they returned. I told him yes, I'd definitely be there. That was the longest week I ever experienced. I still wasn't sure if this was a permanent job. All I knew was I was going back in a week.

Since I was skipping school, I kept this a secret from my family and friends. Finally, I broke down and told my two brothers, Carmen and Steve, about my secret life as a batboy. I told them not to tell our father, that when the time was right, I would tell him. They knew how our father was with us getting a proper education, since he did not have that opportunity back in the old country. So, I prayed, waited, and let the chips fall where they may.

When the Pirates came home to Pittsburgh, I had another pleasant surprise. Schoff told me that in the week they played out of town, the Pirates' batboy had been drafted into the Army. World War II was looming over our young lives. He said I would be promoted to Pirate batboy if I could get someone to be the batboy for the visiting team.

The first person I thought of was my brother Carmen. He was one year younger than me. At this time, he was going to a vo-tech school across town, and it was too far to run and tell him on such short notice. I still wanted Carmen to have this job, but for that day I told my friend, Hallahan, I had a temporary job for him. It turned out not to be so temporary for him, and many Pittsburgh fans may remember him because he eventually became the Pirates' equipment manager. He was with them for many years.

I wasn't able to get Carmen into the job of batboy, but because he hung out with me, the Pirates eventually used him as their batting practice catcher.

We had the time of our lives then! I got to know and sometimes hang out with people like Vince DiMaggio, Pete Coscarart, Frank Gustine, Al Lopez, Elbie Fletcher, and the others. Some of them took me under their wing. They shared their baseball stories and dugout secrets.

They really made me feel like one of the guys. Besides being the official batboy, I was the unofficial beer garden runner. Beer gardens were bars that sold beer. Players were not allowed to drink beer and kids under the age of 18 were not allowed to purchase beer, but somehow we managed to pull it off. The players would send me to the beer gardens, and the vendors would sneak me in the back, load up my backpack with beer, and send me back to the locker rooms. For this undercover job, I earned more than I made in wages. Reflecting on this experience, I think that this was the caper that turned this *batboy* to *badboy*.

Because my brother and I were both cutting classes and working weekend doubleheaders, we had to tell our father. We knew he'd be furious if we cut school. We assured him we stayed in the mornings for the academic classes and only left during electives in the afternoon. As we waited for our punishment, my father roared, "You mean you guys have been batboys for months and I didn't see any of those games?" From that day on, my father came to all the games. Sitting behind third base, he booked his numbers and sport bets, while bragging to all his customers, "See those batboys? They're my sons!"

In June 1943, the reality of the war came to our family. My Italian American dream job ended when, just 18 and not yet graduated from high school, I was drafted into the United States Army. The innocence of my youth would end on that baseball turf of Forbes Field.

With mixed emotions, I handed over my job to Carmen. Although he was happy to be Pirate batboy now, he was just as sad to see me go.

I was in the Army only a few months when I received a check for $400. The Pirates were one of the four National League teams to receive a share of the World Series. They came in fourth place, and as Vince DiMaggio had promised me, they sent me my half share of their winning money. I'll never forget how those guys kept their promise to me while they were hundreds of miles away. It really helped, given that I was so young and so far from home, to know they were thinking of me.

Many years later, I married and had children. I took my eldest daughter, Lisa, to her first Forbes Field game. We didn't realize it then, but it would also be our last Forbes Field game. When I walked into that stadium, I could vividly see my brother and me running around the field as if we owned the place. I could hear the crowds cheering, and I could see my father sitting behind third base and beaming with pride at his sons on the field at Forbes, hobnobbing with the pros!

Joe Bruno
Pittsburgh, Pennsylvania

*Excerpt from his unpublished autobiography, "Batboy to Badboy" by Joe Bruno, edited by Lisa Marie Bruno.*

---

I'm the son of Clyde "Pooch" Barnhart of the Pirates and Forbes Field. My father played in two World Series: 1925 and 1927. Having the chance to play on the same team in the same park as my dad was something else, and meeting some of the players who had played with Dad — Pie Traynor and Paul Waner — and to meet with and talk with Honus Wagner, "Mr. Pirate" himself, was quite a thrill.

Vic Barnhart
Hagerstown, Maryland

*Victor "Vic" Barnhart played shortstop and a few games at third base for the Pirates between 1944 and 1946. His father, Clyde, played his entire major league career with the Pirates (1920–1928) and was the starting left fielder on the 1925 and 1927 World Series teams.*

---

The 1925 World Series Champion Pittsburgh Pirates. Front row (left to right): Mule Haas; Eddie Moore; Bernard Culloton; Tom Sheehan; Jewel Ens, player-coach, with Bill McKechnie, Jr., mascot, seated in front of him; Glenn Wright; Kiki Cuyler; Ray Kremer; Johnny Gooch. Center row: Johnny Oldham; Earl Smith; Pie Traynor; Stuffy McInnis; Max Carey, captain; Bill McKechnie, manager; Fred Clarke, assistant manager; Carson Bigbee; Fresco Thompson; Roy Spencer; George Grantham; George Austen, trainer. Back row: Chick Fraser, scout; Bill Hinchman, scout; Jack Onslow, coach; Pooch Barnhart; Vic Aldridge; Samuel Watters, secretary; Barney Dreyfuss, president; Samuel Dreyfuss, treasurer; Johnny Rawlings; Emil Yde; Babe Adams; Johnny Morrison; Lee Meadows (Pittsburgh Pirates Baseball Club).

As a player for the Pirates, I remember the parking of the batting cage inside the park in center field, 457 feet away. The cage was in play! Forbes Field was no place for a home run hitter then. The Pirates bought the contract of Hank Greenberg in 1947.

Thank God for Greenberg Gardens!

Ralph Kiner
San Bernadino, California

*One of the two greatest home run hitters in the history of the Pirates (Willie Stargell was the other one), Ralph Kiner led the National League in homers for seven straight seasons and averaged 7.09 round trippers for every 100 at bats during his 10-year major league career, second only to Mark McGwire and Babe Ruth among retired players (as of April 1, 2005). He hit many home runs into Greenberg Gardens, which was later renamed Kiner's Korner.*

---

One season, I remember I was engaged in a "pepper game" with Bing Crosby. Made a triple play (with Billy Cox, shortstop, and Hank Greenberg, first baseman), and Clyde Klutz, catcher, threw out Jackie Robinson to me at second base, three times in a single game. I handled 14 chances in a single game at second base (7 putouts, 7 assists) and tied the record.

I had two doubles off Warren Spahn at Forbes Field. We lived four blocks apart in Buffalo, New York, before our pro careers.

A home run by Hank Greenberg in 1947 hit over the center field wall went 500 feet. In the dugout, Greenberg casually said, "I hit it on the end of the bat." Wow!

I also remember having a friendship with Frank Gustine as a teammate. He was truly an outstanding person, a fine human being.

I have some great memories of some awesome home runs by Ralph Kiner, Billy Cox as the best shortstop I ever teamed with, and, of course, the privilege of talking with Honus Wagner.

Eddie Basinski
Milwaukee, Oregon

*Known as "Bazooka" and "Fiddler," Edwin "Eddie" Basinski played shortstop and second base for Brooklyn during the 1944 and 1945 seasons, and then finished his career with Pittsburgh in 1947.*

---

It's nice to turn the clock back over 50 years and remember many happy moments. Enjoying my friendship with Art Rooney and watching the Steelers home football games — they always had tough competitive teams.

Forbes Field brings back many pleasant memories of my playing days with the Pirates, 1947–1953. Although we didn't have a great team, the Pittsburgh fans were very loyal and supportive. I enjoyed playing at Forbes Field — it was a pitcher's park, not like the bandbox fields of baseball today where all players hit home runs. I had a lot of great teammates including Rip Sewell, Kiner, Clemente, Groat, Law, Friend, Haddix, Roe, Face, Garagiola, Thomas, Del Greco, and Greenberg; some great coaches, such as Honus Wagner, Frank Gustine, Milt Stock, Sukeforth, Dixie Walker, Posedel, and Riddle; Rosey Rowswell and Bob Prince, the voices of the Pirate broadcasts; and the Pirate owners: Dreyfuss, Benswanger, McKinney, Bing Crosby, Galbreath, and Johnson.

I was at the 1960 World Series, seeing Mazeroski's game-winning home run against the Yankees and the big celebration in Pittsburgh. I witnessed lots of great Pirate moments at Forbes Field.

Pete Castiglione
Pompano Beach, Florida

*During his time with the Pirates, Peter "Pete" Castiglione was primarily a third baseman, but he also played at least one game at every other position except pitcher, catcher, and center field.*

---

My first major league start was in Forbes Field. As a matter of fact, it was my first start in professional baseball. I was pitching for the Brooklyn Dodgers at the time — 1944. I was then traded to the Pirates in 1947 in time to see Greenberg Gardens.

I was with Pittsburgh for only part of two years, but didn't pitch, as I had returned from Europe during World War II with a bad arm. I was traded to the Chicago Cubs in 1949.

Cal McLish
Edmond, Oklahoma

*Calvin Coolidge Julius Caesar Tuskahoma "Buster" or "Cal" McLish spent 15 years in the majors, compiling a 92–92 record with a 4.01 ERA. His best seasons were 1958 (16–8, 2.99) and 1959 (19–8, 3.63) when he pitched for the Cleveland Indians.*

---

Forbes Field holds a very important place in my life. If not for what happened there in the summer of 1939, I would not have memories of a wonderful 58-year marriage. In brief, this is how it happened:

I was attending a Pirate-Phillies game with my father and a girl friend. We went to see a hometown boy, Lowry by name (a left-handed pitcher), who was having a tryout with the Phillies. He and my husband-to-be (also a pitcher, by the name of Hugh Mulcahy) were sitting on the steps of the dugout. During the game, Lowry and I exchanged glances and some conversation, as we were sitting in a box near the Phillies' dugout.

Hugh asked Lowry if I was his girlfriend, and he said, no, just a friend. So, Hugh said he would like to meet me. Lowry always came to visit me when he came back to town (Beaver), and told me about Hugh. As it happened, I was attending a convention in July 1940 and staying at the Schenley Hotel, where the visiting teams stayed. I told some friends from Philadelphia about Hugh, and they arranged through Stan Baumgartner, a Phillies' sportswriter, for us to meet.

Hugh was returning from St. Louis, having been chosen for the All-Star Team that year. We met at the Syria Mosque, where the convention was being held, and I think we both knew then that we were going to see a lot more of each other. We were married in Memphis, Tennessee, on July 12, 1943, just three years and a day after we had met in Pittsburgh. Hugh was the first major league player to be drafted (into military service) on March 8, 1941.

We have two boys, six grandchildren, four great-grandchildren, and a wonderfully happy marriage that all began because I attended that game back in 1939 at Forbes Field.

Sadly, my husband passed away on October 19, 2001. In his room at the hospital where he died, there hung on the wall, at the foot of his bed, a Norman Rockwell calendar with a picture of an umpire at home plate calling the runner "safe," with the title, "Safe at Home." How very appropriate for my ballplayer-husband, for he is now safe at home.

Ruth Mulcahy
Wife of Hugh Mulcahy
Beaver, Pennsylvania

*Hugh Mulcahy spent nine seasons in the National League, but pitched only briefly for the Pirates in 1947.*

*The editors are grateful to Ruth Mulcahy for contributing her special memory of Forbes Field.*

---

I remember the high fence in right field where the stands were three levels high and the great playing field that was always maintained to high standards by the groundskeepers.

I also remember being the next player after Babe Ruth to hit a home run over the right field grandstand in the early '50s. The Pirates were playing the Boston Braves, and Bob Hall was the pitcher.

Ted Beard
Fishers, Indiana

*A 5'8" native of Woodsboro, Maryland, C. Theodore "Ted" Beard was an outfielder who played 137 games for the Pirates from 1948 until 1952.*

---

It was very nice of you to ask me about Forbes Field in Pittsburgh. I was not there very long (about 30 days). The one thing I remember most was Honus Wagner. When I was there he was a coach (mostly honorary), and he got in uniform everyday and came to the bench. Of course, he was always asked questions, and we all carried on a conversation with him. He was most pleasant and always available to us. He usually stayed until about the seventh inning, and then he would quietly leave. We were told he would visit his favorite bartenders on the way home, but he was a joy to be around. He had a great laugh. That is what I remember about Forbes Field.

Don Gutteridge
Pittsburg, Kansas

*During his 12 seasons in the major leagues, Donald "Don" Gutteridge played for the St. Louis Cardinals, St. Louis Browns, and Boston Red Sox before finishing his career with the Pirates in 1948. He later managed the Chicago White Sox in 1969 and 1970.*

---

Being on the Pirates' roster in 1948–1949 and being able to see Hall of Fame player Ralph Kiner hit 94 of his home runs was certainly an honor, and I'm proud to have been a Pirate, even for a short while. Ralph has been somewhat forgotten in the feats that he performed. There were many thrills and much participation in my short time with the Pirates.

Eddie Bockman
Millbrae, California

*J. Edward "Eddie" Bockman played for three teams during his four-year major league career, spending his last two seasons as a third baseman–second baseman with the Pirates.*

---

I have both pleasant and unpleasant memories of spacious Forbes Field. As a platooning first baseman for the New York Yankees, pennant winner and World Series champion in 1949 under the management of Casey Stengel, I was coming off the 30-game disabled list and hitting .308; we were in first place by five and a half games, and the great Joe DiMaggio was just starting to play center field again.

On August 6, 1949, I was sadly sold to the Pittsburgh Pirates. Joining the sixth-place Pirates, I was fortunate to be playing with National League home run hitter Ralph Kiner, who hit many Forbes Field home runs over Greenberg Gardens, then over the big scoreboard (365' out in left field and 40' high), and into Schenley Park's memorial.

I also remember Truett "Rip" Sewell (famous for the "eephus" or blooper pitch), ex–Yankee pitcher Ernie "Tiny" Bonham, second baseman Danny Murtaugh, and having many conversations with the great "Dutchman," Honus Wagner. Wagner was an honorary coach still in a Pirate uniform, and fond of saying, "Jack, these young boys just don't know how to play this game!"

Jack "Stretch" Phillips
Potsdam, New York

*Jack "Stretch" Phillips played first base and third base and even pitched one game (in 1950) for the Pirates between 1949 and 1952. However, his greatest moment came on July 8, 1950, when, as a pinch hitter, he belted a walk-off grand slam against Harry Brecheen to help the Bucs defeat the Cardinals, 7–6.*

What I remember about Forbes Field is:

1. Playing my first game there in center field next to Ralph Kiner and, later, playing next to Roberto Clemente.
2. Meeting and talking daily to the great Honus Wagner. What a nice man he was.

Tom Saffell
Sarasota, Florida

*During his four seasons with the Pirates (1949–1951 and 1955), Thomas "Tom" Saffell played all three outfield positions, but was primarily a center fielder.*

Being a country boy from a very small town (Meridian, Idaho), I had never been to such a big ballpark as Forbes Field. It was exciting and a very beautiful old park, with ivy on the red brick outfield wall with Schenley Park as a background. I was a bit awestruck at my first sight of this park. I'm sorry it had to be torn down, but I understand progress. However, it sure took a lot of memories and happy times from a lot of fans and players.

I just appreciate my time there and helping to build memories, not just for myself, but for the many fans that we had during the '50s and '60s. Even though they took down that beautiful old park, they can't remove the memories of games played, special players that performed there, and especially the ultimate experience of the 1960 World Series — a series that will live in our hearts forever.

Vernon Law
Provo, Utah

*Playing his entire career with the Pirates (1950–1951 and 1954–1967), Vernon "The Deacon" Law had his finest seasons in 1959 (18–9 record, 2.98 ERA); 1960, when he won the Cy Young Award (20–9, 3.08); and 1965 (17–9, 2.15).*

Forbes Field is very special to me since I played my first big league game there — all fond memories, even though our club didn't set the world on fire. How can one not have fond memories when you played where Wagner, the Waners, Pie Traynor, and all the other old-time greats played?

Back then it was a game — today it's a stage show.

George Strickland
New Orleans, Louisiana

*George "Bo" Strickland began his 10-year career with the Pirates in 1950 before being traded to Cleveland during the 1952 season. However, the move was to his advantage because he became the starting shortstop on the 1954 Cleveland team that won the American League pennant.*

My stay with Pittsburgh was very brief because I injured my arm — bursitis.

Memories include:

1. Forbes Field was the scene of my big league debut versus Cincinnati in 1951.
2. Forbes Field was very important as it was the culmination of my years of baseball and major league hopes.
3. Echoes of the past greats having played there.
4. Hoping to strike out the first batter I faced (Bobby Adams). I did so, but he reached first on a passed ball on the third strike!

Con Dempsey
Redwood City, California

*Cornelius "Con" Dempsey pitched in three games for the Pirates during the 1951 season, starting two of them.*

When I joined the Pirates in 1951, the first time seeing Forbes Field, I thought, what a great ball-park! Being a pitcher, I was doing my running in the outfield. At the end of my workout, I ran one long lap from the left field foul line to the right field foul line and back. When I got to the right field side, I noticed a bronze plaque on the right field wall, so I stopped to read it. It said only two people had ever hit home runs over the upper deck roof: One was Babe Ruth and the other was Ted Beard. I found it hard to believe anyone could hit a baseball that far. I have often wondered what happened to that bronze plaque after Forbes Field was torn down.

Bill Koski<br>Modesto, California

*William "Bill" or "T-Bone" Koski made his major league debut with the Pirates on April 28, 1951.*

---

I wish I could give you some real meaty stuff for your book, but I really wasn't there long enough to settle in. I was in the Pirates system, pitching at Charleston, South Carolina, in the Sally League, a Class A farm club of the Pirates. My contract was purchased by the Pirates in early September 1951.

I worked out a few days to let Mr. Rickey see what he bought. He called me into his office on the morning of September 18th and told me I had to sign a Pirate contract, which I understood. I had a clause in my original contract that called for 20 percent of my sale to a major league club. The contract he offered had no monies for my bonus, and if I wanted to pitch that night—and I did—I had to sign the contract he had on the table. I was a little under 23 years of age and I wanted to pitch, so I signed.

That night I pitched against the Boston Braves in Forbes Field with 8,036 fans in attendance. I won that game (my only win), 6–5, pitched into the eighth inning. So yes, Forbes Field was special to me.

Forbes Field was like a good kitchen with food cooking. It had that smell, the aromas of all the things that make a ballpark: The clubhouse with all its different senses, the trainer rubbing down a pitcher, and all the goings-on prior to the game and after the win or loss.

You can imagine pitching in a ballgame with 800, 900, or a 1,000 people in the stands, and then going out to the mound, a stadium with a capacity of 50,000 to 60,000. To say I was scared, no; nervous, yes. The short time I was there—88 days during 1951–1954—I enjoyed and met and played with some very good people.

Lenny Yochim<br>River Ridge, Louisiana

*Although Leonard "Lenny" Yochim pitched in only 12 games for the Pirates, he made his presence known in the Pirate organization as a scout and senior advisor for 37 years.*

---

In one of my early years—'53 or '54—playing for the Pirates, I was told that I had another person sharing my locker. It happened to be Honus Wagner, a coach, who was one of the greatest players ever. After two weeks, I came to the clubhouse and our locker was gone. Thinking I was being sent to the minor leagues, I went to Honus, who told me our locker had been moved. He stated his original locker had been sent to the Hall of Fame at Cooperstown. I have a picture of our locker at Cooperstown, but my name is not there with Honus Wagner's. I never even had him sign his name on a baseball card. What a big mistake!

Dick Cole<br>San Francisco, California

*During his five seasons with the Pirates (1951, 1954–1957), the versatile Richard "Dick" Cole played every infield position.*

---

My name is Frank Thomas—The Original One—and I played major league baseball from 1951 to 1966.

I have lots of memories of Forbes Field. Pittsburgh is my home and always has been. I got my first baseball from Josh Gibson from the Homestead Grays when I was 12 years old. My dream was to play in my hometown, which I did from 1951 through 1958. I came up from the minor leagues at the end of the minor league seasons in 1951 and 1952. My first full year with the Pirates was 1953, when I played center field and set a record that still stands to this day: I hit 30 home runs and drove in 102 runs in 112 games. My first major league home run was hit in New York, but my first at Forbes Field was in September 1951, off Clyde King.

My first grand slam homer was off Dave Koslo in Forbes Field in April of 1953. Mom and Dad were in the grandstands to see this. The thrill of simply putting on a major league uniform and playing in my hometown of Pittsburgh and in Forbes Field to fulfill my boyhood dream is something you cannot imagine — you have to have experienced it.

Frank Thomas
The Original One
Pittsburgh, Pennsylvania

*A three-time All-Star, Frank Thomas played eight seasons with the Pirates before spending time with the Cincinnati Reds, Chicago Cubs, Milwaukee Braves, New York Mets, Philadelphia Phillies, and Houston Astros. While in a Pittsburgh uniform, he hit 20 or more home runs six times, twice getting 30 or more, and drove in 100 or more runs twice.*

---

I am the wife of Frank Thomas, married to him almost 51 years. My dad, a sports enthusiast with two daughters, took us to every game the Pittsburgh Steelers and the Pittsburgh Pirates played at Forbes Field — bleacher seats, of course, peanuts and hotdogs, and a sunburn.

I graduated from attending Kids Day to attending Ladies Day. We didn't win many games, but I saw the greatest play. Married at 19 to a professional baseball player, it became my way of life. I still enjoy it, though it's a big business today. Forbes Field was home to Honus Wagner, Pie Traynor, the Waner brothers, and I met them all!

Dolores Thomas
Wife of The Original One
Pittsburgh, Pennsylvania

---

In August 1952, as a 20-year-old rookie going to the mound to start my first big league game, I got a real feeling for what that grand old park was: the closeness of the fans and the excitement were unbelievable. Later, as I got a chance to just go through the ballpark, it became sort of eerie thinking about the past Hall of Famers that played there. The great Pirate history still has me in awe of that place. Almost 50 years later, I'm still thankful for having had a chance to play in the great Forbes Field.

Ron Necciai
Monongahela, Pennsylvania

*Ronald "Ron" Necciai pitched in 12 games for the Pirates in 1952, starting nine of them. A minor league phenom, he once struck out 27 men in a nine-inning no-hitter, although it wasn't a perfect game: he gave up a walk and hit a batter, and his teammates committed an error and a passed ball.*

---

My greatest memory of Forbes field is meeting Honus Wagner, Pie Traynor, and Paul Waner in the clubhouse when I was a 19-year-old rookie.

Tony Bartirome
Bradenton, Florida

*A "good field, no hit" first baseman for the 1952 Pirates, Anthony "Tony" Bartirome became an outstanding trainer, serving the Bucs in this capacity from 1967 to 1985.*

---

My first time to see a major league game was when I joined the Pirates from Charleston, South Carolina. It was a fabulous experience. I couldn't believe I was on the same field with Robin Roberts, Curt Simmons, and other players of that caliber. It was a real honor.

Cal Hogue
Centerville, Ohio

*Calvin "Cal" Hogue pitched for the Pirates for three seasons (1952–1954).*

---

In 1952, the first time I was in Forbes Field, an elderly gentlemen was sitting on the bench with some of the coaches. As I walked by, one of the coaches introduced me. "This is Honus Wagner," he said. Then I got to shake the hand of the greatest player of all time.

Jim Mangan
San Jose, California

*James "Jim" Mangan was a catcher for the Pirates during the 1952 and 1954 seasons. He finished his major league career with the New York Giants in 1956.*

---

The 1960 World Series Champion Pittsburgh Pirates. Championship team poses behind Bobby Becker, batboy. Front row (left to right): Smoky Burgess; Gene Baker; Roberto Clemente; Mickey Vernon, coach; Sam Narron, coach; Danny Murtaugh, manager; Frank Oceak, coach; Bill Burwell, coach; Dick Schofield; Don Hoak; Hal Smith. Second row: Bob Rice, traveling secretary; Bob Friend; Harvey Haddix; Rocky Nelson; Vernon Law; Fred Green; Dick Stuart; Vinegar Bend Mizell; Joe Gibbon; Joe Christopher; George Sisler, hitting instructor; Danny Whelan, trainer. Back row: Tom Cheney; Dick Groat; Gino Cimoli; Bill Mazeroski; George Witt; Clem Labine; Bob Skinner; Bill Virdon; ElRoy Face; Bob Oldis (Pittsburgh Photographic Library Collection of Carnegie Library of Pittsburgh).

I grew up in Swissvale and had always been a Pirate Fan, so Forbes Field has many memories for me. In 1947, I played in the *Sun Telegraph* All-Star Game as a junior in high school and won a trip to New York City representing Pittsburgh in the Hearst All-Star Game. I hit a triple to the iron gate for two RBIs and scored the winning run.

My double in the first inning of the 1960 World Series drove in Bill Virdon — what a thrill to have that victory in your own home town.

Finally, there was Mazeroski's home run that gave the Pirates their first World Championship in 35 years. It's the greatest thrill in sports, to win a World Championship in your own home town.

I loved playing at Forbes Field and have always felt hurt to have been traded by Joe L. Brown.

Dick Groat
Pittsburgh, Pennsylvania

*A two-time All-America basketball player at Duke in 1951 and 1952 and the Helms Athletic Foundation's National Player of the Year in 1951, Richard "Dick" Groat was the starting shortstop for the Pirates for nine seasons. In 1960, he won the National League Most Valuable Player award as he helped to lead Pittsburgh to a World Series championship.*

**Pregame activities prior to one of two exhibition games between Pittsburgh and Detroit, April 1956. The expansive outfield and spacious foul territory behind home plate to the backstop were signature features of Forbes Field (Bettmann/Corbis).**

Forbes Field? I remember it was 80 feet from home plate to the back stop. My memories? First is the only time in my career I wanted to be thrown out of a game. The Dodgers were playing Pittsburgh. It was 115 degrees in the shade. Pigeon feathers were hanging in mid-air — but what air? Lindell was pitching, I was catching, and Al Barlick was umpiring. Lindell was out in the third inning. About the sixth inning, I see Big John in the stands eating a little jolly pop with a creamy top.

One inning, Barlick looked at me and said, "You forgot your bib," meaning my chest protector was missing. Well, I thought it was a good time to joke. So, a couple of pitches later, with Hodges hitting, I said, without turning around, "Does the color of the uniform make a difference on balls and strikes?" Well, Barlick had a short fuse! So he flew from behind the plate, and with the little broom, swept back and forth, and then up he came with a big swing. He hesitated, saw me grinning, and stuck the little broom in my mask and said, "You ain't going anywhere!"

Michael J. Sandlock
Old Greenwich, Connecticut

*Michael "Mike" Sandlock finished his five-year major league career by catching 64 games for the Pirates in 1953.*

I had what you call a "cup of coffee" in the majors (National League with the Pittsburgh Pirates in 1953 and 1955). I didn't have a chance to play much, because of "Bonus Babies" keeping the rosters full, and other reasons I'd rather not mention.

Do I have memories of Forbes Field? Of course. I don't remember exactly the day, but I hit my only two home runs (one in each game) of a doubleheader against the St. Louis Cardinals in 1955; it was a Sunday, maybe around May or June. That is for me a very fond memory of Forbes Field, the Pirates, and part of my baseball career of 20 years.

Felipe Montemayor, Jr.
Monterrey, Mexico

*A native of Monterrey, Mexico, Felipe "Monty" Montemayor appeared in 64 games for the Pirates during the 1953 and 1955 seasons.*

---

I remember when I first came up, they had the Greenberg Gardens. It was about 30 feet shorter in left and left center fields. After the '54 season, they removed the gardens, and it was 365 feet down the left field line and 406 in left center. Right field was only 300 feet down the lines, but there was an approximately 25-foot-high screen. Right center was 408 feet, and just left of straight away center was 457 feet. That made it a good park to pitch in, because there were no cheap homers. Also, that's one reason there weren't too many home run hitters on the Pirate teams— 30 or 35 homers was a good year for the hitters there.

ElRoy Face
North Versailles, Pennsylvania

*Known as the "Baron of the Bullpen," ElRoy Face is one of the three greatest relief pitchers in the history of the Pirates (the other two being Kent Tekulve and Dave Giusti). In 15 seasons with Pittsburgh, he saved 188 games (not counting three in the 1960 World Series), led the National League three times in saves (twice outright) and once in winning percentage, and won the The Sporting News National League Fireman of the Year award in 1962.*

---

I didn't get to spend much time in Forbes Field, but I do remember that it was the biggest field in the National League. Also, I had two hits off Don Newcombe the day I ran into the right field wall chasing a line drive off the bat of George Shuba. I didn't catch the ball that time! That game was the last that I played at Forbes Field —1954.

Gail Henley
La Verne, California

*Born in Wichita, Kansas, Gail Henley played his only major league season with the Pirates in 1954.*

---

I loved Forbes Field because of its vastness and because it was a good pitcher's park. My best memory of Forbes Field was the first game that I pitched in.

Playing against the Brooklyn Dodgers, I came in as relief with the bases loaded and nobody out. The first batter I faced was Jackie Robinson, and I struck him out on three pitches. The next batter was Gil Hodges, and I got him to hit into a double play to get out of the inning. That was one of my two fondest and best memories of Forbes Field — that and pitching and starting my first major league game there and winning.

Vernon "Jake" Thies
Florissant, Missouri

*Vernon "Jake" Thies pitched for the Pirates during the 1954 and 1955 seasons.*

---

When I came to the Pirates in 1954, it was automatic: a walk or base hit, man on first base, another hit, and the runner didn't even look at the third base coach, he would race to third base —first and third just like clockwork. But in 1955, the Pirates put a young outfielder in right field named Roberto Clemente, and for the next 17 or 18 years that stopped the first to third situation.

It was just like it was written in the wind: the first or second or third game Roberto played in right, man on first base, a base hit to right. On the second bounce, Roberto picked the ball up and cut a frozen rope about belt high all the way to third on the fly, and the runner was out by six feet. From then on, every third base coach in the league put the stop sign on whenever the runners rounded second.

In 1956, manager Bobby Bragan brought me, Laurin Pepper, in to pitch against the Cincinnati

Reds. I'll never forget that there were men on second and third and two outs. I worked the count to 3 and 2 on big Ted Kluszewski. Catcher Hank Foiles gave me five signs because it was 3 and 2, and the pitch was to be a fastball. All of a sudden, this thought came into my mind. I saw "Big Klu" hit ElRoy Face (the Pirates' great closer for years) on the thigh with a vicious line drive and knock him back about five feet. ElRoy said it came out of the white shirts on a Saturday afternoon, and he knew it was back at him, but couldn't pick the ball up. ElRoy's thigh turned black and blue, and Dr. Finegold and Dr. Jorgensen really were concerned about his leg. It hurt ElRoy so badly, I think that he was out for two games. I saw "Klu" hit another one of our pitchers, and they sent him home for the rest of the season. I had heard of a Philly pitcher that Klu had hit in the jaw, which shattered it. All of this was going through my mind as I wound up, so I ended up overthrowing the pitch, trying to get everything I could on it. It hit "Big Klu" on the head and knocked him down on the ground at home plate. Somehow, Hank caught the ball off Klu's helmet and umpire Frank Dascoli called Klu out — he said it was a foul tip off his bat. Well, you can imagine what transpired after that. Manager Freddie Hutchinson of the Reds came roaring out of the dugout and was immediately ejected from the game along with one of his coaches. Big Klu got up and told Frank that the ball had hit him in the head and, of course, Frank told him no, that it was a foul that was tipped off his bat. I heard later that Klu told Frank to get the ball and he (Frank) would find red paint on it. So Dascoli came strolling over to the Pirates dugout and asked Hank, "Hey, Foiles, where is the ball?" Hank told Frank that he had rolled it back toward the mound. Frank turned and walked back toward home plate and hollered "Play ball." Ted told me in spring training with the Pirates in 1958 that he went back to the dugout, walked downstairs, and asked manager Hutchinson who that was pitching for the Pirates. Hutchinson told him it was some pitcher from Mississippi that the Pirates got out of college. Ted said he made the remark at the time that I would probably kill someone with a wife and kids before they could get me out of the league. Ted Kluszewski was a special man and truly one of the greats of baseball. He stayed with the Pirates for only one year. He went to the White Sox in '59 and helped bat them to an American League championship. They played the Dodgers in the '59 World Series.

In 1958, during spring training with the Pirates, if you were not in the game at 1:00 P.M., you were through around 11:00 A.M. I went to class from 7:00 to 8:00 that morning, and at 11:00 I went in, undressed, got my towel, and went in for a shower. Guess who walked into the shower with me? None other than Big Klu. He looked at me and asked, "Are you getting in good shape, Pepper?" I was surprised that he knew my name. I said, "Yes, in fair shape." I looked at him and asked, "Big Klu, how about your condition?" He said it was not as easy as earlier in his career to get in playing condition, but that in another week or week and a half, he would be able to play a few innings. The Pirates were letting him get into shape at his own pace because Ted was a true superstar and they didn't want to rush him. He looked me in the eye and asked, "Pepper, do you remember the night in Pittsburgh you hit me in the head?" I told him I did, that it was a case of overthrowing and I surely hadn't wanted to hit him in the head. He told me he just hadn't seen the pitch. Klu said that when he hit the ground he was dazed, but then realized he was OK. Then later, after the "melee" was over, he asked manager Hutchinson who was pitching for the Pirates. That's the actual story as told to me by Klu.

Roberto Clemente hit a massive towering ball a little left of center field (from home plate), and manager Bobby Bragan leaped to the second step of the dugout and screamed, "Let's see you catch that one!" This number 24 [Willie Mays] for the New York Giants turned and ran, then just before he hit the batting cage in deepest center field, he stuck his glove up, and you could see the caught ball. With the ball in his glove, he swung inside the cage, holding on to the steel frame, then stepped out and threw the ball underhanded, back to the cut-off man in short center field. Manager Bragan stepped down from the second step, looked at the floor of the dugout, and muttered, "If he's not the greatest, then tell me who is?"

Hugh "Laurin" Pepper
Ocean Springs, Mississippi

*Hugh "Laurin" Pepper pitched in 44 games for the Pirates between 1954 and 1957.*

---

Many questioned the hiring of Bobby Bragan as a first-year major league manager, but after the Pirates got off to a great start, it appeared to have been a brilliant move. In his personality and style, Bragan seemed to match the young Pirates, who in mid–June of 1956 were atop the National League standings. Nobody had expected this kind of success. The Pittsburgh fans and all the players were enjoying the ride. Then-unknown players such as Clemente, Groat, Skinner, Mazeroski, Virdon,

Face, Friend, Law, myself and others began to believe they could win at the major league level. The leadership and amazing offensive production of first baseman Dale Long cultivated confidence in a young team. Long had brief appearances in 1951 with the Pirates and the St. Louis Browns, but failed to gain an identity. His lone identity was in 1955, when Branch Rickey tried to make Long a catcher. Finding a glove for him was the most difficult aspect of the idea. Long threw left-handed, and Rickey had to get Rawlings to make a special catcher's glove. He should have saved the money, as Long used it only for batting practice.

Dale earned his own claim to fame in 1956 and brought the fans and excitement back to Forbes Field. He captured the hearts of Pittsburgh baseball fans late in May, setting a major league record by hitting home runs in eight consecutive games. I vividly recall the excitement and media attention the feat created. In my three years in the majors, all with the Pirates, I won only seven games, and two of them came during Long's record-setting performance. The second of those wins occurred when Long hit a home run in his sixth consecutive game against the Phillies at Shibe Park on May 25. This moved him to within one game of the record and, for the first time in years, the media became visible in the Pirates' locker room. I picked up the victory that night in our 8–5 win, relishing the media attention Long had created. We had an afternoon game the next day, so we showered quickly. I waited on the team bus with the other players to return to the Warwick Hotel. The delay had been longer than usual when someone inquired, "What the hell are we waiting for?" Someone replied, "Long. The writers are still talking to him." Then another replied, "Let him grab a cab, let's go." I got up from my seat, walked to the door of the bus and said, "This bus ain't leaving until Dale Long gets on," then laid down in front of the bus. We all enjoyed a good laugh, and we did wait for Dale Long.

The next day, Saturday, May 26, there was an increase of photographers and writers to see if Long could tie the record. He did so with a dramatic home run. Hitless in three at bats, he belted a home run in his final at bat off knuckle-baller Ben Flowers. After that game, Long and the Pirates were the big stories in the newspapers and, for the first time, *Sports Illustrated* started following the Bucs.

The Sunday game with the Phillies was rained out, setting the stage for Dale to set the record at home in Forbes Field against the World Series champion Dodgers. With no game scheduled for Monday, the Pittsburgh and national media gave it the hype it deserved. Tuesday night May 28, the fans jammed Forbes Field. I was in the bullpen that evening and experienced an atmosphere unusual for an early season game. It was like a World Series game. Carl Erskine, the Dodgers' starter, retired Long his first time at bat. As Long stepped in for his second at bat, the crowd's anticipation and hope grew. Both were realized and the anticipation exploded into a seemingly endless standing ovation when Long hit Erskine's pitch over the screen into the right field lower deck. The ovation continued for three minutes and would have gone on longer had it not been for Jack Berger, the Pirates' publicity director, who was in the Pirate dugout. Long was not aware of the impact the record-setting home run had on the fans, but Berger was. This was a PR guy's dream! Like a wise marketing man, he knew what the fans wanted, and he gave it to them. He literally shoved Long back onto the field. Long humbly waved to the crowd as the ovation continued. It didn't end until he tipped his cap and went back into the dugout.

Branch Rickey, who was in attendance that evening, said, "I have been in major league baseball since 1913, and that is the first time I have ever seen a player called to make a curtain call." Curtain calls now are considered an accepted happening in baseball, but it took place for the first time that May 28 evening at Forbes Field. Fans who attended that game will confirm how unusual the evening and adulation were for that event.

The 1960 team was a group of experienced, mentally tough, hungry, happy, and at times crazy, but always confident, players who produced a fantasy season. The fans and media called them the "Battling Bucs." Benny Benack's Dixieland Band created a loose and fun-filled atmosphere at Forbes Field with "The Bucs Are Going All the Way," a theme song written by an advertising agency for Iron City Beer that had everyone singing. They did go all the way, winning the pennant by seven games. Their trademark, from the start of the season, was coming from behind in the late innings to miraculously win games. They felt they owned the final three innings of every game. Little did fans or players know it would continue to be their trademark through to the final inning of the seventh game of the World Series, when Bill Mazeroski hit his historic home run in the last of the ninth inning at Forbes Field to win the World Series.

The 1960 World Series was supposed to be a mismatch between the favored New York Yankees and the Pirates, and it was a mismatch if you totaled the runs scored. However, the Bucs won all the close games. I covered the Series that year for a small daytime radio station in Latrobe, Pennsylvania, in my first year of broadcasting. Prior to the Series, I interviewed Pittsburgh players asking who they thought would be the star of the Series. Groat, Face, Law, Hoak, Clemente and Virdon were mentioned the most. Haddix, whom I had played baseball with in the Army in 1952, was the only one to choose Bill Mazeroski. I asked him why and, with the wisdom of a veteran pitcher, he said, "Because they'll pitch to him."

The Series began and ended in Forbes Field, and it was as dramatic as you could get. The Bucs won the opener 6–4, but then were blown out in two straight embarrassing losses, 16–3 and 10–0. Their confidence questioned, the Bucs won the final two in Yankee Stadium with strong pitching from Law, Haddix, and Face, the ace reliever who saved all three wins. With the Pirates back in Forbes Field for the sixth and, if needed, seventh game, leading 3–2 in the series, the anticipation of winning the World Series was now a reality for Pittsburgh fans. However, for the second time Whitey Ford shut out the Bucs 12–0, and there would be a seventh game. The situation was best described by *New York Daily News* sportswriter Dick Young. His lead line was one that I will always remember: "As Mrs. Dionne said to Dr. DeFoe, 'Don't go away. There's more to come.'" (Dr. DeFoe was the doctor who had delivered the Dionne quintuplets.)

The series now came down to one final game. It was to be the most memorable baseball game ever played in Pittsburgh and perhaps in World Series history. Blowing an early 4–0 lead, the Pirates trailed 5–4 following Yogi Berra's three-run homer in the sixth off Face and appeared to have wrapped it up with two more off him in the eighth for a 7–4 lead. But, as Dick Young wrote, "There was more to come." In Pittsburgh's eighth, Gino Cimoli pinch-hit for Face and drew a walk. Then the Pirates got a break. Virdon's grounder to Tony Kubek at shortstop looked like a sure double-play ball, but it took a bad hop and hit Kubek in the throat, forcing him out of the game. With nobody out, Groat singled to drive in Cimoli. Bobby Shantz, who had pitched four scoreless innings, was replaced by Jim Coates. Bob Skinner's sacrifice moved Virdon and Groat to third and second. Rocky Nelson flied to Maris in right, with Virdon holding. With two out and a 7–5 lead, Coates would make the biggest blunder of the series. Clemente tapped a slow roller down the first base line, which should have been the final out of the inning. However, Coates was late covering first, Clemente was safe and Virdon scored to make it a 7–6 game. Hal Smith, who pinch-hit for Burgess to lead off the seventh, got what then looked like the Series-winning hit. With the count of 2–2, he hit a crowd-raising, three-run homer to left center that gave the Bucs a 9–7 lead going into the ninth. Bobby Richardson and pinch hitter Dale Long opened the Yankees' ninth with singles to put the tying run on base and chase Bob Friend, who replaced Face. Casey Stengel erred in allowing Long, then the tying run at first base, to stay in the game, but got away with it. Haddix relieved Friend and had to face Maris, Mantle, and Berra. He got Maris to foul out, but Mantle singled, scoring Richardson, to make it a 9–8 score, as Long, the tying run, went to third just ahead of the throw, with only one out.

Stengel finally realized he needed speed at third and Gil McDougald came in to pinch-run for Long. Berra then hit a line drive to Rocky Nelson, who was holding Mantle at first base. Nelson trapped the ball, tagged first, which took off the force play at second, and went to throw to second. But Mantle, who either thought the ball was caught on the fly or made one of the most intelligent running decisions in the game, slid back into first base ahead of Nelson's tag as McDougald scored the tying run. I vividly recall watching catcher Hal Smith after this play. His head and shoulders had dropped in disbelief. The game was now tied and his three-run home run was just a footnote in the box score. Haddix got Bill Skowron to bounce out to end the inning, but the fans' shock and disbelief took them out of the game.

It was eerily silent, as I recall, when Mazeroski stepped in to face Ralph Terry, the fifth New York pitcher. He threw a high fastball for ball one and came back with another high pitch, which Mazeroski hit over the head of Berra in left field near the 406 mark. "Maz" told me, "I didn't know it was out of the park until I reached second base. That's when I began celebrating, waving my hat, knowing we beat the Yankees." The crowd at Forbes Field, people working downtown and everyone in western Pennsylvania began a spontaneous, but amazingly peaceful, revelry that has become rare with such celebrations today. To this day, Pirate fans who took part in the revelry can tell you where they were and what they were doing when "Maz" hit that home run.

Only a year ago while discussing that home run, a fan told me he was driving on Smithfield Street near Kaufmann's Department Store, listening to the game on the radio when "Maz" hit the home run. He jumped out of the car, left the motor running, went into a bar across the street and joined in

**Part of the parade celebration in downtown Pittsburgh after the Pirates won the 1960 World Series, October 13, 1960. Pictured in the window are local residents Louise (Maurer) Gargis, age four, and her aunt, Adele Dugan (courtesy Louise Gargis).**

the revelry. Soon the people in the bar moved out into the street with their drinks, joining in the bigger celebration outside. Confetti was pouring from office buildings in downtown, people were driving with their lights on and honking their horns. Everyone wanted to share in the joy and excitement.

Covering the series for that small radio station, I was lucky to witness the Pirate clubhouse celebration. With the tension and pressure of the season and the World Series now relieved, the Pirates sprayed champagne all over the room as players shared hugs with each other. Bob Skinner and Bill Virdon each wisely grabbed a bottle of champagne and hid them in their lockers. When the clubhouse cleared, they sat and enjoyed the memories and the champagne. Virdon, a strong, quiet man from Missouri, had so much champagne that he made one of the weirdest requests I have ever received. He said, "Nellie, I have had too much to drink and I'm afraid if I get into the shower, I'm going to fall on my ass and get hurt. Will you take a shower with me? I want to make it to the party at the Webster Hall." I did, and he made it to the party.

A history of the Pirates from 1956 to 1975 could not be written without including the most well known person of that era. This was definitely "The Bob Prince Era." No personality dominated Pirates baseball from 1956 to 1975 more than Prince. Known as the "Voice of the Pirates" and "The Gunner," he became an enormous personality in Pittsburgh. The son of a career U.S. Army officer, he was well traveled and worldly wise at a young age. Academically, he attempted law schools at Harvard, Oklahoma, and Stanford, but with limited success. He truthfully remarked that he loved the social scene too much. Jack Henry, a Pittsburgh raconteur, had the best description of Prince's college résumé, stating, "Bob Prince's diploma has more fingerprints on it than Elizabeth Taylor's ass." Everyone will agree that his talents would have been wasted in a courtroom. He was made for radio and baseball.

Prince got his break in 1948. With the aid of a friend, Tom Johnson, then a part-owner of the

Pirates, he began doing Pirates baseball with Rosey Rowswell on WWSW-AM. In those days, all of the team's away games were recreations taken off the Western Union ticker. Rowswell, the first Pirates' broadcaster, was a whimsical personality who developed a strong following in those early days of radio. He and Prince were light-years away in age, but both were strong personalities who yearned for the spotlight. Prince often said it was a tough apprenticeship for him. He did little play-by-play and was assigned mostly to commercials and to handling the sound effects used by Rowswell. When a home run was hit, Rowswell would exclaim, "Raise the window, Aunt Minnie, here she comes." Then Prince would drop a huge metal tray that sounded like a window breaking, and Rosey would say, "Aunt Minnie didn't make it."

Prince did not merely want an identity or affection with his audience. *He needed it!* It was his essence. He gave the word "personality" an identity not familiar in those days. He wore wild, flashy sports coats and had a demeanor to match. You always knew when Bob was in the room, and there was no trouble identifying his voice or style when you tuned him in on the radio. You either loved him or hated him, but you always listened. In the press room, prior to heading to the broadcast booth, he would say in a self-deprecating way, "Gotta go. Twenty thousand listeners are getting ready to turn me off."

He had an uncanny ability to come up with nicknames or colorful and descriptive play-by-play phrases. Nicknames he gave to Pirates are still remembered by their fans: "The Tiger" (Don Hoak), "The Dog" (Bob Skinner), "Deacon" (Vern Law), "Quail" (Bill Virdon), "The Great One" (Roberto Clemente), and "Will on the Hill" (Willie Stargell) easily come to mind. Most memorable were his colorful and descriptive play-by-play phrases: "by a gnat's eyelash" (a fair or foul ball); "a Hoover" (a double play); "an alabaster blaster" (a high bouncing ball off the hard infield at Forbes Field); "a bug on the rug" (a ground ball hit on Astroturf); "We had 'em all the way" or "How sweet it is" (after a Pittsburgh win); and his memorable home run call, "You can kiss it goodbye." The one phrase that always cracked me up was what he used after a Pirates' win that ended a long losing streak. He would loudly proclaim, "We may *never* lose another game!"

During the Prince years, the Pirates had little or no budget for marketing. Prince filled that vacuum with his own wild, but effective, promotions used during Pirate broadcasts. The idea for his first one came from Danny Whelan, the superstitious team trainer. Whelan had a green rubber hot dog that he waved from the dugout to keep a Pittsburgh rally going or to stop one by an opponent. Prince constantly mentioned it on the air and began calling it the "Green Weenie." It caught on, and a sponsor was acquired for "Green Weenie" night at Forbes Field, which brought a big crowd. Fans who attended that game proudly maintain possession of their "Green Weenie," and collectors of baseball memorabilia still search for them.

**Best Major League Ballparks:** The best major league ballparks were the old parks like Wrigley, Ebbets, Crosley, Polo Grounds, Forbes Field, Sportsman's Park, and Shibe Park. All had a distinct personality and great history. I always felt honored to step onto the field in those parks.

**Best Catch I Ever Witnessed:** The best catch I ever witnessed was by Willie Mays at Forbes Field, 1956. Forbes Field was the only park I can recall where the pre-game batting practice cage was in the field of play, placed in center field, the deepest part of the field. I was sitting in the Pirate bullpen down the right field line and had a great view of this one. I can't recall who hit the ball, but it was a deep fly ball to straight-away center field. Mays turned quickly on the ball, looked over his right shoulder ready to make the catch as he neared, and then colliding with the batting cage as he suddenly realized the ball was over his left shoulder. Without skipping a beat, he instinctively threw his glove hand to the left side of his body, caught the ball, and while catching it for the out, pushed off the batting cage with his right hand.

Nelson "Nellie" King<br>
Pittsburgh, Pennsylvania

*Nicknamed "The Crane," Nelson "Nellie" King pitched for the Pirates for four seasons (1954–1957) before an injury ended his major league career. He then made a name for himself as a broadcaster and served the Pirates in that capacity from 1967 to 1975.*

*Excerpts from "The Halcyon Days of Pirate Baseball: 1956 to 1975," an unpublished manuscript, by Nelson "Nellie" King.*

---

Forbes Field is so historic, very similar to Yankee Stadium. So many great ballplayers played there — Pie Traynor, Lloyd and Paul Waner, Honus Wagner — you can go on and on. And there are the greats of today: Roberto Clemente, who I think was the greatest ball player I ever saw — as great an outfielder one would ever see, who could hit, run, field, and hit with power; Willie Stargell; as well as Bill Mazeroski, whose dramatic home run won the World Series for the Pirates at Forbes Field.

And don't forget the monument of Honus Wagner behind the left field wall, which I touched often.

Al Grunwald
Chatsworth, California
*A 6'4" native of Los Angeles, Alfred "Al" or "Stretch" Grunwald pitched for the Pirates during the 1955 season before finishing his major league career with Kansas City in 1959.*

Forbes Field was a great place to play and to see a game. The ivy on the outfield walls, the spaciousness of the field, and the closeness of the fans made it special.

Something that may be of interest is the face that the 1960 World Series ring was made from a picture of the field taken from an airplane. I put a small "x" on a spot where a hotdog vendor was located, and the ring has that small spot on it.

I have a few fond memories of Forbes Field. How about playing with such players as Clemente, Mazeroski, Virdon, Groat, Skinner, Law, Face, and Friend! Also, I can remember getting a base hit in the ninth to beat Cincinnati. I really didn't get to play that much, so that was quite a thrill.

Harding "Pete" Peterson
Palm Harbor, Florida

Roberto Clemente — The Great One — whose hitting, running, and throwing thrilled fans at Forbes Field. Photograph taken 1969 (Pittsburgh Photographic Library Collection of Carnegie Library of Pittsburgh).

*An outstanding defensive catcher on the 1950 Rutgers College World Series team and a second-team All-America selection by the American Baseball Coaches Association, Harding "Pete" Peterson played four seasons with the Pirates (1955, 1957–1959) before a broken arm suffered during his rookie season eventually led to his retirement as an active player. However, he remained with the Pirates for 26 more years, serving as a minor league manager, minor league director, scouting director, vice president of player personnel, and general manager, and helped to build Pittsburgh's 1979 World Series championship team.*

Although my presence at Forbes Field was short, it was very rich and exciting, as anybody chosen to be part of "Las Grandes Ligas" would agree. I use this expression to describe the majors, particularly for a "south of the border" youngster.

So much for the introduction. Allow me to reproduce in black and white some of the main events that I recall about the baseball park. As anybody who has ever been in a major league installation will figure out, it is a dream, a fantasy, a unique sight that embraces the mind of any human being who loves the game of baseball. Before Forbes Field, I don't recall seeing a triple-decker park with that glamour because when you hear about the big leagues and you start getting to know about baseball in the majors, you just can't imagine exactly what the feeling of being there could be. So writing about this cannot possibly describe what you really feel when you walk on the field. You wish you could record everything you are seeing in your memory to remember how it was, but that's difficult.

You walk in there, you see the park, you get to the clubhouse, you get the uniform, meet the guys, then you go to the dugout and have a look. You see the stands, the ball field, the scoreboard, then the people that work as the infield ground crew and the concession stands and sportswriters. You want to know everybody and see everything. Then the best part is when fans start coming in. There are sights and feelings that make wonderful memories for the rest of your life. I can say that what most impressed me was the distance of the fences, the huge scoreboard, and the view behind them of the University of Pittsburgh.

> Choly Naranjo
> Hialeah, Florida

*Born in Havana, Cuba, Lazaro Ramon Gonzalo "Choly" Naranjo pitched in 17 games for the Pirates during the 1956 season.*

---

I remember the great people and fans of Pittsburgh. They don't get any better.

> Hank Foiles
> Virginia Beach, Virginia

*A journeyman catcher, Henry "Hank" Foiles played for the Pirates between 1956 and 1959 and was their lone representative on the 1957 National League All-Star team.*

---

My most vivid memory of Forbes Field is Mazeroski's home run ball sailing over the 406 sign as Yogi Berra stood and watched at the base of the wall.

The outfield was so spacious that, as an outfielder there for 10 years, I was never concerned about running into the walls. To give you an example, our everyday batting cage was placed in left center next to the light tower, and no one knew it was there. In over 10 years of play, I only remember it coming into play seven or eight times.

I also saw the longest home run of my career at Forbes. It was hit by Mantle over the center field fence, which was 460 feet away, and it was 75 feet over my head and not coming down. It had to travel well over 650 feet. This was during the 1960 World Series.

> Bill Virdon
> Springfield, Missouri

*The National League Rookie of the Year while playing for St. Louis in 1955, William "Bill" or "The Quail" Virdon was an outstanding defensive center fielder for the Pirates from 1956 to 1965. He also played briefly for Pittsburgh in 1968 before embarking on a managerial career that saw him win 995 games in 13 seasons with four teams and division championships with Pittsburgh in 1972 and Houston in 1980.*

---

Being an infielder, I felt that Forbes Field had the worst infield in the major leagues. Opposing infielders would not take ground balls before the game. But I got used to it and eventually almost liked it. I have a lot of good memories at Forbes Field, especially October 13, 1960.

> Bill Mazeroski
> Greensburg, Pennsylvania
> *Arguably the greatest defensive second baseman in the history of the major leagues, and perhaps the greatest defensive player at any position to ever play the game of baseball, William "Bill" or "Maz" Mazeroski is best remembered for his famous walk-off home run that won the 1960 World Series for the Pirates.*

**Students celebrate Mazeroski's home run from atop the Cathedral of Learning, October 13, 1960 (George Silk, Getty Images).**

Of the things that I remember, I have four that come to mind: first, the short right field line that Clemente played better than anybody in the game; second, the ivy on the walls; third, how large that stadium really was; and fourth, how the home team always had to find ways to park their cars! Those were the good old days!

> RC Stevens
> Quad Cities, Illinois

*A native of Moultrie, Georgia, RC (his first name) Stevens was a first baseman for the Pirates from 1958 to 1960.*

---

As a player, I remember the players I played with on the 1960 Pirates, for many are still friends today. I remember the fans at Forbes Field, the ushers, the grounds crew, people who hung around the clubhouse, and the dry cleaners, among many things. People who could only make the ballpark what it was, and always will be.

Forbes Field and Pittsburgh will always be special in my heart.

Dick Schofield
Springfield, Illinois

*Nicknamed "Ducky," John Richard "Dick" Schofield was a good fielding shortstop who played 19 seasons in the major leagues, eight with Pittsburgh (1958–1965). However, he is best known for two things: first, for substituting for the injured Dick Groat during a three-week period in 1960, a period in which Schofield not only "held the fort" until Groat could return, but also hit a torrid .403 to keep the Pirates on track to win the National League pennant and the World Series, and second, for being the father of Richard "Dick" Schofield, a good fielding shortstop who played for four teams, though mostly the California Angels, between 1983 and 1996.*

---

I have some special memories of old Forbes Field. One is of Bill Virdon putting spikes in the vines on the wall and climbing to catch the ball. Another is of Roberto Clemente catching a ball over his head and running into the concrete right field wall. He had to have stitches taken in his chin — a big gash.

I also remember in the World Series watching the beautiful, bad hop hit Yankee shortstop Tony Kubek in the throat in the eighth inning to keep the inning going so Hal Smith could hit a three-run homer to put us up.

In addition, I was watching Maz's ninth-inning winning home run in the seventh game go over the wall and came running in from the bullpen to greet him at home plate.

Bob Oldis
Iowa City, Iowa

*Robert "Bob" Oldis was a catcher with the Pirates during the 1960 and 1961 seasons.*

---

I never played in the National League, but I knew about the players in the league. The Tigers and I lost a great player to the Pirates: Hank Greenberg. He was a true friend of mine and an outstanding baseball player.

After I finished my major league career with the Yankees in 1958 as World Series champions, I got out of baseball in 1959. Then, in June 1960, I called Danny Murtaugh about being a coach and batting practice pitcher for the Pirates. I knew Danny from my minor league days. He gave the message to Joe Brown, the general manager, who called me and said what he would pay me. I agreed and joined the Pirates the first of July 1960. They also won the World Series, and I got two World Series rings in three years. I was with the Pirates from 1960 through 1963, and I loved it. The fans and the city of Pittsburgh are the greatest.

Virgil Trucks
Calera, Alabama

*A highly successful pitcher for the Detroit Tigers, Virgil "Fire" Trucks pitched two no-hitters in 1952 and twice led the American League in shutouts.*

---

While two stadiums in Pittsburgh have replaced Forbes Field, none have, nor ever will, replace the majesty of the grand old ballpark. It lacked the modern-day trends, but it had a soul created by countless years of use.

While big and old and in need of repair, it touched the core of the players and the fans as well. Gone now, it remains in the memories of those of us who played or watched the games, and its name brings a smile to the face of most of us. It was truly "one of a kind."

Tom Butters
Durham, North Carolina

*Thomas "Tom" Butters was a pitcher with the Pirates between 1962 and 1965.*

---

I have a special feeling in my heart for "Old Forbes Field." Not only was it my first home field in the major leagues, but also there's the history of that great old place, the knowledge of those who had preceded me there.

Having had the honor of meeting Pie Traynor, playing for Danny Murtaugh, and having teammates such as Maz, Virdon, Smoky, Willie, Roberto, Ducky, Vernon Law, Bob Friend, Harvey Haddix, Johnny Logan, Jerry Lynch, Al McBean, Manny Mota, Earl Francis, Don Cardwell, Ted Savage, Joe Gibbon, Jim Pagliaroni, Don Schwall, Bob Bailey, Frank Oceak, Sam Narron, Don Osborn, Ron Northey, and Tommie Sisk made for great memories!

The Pirates and Forbes Field are very special to me.

Ron Brand
Mesa, Arizona

*Ronald "Ron" Brand, a catcher who played at least one game at every other position except pitcher and first base, made his major league debut with the Pirates on May 26, 1963. However, most of his big league career was spent with Houston (1965–1968) and Montreal (1969–1971).*

---

I remember Forbes Field as being a neighborhood ballpark. The players and their families had very limited parking space. In fact, an attendant would take the cars and pack them in a very small area across the street from the park.

There was a very interesting policeman who "performed" while directing traffic. He was a sight to behold with all his animations, and the children loved to watch him.

Bob Veale, a pitcher, would go to the park early and shoot huge rats that resided under the stands. Billy O'Dell and I shot pigeons, as there was an overpopulation of those birds. They made a real mess!

Our older son, Gary, always wanted to eat a hot dog at the game, and he would invariably become sick on the way home.

Quite often after games, we especially enjoyed dining at the Park Schenley Hotel, which was quite elegant at the time. The food was delicious, and they especially catered to the ballplayers.

Don Cardwell
Clemmons, North Carolina

*Donald "Don" Cardwell pitched in the National League for 14 seasons, winning 102 games with a 3.92 ERA. He played for the Pirates between 1963 and 1966, having his best season in 1965 when he went 13–10 with a 3.18 ERA.*

---

I was a coach for the Pirates during the 1965–1967 seasons, and watching Roberto Clemente perform during the period was quite a thrill. He did things that you don't see every day.

One game stands out in my mind more than others. As you know, the Pirates' bullpen was located in the right field corner and was recessed back in such a way that you had to look over the fans who were sitting behind the first base side in order to see home plate. We were playing the St. Louis Cardinals, and Lou Brock, one of the fastest players in the game, was on third base with one out. The batter hit a high pop foul down the right field line in the direction of the bullpen, and Roberto, coming full speed, caught the ball and in one quick counterclockwise turn threw the ball *over* the heads of the fans and got Lou Brock, who was tagging up, at the plate for a double play.

Hal Smith
Ft. Smith, Arkansas

*Harold Raymond "Hal" Smith, not to be confused with another catcher with the similar name of Harold Wayne "Hal" Smith who also played for the Pirates, spent the overwhelming majority of his major league career with the St. Louis Cardinals, during which time he was twice selected for the All-Star team. However, he caught four games for Pittsburgh in 1965, in addition to serving as a coach for three seasons.*

---

One of my favorite stories in my major league career happened in Forbes Field. I had just been called up to the Pirates in September of 1968. My first appearance was facing Hank Aaron with the bases loaded and nobody out. He hit my first pitch over the clock on top of the scoreboard in left field. Our shortstop, Gene Alley, came in to the mound and said, "You sure got out of that jam in a hurry!" He laughed and then ran back to his position.

Bruce Dal Canton
Carnegie, Pennsylvania

*Nicknamed "The Burgettstown School Teacher" by Bob Prince because he taught biology and general science at Burgettstown High School, John Bruce Dal Canton pitched for the Pirates for four seasons (1967–1970) before playing for Kansas City, Atlanta, and the Chicago White Sox. While with Pittsburgh, he had a 20–8 record and went 7–0 between June 29, 1969, and July 20, 1970; while with Kansas City, he set a club record (which was later broken) by retiring 23 consecutive batters on August 14, 1972.*

---

If not the fondest, certainly one of my most unusual, experiences at Forbes Field was shooting pigeons inside the ballpark with one of my coaches, Don Leppert. A tremendous number of pigeons would roost in the rafters in the grandstands, causing much discomfort for the fans.

My son, the bat boys, and several other coaches' boys would throw rocks into the rafters to dislodge the birds. The boys would then race to mark fallen birds for removal. Never would I have imagined the extent of a manager's duties in the major leagues in 1968. Can you imagine firing a shotgun in any stadium today?

Larry Shepard
Lincoln, Nebraska

*Lawrence "Larry" Shepard won a total of 164 games as the Pirate manager during the 1968 and 1969 seasons.*

---

I remember flying to Pittsburgh the day after graduation, June 1962, and arriving in Joe Brown's box in Forbes Field just in time to see Bob Skinner hit a home run on the roof in right field. What a thrill!

The followings days, after working out with the club, I proceeded to "The Box" and was impressed even more. After seeing Koufax and Drysdale pitch and Willie Davis beat out a two-hopper to Mazeroski, I almost asked Joe Brown, "Do you want the money back?" for I had seen in a matter of seven days the longest ball I had ever seen hit, the fastest pitcher I had ever seen throw a ball, and the fastest runner I had ever seen run, all in a ballpark with intimidatingly long dimensions in the outfield. Forbes Field, the first major league ballpark I had ever seen, to this day remains my favorite.

Carl C. Taylor
Sarasota, Florida

*The stepbrother of slugger Boog Powell, Carl Taylor spent the 1968 and 1969 seasons as well as a few games in 1971 with the Pirates, having his best year in 1969, when he hit .348 in 221 at bats. Primarily a catcher-outfielder, he also played first base and third base.*

---

Playing with Roberto Clemente, Bill Maz, and Stargell was something that I'll never forget.

Orlando Peña
Hialeah, Florida

*Orlando Peña won 56 games and saved 40 during a 14-year major league career (spanning the period 1958–1975), but he pitched for the Pirates only during the 1970 season.*

---

I remember sitting in McDonald's having a cup of coffee about a block from the park and watching people going to the park and how excited they were. I was pitching the second game so I was in no hurry to get there because I didn't want to get too excited so early.

We won the first game 3–2, and when I came out to warm up, there was electricity in the air. The first three hitters got hits to start the game, and it was 1–0 with runners on first and third. Jim Hickman was the cleanup hitter, and the count went to 3–2 before he hit into a unique double play. He hit a ground ball to Hebner at third, who threw to Maz at second, who threw to home to get the runner at the plate. I then got the next hitter to pop out, and the crowd went nuts.

I settled down and didn't give up another run, winning 4–1. After the game, the fans stormed the field and took everything, grass, bases, numbers off the scoreboard — I even saw some old ladies with parts of chairs. It was a real scene.

Jim Nelson
Sacramento, California

*James "Jim" Nelson spent his entire major league career with the Pirates, pitching for them during the 1970 and 1971 seasons. He was the starting pitcher and earned the victory in the last game played at Forbes Field on June 28, 1970.*

---

## The Fans

I was privileged as a teenager to witness the 1924 Pirates play the New York Giants at Forbes Field. I recall most vividly the pregame practice of the Pirate infield. I remember Pie Traynor at third base, Glenn Wright at shortstop, Rabbit Maranville at second base, and Charley Grimm at first base. They fielded ground balls, zipping them to all the bases with amazing speed and skill. Grimm took all throws with his gloved hand. Many fans agreed the warm-up drill alone was well worth the price of admission.

Gilbert B. Rutter
Youngwood, Pennsylvania

---

Being born two blocks from Forbes Field on Boquet 79 years ago, I attended many games at Forbes Field. Saturday was Knot Hole Day, when kids watched the game in the bleachers.

My dad had two tailor shops on Boquet Street, and at one time, made suits for the ballplayers and had a valet service at the Schenley Hotel, where many of the ballplayers stayed.

I was four years old when the 1927 World Series was played, and the Yankees beat the Pirates four games in a row. I remember the Greenberg Gardens. One of my favorite players was Ralph Kiner. The fans went to the stadium just to watch him hit a home run. It was a fascinating era in which to grow up in nearby Oakland.

James Moneck
Bradenton, Florida

---

My first game was in 1932 at age 12, Pittsburgh versus St. Louis, with Steve Swetonic versus Bill Hallahan. It happened to be Opening Day. Some of the Pirate players were Paul and Lloyd Waner, Pie Traynor, and Larry French; some of the Cardinals were Ducky Medwick, who always led the league in doubles, Dizzy Dean, Jess Haines, Pepper Martin, and Jim Bottomley. It cost 50 cents to get in to see the game.

Another highlight was when Leo Durocher, who was an announcer for NBC, came down from the booth toward our box seat and my neighbor bet me he would get his autograph. Durocher gladly obliged.

My wife, Mary, and I went to see the 1960 Series with the Yankees on the day the Yankees won 12–0. Mickey Mantle hit from the right side in this game, and he lined one over the right center field fence to the right of the iron gate. It was rising when it cleared the fence. I never in my life saw a ball hit harder or farther. The measurement on the left center wall was 436 feet, and the iron gate was 457 feet. Can you imagine playing in a field that large now? No cheap home run there.

I saw Babe Ruth, playing in his last year, and possibly his last game, hit one over the right field roof. Willie Stargell did it a number of times since. I remember Greenberg Gardens. They brought the fence in about 30 feet or so in left field to accommodate Hank Greenberg who came over from Detroit to tutor Kiner and be his home-run-hitting partner. But it cheapened the beauty of the field as well as the sport, and was abandoned after Kiner was traded to the Cubs.

Speaking of Kiner, it's true that the fans stayed till he batted last, and then the field emptied quickly. He and Dick Stuart hit some of the longest home runs over the left field wall.

I had some great moments at Forbes Field watching the Steelers play. Bob Waterfield, Crazy Legs Hirsch, Tank Younger, Deacon Dan Towler, and the rest of the Los Angeles Rams came into Pittsburgh on a Saturday night and trounced the Steelers by over 50 points. And I remember when the Steelers' Bill Dudley, out of the University of Virginia, kicked the extra points and field goals, returned punts, and played defense. I will never forget how on punt returns he would field the punt and remain motionless until the opponents were right on top of him. Then he would zigzag and speed up the field for long gains. I also remember the Cleveland Browns before Jimmy Brown. They had a huge 255-pound fullback named Marion Motley, and he killed the Steelers. They also had a punter, Horace Gillom, who stood around 18 yards from the center and kicked the ball 50, 60, 70 yards, and sky high, giving his team plenty of time to cover the kick.

I remember Charlie Conerly, the New York Giants quarterback, breaking single-game passing records against the Steelers with some 50-plus completions. I also remember the game against the Chicago Cardinals, who had Elmer Angsman and Charlie Trippi as running backs. On the first play after the kickoff, Christman, the quarterback, threw a pass to Trippi for a touchdown of 80 yards.

"Greenberg Gardens"— later renamed "Kiner's Korner"— as seen from the left field bleachers (Pittsburgh Photographic Library Collection of Carnegie Library of Pittsburgh).

I had season tickets for many years and got to see some great players: Mike Basrak, Chuck Cherundolo, Ernie Stautner, Fran Rogel, Elbie Nickel, Joe Geri, Lynn Chandnois, Whizzer White, Bobby Layne, and John Henry Johnson.

William Gasper
Youngwood, Pennsylvania

---

Between 1930 and 1936 there was a box in the ground between the Pirates' dugout and home plate where they stored baseballs for the umpire. The ump would lift the lid on this box and take as many baseballs as he needed. At the end of the inning, the bat boy would fill the box again.

Before public address systems, a man with a megaphone would walk up and down the first and third base line and announce to the crowd the battery of the game. When I was 10 or 11, in the early 1930s, I saw the Pirates play the Chicago Cubs. I was on my feet and screaming at every fly ball, grounder, and pop-up. I had laryngitis for a week.

William Fischer
Allison Park, Pennsylvania

---

When I was seven or eight years old (1934 or 1935), my brothers and I used to go to Forbes Field for free. The *Pittsburgh Press* had a section where they would let us in free two or three times a year. It was a big day for us.

Charles E. Cleaver
One of the Old Knot Hole Gang
Pittsburgh, Pennsylvania

My fondest memories of Forbes Field come from going to a Pirate-Cardinal game in the mid-1930s. I got to see all my Pirate favorites: Lloyd Waner, Woody Jensen, Paul Waner (my number one favorite), Arky Vaughan (a very underrated player), Gus Suhr, and Pep Young. But the most memorable moment was when Dizzy Dean approached the left field bleachers where I was sitting, pointed to his arm, and said loud enough for the fans to hear: "My arm and Medwick's bat will win this game."

And I believe they did!

> The late Joseph Louisa
> as told to Angelo Louisa
> Bridgeville, Pennsylvania

---

I have a memorable experience that happened at Forbes Field, one that I'll never forget. A few friends and I attended a police circus show there one very warm evening, and it was a very good show and very entertaining.

About halfway through, a big thunderstorm broke out over the field. Lightning and very loud thunder crashed all around us. Many spectators were really afraid, and a good many were on their knees praying.

The storm finally broke to the relief of everyone including myself. With all that metal around us, we were fortunate that none of us were hit.

In 1935, I was a newspaper boy, and if we got three new subscriptions, the Pittsburgh paper would take us to a Pirates game and give us lunch. Well, I got the customers and went to the game. The Pirates were playing the Boston Braves. Babe Ruth played for them. Before the game, I was standing outside, and I looked up the street and here comes the Babe walking toward me. I didn't make a move, and when I realized who it was, he was completely surrounded by a mob of kids.

In that game, which was his last, he hit three home runs and a single, and he ran to the dugout. I know many people who claimed to be there, but weren't. I can truthfully say, "I was there."

Years later, I went to a night game with my oldest boy, when he was about six years old. We had good seats on the second tier near third base. I used to go to many games hoping to be able to come away with a ball, but no such luck. On that night, Smoky Burgess, the catcher and my son's favorite player because of his name, hit a soft pop foul right directly to me. I reached out, caught it with my bare hands, and handed it to my son, Jim. This had to be about 1960, and we still have the ball.

> Louis Uriah
> Bridgeville, Pennsylvania

---

My memories are when I was a young girl. I went to Ladies Day on a Thursday and got in for 10 cents.

We would get dressed up with white gloves and hats.

> Madeline Vaughn
> Pittsburgh, Pennsylvania

---

I graduated from high school in January 1939. I attended games at Forbes Field from 1939 to 1941. During the three summers, I saw quite a few games.

Most memorable were the "Ladies Day Games." Every Thursday afternoon, if the game was scheduled for Forbes Field, it was Ladies Day. The left field bleachers were reserved for the ladies. There was a gate in the left field fence. Outside the gate, they set up a ticket booth. We would pay tax only to get in. It came to 10 cents. You would not believe the following the Pirates had. The stands in left field were always sold out.

Paul and Lloyd Waner played in the outfield, one in right field, the other in center field. During warm-up sessions, they always talked and joked with the ladies. At the end of the warm-up session, they always threw a baseball into the stands. I was lucky to catch one. At the time I was 17, and never gave a thought to keeping the ball. I really don't know what happened to it. My sister and I have many memories of the times we were at Forbes Field.

> Irene Pividore Louisa
> Logan, Ohio

All through my high school years, I worked at the concession stands in Forbes Field, most of the time along the third base line. Hot dogs were 15 cents each, and we poured soda pop rather than giving the bottle to the buyer. We were paid $2.75 for a single game, and $3.25 for a doubleheader.

I remember Billy Conn and his friends coming over to the concession stand to make their bets. They would bet on anything—if someone might steal home or third base—you name it.

I also remember the broadcasters. There was Rosey Rowswell who always said, "Open the window Aunt Minnie," and then he'd break a piece of glass, and Bob Prince, who followed and was our broadcaster for many years.

Loretta Harris
Pittsburgh, Pennsylvania

I remember going to Forbes Field in the 1940s where my dad was a ticket-taker in the left field bleachers. On one occasion during batting practice, Jim Russell hit a drive to left field that came through the wire fence and hit me right in the bread basket, knocking the wind out of me. When I recovered, I was surprised to see him standing over me and asking if I was all right. He gave me a new baseball and the bat he hit with and told the vendors to let me have anything I wanted to eat. Dad cut the bat down so I could use it, and I often wish I had kept it. Dad was a former big league player, and, oh, how I wish we could play catch again.

Otto S. Jordan
Blairsville, Georgia

As a nine- or 10-year-old boy, I attended a "War Show" at Forbes Field in 1943–1944. It was at night, and I remember tanks and guns and lots of explosions. I remember chunks of the field mud flying up and landing on me. There were flashes, explosions, and gun smoke everywhere. I know it was staged by the Army, and I guess it was to give the civilians a sense of what it was like for the soldiers fighting in Europe and the Pacific. Maybe it was a bond rally where they sold war bonds. It was like the Fourth of July, but way better for a 10-year-old boy! I later went there to watch Ralph Kiner, Bob Friend, Vernon Law, and Roberto Clemente. I also saw the Pittsburgh Steelers play the Minnesota Vikings there in an NFL game in the Vikings' second season. It's a place that I'll never forget.

Jim Coudriet
Riverview, Florida

I have many happy memories of Forbes Field. I attended many baseball games, Steeler football games, and circuses there. My cousin and I had season tickets to the Steelers.

I remember one game the Steelers played against the Philadelphia Eagles. I looked across the field and noticed one of the Eagles standing there with his jersey sleeves pushed up above his elbows, and with his hands on his hips. I said to my cousin, "There is only one person in the whole world that stands like that!" Indeed it was my old friend from St. Vincent College, Bap Manzini. We waved like mad and caught his attention, and he walked over to where we were sitting. Many were the games I saw him play at Bearcat Stadium, while I was a student at Seton Hill.

Mary W. McBride
Pittsburgh, Pennsylvania

In the mid-to-late 1940s, I spent entire summers at Forbes Field. I lived at Centre and Craig, about a 15-minute walk away, and when there was a Pirate day game, my pals and I headed to Forbes Field.

We never used tickets, yet we always got in. When all else failed, one of us would distract the cop outside the right field gate while about 10 of us would leap up onto the metal slats going up the side of the stands. We'd tuck our tennis shoes behind the metal strap, hold the slats and climb to the top. The easiest dismount spot was on the third tier because you didn't have to reach so far to grab the rail. To someone on the ground, we looked like a colony of ants crawling into the game.

Once there, we saw Kiner, Gustine, Billy Cox, Fritz Ostermuller and the rest. Today, I can't believe we did that. But we did—every home daytime game, for the best summers of my life.

George Morin
New York, New York

My fondest memory was going to Saturday games with about 8 to 10 other kids. If you were under 12, you could sit in the right field lower-deck stands for free. This was from 1946 through 1948. No kids ever left until Ralph Kiner had his final at bat. It was a long trip by streetcar from Manchester, but it was worth it.

Herb McFarland
Brentwood, California

---

I am now 67, but I still can remember those wonderful days and nights spent at Forbes Field as I was growing up. I just wish my children could experience baseball and the sounds and smells of old Forbes Field to get an idea of what real baseball and fan support was, even when the team finished last every year.

Memories, yes, there was Jackie Robinson's first trip to Pittsburgh, Bob Friend and Robin Roberts pitching shutout baseball into extra innings, and me and my bride sitting at the top of the right field stands on a hot summer night. And, oh yes, the only MVP in a World Series from a losing team, Bobby Richardson, lives across town from me, and every time I see him he mentions that fateful October afternoon when they lost the Series while playing at Forbes Field.

Dick Brookes
Sumter, South Carolina

---

I attended my first game in May 1947, as an eight-year-old fan. We lived in central Pennsylvania, and back then, it was an all-day trip to a Pirate game. It rained all the way to Pittsburgh. When we got to Forbes Field, they were using buckets to get rid of the water, but the game was played in its entirety.

I have been to many games since 1947 and have seen only one one-hitter. It was by Bubba Church (Phils), with Ralph Kiner, my favorite player, hitting a homer in the seventh over the scoreboard. It may have been in 1950 or 1951.

On June 2, 1968, while sitting in the left field bleachers with my seven-year-old son, I saw Clemente hit the hardest shot I ever saw, sending the ball between the scoreboard and the left field foul pole.

Jim Kearney
Pittsburgh, Pennsylvania

---

I worked at a hot dog stand, and Wally Westlake passed by every game. He would say, "How are you ladies today?"

When they traded him, we all cried.

Also, if you had a seat behind the girders, you would have to stretch your neck to see. I used to see Ralph Kiner pass by. I thought some day he'd be a great player.

We were paid 50 cents a game then and 75 cents for a doubleheader. In those days, 50 cents was a lot.

Joyce Miller
Pittsburgh, Pennsylvania

---

When I think of Forbes Field, I recall the antics of the pitchers. I loved to watch the man on the mound. One of my favorites was Rip Sewell. His blooper ball — an overhand and slow-moving pitch that looked like something a girl would throw — was greeted with cheers and laughter from the Pirate fans and disgust from the man at the plate.

Then there was Fritz Ostermuller, with what the sportswriters called the "windmill windup." To me, it looked more like the exercise where a person bends from the waist, after stretching his arms overhead, and tries to touch his toes. He did this several times before releasing the ball. In retrospect, I wonder how many bases were stolen while he went through this ritual.

I remember Ralph Kiner's attempt to break Ruth's record. There were people who didn't want the record to be broken. Consequently, a lot of pitchers did not pitch to him.

Hank Greenberg was a big guy, who impressed the fans by swinging three bats at one time to warm up before stepping up to the plate. Of course, he was expected to hit one out to Greenberg Gardens in left field.

Roberto Clemente's strong arm, spectacular catches in right field, and power at the plate made him a formidable player at any time.

Danny Murtaugh's ever-present wad of tobacco in his cheek and constant chatter on the field made him an unforgettable second baseman.

I saw Honus Wagner from afar when he was one of the coaches. You couldn't mistake him for someone else — his legs were, among other things, a distinguishing factor.

Anna M. Louisa
Bridgeville, Pennsylvania

Sometime in the late 1940s, when I was living in the Cleveland area, three of us drove to Pittsburgh where I saw the only game I was ever to see in Forbes Field. (Eventually, I saw games in all the parks then in existence except the Polo Grounds.) We neglected to take into account an hour time difference between Cleveland and Pittsburgh and arrived late, only to learn that one of the pitchers, I don't remember for which team, had hit a home run with the bases loaded. I had never witnessed a grand slam and was greatly disappointed by missing it.

I loved that quirky field. As I recall, the Greenberg Gardens were there in left field and the batting cage was on the field in center, so far away from home plate that it was unlikely to interfere with play. I noticed the vast distance between home plate and the foul screen, and scrutinized the grandstand roof in fair territory where the Babe had his last home run.

Robert Boynton
Del Mar, California

I remember Frank Howard's home run that went over the left field scoreboard and almost hit Joe Tucker (a sportscaster) in the parking lot. I also remember the game where Ralph Kiner hit three home runs. The first one went into Greenberg Gardens. His loyal fans in the bleachers booed him. "That should only be an out," they cried. The second homer hit the scoreboard. "That should only be a double," they yelled. Finally, the third one went over the clock. "That's the way to hit 'em," they yelled. Kiner looked up and shook his head. The fans loved the guy.

Edward J. Novak
Pittsburgh, Pennsylvania

The year was 1948, and the place was a rented room, a couple blocks from Forbes Field. A fellow Pitt student and I learned quickly that the greatest obstacle to a formal education that stood between us in our room on Atwood Street and the Cathedral of Learning was Forbes Field.

On those steaming hot summer evenings without air conditioning, our only hope for a breath of air was by throwing our windows wide open in preparation for hitting the books.

Then would come the roar of the crowd — it was pre-game batting practice. A couple more roars and we would look at each other, mutter "what the hell" to ourselves, and head for Forbes Field. We both survived and got our degrees, but it was in spite of the nearness of that greatest of ballparks.

Alex G. Corey
Weeki-Wachee, Florida

I remember fondly attending games at Forbes Field with my uncle, who took me to Sunday doubleheaders in the late 1940s. You could almost count on Ralph Kiner to hit at least one home run, and that is what almost everyone wanted to see. I remember a game in which Elmer Riddle was pitching and the score was tied going into the ninth inning. To everyone's disappointment, Kiner was not in the opening lineup due to having a fever, as reported by the press. However, in the bottom of the ninth, he stepped to the plate as a pinch hitter. My uncle and I always sat in the right field stands to have a clear vision of the scoreboard and the outfield. As Kiner came to bat, there was a tremendous cheer. There must have been a lot of pressure on him, but he did not disappoint the fans. I can still remember the sound of his bat hitting the ball and the ball going on the straight line over the clock atop the scoreboard to win the game. It still brings a lump in my throat as I think about it.

P. Kendall Rankin
Jefferson Hills, Pennsylvania

My widowed mother, my uncle, and I lived on Greendale Avenue in Edgewood during the late 1940s. At least twice a month during baseball season, my uncle and I would hop the #67 Swissvale, Rankin, and Braddock streetcar to watch a Pittsburgh Pirate Sunday doubleheader at Forbes Field. A framed colored picture of the old red #67 streetcar downloaded from the Web hangs in my office.

My mother would pack us each a lunch because we were in the stands from the first pitch of the day to the last pitch of the day (unless the Pirates were losing badly in the second game). We watched many a Ralph Kiner home run ball go over the left field fence before and after the famous seventh inning stretch.

As an addition to my previous recollections, I will never forget Rosey Rowswell, the voice of the Pittsburgh Pirates, with his famous beginning greeting: "Thanks a lot, Bob [Prince], and a cheery hello to you baseball fans of the air. This is Rosey Rowswell..."

R. L. Heinrichs
Austin, Texas

___

When I was a little girl, my father often took me to Pirate games at Forbes Field. That explains my love of baseball.

As a member of my school's safety patrol, I was treated to a Pirate game as a fifth grader, approximately 1948–1949. In trying to get Ralph Kiner's autograph, I became separated from my group and ended up in an Oakland police station. In the meantime, the man who had driven the other safeties and me to the game (the father of one of the girlfriends), left without me and, hard as it is to believe, didn't even call my parents. My dad received a call from the police and drove to the police station to get me. It was an unforgettable game — and experience — for me.

Lois J. Gasper
Yardley, Pennsylvania

___

My favorite memory of Forbes Field was my very first game. It was the opening game of the 1949 season. How proud I was to sit there with my favorite uncle. Those were the greatest hot dogs I had ever eaten. The Reds were the opposition. Here was the batting order for Pittsburgh: S. Rojek, SS; D. Murtaugh, 2B; D. Walker, RF; Kiner, LF; W. Westlake, CF; E. Bockman, 3B; E. Stevens, 1B; C. McCullough, C; and B. Chesnes, P. The Pirates won 5–4 and Ralph Kiner hit a grand slam off starter Howie Fox in the third inning. I will never forget this first game. I have continued to root for the Bucs ever since.

I have many fond memories of Forbes Field from my first game to the Maz's home run. One of my favorites was listening to Rosey Rowswell telling Aunt Minnie to "raise the window," but the Knot Hole games were also special.

By mid-summer, my aunt, whom I spent a great deal of time with, would drop me off to get some peace. I loved watching batting practice, and especially watching Ralph Kiner put ball after ball over the wall. Nothing was better than a Sunday doubleheader. I just loved being at Forbes Field, to smell the hot dogs and peanuts. In later years, when I would return to Pittsburgh for a visit, this always included a trip to Forbes and watching Roberto Clemente swinging out of his cap or throwing a bullet to nail an advancing base runner.

James Meyers
Florissant, Missouri

___

My wife and I worked as vendors at Forbes Field. My wife worked the bleachers, and I worked all through the stands.

We started on a Sunday morning at 9:30, and finished after the game was over and all the cushions were picked up.

The best day we ever had was a Sunday doubleheader with the St. Louis Cardinals. We started at 9:00 in the morning and finished at 8:30 at night for a combined total of $38.00 — and that was tops.

Adam Picciafoco
Pittsburgh, Pennsylvania

___

I can recall as a youngster my family friend who took me to games at Forbes Field. We would wait until Ralph Kiner had his last at bat before we would leave to go home, and many times, he would not disappoint us. Then we would catch the 77/54 Bloomfield streetcar to 34th and Penn Avenue and then catch the 94 streetcar to Sharpsburg. Boy, I sure do miss those days.

Robert Schaeffer
Sarasota, Florida

---

When I was a teenager back in the early 1950s, it seemed like everyone in Pittsburgh was a Pirate fan. My grandmother was a big fan, and once I turned 16 and got my driver's license, I used to take her to Pirate games at Forbes Field. She was getting up in age, and our seats were always on the third tier. The only way up was steep steps, and she used to take forever to get up those steps. It was such a great view once we got to our seats, however. In one game, a player hit a foul ball our way on the first base side, and it bounced on the short tin roof right in front of us and rolled down into the rain gutter. Well, I wanted that ball so bad and was willing to crawl down on the roof to get it, but my grandmother put up such a fuss I didn't. Thinking about that now, maybe it was best I didn't because it was a long way down to the seats below.

Ed Rodenbaugh
Hobe Sound, Florida

---

Throughout the 1950s, my friend Paul Blough and I would often depart early for a day game at Forbes Field. We'd take the city bus from Windber to Johnstown, where we'd get the train to Pittsburgh. Once in Pittsburgh, we'd take the trolley to Forbes Field, stand in line, and get our tickets. Then, after the game, we'd reverse our trip from Forbes Field by trolley and train as far as Johnstown. Because the city bus stopped running late at night, Dad would be waiting to pick us up and take us home.

Paul and I made this trip many times. Of course, it's not possible to make those connections today for a game in Pittsburgh. I'm amazed our parents permitted us to travel by ourselves.

Louis Cicotello
Colorado Springs, Colorado

---

It was on July 18, 1951, and the main event was the heavyweight title match between champion Ezzard Charles and contender Jersey Joe Walcott, who had already lost twice to Charles in 15 rounds. Walcott was the sentimental favorite at the "old" age of 37 years. Charles was not very popular because he defeated the great Joe Louis in his comeback from retirement to regain the title. Walcott had lost twice to Louis, the first time on a questionable split decision, despite the fact he had twice dropped Louis to the canvas.

Walcott, whose real name was Arnold Cream, had started his career four years before Joe Louis. In 1946, he lost to Joey Maxim and Elmer "Violent" Ray, but got revenge the next year against both of them, before he faced Louis for the first time on December 5. Louis won on a disputed split decision, even though he thought he had lost. He KO'd Walcott in the 11th in the rematch.

This fight was historic in that Walcott, at age 37, was the oldest ever in a championship bout. He was the sentimental favorite that night, despite being a 7-to-1 underdog, and was cheered at the end of every round. Walcott knocked Charles out in the first 55 seconds of the seventh round, with a tremendous right hook to the jaw. The champ fell flat on his face, and Walcott, on his fifth try, was finally the heavyweight champion. Everyone knew the crown had changed hands when that punch landed. I sat in the right field seats, just as I did every Saturday afternoon for free, and that punch looked great even as far away as I sat.

The ring was over second base; I had a good view, even if it was some distance away. *Ring Magazine* called it "The Fight of the Year." The next morning all three newspapers (*Press*, *Post-Gazette*, and *Sun-Telegraph*) had "Extra's" out with two to three pages on the fight.

During the '40s, there were fights at this grand old ballpark every summer. Fritzie Zivic fought Charley Burley, Sammy Angott, Lew Jenkins, and Jake LaMotta, to name a few of his opponents; Sammy Angott, in addition to fighting Zivic, fought Ike Williams, among others; and Sugar Ray Robinson fought Ossie Harris.

Herb McFarland
Brentwood, California

---

Ezzard Charles attempts to get up after being knocked down by Joe Walcott's left hook in the seventh round of their heavyweight championship bout on July 18, 1951 (Pittsburgh Photographic Library Collection of Carnegie Library of Pittsburgh).

Forbes Field was one of my Pittsburgh favorites. My most memorable moment there? I was hanging around outside Forbes Field where the players were waiting to get their cars and go home. I asked a handsome young player for his autograph — it was all about handsome. "You don't really want my autograph," he said. "See the old man over there? Go over and ask him for his autograph." So I did, and the old man was so delighted to be asked. His whole face lit up. He signed my autograph book. It wasn't until much later that I realized it was Honus Wagner.

Carol Prisant
Roslyn, New York

*A slightly different version of Ms. Prisant's memory was first published in* Pittsburgh Home and Garden *(Spring 2004) and is reprinted with the author's permission.*

In the early '50s, I attended a night game at Forbes Field. Sid Gordon was in right field, Ralph Kiner having been traded to the Cubs about a week before. Sitting in right field, I listened to a constant stream of criticism shouted at Sid Gordon. A base hit dropped into right field. "Should have had it, Sid," the crowd called. Sid singled to right center and was greeted with, "Should have had two, Sid."

Sid paid no notice to this constant badgering. Suddenly, all the outfield lights failed and the field was lit by three infield light standards. A voice called out, "How bout that, Sid?" A voice from right field responded, "Just cutting expenses, just cutting expenses."

Robert Luckey
St. Louis, Missouri

I remember being excused from school to go to "Opening Day" and seeing Curt Roberts, the first African American of the Pirates, hit a double. We all hoped he would become the next Jackie Robinson.

I also remember taking the streetcar to the end of the line where Mom picked us up and drove us home to Penn Hills. How did I get excused from school? My dad was the superintendent.

John M. Linton
Chicago, Illinois

I started going to Forbes Field in 1954 with my dad. I was fortunate enough to go there through grade school, high school, and college. Some of my favorite memories were:

• Seeing Roberto Clemente and Hank Aaron hit grand slams in the same game. Pittsburgh was losing big, but came back to win.
• Seeing Roberto Clemente hit a home run off Sandy Koufax. The line drive was still rising as it hit the light tower in left center field.
• Seeing a World Series game in 1960: Game 2, New York Yankees, 16, Pittsburgh, 3. Mickey Mantle had two home runs — he hit one of them right-handed over the exit gate in right center field! He was the only player ever to do it.

Gregory M. Gyauch
Johnstown, Pennsylvania

I have so many fond memories of Forbes Field. There will never be another park like it. My memories begin with working in the concession stands. Although, as the newest employee, it was my job to chip the ice to cool the Coca-Cola bottles and to clean the grill used for the wonderful tasting grilled hot dogs, I loved every minute of it — well, except for the time Myron O'Brisky (who managed the concessions) caught me sitting on the Coke cases eating a hot dog. Remember those great-tasting grilled hot dogs and ice-cold Cokes?

When I began working for Gulf Oil Company in Bloomfield, I took a one-week vacation in half-day increments so that I could enjoy Ladies Day ballgames in the right field stands watching my favorite, Roberto Clemente, roam right field.

Amanda Hatfield
Fort Myers, Florida

I moved to Pittsburgh when I was eight years old in 1955, from South Carolina. First we (brothers Bobby and Billy and sister Rose Mullins) lived on Atwood Avenue, and then we moved to Bouquet Street across the street from Forbes Field in the Oakland neighborhood. I went to Frick Grade School and Schenley High School, and then we moved from Pittsburgh to Florida in 1963, when I was 16. I sold newspapers outside of Forbes Field before some of the games and spent the money at Gus Miller's pinball place. I knew all of the ways

**CONCESSION PRICES**

| | |
|---|---|
| Breakfast Cheer (hot coffee) | .15 & .25 |
| Coca-Cola | .15 & .25 |
| Orange Drink | .15 & .25 |
| Hot Chocolate | .25 |
| Meadow Gold Ice Cream | .20 |
| Armour Red Hots—Manos Roll. | .30 |
| Snax Peanuts | .15 |
| Reymers Blennd | .25 |
| Meadow Gold Orange | .25 |
| Gold Label Palmas (4-Pack) | $1.00 |
| El Producto Cigars | .15 |
| White Owl Cigars | .15 |
| Muriels | .10 |
| Muriel Air Tip (5-pack) | .35 |
| Muriel Coronella (5-pack) | .30 |
| Robert Burns Tipparillos (5-Pack) | .30 |
| Score Card | .20 |
| Pencils | .10 |
| The Sporting News | .25 |
| PIRATE YEARBOOK | .50 |
| Cushion Rental | .25 |

**(PLEASE NOTE:)** All Vendors and Stand Employees have uniform numbers. Any complaint can only be rectified when having EXACT UNIFORM NUMBERS.

*Myron O'Brisky*
Gen'l Mgr., Concessions and Advertising

Concession prices in 1965 as advertised in a scorecard (Pittsburgh Pirates Baseball Club).

to sneak into Forbes Field, such as over the outfield wall by climbing the trees and through the vendors' entrance. Also, in the seventh inning, the gates were opened to everyone. When we snuck in before a game, we would hang out in the right field stands and wait for batting practice home run balls.

The ushers would chase us, and we would hide until they left. Back then, the players would talk to us from the bullpen. I can remember during the spring and night games, the roar of the crowd would keep me up on school nights. So many times after a game, we would go on the field and run around and then go out to an old iron gate that opened out where we played little league. Also, there was a fountain called the Turtle Spit. The back of right field is where the Knot Hole Kids entered into the game.

Jerry Mullins
Neptune, New Jersey

My brother took me to Forbes Field for my birthday on July 25, 1956. The Pirates were fighting for last place, as usual, in those days. We were losing by three when somehow we got the bases loaded and Clemente hit a ball off one of the light standards in left field. He was told to stop at third, but he kept coming and, in a cloud of dust, he completed an inside-the-park grand slam. It was amazing! Since much of the crowd had left early, we were able to move down to the box seats and see his mad dash from third to home up close. We could see the fire and determination in his eyes as he flew home. Maybe he didn't care that the Pirates were in last place.

Rich Engel
Riverview, Florida

I attended a game in 1956, and we were playing the Cubs. The old Greenberg Gardens had been removed from left field so that play went right up to the scoreboard. We were losing 8–5, with no one out in the bottom of the ninth and the bases "F.O.B." (Full of Bucs, as Rosey Rowswell would have said).
A young Roberto Clemente stepped up to the plate and hit one off the scoreboard. The left fielder was expecting the ball to come straight back to him, but instead it took a weird carom toward center field. While the left and center fielders were pursuing the ball, the bases cleared and El Roberto went flying around the bases for an inside-the-park grand slam and a Pirate victory. Oh, what a ballplayer he was!

Jim Malarky
Norco, California

I was 15 when I won a brand new Plymouth on Prize Day in 1956 (also my mother's birthday). My cousin and I had 99-cent bleacher tickets, and the ballpark people pulled the winning ticket out of a drum. They had over 44,000 at the game. They also were giving away a pony, and when Joe Brown noted that I wasn't old enough to drive, he said that they were going to give me the pony. I said something to the effect of, "Give me the (bleep) car!" over the loud speaker system, much to the crowd's amusement. And so I got the car.

Andrew Simko
Norwell, Massachusetts

My dad and I (and sometimes my mom) attended many Pirate games, especially during the 1950s, before I went to college. My favorite player was Roberto Clemente, who I remember taking a ball hit by the muscular Ted Kluszewski of the Cincinnati Reds off that notorious right-center wall (out near the end of the fence), spinning, and falling down as he threw a line drive to third base as Ted tried to rumble in for a triple. The ball *never* touched the ground, and big Ted was out by a mile! The whole crowd stood and cheered as Roberto picked up his hat and gave a humble wave like it was nothing. I have not seen anyone else play his position as he did.
I remember Bill Mazeroski, the magician with the quickest double play turnaround *ever* in base-ball. Most folks remember the famous home run in the 1960 World Series to beat the almighty Yankees, but I also remember his fielding.
In Forbes Field, there was a runway behind first base and before the Pirates bullpen down the right field line. During one game that my Dad and I attended in the 1950s, an opposing player hit a pop-up that seemed unplayable, but Maz, with his tremendous hustle and not-so-tremendous speed, actually caught the ball on the run, going up that runway into the locker rooms. He disappeared at first and then came out with the ball in his rather small glove, and the umpire, who had followed the play, signaled an "out," much to the delight of an unbelieving partisan crowd. What a player he was!

Richard Morgan
Lake Hopatcong, New Jersey

**Fans lining up at one of Forbes Field's gates on Boquet Street, July 21, 1957 (Pittsburgh Photographic Library Collection of Carnegie Library of Pittsburgh).**

My first trip to Forbes Field was in 1957 as a nine-year-old little leaguer. The Bucs had a special promotion for kids called the Knot Hole Club. We got a cheap ticket in right field and some snacks as well as our own Knot Hole Club membership card. They treated us really great. I don't remember anything about the game other than I got sick 'cause I ate too much popcorn.

I got to see the Cubs' great third baseman Ron Santo make his major league debut in Forbes Field. On June 26, 1960, Dad took me to the game as a birthday present. We sat in the upper deck in right field just inside the foul pole. The Bucs won both games, as I remember, with the highlight of the second game being Smoky Burgess taking potshots at the right field foul pole. He hit about three shots just foul, and on the fourth try, he hit it right on the nose.

We also sat in the left field bleachers a good bit. It was only a buck to get into the game, and we had lots of fun watching the men get drunk from the booze they brought to the game in their paper bags. (In those days, no alcohol was sold at Forbes Field.) I do remember a game there in 1960 against the Braves, who were in Milwaukee at the time. We sat in the bleachers and carried on a conversation with the Braves' relief pitchers. But the best was yet to come.

Al Spangler was in left field that night, and didn't always go into the dugout when the Braves came to bat. He would instead sit in the Braves' pen. We started to get on him a bit, just friendly kidding. He kidded back and even threw us a ball. I didn't win the battle for it, but I did enjoy the kidding and the error he made that night in left field. After the error, we really got on his case.

Another memory that sticks out is that during the mid-'60s, the Bucs had a promotion against the Dodgers called "Long Ball Fan Night." Everyone was given a big stiff paper fan to wave when the Bucco hitters were up to create a breeze and help the ball fly out of the park. Along about the third inning, Don Drysdale, the Dodger pitcher, complained to the ump that the fans were distracting him, so an announcement was made over the public address system to the fans asking them not to wave the fans. Well, as you may guess, about 25,000 fans were rained onto the field. It took about 20 minutes to clean up things, and of course the Bucs proceeded to pound the daylights out of Drysdale.

Finally, though it may not be too well known, the Steelers played their games at Forbes Field for many years. The field ran from home plate out to right center field. I saw some great players at those games. Many of the Steelers were, by then, over the hill. The most memorable game was in 1960 when the Philadelphia Eagles came to town. We sat in the upper deck on the third base side of the field — they were end zone seats. It snowed so hard that the fans couldn't see beyond the 50-yard line. There was no way to sweep snow off the field like today, so they had to improvise to make the calls on out-of-bounds plays and other such matters. The Eagles won the game, which was close for a good while, on a Norm Van Brocklin to Tommy McDonald pass. The Eagles went on to win the NFL title that year, and it was the last game that Philly great Chuck Bednarik played in Pittsburgh.

Bryce D. King
Scottdale, Pennsylvania

It was 1958. I was 8, and our neighbor Wayne's father, Dean, took Wayne, my brother, and me to what was my first major league game on a Saturday afternoon at Forbes Field. The Pirates took on the Cardinals and their star, Stan Musial, and it was Vernon Law versus Sam "Toothpick" Jones on the hill. The Bucs pushed one across in the first with a bunt and a single, and that's how it went late into the game, when, indicating the man at the plate, Dean announced, "That's Stan Musial!" It was downright frightening. I don't remember all the details, but the game was saved by Bill Mazeroski, whom I can still see in my mind's eye, flat on his back, tossing the ball to first for a crucial putout.

Bill Sabol
Gulfport, Florida

At 10 years of age, in 1958, and living in Clarion, Pennsylvania, I experienced my first professional baseball game at Forbes Field. It was a Sunday afternoon, and my father and my young brother and I were listening to the ball game, the first of a doubleheader. After an inning or two of the first game, Bob Prince, the unforgettable announcer, made a casual comment: "There are still plenty of good seats, so come on down to the ballpark." With that, my dad perked up. "Let's go, boys," he said. "We're going to the ball game." About an hour and a half later, with the second game about to begin, we bought our tickets, and then — who can ever forget their first steps through the grandstand gate as the glorious vista of the pristine green field opens up before one's eyes? It literally took my breath away. It was a feeling that today, over 40 years later, I remember vividly. Indeed, we had terrific seats behind the third base dugout, and we even had an additional moment of excitement when a hard line-drive foul ball bounced off our seats while my Dad made us "duck for cover." It was unforgettable for me: a father and his sons sharing a timeless experience in a grand old venue is how I fondly remember Forbes Field.

Mark Nicolas
Wayne, Pennsylvania

Much of the summers of my junior high school and high school years were dedicated to Forbes Field. My father worked for one of the major banks, and one of the "benefits" he received from his business associates was a seemingly inexhaustible supply of Pirates' tickets. About 75 percent of the time, the tickets were located in the boxes in the front of the second deck behind home plate and over the broadcasting booths. The other seats were almost always in the boxes behind one of the dugouts. I was in attendance for many a win, loss, home run, and catch, but the following two stories involve one of the more memorable characters in the history of Forbes Field, Bob Prince, the "Gunner."

## THE GUNNER LOSES HIS SHOES

It was a night game against the Braves in the mid-to-late 1950s when the team from Milwaukee was king of the National League. For whatever reason — perhaps our trolley connections worked well that night — we arrived early and took our seats in a box behind the visitors' dugout. Bob Prince, looking natty in a sports coat and slacks, was pacing back and forth on the field waiting for wires to be strung and TV cameras to be moved into place. Soon he was joined by Warren Spahn for a pre-game interview.

Lew Burdette emerged from the Braves' dugout and sized up the situation. He moved toward Prince and Spahn, and as he got close, he got down on his hands and knees. At first I couldn't tell what was going on, but it soon became obvious that Burdette was trying to steal the Gunner's shoes, a pair of loafers without ties, as I recall. The Gunner, of course, was trying to resist him, but the best that he could do were some halfhearted kicks because he was talking to Spahn and the cameras were rolling. Burdette finally pried the shoes off Prince's feet, crawled out of camera range and ran to center field, where he threw the shoes over the wall. I can only guess what the Gunner did for footwear the rest of that evening.

## "I Wanna Talk to the Gunner"

I can't remember the year—it was the 1950s—and I can't remember the opponent, but as you will see, neither of those details is important. I was sitting in a front box in the second deck, behind home plate. The boxes in this area consisted of two levels, with two metal folding chairs on each level. Just before game time, three men with a cooler showed up to sit in the box immediately to my right. As I recall, there was a bit of a discussion with the usher as to whether the cooler was permissible, but the issue was settled when tickets were presented for all four seats in the box. In other words, this wasn't a cooler, it was "Mr. Cooler," and he was here to see the game.

As the game progressed, it was becoming increasingly obvious that Mr. Cooler was dispensing more than sandwiches and lemonade. His human companions were becoming more and more boisterous—even humorous at times. Somewhere in the middle innings, one of the men in the front row discovered that the box was located directly over the Pirates broadcast booth, which was suspended under the second deck. He spent the next inning or so after that leaning out of the front of the box in an attempt to establish a dialogue with the Gunner. Eventually, the combination of adult beverages and frustration caused him to announce to his friends—and almost everyone else behind home plate—"I wanna talk to the Gunner." As he leaned forward, his friends grabbed his legs and lowered him down in front of the broadcast booth. A squadron of ushers descended on the box and the occupants, including Mr. Cooler, were persuaded to continue their party on Sennott Street.

That couldn't be the end of it. I had to know what actually happened. I rushed home to ask my father if he'd listened to the game and if Prince had made any comments. Unfortunately, he had not had the game on the radio, and it was too late to call any of my friends who I knew listened to every game. I burned up phone lines the next morning, and the first person I called said that he heard the whole thing. He said that there was a lot of noise but that you really couldn't understand anything, and then the Gunner screamed, "I don't come to your place of business and bother you when you're working!"

Tom Davis
Allentown, Pennsylvania

My grandfather managed the movie theater outside Forbes Field through the '50s and '60s. In those days, it was common for the players to have a White Tower hamburger and see a movie after the game. My grandfather would have us stop in to see him in hopes we might get lucky enough to meet some players.

One afternoon, we met Bill Mazeroski and Ted Kluszewski. Those were wonderful, carefree summer afternoons. We lived for baseball. What it felt like to meet those guys will be with me all my life. One evening, my cousin and I were there to see a movie, and my grandfather came and got us from the balcony to meet Bob Prince. I couldn't sleep all night after that.

Jack Bailey, Jr.
Salem, Virginia

My first memory of Forbes Field was from August 22, 1959. I was five years old at the time. I had received a whiffle ball and bat for my birthday in July, and I had started to become interested in baseball. My grandparents, who resided in Glassport, decided to take me to a Pirates game. I had no memory prior to this of ever being in Pittsburgh. The ride to Pittsburgh in their car was quite an adventure. I distinctly remember driving over the old Glenwood Bridge with its wooden planks (I thought the noise was from people banging with hammers below the bridge). I also remember passing by the old trolley barn in Hazelwood on Second Avenue with all the trolleys (to a five-year-old, this was a great thrill).

We parked next to the burial vault company on Bates Street and walked to the park. I remember thinking the homes on Bouquet Street were quite old and foreboding. We entered the park, and my grandfather bought a program and a hot dog and a Coke for me. I didn't know why we were entering this dark place. We walked up the ramp and out, and suddenly the green of the field appeared. It was quite surprising and breathtaking. I remember the Pirates in their white home uniforms and the Dodgers in their gray and blue uniforms. I remember the blue and gray seats. We sat behind third base in the second deck. The Pirates won 2–0. I know that Bennie Daniels started and won the game. I also remember that there was a home run by one of the Pirates. The bottom line, though, was that I was now hooked as a baseball fan. This was perfect for my grandfather, who had played shortstop in high school and was a long-suffering Pirates fan. My mother was an only child, and my father was not into sports. My grandfather and I had found a common link and became soul mates. I became the son he never had, and he educated me in all the fine points of the game.

I remember seeing one more game there that year, which I believe was an extra inning win over the Reds. I believe Maz may have hit a homer to win the game, and he now became my favorite player.

I saw three games at Forbes in 1960, the last being on July 2 with Tom Cheney losing to the Dodgers 6–1. I remember this because I had a perfect record before this in that the Pirates had won all their games I had attended.

In 1961, I remember attending a game in May on a Saturday when Don Blasingame was the leadoff hitter. He got hit in the face with the first pitch and was down for 15 minutes with his face bloodied. I think this was when I first realized the danger involved with the game.

In July of '62, I remember attending a game with the Glassport Rotary Club in my father and grandfather's company and that of a number of children my age who were neighbors of my grandfather. Johnny Logan hit his first and only homer of the year to win the game — a grand slam at that — against St. Louis. I also remember the fans cheering for Musial when he was introduced.

In '62, I remember attending a doubleheader in which Harvey Haddix hit a three-run homer versus Houston into the upper deck. Unfortunately, he did not last long enough to enjoy his homer, and the Colt 45s ended up winning.

On June 1, 1965, I witnessed Bob Veale, in a twice rain-delayed game, set the Pirates strikeout record at 16 in a 4–0 win over the Phillies. I also remember the fans giving Dick Stuart a hard time in fielding practice before the game for the Phils. This was another game I attended with my grandfather's Rotary Club. I remember that a contingent of the men played craps in the back of the bus, despite the presence of us kids. It was an introduction to manhood in some ways.

I saw one game in '66 during the Bucs run at the pennant and did not see another game after that until my best friend's dad took me to a Braves-Pirates contest in August 1969. I remember that game because we sat in the upper deck in right field, and Stargell jacked one over our heads and over the roof.

Forbes was also the site of my first Steelers game. I remember it being a loss in the rain to the Giants, 21–16, in 1959. My father, grandfather and I sat under the overhang in the lower deck on the third base side. I remember watching the Steelers beat the 49ers there in 1961 and beating the Cardinals there, 19–7, in '62 (Lou Michaels kicked a then-astonishing four field goals for the Steelers).

I have fond memories of attending Knot Hole games with the White Oak Athletic Association (my little league organization) in '63 and '64 with my contemporaries. There were no parents other than a coach or two to supervise us. We sat in the right field pavilion on a Saturday afternoon. The seats were free, and it cost us $1 for a round trip on the bus. I felt like a man of the world, on my own in the big city. This is not to mention I usually spent every dollar in my wallet on hot dogs, Coke, Lemon Blend, popcorn, and a real telescope (to better view the action). One of our group's proudest moments was hitting Rusty Staub with an Oreo cookie on the back of his leg. Even better, the next inning, Clemente picked up the cookie and threw it off the field (a true brush with greatness).

My most poignant memory of Forbes Field was going to the last game there (actually a doubleheader). We came home from 10:30 Mass on Sunday, and I was reading the Sunday Press in the living room. All of a sudden, to my surprise, my dad announced he would like to go to the game. He called my grandfather, and we drove down to the ballpark. My grandfather, at the time, was in the beginning stages of Alzheimer's disease. We got stuck in traffic on the Parkway outside of the Squirrel Hill tunnels. We finally made it into Oakland and my dad found a parking spot on Forbes Avenue by the old A&P store. When we got to the park, all that was left was standing room tickets. When we went in, we at first stood at the top of a ramp exit. The usher told us we could not stand there. My dad said something to the usher, who thought my dad was being a jerk and was ready to deck my dad (the only time I actually saw my dad close to becoming embroiled in a physical altercation). Eventually, we found a place to stand on the catwalk behind the last row of seats in the lower deck behind third base. We watched both games. My grandfather, who was 70, eventually was able to sit down in a seat in front of us for the last few innings. I remember Maz making the last out and the fans, in complete disregard to Bob Prince's pleadings, storming the field, digging up patches of grass, climbing the scoreboard and taking numbers, breaking seats for souvenirs, and taking everything not bolted down (including a Ladies Room sign). Looking back, however, it was a great day for my family.

John Bodnar
Oshkosh, Wisconsin

---

About the time I started playing baseball, I became aware of the "Bigs," and of the Pittsburgh Pirates in particular. Growing up 30 miles from Pittsburgh, I readily became a Bucs fan.

On my first day at a major league ballpark, my parents and I attended a doubleheader between the Pirates and the Los Angeles Dodgers at Forbes Field. It was Sunday, August 23, 1959. We sat in reserved seats high above and directly behind home plate. The Pirates won both games: 9–2 and 4–3 in 10 innings. Don Drysdale was the losing pitcher in both, first as a starter and then as a reliever. He ended the day with a 15–9 record. Pirates' relief pitcher ElRoy Face won the second game to make his record 16–0 en route to an 18–1 season. Face still holds single-season major league records from that year for most consecutive wins (17) and total wins by a reliever and highest winning percentage (.947) by any pitcher with 16 or more decisions. Buc center fielder Bill Virdon was the batting star of the day, going 8 for 9. In the second game, Dick Stuart drove in the tying run in the ninth inning, and the winning run in the 10th, both times with two outs. It proved to be quite an ironic day for the Dodgers. They won the World Championship that year, and Drysdale ended up in the Hall of Fame.

My father took me to Forbes Field once each year, and he always bought tickets in advance for a Sunday afternoon doubleheader in the midsummer. He liked the idea of seeing two games for the price of one, and insisted on going only when the weather was certain to be warm. In 1960, there was more irony on my day at the ballpark. On Sunday, June 26, we saw the last place Chicago Cubs sweep both games of a twin bill from the front-running Pirates, who went on to win the World Series. More than 30 years later, I learned in a newspaper column that Ron Santo, the Cubs' star third basemen of the '60s and early '70s, had made his major league debut that day.

I came to love Forbes Field. The ballpark exhibited so many unique and beautiful features. There was the 12-foot-high ivy-covered brick wall in left and center fields, far from home plate, with Schenley Park beyond. The 25-foot hand-operated scoreboard built against the left field wall, providing an inning-by-inning account of every major league game in progress and final scores of completed games that day, and surmounted by the 14-foot-square Longines clock. The right field wall, just 300 feet down the line from home, with a 15-foot, eight-inch screen atop it between the 300 and 375 feet signs, required a high trajectory of long balls hit in that direction if they were to reach the grandstand beyond for a home run. The monument to Barney Dreyfuss — the Pirates owner who was instrumental in the construction of Forbes Field — located in play on the center field warning track to the right of the flagpole and the angle in the wall at the 457 feet sign, appeared from my faraway seat to be a headstone. I once wondered, was someone really buried there?

The batting cage, also in play during games, was stored just to the left of the 457 feet sign, its open end against the wall. The iron gate in the wall in right center at the end of the grandstand served as an exit in that part of the park. The lower deck general admission seats were near the infield with a view partially obstructed by support columns and the upper deck overhang. The bleachers were down the left field line in foul ground near the scoreboard. The infield tarpaulin wound onto its long cylinder and lowered into the ground off the third base line, so that the top of the cylinder's housing met flush with and became part of the playing field. And there was real grass.

Larry Pansino
Canonsburg, Pennsylvania

I saw my first and only professional football game at Forbes Field. The Steelers were playing the Lions, it was a night game, and they were using a white football.

I also attended Pirate baseball games and usually sat in the left field bleachers (I was a bleacher bum). In those days, I could see a doubleheader for 50 cents, and get a hot dog and a Coke for $1.00. I can still see Joe Christopher playing left field, making a diving catch for the last out of the game, and coming up smiling and waving to those of us in the left field bleachers.

I was in attendance when Clemente made a running catch in right field at the iron gate and then somehow twirled around and threw out a runner trying to tag and score from third base. No matter who is playing there now, nothing will ever take away my memories of Forbes Field and the great players that made it a part of my young life.

Paul McKeever
Lexington, South Carolina

---

I'm from West Mifflin, and I remember being at Forbes Field and watching the Steelers play. I remember the thrill of Opening Day as they opened the gates and I saw the Washington High School band march onto the field. They looked so proud to be performing for the crowd.

I also went to Pirate games there. I remember seeing Dick Stuart play ball. I would watch him hit a line drive, and just as it was going to be caught, the ball would start to rise like it had wings on it.

I also remember paying $2.00 for parking and thinking that was a lot of money.

Mike Chonko
West Mifflin, Pennsylvania

---

I'm almost 53. The left field bleachers at Forbes Field was the place to be. In my early years, I was a Dodger fan and used to love leaning over the fence into the visitors' bullpen and feeding the Dodger pitchers peanuts. I remember that one afternoon I gave Ed Roebuck too many!

After one game, I caught both Don Drysdale and Sandy Koufax walking down the street outside of Forbes Field. I asked for their autographs, but they insisted they had to catch a train. Being a kid, I believed them!

Rex Rutkoski
Freeport, Pennsylvania

---

Some of my earliest memories are of going to Forbes Field in about 1959–1960. Dad didn't have much money, so we sat in the right field bleachers. I believe that the seats were a buck apiece. They were logistically probably the worst seats in the house, except that you could almost reach out and touch Roberto Clemente, which made them the best seats in the house in my young mind. I have never been anywhere quite like it since.

I am sure I never will.

Paul Esposito
Omaha, Nebraska

---

I remember going to Forbes Field to hear a young man speak. It was the first time I heard of this person — it was in the late '50s or early '60s, I don't remember the date. I really went to hear Mahalia Jackson sing. That was the most entertaining show I had ever seen. This man spoke so well, he kept 10,000 people quiet to hear him.

You could have heard a pin drop. Mahalia Jackson sang so beautifully we were glued to our seats, and she danced when she sang.

I really enjoyed both of them.

Rosalie Augustus
Verona, Pennsylvania

---

May of 1960, Pirates versus Phillies, was my first time at Forbes Field. I was 11 years old and at my first major league game. The air smelled of cigar smoke and stale beer, the playing field was a perfect green, and the players were all larger than life.

In mid-game, Roberto Clemente broke out of a rundown on the third base line and crashed into the Phils' catcher, who dropped the ball. After the collision, Roberto was on the ground with the catcher on top of him past home plate. Before the Phils could retrieve the ball and tag him out, Roberto wriggled free and touched home. The game went into extra innings, and Don Hoak won it in the 13th with a three-run homer over the right field screen. The 1960 Buccos were pure magic, and baseball has never been better (or even as good).

Guy Tweed
South Euclid, Ohio

I was at Forbes Field once as a 10-year-old to see the Pirates play the Giants in a Sunday double-header. The ballpark was like Ebbets Field in that it was a fan's ballpark, putting you close to the action it seemed. It was great to see Cepeda, Mays, and Dark play for San Francisco. The Pirates — Maz, Virdon, Clemente, Stuart, Groat, and Skinner — were in their prime. I recall the Pennsylvania Sunday curfew law on baseball, which meant the second game was stopped. It was a great old ballpark for a kid from New Jersey to see.

Pete Cullen
Clifton, New Jersey

The first game I went to was when I was in third grade. It was the last Friday night of the season in September 1960. My dad took me to the game against the Braves. The Pirates had already clinched the pennant. It was the first season I ever closely followed baseball. I recall "Beat 'em Bucs" stickers plastered on every car bumper in the city that year. The thing I recall most about my first game was that we sat in the left field bleachers, which is strange, since that was the only time I ever sat in that section. Over the next 10 years, I went to about 25 games and never sat in the bleachers once. Anyway, I recall that it was already dark when we got to Forbes Field for the Bucs-Braves game. I think in those days, the games didn't start until 8 P.M. As a result, my first memory of walking into the park was pretty much the way Billy Crystal, in *City Slickers*, described his experience of going to Yankee Stadium for the first time as a kid. The grass never looked greener to me after that. As for the game, Smoky Burgess hit a home run for the Pirates, but they got whipped pretty good. For the next 30 years, I thought the final score was Braves 10, Pirates 1, but I found out in 1990 that the actual final score was 13–2. I had forgotten that my dad and I left the game in the seventh or eighth inning. On our way out of the park, my dad bought me a 1960 National League championship pennant with the names of the players listed on the left side. I wish I still had it.

David Assad
Pittsburgh, Pennsylvania

When we drove to Oakland for the Pirate games in the 1960s, we would more often than not pay someone a buck to park in their front yard. I don't remember ever parking in a paid parking lot. And on the porches of the private little lots, the guy collecting the money was holding his Iron City, Fort Pitt, or Duquesne beer, and had a KDKA pregame show on the radio.

The sponsors were Sealtest Ice Cream (gallons given away for home runs), Atlantic Gasoline ("Which keeps your car on the go, go, go; so keep on the go with Atlantic"), and Iron City Beer.

After the games, we did the best we could to find a place at the bar in Frankie Gustine's. We swapped stories and listened to the scuttlebutt; we got the real story behind the Bucs from the regulars at Gustine's. Somehow, someone always seemed to know what was really going on.

But, for what it may be worth, here are a few of my memories from the magical 1960 season.

## DICK STUART: DR. STRANGEGLOVE

I once watched Stuart during warm-ups reach out to take a throw from Don Hoak. His glove outstretched, Stuart took the throw dead in the gut. Another time, he received an ovation for fielding a soft drink cup as it blew by his position.

## ROCKY NELSON

Nelson seemed like a throwback — a player from another time. He was a little old it seemed, with a wad of chew stuffed in his cheek, stains on his shirt, and a curious battling stance that we came to rely on for a hit at the right time.

## BILL MAZEROSKI

Much has been written in Hall of Fame discussions, but he could really get rid of that ball. Somehow, it seemed that on a double play, the ball never stopped at second — Maz simply redirected it. He made a good shortstop out of Groat. Groat was fine, but a better shortstop would have allowed records that would never be broken for the number of double plays turned. He was "The Kid" for some time, and then he was "Maz." And it never failed — at least once a season on a pregame or postgame show, we would see Maz showing his tiny glove to Bob Prince and to us. He had used the same glove forever it seemed — small, worn, and patched.

## ROBERTO CLEMENTE

"Arriba!" "Bobby" walked up to the plate, almost always with a crick in his neck. He worked it out as he stepped into the batter's box. Clemente would swing at absolutely anything. He sometimes seemed to be falling away from the ball as he lashed it to right field. I remember so many line drives banging off that wall as he flew around the bases, one of those runners who, with his feet wide apart, pushing himself along at a clip that we used to wonder: "How many steps does Clemente take between first and second?"

Lou Florimonte
Valencia, California

---

I remember the day Mickey Mantle hit a tremendous shot over the right center field wall. I was in Schenley Park and had a chance to get the ball.

But my greatest memory of Forbes Field is the game when I was sitting in the right field stands. There was a man on third and a ball was hit into right field. Roberto Clemente caught the ball and rifled it to home plate, getting the runner out. What made this amazing was that Clemente was at the warning track and threw a perfect strike into home plate.

Vinny Pietropaoli
Fort Worth, Texas

---

I went to many games at Forbes Field. I paid 10 cents for the street car and 50 cents for bleacher tickets in left field during the 1940–1960 period.

But there was an event that I will never forget — Bill Mazeroski's home run in the seventh game of the 1960 World Series. It was very emotional. Nobody left the ballpark for a whole hour after Maz hit his home run.

Our bank gave me a ticket for the seventh game before the World Series. I was a little disappointed because I didn't think the Series would last past the fourth or fifth game, but as it turned out, I really got lucky with that ticket.

James Palumbo
Bridgeville, Pennsylvania

---

Born and raised three blocks from Forbes Field, I spent many summers in the bleachers. My dad was a policeman in Oakland. He would give me $2, and I would get a ticket, a Coke, and popcorn. Best of all was, if you stood at the press gate, the players would come out and give us little guys balls, hats, and just stand and talk with us — unlike the unfriendly businessmen ballplayers of today. When Smoky Burgess gave me his old mitt, I slept with it for years under my bed. When Roy Face and Dick Groat took me by the hand and walked me to my seat, I was the talk of my little school.

I was 10 years old when Maz hit the homer to win the '60 series, and my old man said, "Remember this, it's Pittsburgh history." I did.

Mark Fajnili
Pittsburgh, Pennsylvania

---

Having grown up in Grove City, Pennsylvania, I can remember going to see the Pirates play about five or six times every year between 1961 and 1969. Most of the time, we sat in the right field grandstand where I could see my idol, Roberto Clemente, play. I can remember going to games with my Dad or with some group such as the Safety Patrol, Boy Scouts, or another group. I seem to remember

**View from the upper deck in the right field stands, ca. 1968–1970 (Library and Archives Division, Historical Society of Western Pennsylvania, Pittsburgh, PA).**

that after the game they would open that big door in right center field, and we could leave the stadium over the right field grass. I also remember the kids climbing the trees outside the left field wall to see the game.

Dana H. Teufel
Derry, New Hampshire

My first vision of Forbes Field was an event that I would repeat from the years of seven to 12. Every summer for a week, my dad and I would take the train from Windber to Pittsburgh, and be met at the train station downtown by his Uncle George, who lived on Ann Street in Munhall.

All week long, while visiting my cousins in Pittsburgh, we would do the things kids of that age do during the summer, but as the afternoon turned to night, Uncle George and I would get on a trolley and head for Oakland.

The first time I saw Forbes Field I was awestruck as I watched people bustle along to their favorite pregame restaurant. We had two: Gustine's, and The Moose in Homestead. Gustine's had the greatest hamburger I had ever eaten up to that point, while The Moose had a huge jar of pickles sitting on the bar. Funny, I never saw anyone get a pickle out of that jar.

Uncle George insisted we always sit somewhere along the third base line so that we had a direct view of "The Great One" in right field. Tonight would be no exception because in the third inning, someone from the Dodgers hit a shot to right, and everybody was anticipating a double at least, which would score two runs.

My eyes were riveted on Number 21 as he gauged the trajectory of the ball, and at the very last moment, scaled the right field fence, sprang off the fence, and caught the ball. He landed with his back to the diamond and, with the same motion, spun to face the field and fired a strike to double up the runner. No one moved, no one said a word for about a second or two, and then the entire crowd gave witness to what had just happened and erupted into an applause that by closing my eyes tightly, I can still feel and hear today. As Roberto Clemente trotted in from right field at the end of the inning, he gracefully and with great panache acknowledged the applause from the crowd.

I have never experienced that feeling again, nor would I want to—it is too precious and too surreal to repeat.

Richard S. Morgan
Pittsburgh, Pennsylvania

So many memories—where does one begin? Those that come to mind are:

• The Benny Benack band in the 1960s: They rode the '60 Series as good luck and were later banned because the band brought bad luck.

• Dizzy Bellows: He ran the press box from the '40s until Forbes Field closed, then later did the same thing at Three Rivers. When he died, Dizzy was eulogized in *Sports Illustrated*. Every reporter visiting Forbes and Three Rivers for four decades knew Dizzy.

• The "Cheap Seats" in the left field bleachers, made of concrete. They were still affordable when I was at Duquesne University in the '60s. Using a syringe, we would load oranges with vodka (cheaper than beer). Then we would go to Oakland, pay a buck, and root for the Bucs.

• The Cathedral of Learning viewed from the right field stands.

• Roberto Clemente throwing out runners rounding first on a single.

• Bob Skinner running down the sure double in left and Bill Virdon doing likewise in center.

• A easy grounder going right through Dick Stuart's legs—"Da Bum!"

**Benny Benack and the Iron City Six entertain fans prior to the first game of the 1960 World Series at Forbes Field (Bettmann/Corbis).**

• Bob Prince saying: "They're not booing Stuart. They're saying, 'Stu! Stu!'..." No, they were booing Stuart!

• Myron O'Brisky's hot dogs—They were scrawny, but none tasted better.

Tom Gallagher<br>Carrollton, TX

I don't have one specific memory of Forbes Field, but rather a compilation of them from over the years. At the time, we didn't realize that we were witnessing history, as we watched Roberto Clemente, Bill Mazeroski, and ElRoy Face every summer. Those games were just fun, family outings.

Often I went to Forbes Field with my granpap and my brother. We lived in Carrick, and so we would take the 77/54 streetcar over to Oakland. The stop on Forbes Avenue was in front of Frankie Gustine's, and from there we walked over to the field, taking in the sights and sounds. We usually packed a brown bag lunch, and Granpap would always buy us Cracker Jack, the ultimate baseball snack.

We would go on Saturday afternoons, called Knot Hole Days. That was a club the Pirates started to encourage kids to come out to the ballpark. For a mere 50 cents, kids went through an entrance in right field and had a beautiful view of the entire diamond. We sat close enough to talk with Clemente when he came back to the outfield after each inning. Sometimes he would toss a ball to the kids, but not only did we see him, we also saw Willie Mays and other greats from the opposing teams, up close and personal.

After the games were over, we would wait by the players' exit and hope to catch a glimpse of our heroes or get an autograph. One day, Dick Schofield stopped and talked with us a little and signed autographs on our programs. We were so excited and talked about it for days afterward. I was often too shy to approach the players, but I still enjoyed just seeing them go by. Those moments forged a strong connection between the players and the kids. Back then, there weren't people waiting to buy autographs, and the players weren't charging to sign their names. We were there out of sheer admiration for them, hoping to get a memento to show our friends and keep in our rooms. If I close my eyes, I swear I can still smell the hot dogs, still see the ivy-covered walls, and still hear the organ playing at old Forbes Field!

Jan Snyder<br>Spring, Texas

I'm 49 years old, so my memories are as a kid watching the 1960s Pirates. My dad would take us to three to four games each year, and we'd always sit in the left field bleachers. Walking beneath the third base grandstand to get to the bleachers was always my favorite part because it was dark and dank and served as the antithesis of what was about to happen. Turning the corner and catching a first glimpse of what had to be the greenest grass on earth and the bright lights was as great a thrill as I had as a kid. I equate it to those people who have been brought back from death and claim they were moving down a tunnel toward a bright light they could only describe as God. I would break free of my dad and run to the end of the tunnel so I could take in the entire park at once.

I can't imagine sitting anywhere else in Forbes Field was as good as sitting in the bleachers. The cigar smoke was intoxicating. Even today, I'll catch a whiff of that smell and a rush of memories comes flooding back. All the men and boys in the bleachers (Forbes was like a male sanctuary) talked baseball and watched the scoreboard for out-of-town pitching changes. Sometimes we'd walk down to the visiting pitchers' bullpen to see if we could get those guys to talk with us, but they never did.

Some of my best baseball memories include Dick Groat hitting an inside-the-park home run down the right field line and Willie Mays striking out three times in one game.

Dennis Fischer<br>Allison Park, Pennsylvania

I have numerous fond memories of Forbes Field from my youth, but some of my best include opening days, attendance with my grandfather, an incident involving Smoky Burgess catching a fly ball, and of course, the final game at Forbes.

Beginning when I was 10 years old in 1960, Mom and Dad always gave me a traditional birthday gift (they still do): tickets for the Pirates' opener. What a thrill it was for me to be at Forbes Field each opening day screaming, "Beat 'em, Bucs!" I enjoyed watching my heroes, the Bucs. My favorites were Roberto Clemente and Bill Mazeroski. Believe me, I felt like I'd died and gone to heaven.

One opener at Forbes was particularly special because I went with my grandpa, Dick Cooley, who was a former professional catcher and umpire in the minors. Grandpa called me "Bucky" because we were both great fans of the Bucs. He had taught me everything about baseball; therefore, attending a game at Forbes with Grandpa was quite an event.

I recall a game at Forbes when Smoky Burgess lost his "cool." It was Smoky's turn at bat. Unfortunately, he flied out. Smoky was so angry with himself that he repeatedly jumped up and down on the plate. Although I felt sorry for Smoky, the incident was rather humorous.

At one game I attended with Mom when I was 10, we were fortunate to obtain seats along the third base line in the front row. The Bucs' rivals that day were the St. Louis Cardinals; Curt Flood was at bat. He hit a foul ball right into the stands. Both an adult and I attempted to get the ball, but I caught it! I remember that the adult grabbed at the ball, trying to wrench it from my small hands, but I gripped it tightly and took the ball home!

Finally, the last game at Forbes was bittersweet. Although I realized that the new stadium would provide improvements over the old, part of me just couldn't say good-bye to Forbes Field forever. Wanting to take something home as a remembrance, I pulled out one of the seats. In recent years, I've acquired a replica of Forbes Field as well as other Forbes memorabilia because it was indeed a very special place.

Richard J. Gallagher
Allison Park, Pennsylvania

One of the earliest memories of the house that I spent the first 24 years of my life in was that as a very young child, I could see bright lights shining into my third-floor bedroom window on a lot of summer nights.

As I grew a little older, I found out that the illumination in my room was coming from one of the light standards at Forbes Field, which was just a couple of blocks away from our house, on Atwood Street in Oakland. I remember hearing the cheers from Forbes on hot summer nights while sitting on the front porch with my family, and earlier in the evening, seeing the crush of cars that would come into Oakland looking for parking.

One of my friend's grandfathers, a feisty old guy from across the street, would sell "parking spaces" at a dollar a pop and put cars in "spaces" he created off an alley between Atwood Street and Meyran Avenue. He'd park 'em anywhere they would fit.

As I got older, and maybe because of sheer proximity to the ball yard, I became addicted to baseball, and specifically the Pirates. My friends and I developed creative ways of getting into Forbes during the '60s to see our beloved Bucs, one of them involving a tree branch, readily available from any tree in Schenley Park (the edge of which was adjacent to Forbes), and a certain unattended gate that was at the bottom of a right field ramp and was only legitimately utilized on Saturday afternoons for Knot Hole games (special youth group admission days). The branch was used to gently jack up the gate just high enough to let us all slide under and into the ball yard, with a makeshift stack of whatever stones we could find in the woods used to hold the gate up, until we were all in. Then we were in the right field seats and mostly stayed put there, getting to watch Roberto Clemente up close. We loved how he played the tricky caroms off the right field sculpted wooden wall, with its many carved indentations, how he galloped after the ball, and how he gracefully swirled and then rifled down anyone young enough or foolhardy enough to think he could go from first to third. I also remember getting to see the ballet-like moves of Mazeroski and Alley turning the double play, and a young "Pops" planting balls on the right field roof over us where the likes of the Babe back in his Boston Braves' swan song days had done before.

After the "Old Lady of Schenley" closed her doors for the final time in 1970, we continued to enjoy the wonders of Forbes, going in at night and standing in right field exactly where we saw "The Great One" stand for those many years, and getting to run the base paths and sit in the dugout where our heroes had actually been assembled. What a childhood! How fortunate I was to get to grow up right next door to my very own Field of Dreams.

Pete Ridge
Hershey, Pennsylvania

I grew up in the South Side of Pittsburgh and later in Bethel Park. I remember walking about one mile to Forbes Field with my cousins. We would begin at St. Casmir's on the South Side, cross the

22nd Street Bridge and go up Forbes Avenue to the ballpark. We would usually pay the admission to the left field bleachers and watch Bob Skinner roam left field. We had an excellent view of the manual score board from there, and I could see the numbers being changed and heads looking out of openings in the scoreboard. As a kid, I thought that would be a great job — to actually get paid to watch a game and keep score.

When we moved to Bethel Park, my friends and I would ride the streetcar into town, obtain a transfer to Oakland, and get off on 5th Avenue at the White Tower restaurant. We would go into the general admission area of the ballpark and, after the sixth inning, sneak up to the corporate boxes, which consisted of green painted metal rooms with folding chairs (this was before the luxury boxes of today). We would watch the last few innings of the game from here and thought we were really special to be in those seats.

Forbes Field was a unique ball field, with its vast center field and left field and its short right field. Anyone who watched a ball game at Forbes Field would remember the batting cage parked in dead center.

I was in attendance at the last game played at Forbes Field, which I believe was a doubleheader against Chicago. At first, I couldn't believe the mass destruction going on, with fans jumping and kicking the seats to try to break them apart and other fans running on the field trying to steal the bases and get out to the scoreboard. It was mayhem and took me awhile to understand it, but I finally realized they were just trying to get a piece of history.

What I remember most about Forbes Field is the number of great Pirate players and teams that the organization fielded during my youth. The greatest all-around player to ever play professional baseball roamed right field for the Pirates: Roberto Clemente. Watching "Arriba Roberto" throwing strikes to third and home from the warning track was awesome and spellbinding. The thing that really amazed me was when opposing players on second or third would hold up during long fly balls hit to right. This was the ultimate respect for Clemente's arm. He would still throw a flame to the appropriate base.

Another thought concerning Roberto Clemente was his base running. I can remember vividly how he would try to stretch a single into a double or at least be in position to take second if the outfielder bobbled the ball or was lackadaisical. He would sprint to first and make the turn toward second. If he couldn't take the extra base, he would go down (slide) on his right shin to stop and return to first. Roberto was a great player, but I never did like his basket catches, and I can remember at least once when (as Bob Prince would say) "the can of corn" was dropped by a Clemente basket catch.

It seemed like any hard shot down the right field line could take a hundred different bounces off the wall. I can't remember how many times these balls down the line would elude Clemente, and it had to be his greatest frustration at Forbes Field.

Joseph G. Capasso
Mechanicsburg, Pennsylvania

---

Believe it or not, my best memory of Forbes Field was not a baseball game: It was in the 1960s, and the Three Stooges were appearing "live." I took my two young sons, who were absolute fans. The Three Stooges (seated in the back of a convertible) entered, circling the full-capacity crowd. The people went wild. Everyone was standing and screaming. I sat there shouting, "Sit down! Sit down! We can all see!"

Well, much to my embarrassment, the "Star Spangled Banner" was being played, so we stood.

Patti Faloon
Pittsburgh, Pennsylvania

---

It was a hot Saturday afternoon in July of 1962. We had tickets for seats in the right field bleachers, behind the screen and above the ivy-covered walls. A friend of mine, his father, my father, and I made the drive from Grove City, 60 miles north of the city. I watched in reverential joy as the Pirates played. I had the privilege of seeing "The Great One," Roberto Clemente, make a perfect throw from the corner in right to cut down a runner racing from first to third — the runner never made it. Having watched Clemente on TV and listened to the games on radio, I was thrilled to see for the first time in my life the greatest all-around player of the game.

After one game in person, Roberto Clemente came to be more than a baseball player. He came to represent the class and dignity that sports heroes are supposed to have. After seeing his catches and throws during my first game, I never sat anywhere at Forbes Field other than behind the screen in the right field corner.

I will never forget the joy and beauty of the old friendly confines of Forbes Field. The one thing my father and I always had in common was and still is the love of the game. May many more fathers and sons grow together and share the joy and memories of baseball in the late afternoon in the Steel City. PNC Park may never bring the nostalgic feel of Forbes Field back, but here is hoping that many more eight-year-old boys can hang their hopes on a hero at a ballpark with the class of our heroes. That 9–5 putout on that hot Saturday afternoon is still fresh in my mind 38 years later.

Bill Perry
Pompano Beach, Florida

In the spring of 1963, I was working in western Pennsylvania as a college text sales rep for Harper Collins. The University of Pittsburgh was my most important customer, and I spent many days on the campus. I also spent many evenings at Forbes Field. I would habitually arrive early, sit in the right field grandstand, and watch Roberto Clemente put on a dazzling show during fielding practice, gliding after fly balls and whirling and throwing perfect one-bounce bullets to second, third, and home. One evening, I sat alone in the upper right field grandstand, and a tall, powerful-looking batter sent a line drive straight at me. The ball caromed off a nearby seat and plunked into the seat next to me, and I had only to reach over and pick it up. I looked at my scorecard to see who had provided the souvenir. It was Willie Stargell, beginning his first full year in a Pirates uniform.

Christopher Jennison
New York, New York

I grew up in Greenwood, Delaware, as a fan of the Pirates and Steelers. I came to Washington County, Pennsylvania, every summer to visit my grandparents and other relatives. My Uncle Don, freshly home from the Navy, took me to my first Pirate game at Forbes Field in 1963. I was in awe of the hallowed place and most impressed (at the age of 10) by the ivy on the left field walls and my hero, a young player named Roberto Clemente. On that day (as my memory has it), Clemente caught a long fly at the base of the right field wall and threw out a runner at home plate with a perfect strike. It was the greatest throw I ever saw an outfielder make! I think my uncle had a lot of fun, too, since he bought me a program to take home with me. Now if I could only find it.

Walter Chambers
Uniontown, Ohio

My Uncle Lou Pantano, who lives in Brentwood, somehow smoked enough Phillies cigars to redeem the wrappers for a baseball glove. He gave me that glove, which was a Frank Malzone model for little leaguers. Malzone was a third baseman for the Red Sox and I was a Pirate fan, but it mattered little, because along with the gift of the glove were tickets to a game at Forbes Field.

We sat through a doubleheader in the bleachers down the left field line. The Milwaukee Braves were in town. The Pirates and Braves split the games, with Clemente homering in the second one.

Years later, my uncle confessed that although he liked the Pirates, he was never a big enough baseball fan to want to sit through a doubleheader. But he did for me in the summer of 1963. I was seven.

Albert J. Torquato
Windber, Pennsylvania

My first game was at the age of 12. My father took me on a train and we walked from the station to Forbes Field and back! It was my first train ride and my first ballgame. I have the box score of the game and autographs of Warren Spahn and Alvin O'Neal McBean. Five Hall of Famers played in that game: Clemente, Mazeroski, Aaron, Spahn, and Mathews.

My fondest memory of Clemente came at Forbes Field in 1967 or 1968. The Bucs were playing the Cardinals. Orlando Cepeda was on third base, and someone hit a fly to deep right field. Clemente caught the ball on the warning track and threw a no-bounce-on-the-fly strike to home plate, gunning down Cepeda. I was completely flabbergasted, and I can't imagine what Cepeda thought.

Kevin Ogle
Cumberland, Maryland

Forbes Field is where my love for the Pirates all began. I remember Forbes Field also when I was there to watch a WPIAL High School Football title game that Butler High School was playing in (I was from Butler). I remember the wooden seats and the support poles that blocked the view during a baseball game.

I always enjoyed going to Forbes Field, although it was only a few times since we just didn't get to Pittsburgh that often.

Thomas L Monteleone
Greensburg, Pennsylvania

In my first game, Woody Woodward, who I believe was a rookie, hit a drive off the right field wall. Clemente, who was in right field, fielded the ball and threw to first base. As Woodward made the turn at first, the first baseman tagged him out.

What an arm Clemente had!

Johnny Ace
Palmer, Alaska

When visiting my grandparents, who lived in Natrona Heights, my father and uncles would plan the trip around when the Pirates were home. All the sons-in-law would go to a game while their wives visited with my grandparents. Occasionally, they would take us grandkids with them. I remember walking through Schenley Park and approaching the park, with the smell of roasting peanuts, hot dogs on the grill, cigars, and stale beer in the air. We always sat in the bleachers down the left field line. It was a thrill to exit the game through the exit gate in the outfield. Just to walk on a major league field was amazing. I had never seen such a beautiful patch of green grass and ivy in my life. On one occasion I picked some of the ivy off the left field wall. I still have all of my score-cards from the games we attended, and that piece of ivy is pressed between the pages of one of the scorecards. Any chance I got to attend a game at Old Forbes was a thrill to be remembered forever.

Paul Dorman
Tempe, Arizona

My best memory of Forbes Field was my first major league game there, in 1964. I was seven years old. My great-aunt, Ann Schutzman (nicknamed "Palsy"), was a lifelong Pirates fan. She took my father and me to the game. She had purchased a ball cap, yearbook, pennant, and baseball, all which I still have as part of my Pirates memorabilia collection. She even took me over by the Pirates dugout in order to get some autographs on the baseball.

We got the autographs of players Gene Freese and Jim Pagliaroni, as well as coach Sam Narron. Then Palsy saw Roberto Clemente signing autographs and took me over to him. It was the first time that I had ever heard anyone speak Spanish. We were just one fan away when Clemente had to leave and get ready for the game. I still have the ball, but the autographs have faded a bit. Needless to say, I would have liked to have had Clemente sign that ball. But I still enjoy telling the story!

Donn Frizzi
Peoria, Illinois

Once a season, the Perry Athletic Association little league teams would pile into a couple of old "rattletrap" buses for our annual pilgrimage to Forbes Field. Off we'd go, down Spring Hill through Millvale, across the Washington Crossing Bridge, and up through Lawrenceville toward Oakland. Hanging out the windows of that borrowed school bus on the old Bloomfield Bridge, we'd scream our lungs out that the bridge is going to collapse, "We're going down! We're all gonna die." Rolling into the streets of Oakland we sang "99 bottles of beer on the wall." We'd march around the ivy-patched brick outfield wall to the cheap seats in the right field stands, with the coaches trying their best to keep us from running ahead. Walking by Bill Mazeroski Field, we thought how lucky the kids around here must be to play there, but never saw anyone playing there. Game time would come and we'd take our seats and scream.

One time Gene Alley doubled off the right field screen in front of us. Those of us sitting in the front row sticking our fingers through the fence tried to catch the ball, not thinking that it would have broken our fingers if we actually had! Then there was the heartbreak of seeing our hometown hero, Dick Groat, in a St. Louis Cardinal uniform. We never really understood how Dick could no longer be a Pirate. We'd hang onto the screen behind the great Roberto Clemente in right field — and there was Maz, who made everything look so easy and automatic, at second. Every year the coaches would retell the story, "Ya know, boys, 'The Babe' hit one over the roof above our heads." And year after year, we'd all look up in amazement and say almost in unison, "No way!"

On the journey home, as if to show us the town, the bus driver would loop back to the North Side on the Parkway East. The bus ride home would be past the J&L steel mills along the Monongahela River. The boys would hang out the bus windows, watching the skip cars climb up and dump into the top of the blast furnaces. I don't think I was the only one thinking, "If I can make it to the Pirates, maybe I won't have to work at the mill like our dads and granddads." But by the time we were grown, the mills were gone and so were our dreams of playing Big League ball. The mills became part of Pittsburgh's past, just like Forbes Field.

Glenn Logan
Colstrip, Montana

---

I must have gone to over 100 Pirate games as a youngster between the ages of eight and 12. Many of those were promotional games, such as Bat Day, Ball Day, and Cap Day. Youngsters under 12 had to have a parent with them to get a souvenir. Dad was always at work, but Mom would let me go anyway. I don't remember how far the field was from the house — just a few miles away I guess. We lived near the Highland Park Zoo, and I would ride the streetcar there. Pittsburgh had electric trolley cars back then. When I got to Forbes Field, I had to be very forward with strangers and ask if they would be my dad so that I could get a souvenir. It was scary, but I always got the "autographed bat."

Another memory is when I caught a home run ball. I persuaded Dad and Grandma, who was visiting from out of state, to go to the game. It wasn't actually a home run — it was batting practice. All of the batters were socking them into the upper deck in right field. I pleaded with Dad to let me go sit there till the game started. He said OK, and I took off running for the upper deck. I no sooner got there when Ron Fairly of the Dodgers cracked one. I had anticipated and positioned myself just right. I stood up and raised my hands to catch it. I played street ball with the neighborhood kids, so I knew I could catch it. I also knew it was going to hurt my bare hands. The closest person to me was about five rows back, so that ball was all mine. Just in time, that person shouted a warning: "Don't catch it, don't catch it." I let it hit the seat. By the sound of that ball hitting the wooden seat, I was glad I didn't catch it. I merely bent over and picked it up. Dad and Grandma were just as thrilled as I when they saw me running back. It wasn't actually a home run and I didn't actually catch it, but it certainly is one of my best souvenirs.

Stevo Morris
Ann Arbor, Michigan

---

Though I grew up in suburban Cleveland, the first major league game that I ever attended was in Forbes Field in the summer of 1965. I was seven years old and already a huge baseball fan. I had been asking my father to take me to an Indians game, but he thought I was too young to sit through a whole game.

Well, that summer, my brother had to play his accordion in a music competition in Pittsburgh, so our family rode a bus there with other families from the studio where my brother took his music lessons.

We stayed in a big downtown hotel, and I was thrilled when another father and son that we knew invited us to take a cab and go to the Pirates-Mets game with them. I can still remember stepping out of that cab onto the sidewalk and being shocked when I was told that the building right there, just the sidewalk's width from the curb, was a stadium. I had no idea that a baseball field could be built like that. My dad said that it was much like old League Park in Cleveland. We sat high above third base (I can still picture it in my mind), on the third level. There were only a few rows of seats up there as I recall, but we were right in front with a spectacular view, seemingly right over the field. I had sure never seen anything like this on our black and white Zenith TV.

My only memory of the game is that view of the field, the scoreboard, and a foul ball that went right through my dad's raised hands. He slowed it down enough to make it an easy catch for the guy right behind us.

I always remember that the Mets won 1–0, and even found the box score on newspaper microfilm one day in the library when I was in high school, about 10 years later. I must have really paid attention to that game, because about a week later, my dad took me to the huge Cleveland Stadium for the first of many times. I'll never forget any of them — especially that feeling of being at a big league game for the first time ever.

Ken Krsolovic
Havertown, Pennsylvania

I have very special and fond memories of my first trip to Forbes Field. I believe it was 1965, and I was nine years old. I got out of school early because it was about a two-and-a-half-hour trip from my home in Oakland, Maryland (near Deep Creek Lake). We had seats on the right field side, about midway between the infield and the fence. My seat was behind one of those big steel beams, so I had to twist and turn constantly to see the action. The Pirates were playing the Phillies, and Roberto Clemente had a couple of home runs and a couple of doubles. The game went extra innings and didn't end until very late. We got home about 2 A.M., but I wasn't the least bit tired.

Brad Frantz
Oakland, Maryland

As one of the editors of this book, some of my Forbes Field memories have already been included in the "Introduction," but I couldn't resist sharing a few more of them.

July 21, 1965
• Seeing Al Jackson of the New York Mets pitch a no-hitter for seven and a third innings before Willie Stargell stopped it with a single to left. Ozzie Virgil would later (in the ninth inning) beat out an infield grounder for the second and final hit off Jackson, who won the game, 1–0.

June 23, 1968
• Sitting with my Uncle Andrew, Aunt Anne, and cousin Stush in the roof box seats. Everything seemed below us, including the pop-ups.
• Watching Willie McCovey of the San Francisco Giants hit two home runs off Jim Bunning, the first one being a smash onto the right field roof in the first inning. These were the only two runs the Giants got, as they beat the Pirates, 2–1.
• Seeing Jim Ray Hart follow McCovey to the plate in the first inning and hit a shot to the left field scoreboard. Willie Stargell raced after it, caught it running full speed towards the scoreboard but looking in the opposite direction, turned his head and immediately smashed his face into the scoreboard, knocking himself senseless. He fell to the ground, but continued to hold on to the ball, and Hart was called out.

Undated Memories
• Sitting in the roof box seats with my cousin Stush and one or both of his parents during some game in the mid-to-late '60s and laughing at a man in the next box over who had eaten so many peanuts that the shells were about three inches deep around his feet. After Donn Clendenon struck out for what seemed to be the 100th time, the "peanut eater" shouted at the top of his lungs in a heavy East European accent, "You strike out again, you big galoot!"
• At another game in the mid-to-late '60s, listening to the conversation between a child and a woman sitting a few seats away from me. The child was full of questions, the woman was full of ignorance, so the conversation went like this:
CHILD: Why did the man hit the ball?
WOMAN: I don't know.
CHILD: Why did the man run after hitting the ball?
WOMAN: I don't know.
CHILD: Why did the other man grab the ball?
WOMAN: I don't know. I don't know anything.
• Attending a Pirate-Cubs game and seeing Don Kessinger hit a line drive at Pirate center fielder Matty Alou, who was never confused with Tris Speaker or Willie Mays when it came to defensive prowess. Alou came in and the ball went out — over his head and into the vast space called center field. Needless to say, by the time Alou caught up to the ball, Kessinger had crossed the plate with an inside-the-park home run.

Angelo J. Louisa
Omaha, Nebraska

I remember my dad taking me into Forbes Field in the middle '60s. It was Bat Day, and I was handed my bat as I entered the gate — it was a Roberto Clemente H&B bat. I jumped for joy, only to find out later that very few Clemente bats were given out that day. I still have that bat and it's been kept in mint condition, never used. I have been offered $500 to $700 by collectors, but I won't part with it.

Larry Regrut
Washington, Pennsylvania

My dad is a devoted Bucs fan forever. I believe I was around six or seven years of age when he took my friend Janice and me to Forbes Field on what was called "Long Ball Fan Night." All the fans attending were given a cardboard fan, sponsored by Iron City Beer, with instructions on it to fan fast for the home team's hits so they would go out of the park, but to not fan for the opposing team. Don Drysdale was pitching for the Dodgers that evening, and he stopped pitching to complain to the umpire that the fans were distracting him. When this was announced over the PA system, the fans waved their fans even faster, which infuriated Drysdale even further.

Forbes Field was so special because you were so close to the field and players. You felt like part of the game!

William Salyan, Jr.
Gig Harbor, Washington

**Sold at Forbes Field during the 1960s, the Green Weenie was used as a hex and rattled when shaken. Directions on back instructed fans to "Point at opposing player and give 'em the Green Weenie sound. Caution — Use only when in deep trouble" (collection of David Cicotello).**

I remember...

• My friends and I going to the twilight doubleheaders and shaking the heck out of our Green Weenies.
• My friends and I buying general admission tickets and sneaking down to sit in empty box seats. Sometimes we got caught, and sometimes we got away with it.
• Before the game would start, my friends and I would walk down to the first row of the box seats, hang over the railing, talk to some of the Pirates, and get autographs, too.
• Watching with such amazement every time Roberto Clemente threw the ball from right field to home plate, right on target.

Geraldine Raffaele
Pittsburgh, Pennsylvania

Having grown up in northern West Virginia, I spent many a night listening to Pirate baseball. I fell asleep countless times with Bob Prince broadcasting a game from the West Coast. The first game I saw in person was a doubleheader between the Pirates and Cubs in the mid–1960s. My most vivid memory is of Ernie Banks hitting a ball off the clock above the scoreboard. I was also at Forbes Field on the last day, June 28, 1970. I still have my ticket stub and one of the numbers that was used on the scoreboard.

John Marra
Grand Rapids, Michigan

I have so many memories. I remember the left field bleachers with the hot dogs cooking right in front of you, and being on top of the visitors' bullpen, being in the right field bleachers behind Clemente, even though we didn't appreciate him then, and attending Camera Day, sitting in the first base boxes. But my most vivid memory comes from 1965, I think — it's the combination of Tommie Sisk and Joe Gibbon beating Sandy Koufax 3–2 in the first game of a doubleheader and Vernon Law going the distance to defeat Don Drysdale in the second game, 2–1.

Jim Saint
Rotterdam, New York

I was 16 years old and had grown up a Pirate fan in Ellwood City. I was able to go to some of those special Kids Days and see my Pirates. Clemente was my hero. The World Series of 1960 was etched in my brain. When I was playing baseball in my high school days, I was given the opportunity by the Pirates to play in Forbes Field. It was a hot summer day, and the Pirates were out of town.

We were led through the cave tunnels into the Pirate club house from the Sennott Street offices. I was in awe. I saw all the lockers of my heroes, and set all my equipment down in front of Gene Alley's locker. Everything was wooden and old. Names were scratched into the benches in the locker room.

We were led down the ramp into the Pirate dugout. I thought I was in a cave. All of sudden, there we were, looking out on the field into the bright sunlight. I got on that field and felt like I was in heaven. I ran to center field to see how far that batting cage screen was from home plate. Home plate seemed liked it was in another county. Matty Alou was the center fielder. Then I pretended I was playing center field, and suddenly it came to me: Where would you stand? Center field was immense. I looked over at those iron gates in right center and they seemed to be part of a building in another state!

I pitched that day at Forbes Field. I got to warm up in the bullpen. The coach had to scold me for not warming up because we were playing with the phones in the bullpen that rang in the dugout.

When I stood on that mound, I was overcome. I looked up into those stands and stared at the 35,000 seats with not a person in them. It was awesome. In the first inning, a left-handed batter hit a fastball off the right field screen on me. What a thrill! When I got back to the dugout my coach said to me, "Welcome to the big leagues, kid!"

I'll never forget playing in Forbes Field that day in the summer of 1966. What a great piece of history to be a part of.

Bob Haine
Royal Palm Beach, Florida

My first visit to Forbes Field was in the summer of 1966. The Cubs were playing the Pirates. Bob Veale pitched for the Bucs, and Dick Ellsworth pitched for the Cubs. It was a night game. I vividly remember the smells, sounds, and sights of the ballpark: the vendors selling their wares, the scorecard lineup barkers, the Kennywood–like atmosphere, the smells of popcorn, hotdogs, and cigar smoke permeating the dark mezzanine as we made our way to the field. Up the ramps we walked to the third base side, second level where my dad's company had seats. We stepped out of the darkness to the shining emerald-green ball field in all its glory. Wow!

Herb Carpenter
Waynesburg, Pennsylvania

My memory of Forbes Field is brief, as I attended only one Pirate game there. The year may have been 1966 (I'm not sure of the month), and my Little League Association took us kids to a game as part of the "field trip" experience.

My group sat about half-way up the bleachers in right field and got to see Roberto Clemente play outfield. I believe the Buccos were playing either the Cubs or the Cardinals that day, and the Pirates won, if I remember correctly. I'll never forget the sounds as the fans cheered on the home team, and kicking the base boards behind the seats created a unique sound!

We all went crazy when Pittsburgh would score, but my greatest and fondest memory was seeing the Pirates play for the first time in my life. At age 10, it was wonderful. But I will always remember seeing Roberto Clemente make some spectacular catches that day with his familiar basket catch, then quickly throwing the ball back to the infield. That will stay with me forever. That one summer afternoon was a onetime thrill.

William G. Horner<br>
Johnstown, Pennsylvania

---

I am 50 years old and attended my first ballgame at Forbes in 1959. Over the years until its demolition, I attended probably about a dozen games a year there, more or less. I will be honest and say that, "No, I was not at Game Seven on October 13, 1960," as many claim to have been, but that has to be the top memory of Forbes Field for everyone. Nor was I at the 1970 finale when the mobs destroyed the ballpark. I'm glad I wasn't, but if it is an "in-person-I-was-there" memory you want, I have one for you.

It involves Roberto Clemente and the 1966 Pirates, a team that finished in third place, and is still one of my favorite Pirate teams. Everyone remembers Clemente's 3,000th hit. The fact that it turned out to be his last hit makes it particularly memorable. However, no one ever talks about his 2,000th hit and that occurred in 1966, his MVP season. It was September, I don't know the exact date, but everyone knew he was sitting on 1,999 hits, and the impending milestone was a topic in the papers. On this particular night, the Pirates were playing the Cubs, and my Dad was able to get a couple of third base box seat tickets. I think they were his office's tickets.

Again, I do not remember the exact date of this game, but Ferguson Jenkins was pitching for the Cubs, and when hit number 2,000 came, it was a dramatic one — a home run into the right field upper deck at Forbes. The Pirate bullpen was down the right field line, and I remember the guys in the pen coming out onto the field, and waving for the person in the stands to bring the ball down to the field. I don't know if they did or not. The fact that the Bucs were in a pennant race made it all the more dramatic.

Another memory of Forbes, same season, is of attending a doubleheader against the Giants on a Saturday afternoon, the next to last day of the season. It was cold, rainy, and miserable, and the Pirates needed to win that doubleheader and the game the next day (and maybe have the Dodgers lose their games; I'm not sure) to stay alive in the pennant race. I remember that Clemente homered in game one, but I also remember that the Giants won the game, which ended the season for the Pirates. We didn't stay for the second game.

I have many fond memories of Forbes Field, but not many of any specific games, other than the two described above. Mainly, I will remember time spent with my dad and brothers at these games. It is also easy to idealize Forbes Field long after it is gone. I loved the place, but make no mistake, it was old and outdated and needed to be replaced when it was.

Bob Sproule<br>
Pittsburgh, Pennsylvania

---

Probably my favorite memory of Forbes Field is one that I wish I could confirm. It happened to involve "The Great One." I swear I remember one game where Roberto hit a triple, was thrown out trying to extend it into a home run, and then later in the same game, did get an inside-the-park home run. All I can be sure of was that it was a night game around the mid–1960s.

Bob Gerald<br>
Pittsburgh, Pennsylvania

---

I was born in 1961 and grew up in Alliance, Ohio. I was not a Cleveland fan like my father and brother. As a young boy, what I can remember of my trips to Forbes was riding in a nine-passenger Dodge wagon, buying gas for 30 cents. And then, once we were in Pittsburgh, the smell of the steel mills, walking to the stadium, and most of all, how steep the seats were and that first view of the field as I walked out of the tunnel.

George Kennedy<br>
Saint Louis, Missouri

---

It was during 1966–1969 that I attended the Liliane S. Kaufman School of Nursing at Montefiore Hospital in Oakland. Tickets to the Pirate games were provided free to the school on a regular basis. My friends and I often made use of those tickets, walking the short distance to Forbes Field to sit in the "peanut gallery" and watch my two favorite players, Roberto Clemente and Willie Stargell.

Sharon Childs
Somerset, Pennsylvania

Most of my memories from Forbes Field are Pirate–St. Louis games, as my father was from Missouri. We went to many games in the late '60s to see Gibson, Cepeda, Brock, Flood, Maris, and the other Cardinal greats.

At one game, Stan Musial was in attendance and sat near us, and I was able to get his autograph. In 1968, we went to a Bat Day — it was a doubleheader. I got a Willie Stargell bat that I still have. Willie hit a home run in each game, and in the second game, he and Clemente hit back-to-back homers. After the games, I remember walking on the field and leaving through the center field gate.

John Vaughn
Greensburg, Pennsylvania

My Forbes Field memory: The bases were loaded, and the pitcher was due up. As the pitcher made his way to the box, my dad was hollering for him to be pulled for a pinch hitter. An elderly gentleman, dressed in a suit and tie and wearing a fedora, who was sitting behind us, tapped my dad on the shoulder and said, "You know, mister, he can hit that ball sometimes."

As he finished the sentence, a grand slam was launched from that Pirate pitcher's bat and a joyful memory was secured for a young boy. One of three generations interacting, of strangers interacting, of different races interacting, joined together in celebration of the simple pleasure of our national pastime.

I believe Al McBean was the star of this feat, and it occurred at the end of July in 1966 or 1968, because I think my dad had taken me to the ballgame to celebrate my birthday.

George Campbell
Pittsburgh, Pennsylvania

*It was indeed Al McBean who hit the grand slam on July 28, 1968.*

I watched my first game at Forbes Field in August 1968. We sat in the upper deck on the first base side. Bob Gibson beat Bob Veale 8–0, if I remember right. I saw many games before Forbes Field closed. I usually sat on the first base side and in the upper deck right field. I always went with my dad. I once went to a game in 1970 and bought a second row box seat with money I earned from my paper route. I sat right next to the Pirate dugout, and it was neat to be able to look into the dugout because the front rows were added for the 1959 All-Star Game and were at dugout level. You had to turn and look to your side and behind to see the dugout.

I remember the hawkers selling programs upon entering the park, the smell of hot dogs, stale beer and cigar smoke, the wretched bathrooms with troughs, the trees and ivy making a green backdrop and kids climbing into the trees and guards getting them out. We always parked in the Panther Hollow and walked up to Forbes, approaching from below the right field grandstand and walking past the clubhouse entrances to the main entrance behind home plate. Nothing will ever replace Forbes Field.

Don Lancaster
Indiana, Pennsylvania

I remember going to a 4th of July doubleheader in 1969 with my father. It was a very hot day and we both got sunburned. It was the Pirates versus the Amazing Mets of '69. I remember that the Mets started Tom Seaver and Don Cardwell. What a day that was! The Mets crushed the Pirates in both games. But I believe that Willie Stargell performed very well in both games and hit a home run over the right field roof in the first game.

John Perkun
Pittsburgh, Pennsylvania

From 1969 to 1972, I lived in Wilkinsburg. Very often, we'd be out and about in Pittsburgh in the evening, but to get back to Wilkinsburg, we would drive through Schenley Park. Often during a Pirates night game, if there was an empty parking place on the street outside of Forbes Field (I don't recall the exact name of the street), we'd simply pull in, walk through the unattended gate, and catch the last few innings of the game. It was the best and cheapest entertainment in town. When we really felt extravagant, we'd pay $1 for a left field bleacher seat and see the entire game. Those left field bleacher seats were better than any third base box seat in the majors today — with the possible exception of some newer stadiums (e.g., Camden Yards and Jacobs Field).

An added benefit of the left field bleacher seats was the close proximity of the visiting bullpen. It was possible to converse with the players in the visiting bullpen. I recall interesting conversations with Duffy Dyer, who was then a back-up catcher to the Mets' Jerry Grote, and Pat Corrales, then either a reserve or bullpen catcher for the Cincinnati Reds. I don't recall specifics of any one game, other than the final game at Forbes, but my general feeling is that I never had a bad day at Forbes.

The last game was something. While the Pirates organization was waiting to award prizes, some fans were busy dismantling Forbes. I can still visualize people walking out with rows of seats. Others pulling ivy off the outfield walls. People taking signs down — everything from section signs to restroom signs. I heard that when they wanted memorabilia for the Stadium Club at Three Rivers, stadium personnel had to issue a call for the Forbes scoreboard numbers—fans had walked off with all of them. I'm surprised somebody didn't come to the last game with a jackhammer and take the wall over which Mazeroski hit his greatest home run.

James Campbell
Lewisburg, Pennsylvania

---

The only ticket I ever held, for dozens of games at Forbes Field, was for the bleachers. I knew by theory that the other seats were better, but I didn't know that I was missing anything, so I was satisfied. The couple of times we snuck through a tunnel to seats closer to home plate, late in the game, we were so nervous about being caught that we couldn't enjoy anything. Besides, the bleachers were great. As I got older (past 12), I learned to move to a spot next to the visitors' bullpen, in which relievers sat inches from any fan who pressed himself against the wire fence that separated mundane life from the major leagues. I developed a habit of dropping my pen or pencil through the wire fence, onto the field, inches from the bleachers wall, so that I could attract the attention of a major league ballplayer: "Mister, I dropped my pen. Could you help me please?" I assembled a small collection of Bic pen caps, pencils and other small keepsakes that had been touched by major league ballplayers. Once, my best friend, Gary Clark, grabbed a pen cap just as it was being passed between worlds, before I could take it from a major leaguer's hand, and rubbed all of the player's "cooties" off the cap. After that, I was more careful. And once, I was more bold. I took a pen cap and threw it as far as I could, barely — but officially — into fair territory along the left field line. I bugged a seated opposing pitcher (I'm not sure who it was) who had already retrieved one item for me that day. He looked near his feet, muttering, "Man, kid, you need to be more careful with your stuff. I don't see no pen cap. Where is it?" I pointed toward the left field line. The pitcher smiled at me and looked me in the eye, recognizing the scam, maybe even appreciating it. "You'll have to wait until the next inning." Between innings, he trotted onto the field, picked up the cap, and passed it through the fence to me. He said something about not "dropping" it so far next time, but I was transfixed by my hand, which held a piece of plastic that had been on a major league field, in fair territory, during a major league game. I stared at my palm's contents, scarcely believing my palm could come to be in contact with such a treasure, not knowing how I would or could properly safeguard an item of such unfathomable importance — which was just as well, because Gary Clark promptly snatched it and rubbed all of the cooties off it.

Cris Hoel
Wexford, Pennsylvania

---

I was at the last Prize Day/Fan Appreciation Day at Forbes. It was a cold chilly day, the Pirates playing the Cubs. A couple of unforgettable events happened during the game. First, a fan ran onto the field and shook Dave Cash's hand at second base. When the police got close to him, he bolted out to left and shook Stargell's hand. Then he ran to center, with three or four officers right on his heels, and shook Matty Alou's hand, without breaking stride. He then darted to right center and ran up the batting cage and over the fence to freedom!

On top of that, a deaf man gave my sister and me — we were ages 10 and 11— his family's tickets for prizes. We also learned that our dad, who seemed to us to communicate more by force than verbal skills, could talk sign language. Before leaving he thanked the man in sign.

We won a few small items, maybe ice cream certificates, but since we had to wait around to find out who won what prizes, we got to meet Mr. Cub, Ernie Banks. He was Bob Prince's postgame guest, and he skittered right by us in his cleats, on his way to the press box for the interview.

In spite of the cold day, we still remember the last Prize Day at Forbes Field.

Ken White
Charlotte, North Carolina

---

As a boy, we would go to Pirate games with Knot Hole Club youth tickets. Organizations like church groups or youth sports leagues would get the tickets for free. We would go on a Saturday in bus loads. All the buses would be parked in Schenley Park along the street that seemed to stretch forever. Everyone would walk into the park through the right field gate and find seats in right field. It was probably a rite of passage that every Pirate fan had to sit and watch games from behind that big screen in right field.

I remember going to the next to the last game at Forbes as a Knot Hole ticket holder. I was 11. I recall the smell of the hot dogs and popcorn, and I think the Pirates won.

Joe Zaccagnini
Leechburg, Pennsylvania

*The Pirates did win that game.*

---

Having been raised in McKeesport, Pennsylvania, I always turned on KDKA to hear our Buccos. I was working for United States Steel in Duquesne when the mill shut down early on Sunday, June 28, 1970. Arriving home at noon, I asked my bride of four months if she wanted to go to the last game. In a moment, we were heading "downtown" to Forbes Field.

We had to park by Phipps Conservatory and walk down the hill. Having no tickets, we arrived around 2:00 P.M., and I found a wonderful policemen who took our $4.00 "donation" and allowed us into the game. There was standing room only, but we managed to find two seats on the first base side and saw the Bucs win a doubleheader.

We stayed after the game to hear Bob Prince raffle off ticket numbers for those lucky enough to receive mementos of Forbes Field. Then it was over, and it seemed people were "walking" off with everything. We even saw four men carrying off a turnstile. We took some ivy from the outfield wall and even helped ourselves to two blue metal folding chairs which remain two of our prized possessions to this day. It was such a memorable day for us— but, oh, how we wish we had had a camera!

Wayne and Betty Bostak
Winter Park, Florida

---

My father took me to my first game at Forbes Field in the 1960s, and I closed the place in 1970. I remember that the Buccos swept the Cubs in a doubleheader and that the Mets lost, putting the Pirates in first place. Once the final out was recorded, the place erupted and people began tearing the park apart. I took a folding chair from a box seat and broke pieces out of the old bench seats.

I have a lot of great memories of Forbes. I used to sit in the right field stands and just study Clemente, who was my first baseball hero.

George Bertha
York, Pennsylvania

---

My father and I attended the last game at Forbes Field in 1970, just before the All-Star break. The last game was the second game of a daytime doubleheader against the Cubs. The Pirates won both games. Roberto played in the first game, but not the second. The day was sunny. We sat in the bleachers with the famous Chicago "bleacher bums." After the game, there was to be a special presentation on the field, with some giveaways, and Bob Prince as MC at home plate. As the presentation proceeded, the crowd inched closer to home plate, then I heard banging in the outfield, and I turned to see guys on the scoreboard, pounding the numbers, trying to take some. I saw a guy picking up dirt in the infield and putting it in his handkerchief. As we walked around the place, I saw people trying to break pieces of the seats, some guys taking a neon telephone booth sign down. We went up to the Terrace Reserve section, and there were dozens of empty metal fold-up chairs, painted blue with dozens of coats of paint. My father and I each took one chair. I still have one of them. I saw no violence among people, just guys taking souvenirs.

John Forgach
Pittsburgh, Pennsylvania

---

I saw the last game at Forbes; I was 15 years old and went with my two cousins. My younger cousin, Vince Petrilena, was one of the many who climbed the old scoreboard and tossed numbers like Frisbees. I tore off some vines from the outfield wall, took them home, and put them in a freezer in my garage. I went away to California to go to college and when I came home the first summer, in 1976, I checked the freezer and found my mom had pulled the plug. To my horror, I discovered that my Forbes vines were now brown and gooey! But I still had a piece of that weird strip of artificial turf they had behind home plate; a guy had been cutting it up with a knife, and I got a piece. I remember seeing people leaving the stadium with big sections of reserved seats. It was an awesome day.

Frank Garland
Angels Camp, California

---

Two things stick out in my mind concerning Forbes Field. First, it had the largest outfield I have ever seen. It's easy to see why there wasn't a no-hitter pitched there. And second, in its last couple of years of existence, the place had become a dump. It was filthy and in need of refurbishment or demolition. At the time, I was in favor of demolition. However, on July 16, 1970, after spending my first five minutes sitting in Three Rivers Stadium, I would have done anything just to be back at Forbes watching a game.

Also, there are two sounds of Forbes Field you don't hear anymore: rhythmic applause and kids in the grandstand yelling, "We want a hit!" "We want a hit!"

Andrew "Stush" Carrozza
Bethel Park, Pennsylvania

---

Let me add one memory about the grand old place from when I was 11 years old. In 1971, several months before my grandmother died, she was in one of the hospitals in Oakland. We had just visited

Forbes Field in the process of demolition, April 19, 1972 (photograph courtesy University Archives, University of Pittsburgh).

her and were going home to Wilkinsburg when we drove past the ballpark, which had been closed for about a year at the time. When my dad reminded me that we were about to pass Forbes Field, I sat up in the back seat to see as much as I could. Suddenly, I yelled, "Dad, stop!" (I must have startled him, but fortunately he didn't wreck the car.) The center field gate was open, and I just had to go in. Years later, of course, I realized that this was a sign of how much my father loved me — that he would try to find a place to pull over in Oakland so his kid could walk into a closed ballpark. I remember the grass being about knee high (but of course my knees weren't as high back then), and I remember being really impressed at how far home plate was from center field. I could picture Matty Alou, one of my favorites when he was here, standing where I was standing. And then I walked over to right field, and I couldn't believe I was standing in the great Roberto Clemente's territory. I just wish I'd grabbed some ivy or something.

Father John Hissrich
Pittsburgh, Pennsylvania

I don't think I ever attended a ball game at Forbes Field, but I went to a Billy Graham Crusade there and the Ice Capades. As a teenager, I remember the awesome experience of walking out on to the seating decks and seeing the lighted field. Some experience for a farm boy who hadn't been to the big city.

Also, I was attending the University of Pittsburgh when they dismantled Forbes, and remember the feeling of "losing a friend" as we watched from the windows.

Hervey A. Steiner
New Stanton, Pennsylvania

I grew up three blocks away from Forbes Field and attended countless Pirates games, Steeler games, and even the circus when it came to town. During the demolition of Forbes Field, I was fortunate enough to collect a complete set of decorative arched stones from above one of the entrance gates. The stones are cast concrete, bearing floral arrangements and the Pittsburgh Athletic Club logo cast into their surfaces. I still have the stonework. It's the best reminder of all the memories of Forbes Field.

Ed Dombrowski
Pittsburgh, Pennsylvania

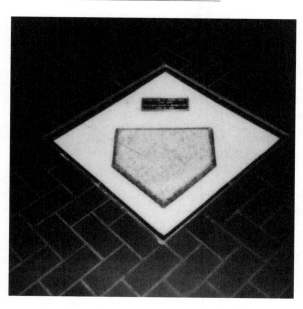

Home plate of Forbes Field, now under Lucite and located in Wesley W. Posvar Hall on the University of Pittsburgh campus (courtesy Barry Chad, Carnegie Library of Pittsburgh).

## *The Media*

I haven't thought about Forbes Field in years, but here is an excerpt from something I wrote for the *Pittsburgh Press Sunday Magazine* of April 10, 1983. In a piece written to coincide with the opening of the season I wrote that in 1982 more people than ever watched major league baseball, and went on to say the following.

If there's an attendance boom, the Pirates have missed out on it. Attendance last year was the lowest in the National League.... Nobody pretends to believe any more that Pittsburgh is a red-hot baseball town. As for the whys and wherefores, we've been hanging them out to dry since Three Rivers Stadium opened: The Pirates don't draw because the Parkway East is perpetually shut down for repairs. The Pirates don't draw because you can't get in or out of the parking lots at the stadium. The Pirates don't draw because the stadium itself, undistinguished in any way from any other concrete cylinder anywhere, lacks intimacy, lacks character, lacks charm.... [However], paid for by the city, $17 million worth of ... improvements are in the works. There will be new artificial turf. There will be a fancy new scoreboard, equipped with a giant screen for instant replays and for highlight films during rain delays. There will be new general admission seats close to the action. By eliminating a couple of 20-foot gaps between the stands and the outfield, says [Jack] Schrom [the Pirates' vice president in charge of public relations and marketing], "we have made the park smaller while making it larger."

Forbes Field, where the Pirates set their all-time attendance record [1.7 million in 1960], was so small it had a community life of sorts. "The crowds there," said Willie Stargell not long ago, "were like a gathering of folks. You could see the expressions on people's faces. And, man, when you did something...."

Forbes Field was a park of ivy-covered red brick walls that bordered but did not enclose. The view in the distance was of grass, trees, and sky. Less romantically, it was also a park of dank inner passages, of heavy iron posts and girders obstructing the view, of dirt and spilled beer and rancid smells of decay. All forgotten. Forbes Field was the good old days.

Were the good old days all that good? It depends on your outlook. The "gathering of folks" included special characters. Bruce McAllister, the Human Screech Owl, was a denizen of Forbes Field. "Human Screech Owl" is a slight misnomer. He was more like a Human Factory Whistle. There's a story that management eventually shut him up with the bribe of a lifetime pass. But McAllister cared [about the Pirates]. In a 1941 divorce suit, his wife made the complaint that he would rather be at the ball park, screeching and hooting and blasting away, than with her.

An usher called Big Bob, an agreeably cynical man weighing 260 pounds in his prime, once said that night ball, an innovation of the 1930s, changed the fabric of the crowds at Forbes Field, bringing family groups to the park, friendly, tolerant people looking for fun. Before that, when daylight games started at 3:15, such patronage as there was came from the leisure class. The third-base side of the park belonged to the gamblers. "In a crowd of 1,500," Big Bob has estimated, perhaps exaggerating somewhat, "you could count on 1,000 being racket guys." They stood behind the last row of seats, waving 50-dollar bills as they called out their bets, and if the game wasn't going right, it had to be somebody's fault. With savage invective, they chased a Pirate third baseman named Bob Elliott out of town. Traded to the Boston Braves, Elliott found love and appreciation, which was all he apparently needed to win the National League Most Valuable Player award.

The heckling went on after Elliott's departure. There was the man who liked to quack at Ducky Schofield when Schofield played shortstop for the Pirates. As Big Bob told it, by the sixth or seventh inning Schofield would be raging, and one night he walked toward the stands. Singling out the source of the quacks, he said, "I'll see you after the game." His tormentor stood up. He was huge, maybe six inches taller and 60 pounds heavier than Schofield. "I don't think Schofield saw him after the game," said Big Bob.

Another loud fan took to booing George Metkovich, a Pirate first baseman in the 1950s. Metkovich, with the abuse in his ears, swung at a pitch and missed. The bat flew out of his hands and into the stands. "And so help me," said Big Bob, "it hit the guy who was booing him right on the head." Big Bob had a taste for parables.

Affection for Forbes Field exceeded all bounds after the last out of the last game ever played there, on June 28, 1970. The gathering of folks went berserk, overrunning a scheduled ceremony. It was like the Visigoths pillaging Rome. They tore down the scoreboard, uprooted the seats, ripped the ivy from the walls, and carried away everything portable. It could be thought of as an aspect of the social revolution. To show disdain for authority, what with Vietnam and all, you smashed something, and this was good practice....

Enthusiasm at Three Rivers is the orchestrated kind. In response to any given situation, fireworks go off, the scoreboard lights up, the Pirate Parrot capers, the organist thunders through "Let's Go, Bucs." Forbes Field was for individualists.

Roy McHugh<br>Pittsburgh, Pennsylvania

*Roy McHugh is a former sportswriter and columnist for* The Pittsburgh Press. *This piece is reprinted, with a few modifications, by permission of the author.*

---

At age 73, the early years are fuzzy at best, but I do recall 1938, at age 10, when my father took me to a Pirate–New York Giants doubleheader at Forbes Field. It was sold out, and I was a very dejected young man.

Then my father purchased scalper's tickets. I recall standing alongside hundreds of other fans outside the field behind home plate. It was a hot Sunday afternoon. To my recollection, Carl Hubbell and Hal Schumacher were the scheduled pitchers for the Giants, and Ken Heintzelman and Mace Brown were tabbed to hurl for the Pirates. I had known Heintzelman as a pitcher for Jeannette in the Penn State Association. I would have to lie to you if you would ask me who won the games, but it was standing room only.

I later attended many games at Forbes Field and many times as an adult, taking the train from Greensburg to East Liberty and back. When Ralph Kiner was in his prime, we, like many others in the stands, awaited his final at bat, and then left the field, whether the Pirates were winning or not.

In later years, starting in 1958, I became sports editor of the *Greensburg Tribune-Review* and had the luxury of receiving season tickets for all the home games.

In one way, it was great. In another way, it was difficult because the seats were on the third base side and I couldn't see the left field fence.

I had the pleasure of covering the 1960 World Series, but there was a catch to that also. I had to take a bus to make sure I made it home in time for the early edition and missed all the celebrations.

Huddie Kaufman<br>Greensburg, Pennsylvania

*A graduate of Saint Vincent College, Howard "Huddie" Kaufman was the sports editor for* The Greensburg Tribune-Review *from 1958 to 1967. After a six-year hiatus spent in private industry, he returned to* The Tribune-Review *in 1973 and continued working there until he retired in 1993.*

---

There was a ceremony in the Hill District last month, commemorating the unveiling of a historic marker honoring the memory of Josh Gibson, the great Negro League catcher for the Homestead Grays. It brought back memories of one of the many wonderful experiences I shared with my father. Sometime during World War II, probably in the summer of 1943, he came home from work and asked me if I wanted to see a ballgame that evening. My response was, "Of course, but the Pirates are playing in St. Louis tonight." I was politely advised that there was more to baseball than the Pirates. "This is your chance to see Paige and Gibson."

Sure enough, the Homestead Grays were entertaining the Kansas City Monarchs at Forbes Field that evening, and Satchel Paige was scheduled to pitch for the Monarchs. So we hurried through dinner and headed for Oakland. I suspect that we caught a Bigi bus "downtown" and then a streetcar out to Forbes Field. I am reasonably sure we didn't drive to the game. There was gasoline rationing at that time, and we only got three gallons a week. The only way we could make the occasional trip to my father's home near Chambersburg or my mother's in Emporium was to limit our use of the car to a bare minimum.

I suspect that the first familiar thing we encountered when we got close to Forbes Field was the old black preacher who sold peanuts outside the ballpark. He was a permanent fixture at every major sports event in those days, with his paper bags of peanuts which he claimed came straight from "Indooo China." Buying a bag of peanuts from him was a ritual. We always did our bit to support his church and those poor folks in "Indooo China" who relied upon him for their living.

One distinct memory about the game was the fact that they didn't turn on the field lights until the game was ready to begin. I suspect this was a combination of the need to preserve energy during the war and the financial state of the Negro League. When the lights came on and we were able to see the rest of the grandstand, it was obvious that there was a large crowd there and that, for once, we were the minority! I also remember that this was a festive crowd, eager to enjoy the game. At one point a girl sitting behind us accidentally burned a hole in my father's sweater with a cigarette. She immediately started to apologize. When he told her not to worry about it, she replied "That's good. My motto is 'No fool, no fun.'" I'm sure she had a lot of fun that evening.

Satchel Paige did indeed start the game, but left after pitching only three innings. In those days he was the major box office attraction in the Negro Leagues, so he pitched at the beginning of nearly every game. I remember that he appeared to have abnormally large feet and that he kicked his left foot high in the air as part of his delivery, making it seem that the ball was coming from behind his enormous left shoe. I don't think the Grays got any hits off him during the short time he was in the game. It was a real thrill for me that Satchel finally was allowed to pitch in the major leagues and to participate in the 1948 World Series as a Cleveland Indian. Although his true age was always a mystery, there was some proof that 1948 was his thirtieth year in organized baseball.

My father was as excited about seeing Gibson as he was about Paige. For some reason he always was impressed with catchers, and he thought Gibson was something really special. I am reasonably sure he told me he had seen the Grays play in Bridgeville sometime late in the 1930's, probably in the ball field across Chartier's Creek from the Presbyterian Church. I would be interested in hearing from anyone who could confirm that recollection. I think Gibson did hit one of the 800 home runs with which he is credited, in the game we saw, but I'm sure it wasn't off Satchel Paige.

A few years later, when the black players were finally allowed to play in the major leagues, we tried to match the names of the new recruits with our memory of those we had seen play. For some reason I didn't manage to keep any record of that specific game — that is one scorecard I really wish I still had. And that is one evening I would be very happy to relive.

It is gratifying to hear of things like this recognition of Josh Gibson. We can't do anything today for the black athletes of that generation that will make up for the unjust way they were treated, but we can make certain that they are remembered and honored for the contributions they made to their culture.

John F. Oyler<br>Pittsburgh, Pennsylvania

*Dr. John Oyler is a retired engineer who writes a column for the* Bridgeville Area News.
*This piece is reprinted, with modifications, by permission of the author. Copyright © 1996.*

---

I have a lot of memories of Forbes Field! I saw my first baseball game there at age six in 1944. The recollection is so vivid that I can still remember most of the St. Louis Cardinal lineup from that July doubleheader. I know Stan Musial had three hits in each game. The Cards' infield was Stan Musial, Red Schoendienst, Marty Marion (one of the game's great fielding shortstops and maybe as good as Ozzie Smith) and Whitey Kurowski, a fireplug who played third base largely with his chest and collarbones. My mom packed us a huge lunch: tuna salad sandwiches, chocolate cake, and deviled eggs. It's funny, but I don't remember much about the last game played there, which I covered and watched many fans dishonor and virtually plunder the place in a truly mad obsessiveness to collect a last souvenir. Bob Prince was on the field and tried to MC a final ceremony and ran for his life.

What made Forbes Field arguably the most charming ballpark ever — and I include the new "old" ballparks in that comparison — was its capacity to invade all the senses. Sound, for instance, carried there far better than it did later in Three Rivers, where they had major sound system problems the first year. When a game occasionally turned quiet, you could hear the infielders' chatter, the clatter of the chain that anchored the flag against the steel pole in distant center field, and the refreshment hucksters who would bark and plead and cajole.

Forbes Field had a thousand odors. Outside in front of the ticket windows, the air was thick with the smoky smell of roasting peanuts sold by an aging black preacher who treated everyone with great dignity, called even small boys "sir," and taught more that one young generation the meaning of the word "civility." When you came into the seating area from the concourse, though, you did so through tunnels that were damp and dank and had a mildewy smell that suggested a dungeon. It was a ripe, pungent odor that announced this was no antiseptic structure, but a place where serious men engaged in a kind of serious and mortal combat. And a boy could sit there and watch them and daydream about the day he would be out there in white flannel on that thick grass among them.

Still, the dominant sense of that place was sight. Oh, the dewy odor was still thick in your nostrils, but suddenly you emerged from the dark tunnel into a fresh breeze, and a sweeping green pastoral scene clutched at your eyes. And make no mistake, if you had a box or decent reserved seat, you were on top of the game. I'd be very curious to know exactly how far it was from the last row of box seats to the baselines, but I guarantee you it was closer than you'd be at PNC Park. Or maybe I'm just getting old and my vision is not what it was.

The broadcasting booth, located in the "Crow's Nest," provided announcers with a lofty perspective of Forbes Field (*The Sporting News*).

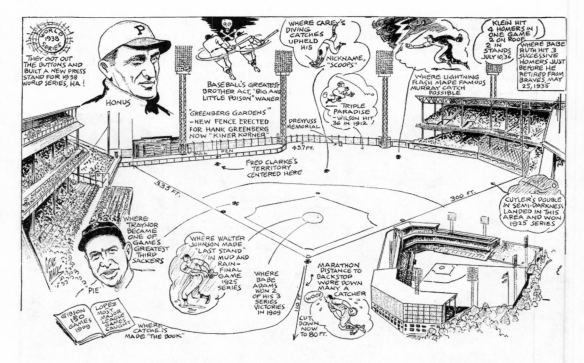

**Gene Mack's illustration of Forbes Field, 1947 (family of Gene Mack).**

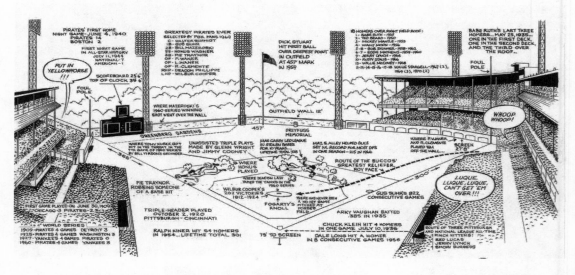

**Illustration of Forbes Field published in the "Forbes Field Farewell" souvenir poster, June 28, 1970 (Pittsburgh Pirates Baseball Club).**

Putting sentimental rambling aside, Forbes Field was simply prettier — greener, with background colors that complemented each other — than any other major league park, with the possible exception of Wrigley Field. I say that having seen all that were still around as late as 1985. Certainly no other venue of its time was so easy on the eye and soothing to the soul and ideal to host the national game than Forbes Field. And no ballpark more clearly signaled that what would take place within its

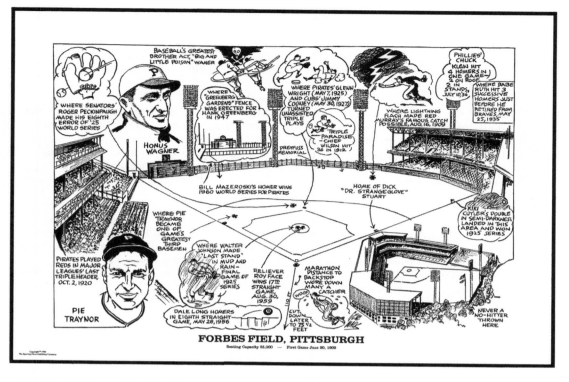

**Gene Mack's illustration of Forbes Field updated by Amadee and published in *Take Me Out to the Ball Park* in 1983 (*The Sporting News*).**

embrace was the real royal sport, baseball, as it was before a floodtide of money changed it in too many ways to count.

Making the transition from fan to professional observer, as I did when becoming a baseball writer in 1969, necessarily changed my perspective on Forbes Field. It became a place to work, and I think I viewed it with a more critical eye. But one thing is sure, I never found it less than unique, which in addition to beauty, was its chief virtue. No other ballpark was quite like it. Not other park had its angles and oblique geometry. Where else could you line a ball off a screen in the right field corner and be routinely erased if you had the temerity to try to reach second base? Where else — but the Polo Grounds in New York — were the power alleys so distant? And so different, a batting cage within hailing distance in one (at 457 feet) and the other guarded by an iron gate breached, I think, by only one hitter in the park's long history. Where else did a home run hit down the left field line have to travel so far (365 feet) and so high (the scoreboard was 25 feet high, I believe)? In fact, where else did they change the basic scope of the place to accommodate one hitter?

I've been asked before what my most vivid memory of the Pirates was and, other than Willie Stargell walking 150 feet to pour me a glass of exceptional chardonnay after he won the seventh game of the 1979 World Series, it was watching Roberto Clemente play right field at Forbes Field. Specifically, I recall the three or four times I saw him come racing in, drop to his knees, slide across the ground, and raise twin geysers of water up around his shoulders as he snatched a soft liner off the grass. Both Steve Blass and I agree it was the coolest thing we've ever see in baseball. There was also the time I saw him throw behind Willie Mays as the Giant Hall of Famer made the turn at first base too wide. The ball was on top of Mays so quickly that he never moved toward first base as Al Oliver tagged him out. Oh, yeah, and the time he caught a short fly ball along the right field line, dug his spikes in, and threw the ball over the box seats where they jutted out near the baseline, and every last fan sitting there ducked. The ball hit the Pirate third baseman's glove on the fly, at knee level. Somebody on the other team — I think it was veteran infielder Don Blasingame — said it was the greatest throw in the history of baseball. Personally, I found him guilty of understatement.

Yeah, I have a lot of memories of Forbes Field. It was to ballparks what Frank Sinatra was to soft, smoky ballads.

Philip W. Musick, Jr.
West Deer, Pennsylvania

*Phil Musick is a former sportswriter and columnist for* The Pittsburgh Press *and was a local talk-show host.*

---

Forbes Field, with her ivy-covered outfield walls and a grand view into Schenley Park, was for the most part a fine place to watch a ball game. But those who express nostalgia for Forbes Field often forget that the sight lines were terrible. If seated in the lower grandstands, for example, one lost sight of fly balls because of the overhanging second deck and had to follow the outfielder's path to know where the ball had been hit. You did not see it again until it descended into the outfielder's glove.

For its time, however, Forbes Field was a good place to watch baseball. For football — well, that was another matter.

Myron Cope
Pittsburgh, Pennsylvania

*Eccentric, creative, and hilarious, Myron Sydney Kopelman was to the Pittsburgh Steelers what Bob Prince was to the Pittsburgh Pirates — a one-of-a-kind entertainer who made listening to games even more enjoyable than watching them. But what many Steeler fans and other Pittsburghers may not know is that Cope was an outstanding sportswriter who authored five books and received several awards for journalism.*

# APPENDIX A—FROM 0 TO 1,705,828: A NUMERICAL REVIEW OF FORBES FIELD

*David Cicotello* and *Angelo J. Louisa*

0      The number of no-hitters pitched at Forbes Field.

1      The number of dollars it cost to purchase a ticket for a reserved grandstand seat to a Pirate game in 1909; the number of dollars it cost to purchase a ticket to sit in the left field bleachers for a Pirate game in 1970.

1.25      The number of dollars it cost to purchase a box seat ticket (field level or on the roof) to a Pirate game in 1909.

1.75      The number of dollars it cost to purchase a ticket for a general admission seat to a Pirate game in 1970.

2      The number of times the Pirates clinched the World Series at Forbes Field (1925 and 1960). Also, the number of the times that Franklin Delano Roosevelt gave speeches at Forbes. The first time was October 19, 1932; the second time was October 1, 1936.

3      The number of World Series championships the Pirates won while occupying Forbes Field (1909, 1925, and 1960); the number of dollars it cost to purchase a reserved seat to a Pirate game in 1970.

4      The number of Philadelphia runners Fred Clarke threw out in a game played on August 23, 1910; the number of dollars it cost to purchase a box seat ticket to a Pirate game in 1970.

5      The number of undefeated football teams that the University of Pittsburgh had while occupying Forbes Field. The 1910, 1915, 1916, and 1917 teams were undefeated and untied; the 1920 team was 6–0–2.

6      The number of hits Paul Waner got in a game played against New York on August 26, 1926. Waner used a different bat for each of his hits.

7      The number of home runs Willie Stargell hit over the right field roof during his career as a Pirate — the most by any player.

7-5-09      The date of the first home run hit in Forbes Field. The batter was Mike Mitchell of Cincinnati, who would later play for the Pirates in 1913 and 1914.

7-18-30      The date of the first nighttime baseball game played at Forbes Field. The Homestead Grays and the Kansas City Monarchs competed by using portable lights, with the Grays winning in 12 innings, 5–4.

Game action of Pittsburgh (light uniforms) against Detroit (dark uniforms) during the 1909 World Series (Library of Congress, Prints and Photographs Division, Detroit Publishing Company Collection).

7-18-51    The date of the only heavyweight boxing championship bout held at Forbes Field. Jersey Joe Walcott knocked out Ezzard Charles in the seventh round.

7-21-42    The date of a game played between the Kansas City Monarchs and the Homestead Grays in which, according to some baseball historians, the Monarchs' Satchel Paige purposely walked two men in the bottom of the seventh inning to load the bases so that he could face the Grays' great slugger, Josh Gibson. He then struck out Gibson on three called strikes. What really happened, according to the *Pittsburgh Post-Gazette*, was that in the bottom of the ninth inning, with the score tied at four and with two outs and a man on second for the Grays, Paige purposely walked Howard Easterling to face Gibson and then got him to fly out.

8-4        The score of the Negro League World Series victory by the Kansas City Monarchs over the Homestead Grays on September 10, 1942. In the bottom of the seventh inning, with the Monarchs leading 2–0, the bases loaded, and two out for the Grays, Satchel Paige struck out Josh Gibson on three pitches: two foul balls and a third strike swinging. Some baseball historians have claimed that this was the game in which Paige purposely walked two men to load the bases so that he could face Gibson and then struck out Gibson on three called strikes. (See 7-21-42.) However, in this game, all three base runners got on base by hitting singles and Gibson went down swinging.

10-13-60   The date of Bill Mazeroski's famous home run that sunk the Yankees and won the seventh game of the World Series for the Pirates in the bottom of the ninth inning by a score of 10–9.

10-16-09   The date of the first football game played at Forbes Field. The University of Pittsburgh defeated Bucknell University, 18–6.

11         The number of boxing matches Harry Greb is known to have fought at Forbes Field.

11-1-29     The date of the Duquesne University–Geneva College football game that was the first night game of any sort played at Forbes Field. Duquesne rented portable lights and defeated Geneva, 27–7.

11-23-18    The date of the University of Pittsburgh-Georgia Tech football game in which Pitt destroyed the powerful Golden Tornado, 32–0.

11-27-24    The date of the last University of Pittsburgh football game played at Forbes Field. Pitt bid Forbes a fond farewell by defeating Penn State, 24–3.

12-2-62     The date of the last Pittsburgh Steeler game played at Forbes Field. The Steelers ended their stay on a positive note by beating the St. Louis Cardinals, 19–7.

14          The height in feet of the Longines clock on top of the left field scoreboard.

15          The number of rounds of the New York State Athletic Commission and National Boxing Association World Middleweight Title bout fought between Teddy Yarosz and Vince Dundee on September 11, 1934. Yarosz won on points. Also, the number of rounds of the New York State Athletic Commission and National Boxing Association World Middleweight Title bout fought between Teddy Yarosz and Eddie "Babe" Risko on September 19, 1935. This time, Yarosz lost on points.

18          The total number of home runs hit over the right field roof.

19–0        The score of the football game in which Carnegie Tech upset undefeated, untied, and heavily favored Notre Dame before a crowd of 45,000 on November 27, 1926.

23–2        The score of the first Pittsburgh "Steeler" game held at Forbes Field, with the "Steel-

Amateur baseball game action at Forbes Field in 1943 with Marine Corps figure and war bonds sign along the left field wall (Pittsburgh City Photographer Collection, Archives Service Center, University of Pittsburgh).

ers" on the losing end of the points. The game was played on September 20, 1933; the opponent was the New York Giants; and the Steelers were then called the Pittsburgh Pirates.

24          The height in feet of the left side of the right field screen; the number of triples Chief Wilson hit in Forbes Field during his record-setting season of hitting 36 triples in 1912.

25.42       The height in feet of the left and right sides of the left field scoreboard.

27          The height in feet of the middle of the left field scoreboard.

27.67       The height in feet of the right side of the right field screen.

30–17       The score of the first Cleveland Brown–Pittsburgh Steeler game played at Forbes Field. The date was October 7, 1950, and unfortunately for Steeler fans, the Browns had the 30.

32          The height in feet of the wooden Marine sergeant that was placed to the right of the scoreboard from June 26, 1943, until the end of the 1943 season. Other than the Marine and promotional banners for war bond sales, no commercial advertising was ever permitted on the outfield walls at Forbes Field.

38          The number of home runs hit by Eddie Mathews at Forbes Field, the most hit by a visiting player.

50          The number of cents it cost to purchase a ticket to sit in the left field bleachers for a Pirate game in 1909.

75          The number of cents it cost to purchase a general admission grandstand ticket in 1909.

86          The height in feet of the right field roof.

122         The number of days it took to build Forbes Field.

175         The number of home runs hit by Ralph Kiner at Forbes Field.

200         The smallest crowd to see a Pirate game at Forbes Field watched Pittsburgh lose to Philadelphia by a score of 3–2 on June 10, 1938.

1909        The year when Forbes Field was built.

1934        The year when the Barney Dreyfuss Monument was erected.

1938        The year when Forbes Field became the first major league park to have an elevator; the year when regular radio broadcasts of Pirate home games began.

1944        The year when the Major League All-Star Game was played for the first time at Forbes Field.

1951        The year when scenes for the movie *Angels in the Outfield* were filmed at Forbes Field.

1959        The year when the Major League All-Star Game was played for the second and final time at Forbes Field.

1970        The year when the last Pirate game was played at Forbes Field.

1971        The year when Forbes Field was demolished.

2,126       The number of regular-season losses by the Pirates at Forbes Field.

2,599       The number of regular-season victories by the Pirates at Forbes Field.

3,789       The number of major league home runs hit at Forbes Field.

4,760       The number of regular-season games that the Pirates played at Forbes Field (not all games resulted in decisions).

23,000    The seating capacity for the first Pirate game played at Forbes Field.

30,338    The attendance at the first Pirate game played at Forbes Field.

35,000    The seating capacity for the last Pirate game played at Forbes Field.

40,916    Size of the largest crowd to see a Steeler game at Forbes Field. At that game, on September 30, 1962, the home team fell to the defending National Football League Eastern Conference champion New York Giants, 31–27.

40,918    The attendance at the doubleheader played on June 28, 1970, the last two Pirate games played at Forbes Field. The home team ended its relationship with the park by sweeping the Chicago Cubs, 3–2 and 4–1.

44,932    The largest crowd to see a Pirate game at Forbes Field watched their beloved Bucs lose to the defending World Series champion Brooklyn Dodgers, 8–3, on September 23, 1956. Interestingly enough, this game was suspended in the top of the ninth inning because of rain and the Pennsylvania Sunday curfew law, and finished the next day.

139,620    The Pirate attendance for the 1914 season, the worst season for Pirate attendance at Forbes Field.

250,000    The approximate number of dollars that it cost Barney Dreyfuss to purchase the land on which Forbes Field was built.

750,000    The approximate number of dollars that it cost to build Forbes Field.

1,705,828    The Pirate attendance for the 1960 season, the best season for Pirate attendance at Forbes Field.

# APPENDIX B—OFFICIAL GROUND RULES

*Editors' Note: The following information was taken from a 1965 Pittsburgh Pirate scorecard.*

1. Fair hit ball sticking in screen in front of right field grandstand — TWO BASES. Same if touched by a spectator and would not have gone into stand.
2. Fair hit ball hitting foul pole in right field above top of screen; hitting foul pole in left field above top of fence; hitting guy wire in left field supporting flagpole; or hitting supports of screen in front of right field grandstand — HOME RUN.
3. Fair hit ball going through screen in front of right field grandstand — TWO BASES.
4. Batted ball hitting light towers above fence, or dropping inside same — HOME RUN.
5. Players' bench extends from railing to railing on both sides of bench. Ball hitting railing shall be considered in play unless going in bench. Bats are not part of the bench.
6. Ball thrown by pitcher from the rubber to catch base-runner off first or third base that is touched by a spectator and goes into the stand or dugout — ONE BASE.
7. A pitched, thrown or batted ball that hits anyone on the playing field, except as otherwise provided for in the Playing Rules, is IN PLAY.
8. Batted ball striking screen on top of fence in left and center fields, and bounding back into playing field, is IN PLAY.
9. Batted ball striking clock on top of left field scoreboard or framework of football clock — HOME RUN.
10. Batted ball striking any part of left field scoreboard and bounding back into playing field, is IN PLAY.
11. Batted ball going into hole or opening in face of left field scoreboard — TWO BASES.

# EDITORS AND CONTRIBUTORS

**Sam Bernstein** has been a social worker in a variety of settings. A lifelong New York Mets fan, Bernstein is a member of the New Jersey chapter of the Society for American Baseball Research (SABR). On weekends, he is an umpire for vintage baseball teams in New York and New Jersey.

**Gene "Two Finger" Carney** is the author of *Romancing the Horsehide: Baseball Poems on Players and the Game* and the historically based baseball musical, *Mornings After*, as well as numerous short stories. Since March 1993, he has edited "Notes from the Shadows of Cooperstown," which is available for interested readers at www.baseball1.com/carney. He is the author of *Burying the Black Sox: How Baseball's Cover-up of the 1919 World Series Fix Almost Succeeded* (2006).

**David Cicotello** is a member of the Society for American Baseball Research (SABR). He is the webmaster of forbesfieldforever.com and has written biographical articles for both volumes of SABR's *Deadball Stars*.

**Angelo J. Louisa** taught at various academic institutions, served as the assistant to the Minnesota State Director of the National History Day program, and is a member of the Nebraska State Historical Records Advisory Board. He has written articles on sports figures and other subjects for books, journals, and websites.

**Richard S. Morgan** is an observer and note taker of the curious and quaint activities of the human spirit. He dedicates his portion of this book to Dr. Hunter S. Thompson.

**Jim O'Brien** has been hailed as "Pittsburgh's premier sports historian" by sportscaster Myron Cope. He has written 18 books, 15 of which deal specifically with Pittsburgh sports, including two on the Pirates. His most recent books are *Steelers Forever* and *Always a Steeler*.

**David C. Ogden** focuses his research on cultural trends in baseball, specifically the history of the relationship between African Americans and baseball, and he has been a frequent presenter at the annual Cooperstown Symposium on Baseball and American Culture.

**David Rocchi's** interest in Forbes Field grew from an assignment on a local historical landmark while he was attending graduate school at Duquesne University in Pittsburgh. He is and always will be a die-hard Pittsburgh sports fan.

**Ronald M. Selter** is a longtime member of the Society for American Baseball Research (SABR), concentrating in the areas of ballparks, minor leagues, the business of baseball, and the Deadball Era. He is an economist with the United States Air Force Space Program.

**Rich Sestili** played Little League ball at the old Plaza Field behind Forbes Field's center field wall. As a reporter, he won Associated Press awards for breaking the shotgun-slaying story of a Hell's Angels member in 1972. He is the author of two books, *For Your Penance* and *The Healer's Cross*.

**Robert Trumpbour's** research focuses on the intersection of media, sports, and society. He has written on the issue of Olympic stadium construction in New York City for the *Village Voice* and is currently working on a book about stadium construction in the United States.

# BIBLIOGRAPHY

Adomites, Paul, and Dennis DeValeria, eds. *Baseball in Pittsburgh: An Anthology of New, Unusual, Challenging and Amazing Facts About the Greatest Game as Played in the Steel City.* Cleveland: The Society for American Baseball Research, 1995.

Bonk, Daniel L. "Ballpark Figures: The Story of Forbes Field." *Pittsburgh History* 76 (Summer 1993): 52–71.

Burtt, Richard L. "Triples, Pirates, and Forbes Field." *The Baseball Research Journal* 9 (1980): 106–111.

Enders, Eric. *Baseball Parks: Then and Now.* San Diego: Thunder Bay Press, 2002.

Finoli, David, and Bill Ranier. *The Pittsburgh Pirates Encyclopedia.* Champaign, IL: Sports Publishing, 2003.

*Forbes Field 60th Birthday, 1909–1969: Pittsburgh Pirates Picture Album.* Pittsburgh: Century Printing Co., n.d.

Gershman, Michael. *Diamonds: The Evolution of the Ballpark.* Boston: Houghton Mifflin Co., 1993.

Guilfoile, William J., and Joel L. Chadys, eds. *Three Rivers Stadium Souvenir Book.* Pittsburgh: Pittsburgh Baseball Club, 1970.

Lancaster, Donald G. "Forbes Field Praised as a Gem When It Opened." *The Baseball Research Journal* 15 (1986): 26–29.

Leventhal, Josh. *Take Me Out to the Ballpark: An Illustrated Guide to Baseball Parks Past and Present.* New York: Black Dog & Leventhal Publishers, 2000.

Lowry, Philip J. *Green Cathedrals: The Ultimate Celebration of All 271 Major League and Negro League Ballparks Past and Present.* Reading, MA: Addison-Wesley Publishing Company, 1992.

Martin, Len, and Dan Bonk. *Forbes Field: Build-It-Yourself.* Oakmont, PA: Point Four, 1995.

Morgan, J. D. "Should Pittsburgh Save Forbes Field?" *Architectural Record* 150 (July 1971): 119–122.

Palacios, Oscar A. *The Ballpark Sourcebook: Diamond Diagrams.* 2d ed. Skokie, IL: STATS, 1998.

Reidenbaugh, Lowell. *Take Me Out to the Ball Park.* St. Louis: The Sporting News Publishing Co., 1983.

Ritter, Lawrence S. *Lost Ballparks: A Celebration of Baseball's Legendary Fields.* New York: Viking Studio Books, 1992.

Rosen, Byron. "Farewell to Forbes Field." *Baseball Digest* 29 (October 1970): 80–85.

Rosen, Ira. *Blue Skies, Green Fields: A Celebration of 50 Major League Baseball Stadiums.* New York: Clarkson Potter, 2001.

Selter, Ron. "Forbes Field, Hitter's Nightmare?" *The Baseball Research Journal* 31 (2003): 95–97.

Shanley, John. "Forbes: One Kid's Memory." *Elysian Fields Quarterly* 14 (Spring 1995): 54–57.

Shannon, Bill, and George Kalinsky. *The Ball Parks.* New York: Hawthorn Books, 1975.

Smith, Curt. *Storied Stadiums: Baseball's History Through Its Ballparks.* New York: Carroll & Graf Publishers, 2001.

Smith, Ron. *The Ballpark Book: A Journey Through the Fields of Baseball Magic.* St. Louis: The Sporting News Publishing Co., 2000.

Supple, J. Edward. "The New Park at Pittsburgh." *Baseball Magazine* 3 (July 1909): 11–14.

# INDEX

Numbers in *bold italics* indicate pages with photographs.